Tempstaff Universal supports non-Japanese job seekers with finding excellent working opportunities in Japan.

For further details about the careers we are able to offer or to register for employment opportunities, visit our website at: www.tempuniversal.co.jp

TEMPSTAFF UNIVERSAL

We are always seeking intelligent, committed persons of all skill backgrounds to register with us. If you feel you fit the bill and are looking to further your career in Japan, visit our website at www.tempuniversal.co.jp to learn more about us and to register for employment opportunities.

Some typical examples of the type of work we deal with;

Translation	Accountancy
IT/ Tech based positions	Proofreading/ Editing
Copyediting	Advertising/ PR
Media	Acting/ Voice acting
Human resources	Engineering
English tutoring/ programme coordination	

テンプスタッフ・ユニバーサル 株式会社

What Western women say about the Being A Broad network

One of the greatest frustrations in Japan is the unavailability of information and networking for women. Being A Broad was a pioneer in overcoming that obstacle and bringing together Western women. That is an achievement anywhere, but all the more in Japan where the 'spirit of sisterhood' is lacking. Being A Broad, from its beginning as a rough homemade magazine to its transformation into an information-and-support system on the Internet, has remained a flower in a bleak landscape. Hats off to Being A Broad!
—Alison, age 43, American

Being A Broad is your one stop place for finding out anything and everything you need to know about living in Japan. Caroline Pover, through the Being A Broad Website, monthly newsletter and chat group, has developed a 'Virtual Community' that supports every aspect of your life in Japan.
—Andrea Besnard, age 31, Australian

Living far from an urban area, the Being A Broad network of communication is a lifeline for me. Thanks to Caroline's savvy, news, guidance and unique friends from around Japan and the world are now at my fingertips. Considering the successes of the magazine, Website and newsgroup, this book will be a must-have for women living in Japan.
—Michele Mills, age 29, American

Caroline Pover is one of the most impressive people I know. She built something out of nothing and it touches countless women and their families on a daily basis. I can't imagine what it was like for Western women in Japan before. Because of Being A Broad I was able to meet people and do things that I never would have had the chance to otherwise. Not to mention the life-saving (sometimes literally) information that's available.
—Greta Poulsen, age 36, American

Being A Broad is the best networking tool I have ever known in my 20+ years in Japan. Whatever you are looking for, somebody, somewhere will know about it! I have helped people and been helped by people, found old friends and made new ones, all through the fabulous Being A Broad!
—Libby Kaiho, age 46, American

Being A Broad does something simple but very important: it gives me a sense of inclusion. Being an ex-pat brings with it all the ups and downs of trying to learn a new culture and a new language, or simply making new friends. Being A Broad makes the practical side of that easier and the emotional side a little less lonely.
—Kristin Reimer-Herold, age 31, American

Being A Broad is wicked! The yahoogroup has been a constant source of information, help, and fun. I'm really excited about reading the book as it has lots of important information relevant to ANYONE, not just gals, living in or thinking about coming to Japan. Caroline Pover always has good advice and Being A Broad has helped give me back some of the confidence I lost from living in a 'world' full of unrealistically skinny women!
—Julie Collins, age 26, British

In my research to discover how independent, strong women like myself fared in Japan, I grew dismayed when all I could find were a few books that targeted single males—never mind the women—single or involved! However, since I have blissfully found Being A Broad, I know that there is a source of information from other women like myself and I can rest easier knowing that there is a resource for me whenever I need help.
—Robin, age 24, American

Website http://www.being-a-broad.com

Being A Broad in Japan

Everything a Western woman needs to survive and thrive

Caroline Pover

Alexandra Press

Being A Broad in Japan
Everything a Western woman needs to survive and thrive
Author: Caroline Pover
Editor and Proofreader: Cindy Fujimoto
Ilustrator: Aipu
Contributors: Judith Sullivan, Elise Mori, Tracey Delaney, Jeanmarie Todd
Advertising and Sponsorship: Caroline Pover, Judith Sullivan, Lori Irwin, Tomoko Hamaguchi
Author Photo: Kristen Elsby

ISBN 4-9900791-0-8

For my mother, Alexandra Pearce. I carry your love, strength, and belief in me, wherever I am.

And for Cressie. Our time together in Japan was too short, but the friendship will last forever.

Being A Broad wishes to thank the following individuals and organisations for their kindness, generosity, and support in making this first edition of *Being A Broad in Japan* possible:

Paul Goldsmith

PANACHE
Computer Consulting & Services

Takaharu Torikoshi

IMPACT 21
www.impact21.co.jp

Yasuko Nagano

Office Nagano

Acknowledgements

This book would have been impossible to write without the help of a great many people whom I would like to thank.

Tina Derrick, Lucy Sturnam, Kathy Klump, and Debbie Gardiner, for your assistance in compiling and typing the resources. Tina, you have been an especially supportive friend, particularly as this book neared completion—the countless snacks and cups of tea you brought me, in addition to listening to me talk incessantly about the book, gave me energy when I thought I had nothing left. I will try to become a more 'normal' friend now, but I'm not making any promises!

Suzanne Kamata, Alison Finnegan, and Samantha MacIntosh, for taking hours out of your busy schedules to read the first draft. Thank you for your time, patience, support and great understanding of what I was trying to do.

My Japanese friends—Ai Kawabe, Shinobu Kato, Seiryu Ida, Atsushi Teratani, Kaoru Yamada, and Masashizu Hirahara—who endured endless questions about why some things are the way they are in Japan, patiently tried to explain them to me, and helped me with so many practicalities. Also Naomi Nishimura, for her constant encouragement, enthusiasm, and valued friendship. I am very grateful.

Judith Sullivan, for your great work on the Mothers chapter. You managed to write your sections whilst being a single mother of two with a full-time job and living in a foreign country—a great achievement indeed. I wish you good luck with your new writing venture and thank you for embracing me and my book with such enthusiasm! Elise Mori, for sharing your culinary expertise and characteristic sense of humour in the Food section—and I do apologise for taking time away from your frantic attempts at conceiving! Tracey Delaney, for sharing your experiences and research into women's centres in Japan, and Jeanmarie Todd, for all your help in compiling the book information in Chapter Ten.

Others whose wisdom and knowledge they shared with me for specific sections of the book: Monique Stewart, Anne Van Pletsen, Ken Suzuki at Japan Helpline, Elissa and Estelle at Sin Den, Dr Nakashima at Nakashima Dental Office, Mike Nendick formerly at Tokyo English Life Line, Jack Bayles at Tengu Foods, Rosalyn Hagiwara, Hari Tahil, Lynette Airey, Ana Kishida, Prem Dana Takada, David Bryan Thomas at the Children's Rights Council Japan, Brett Cocreham, Anne Makepeace and Alisha Meshii-Inouye at Foreign Executive Women, Gretchen Shinoda, Ulla Hjulmand, Annette Goulin, Susan Cole, Diane Connell, and all the people who prefer to remain anonymous due to the nature of their work. I know who you are and I thank you too.

The women who told me about their jobs and businesses, whose names can be found in the Working chapter. Thank you for your time and humour in sharing your working lives with me in order to help others.

Ai Kawabe, Makiko Sato, Mina Shimoyama, Shinobu Kato, Naomi Ozawa, and Takahiro Yamamoto, for all your hard work in translating the useful Japanese phrases, and Miyu Hinata and Shigemasa Fujimoto for editing them. I am very grateful, as will the readers of this book be, I am sure.

I'd like to thank Ai Kawabe again. Your wonderful illustrations manage to capture so well the spirit I want to create through this book: warm, friendly, and sensitive, with a touch of humour. May this be the first of many projects for you.

Cindy Fujimoto, I am deeply indebted to you for your tireless work in editing this book, especially as it came at a time when you were relocating to Canada. Your attention to detail, positive energy, and encouragement throughout are very much appreciated. You really made this book what it is now. I sincerely hope to have the privilege of working with you again.

My 'publishing' mentors and friends: Anne Bergasse, Kristen Elsby, Roger Boisvert, Larry Greenberg, Alison Pockett, and Alan MacKenzie. You put up with my panic-stricken phone calls and requests at all times of the day and night. I don't know what I would have done without you.

Paul Davies, who lived with this book for eighteen months. You were there when I lost my magazine, you were there when I first had the idea for this book, you were there to read several drafts and give me the benefit of your knowledge and wisdom, you were there during the many times my computer crashed, you were there to listen to my joys and frustrations. In short, you were always there, and I am lucky that you were. Thank you.

Finally, but most importantly, I thank the Western women I interviewed for the main part of this book, who shall remain anonymous. You selflessly answered my questions about so many aspects of your lives in Japan. You trusted me with the most intimate details of your lives. You made me laugh, and some of you made me cry. This book really would have been impossible without you, and I hope that I have done you justice. My most sincere thanks go to all of you.

Caroline Pover

Being A Broad Girls' Night Out

Suntory supports active international women in Tokyo!

Being A Broad holds a Girls' Night Out every month at the Paddy Foleys Irish Pub in Roppongi. It's a great chance for women of any nationality to get together and make some new friends. Come alone or come with a friend - you will be made very welcome!

Girls' Night Out is supported by Suntory, who gives one bottle of Macadia Sparkling to everyone attending in 2005.

The Girls' Night Out is held on the third Wednesday of every month, from 7pm until late. Contact us for information about the next one.

Being A Broad Girls' Night Out
Email: info@being-a-broad.com
URL: www.being-a-broad.com

About the Author

Caroline Pover was born in the UK in 1971. She attended Exeter University where she developed an interest in girls' and women's education and graduated with a First Class Honours degree in Mathematics and Education. After spending one year as a primary school teacher in her hometown of Plymouth, England, a desire to seek adventure led her to Japan in August 1996. When she arrived, Caroline found work teaching English at a technical college. Six months later, she founded and published *Being A Broad*, a monthly magazine, the purpose of which was to connect and support English-speaking women in Japan. The magazine sparked events to promote foreign women performers, a Website, a monthly email newsletter, and the growth of an extensive network of predominantly Western women all over Japan. Financial difficulties caused the magazine to cease publication in November 1998, but the network and the demand for information continued.

Caroline has given speeches and seminars to groups of foreign and Japanese women throughout Japan. She has been interviewed by BBC Radio's 'Woman's Hour', *Working Woman*, *Forum on Gender and Culture*, the *Japan Times*, the *Asahi Evening News*, *Tokyo Classified*, *Kansai Timeout*, and *La Vie de 30 ans*, and was the subject of a short documentary by NHK. The wealth of experiences, information, and resources gathered during her years in Japan are brought together in this book.

Caroline lives in Tokyo. Contact her by email at broads@gol.com.

Foreword

Why would anyone want to publish anything for that audience?
There's far too much fuss made about women's issues these days.
— Princess Anne to the author, 9 March 1999

I'm not in the habit of hobnobbing with royalty. When I was publishing *Being A Broad* magazine, I was invited to a lunch 'in the presence of HRH The Princess Royal', along with several other young Brits in Tokyo who were classified as 'movers and shakers'. I was introduced to her, and the above was her response when she was told what I was doing in Japan. Any woman who has spent less than one week in Japan might say the same thing. In some ways, Western women are the 'privileged' foreigners in Japan. They are idolised by Japanese men and women alike; fashion magazines, billboards, TV commercials, and the most popular movies all feature Western women. Japanese men are often too in awe to speak to them, Japanese women are often wondering whether Western women's boobs are real and how they get their bodies to curve like that. Aside from what is perceived to be a 'glamorous' appearance, many Western women in Japan have fulfilling and challenging jobs, beautiful homes, financial independence, and opportunities for personal development far beyond those we would have in our home countries, and certainly beyond those of most other foreign women in Japan.

But that doesn't mean that we don't have questions or need support, information, and guidance during our lives here.

When I first came to Japan in 1996, I wasn't prepared. Twenty-one thousand Western women move to Japan every year and most of them aren't prepared either. I don't mean being prepared for the language or the culture; I mean being prepared for what it is like to be a Western woman living in Japan. There are many differences between being a Western woman in Japan and being a Western man in Japan. And being an African, Middle Eastern, South American, or non-Japanese Asian woman in Japan raises issues that justify books of their own—books that I am not qualified to write.

I started *Being A Broad* magazine because I sensed a need amongst Western women in Japan. Whenever I saw a group of such women get together, they discussed the many aspects of their lives here and asked questions that often went unanswered. When I travelled around Japan, I met some of the three thousand Western women who live in the countryside. They told me of the sense of isolation they felt, especially if they were the only foreigner in their town. My magazine aimed to support and connect Western women, while providing information and a forum for discussion and expression. I tried to make the magazine humorous, and to encourage us not to take ourselves, or certain elements of being a woman here, too seriously (just look at its title). From the feedback I received, I think *Being A Broad* magazine achieved those aims and I still feel sad about having to cease publication due to a lack of funds.

After the magazine stopped, I received a flood of correspondence from Western women in Japan, as well as those in other countries. These women asked me many and varied questions about living here: from treating a yeast infection to getting a mammogram, from finding an apartment to shipping everything home, from finding work to taking an employer to court, and probably just about everything else you can think of. The need for information and support was still there. After about six months of this, I looked at the information taking up an increasing amount of space in my apartment and decided to turn it and the 'Being A Broad' name into this book.

Throughout 1999 I interviewed about two hundred Western women living in Japan. Most of them were women from the United States, Canada, Europe, Australia, and New Zealand. They were from different ethnic and social backgrounds, and of different ages and sexual orientations. Employment and marital statuses differed. Some were here for six months, some for most of their adult lives. It was a diverse group of women, each with unique experiences, but they all had one thing in common: they were Western women in Japan. I was touched by their willingness to share their experiences to help prepare and support others like them.

These interviews form the foundation of this book. With other research, interviews with specialists in certain fields, some of my own experiences, resource sections and useful Japanese phrases, I have tried to create a comprehensive guide for Western women in Japan.

If that's making a fuss about women's issues, then off with my head!

Table of Contents

Introduction

Being A Broad in Japan is for every Western woman who is either thinking of living in Japan or who is already here. Newcomers will find out what they can expect from life in Japan, and how to cope with difficulties—they will read about the experiences of women who have been there and done that. Oldtimers may find answers to questions that they have had for years, validation of feelings they may not have had the opportunity to express with others before, and comfort in the knowledge that they are not alone in their experience in Japan. Everyone has a different experience, and I have tried to reflect that where possible. I hope you find the many humorous comments by Western women to be a reminder not to take all the inevitable challenges that come with living overseas too seriously. Quotes have been left in the interviewees' native form of English, so you'll find British and American English throughout. All should find the contact information for useful companies, services, and organisations to be an invaluable resource.

Being A Broad in Japan is also for men who want to understand women's experiences and perceptions of Japan, which can be very different to their own. Whether those men are friends, partners, colleagues or employers, I think we all benefit from their having more awareness of what life in Japan is like for women.

Many Western women come to Japan as a result of their partner's relocation. These couples often receive 'ex-pat packages', where the company provides accommodation, information, high salaries, etc., but rarely provides practical or emotional support specifically for a female partner. This is not through neglect on the part of companies, as they often tell me that they search for information for the partner

1

but none is available. Well here it is. This book is for all those companies who want to support their new staff's partners.

It is also for partners, friends, or family who have been 'left' at home—people who want to understand their loved one's new life. Often when a Western woman returns home, people find that she has changed and there is a difficult adjustment period for her and those around her. When she returns home, either on holiday or for good, understanding how different her life and experiences in Japan were will help all concerned.

This book contains information and perspectives not found in any other guidebook to Japan. Survival tells you why you may feel increasingly aware of your appearance and what to do about it. Elise Mori shares her expert knowledge of Japanese food. It also discusses safety issues for women, money matters, and other general survival information. Home tells you how to find a place and how to deal with the practicalities once you have one. Health discusses general health issues such as doctors, dentists and fitness, as well as women-specific health issues. Gynaecologists and general practitioners in Japan have caused Western women much concern; the list of clinics and hospitals in this chapter will save you a lot of trouble. About half of the Western women in Japan are single. Relationships provides information for the single woman in Japan, why she is likely to remain so even if she doesn't want to, and how to develop new perspectives if this is a problem. Women already in relationships may face challenges if they move to another country, or if their partner is Japanese. This chapter also explains how to deal with those challenges in a way that brings you closer together. Japan is one of the easiest countries in which to get married and can be one of the most complicated in which to get divorced. You'll find everything you need to know about the legal aspects of marriage and divorce. Judith Sullivan has assisted me in writing a chapter for Mothers, from pregnancy to schools, including fertility and adoption information. In Working you'll find out about how to get work, the kinds of jobs available, starting your own business, and volunteer work. This chapter also includes an extensive section of interviews with Western women about their jobs in Japan.

Learning provides information on studying Japanese and gives details on the wide range of other classes available. Going Home discusses preparation for leaving Japan and relocation in your home country or another country. Women's Organisations is a directory of the many women's groups throughout Japan, with details about their activities and contact information. Tracey Delaney has also compiled some useful resources on women's centres in Japan. Last, Jeanmarie Todd has helped me in compiling the Reading List, which contains publications by, for, and about Western women in Japan, as well as other necessary and useful reading material.

Each section of the book is followed by useful Japanese phrases written in *romaji* (a method of writing Japanese words using the English alphabet). To help you with the pronunciation, vowels in Japanese are pronounced as follows:

a as in marvellous Marlene
i as in eager Eileen
u as in super Susan
e as in ecstatic Ellen
o as in jokey Joan

'r' and 'l' are pronounced in the same way, and sound like a combination of both.

Following the translations you will find a resource section, which often lists companies or organisations specifically recommended by Western women already in Japan. Some of those recommended companies, along with past sponsors of *Being A Broad* magazine, have been invited to advertise their services within the book. Please support them, as they have assisted in making this book possible.

Feel free to send me any additions to the resource sections so that I can update them for the next edition. I also welcome your feedback about the book, and would love to hear about your own experiences.

I hope you enjoy *Being A Broad in Japan*!

General Useful Japanese

Numbers

1	*ichi*
2	*ni*
3	*san*
4	*yon/shi*
5	*go*
6	*roku*
7	*nana/shichi*
8	*hatchi*
9	*kyuu*
10	*juu*
20	*nijuu*
30	*sanjuu*
40	*yonjuu*
50	*gojuu*
60	*rokujuu*
70	*nanajuu*
80	*hatchijuu*
90	*kyuujuu*
100	*hyaku*
200	*nihyaku*
300	*sanbyaku*
400	*yonhyaku*
500	*gohyaku*
600	*roppyaku*
700	*nanahyaku*
800	*happyaku*
900	*kyuuhyaku*
1000	*sen*
2000	*nisen*
3000	*sanzen*
4000	*yonsen*
5000	*gosen*
6000	*rokusen*
7000	*nanasen*
8000	*hassen*
9000	*kyuusen*

Countries

UK	*eikoku/igirisu*
England	*igirisu*
Ireland	*airurando*
Scotland	*sukottorando*
Wales	*ueerusu*
US	*amerika*
Australia	*oosutoraria*
New Zealand	*nyuu jiirando*
Canada	*kanada*

Days

Monday	*getsuyoubi*
Tuesday	*kayoubi*
Wednesday	*suiyoubi*
Thursday	*mokuyoubi*
Friday	*kin'youbi*
Saturday	*doyoubi*
Sunday	*nichiyoubi*

Months

January	*ichigatsu*
February	*nigatsu*
March	*sangatsu*
April	*shigatsu*
May	*gogatsu*
June	*rokugatsu*
July	*shichigatsu*
August	*hatchigatsu*
September	*kugatsu*
October	*juugatsu*
November	*juuichigatsu*
December	*juunigatsu*

Dates

1st	*tsuitachi*
2nd	*futsuka*
3rd	*mikka*
4th	*yokka*
5th	*itsuka*
6th	*muika*
7th	*nanoka*
8th	*youka*
9th	*kokonoka*
10th	*tooka*

11th	*juuichi-nichi*	**Time**	
12th	*juuni-nichi*	day	*nichi/hi*
13th	*juusan-nichi*	today	*kyou*
14th	*juuyon-nichi*	yesterday	*kinou*
15th	*juugo-nichi*	tomorrow	*ashita*
16th	*juuroku-nichi*	the day after	
17th	*juushichi-nichi*	tomorrow	*asatte*
18th	*juuhachi-nichi*	week	*shuu*
19th	*juuku-nichi*	this week	*konshuu*
20th	*hatsuka*	last week	*senshuu*
21st	*nijuuichi-nichi*	next week	*raishuu*
22nd	*nijuuni-nichi*	month	*gatsu/tsuki*
23rd	*nijuusan-nichi*	this month	*kongetsu*
24th	*nijuuyon-nichi*	last month	*sengetsu*
25th	*nijuugo-nichi*	next month	*raigetsu*
26th	*nijuuroku-nichi*	year	*nen/toshi*
27th	*nijuushichi-nichi*	this year	*kotoshi*
28th	*nijuuhachi-nichi*	last year	*kyonen*
29th	*nijuuku-nichi*	next year	*rainen*
30th	*sanjuu-nichi*	hour	*ji*
31st	*sanjuuichi-nichi*	minute	*pun/fun*
		... o'clock	*... ji*
		Half past ...	*... ji han*

Basic phrases

Hello.	*Konnichiwa.*
Goodbye.	*Sayonara.*
Good night.	*Oyasumi nasai.*
How are you?	*O-genki desu ka.*
How do you do?	*Hajimemashite.*
Excuse me.	*Sumimasen.*
Please.	*Onegaishimasu/o kudasai.*
Thank you (very much).	*(Doumo) arigatou (gozaimasu).*
I am [name].	*... desu.*
I am [nationality].	[country] *jin desu.*
I am ... years old.	*... sai desu.*
I live in ...	*... ni sunde imasu.*
My job is ...	*Shigoto wa ... desu.*
I work for ... company.	*Kaisha wa ... desu.*
Where is the ... ?	*... wa doko desu ka.*
How much is it?	*Ikura desu ka.*
Please help me.	*Tasukete kudasai.*
Do you have the time?	*O-jikan wa arimasu ka.*
I can't speak/understand Japanese.	*Nihongo hanashimasen/wakarimasen.*
Do you speak/understand English?	*Eigo hanashimasu/wakarimasu ka.*

General Resources

Helplines

English Hotline 03-3210-8523
    Tourist and resident information for all of Japan.
Japan Help Line 0120-461-997
    24 hour information, advice and assistance for all of Japan.
    http://www.jhelp.com
Japan Travel Phone Tourist 0088-22-4800
    Traveler and resident information for all of Japan.
    http://www.jnto.go.jp
Tokyo English Lifeline (TELL) (see display ad, page 196) 03-5774-0992
    Living information and phone crisis counselling.
    http://www.tell.gol.com

Organisations

Each district has an affiliated organisation (often called the 'International Association') specifically to meet the needs of foreigners in that area. Check with your ward office for your local organisation. Many of the following organisations have branches throughout Japan, so tell them your area and they will give you the contact information for your local branch.

Asian People's Friendship Society Support 03-3964-8739
    Telephone and in-person problem solving for all of Japan.
    http://www.jca.apc.org/apff/index.html
Council of Local Authorities for International Relations 03-5388-3163
    General living information for all of Japan.
    http://www.clair.nippon-net.ne.jp
Foreign Residents' Advisory Centre 03-5320-7744
    Information, problem solving, emergencies and culture
    enquiries for all of Japan.
International Committee of Kansai 078-881-9533
    Liaises between the Japanese authorities and foreigners in
    Kansai, to help solve any problems.
United Front Japan (UFJ) 0471-20-8407
    Information, newsletter, and mailing list for long-term and
    permanent foreign residents and foreigners married to
    Japanese citizens.
    http://www.ufj.gol.com

Orientations

HRS 03-5563-3880
    Personalised orientation programs for all of Japan.
Tokyo General Agency 03-3409-2031
    Orientation programs for all of Japan, publish TGIEYE
    magazine, telephone consultation service, tours throughout
    Japan with English-speaking guides.

Tokyo Orientations 03-3585-0759
    Personalised services to individuals, families, and
    multinational corporations relocating to Japan.
Welcome Furoshiki 03-5472-7074
    Free home visit and information package for newcomers in
    Tokyo, Nagoya and Osaka.
    http://www.oakassociates.co.jp

Websites

Accessible Tokyo
    Transport, shopping, daily life information for disabled visitors and residents.
    http://www.jwindow.net/LWT/TOKYO/REDCROSS/redcross_index.html
Japan Information Resource Centre
    General information.
    http://www.konradh.net/jp.html
Japan Traveler
    General information.
    http://www.tic.joho.com/
Japan Unlimited.com
    General information.
    http://www.japanunlimited.com
The Community
    Concerned with eliminating discrimination against foreigners in Japan.
    http://www.voicenet.co.jp/TheCommunity/
Japan Window
    General information.
    http://www.jwindow.net/
Living in Japan
    A cyber community Japan forum.
    http://www.livinginjapan.com/
Living Manual for NTT R&D Centres
    General information.
    http://home.ntt.com/japan/living/lm.html
Marco Polo
    General information.
    http://www.marcopolo.com/cities/tokyo/tokyo.html
Schauwecker's Guide to Japan
    General information.
    http://www.japan-guide.com/
Tokyo Orientations Living in Japan Links
    General information.
    http://www.tokyoorientations.com/injapan.htm

Survival

1

Your Status

When you enter Japan your passport will be stamped, indicating your status and permitted period of stay. You may later apply to change your visa status or extend your period of stay.

Tourist or temporary visas

You are eligible to stay in Japan for ninety days and this may be extended for a further ninety days providing you have sufficient funds, a return flight, and a valid reason for staying (such as travelling around Japan, visiting friends, or participating in lectures or business meetings). To extend a tourist visa, visit the nearest immigration office and complete the necessary paperwork. If successful, you will receive your new visa the same day. You cannot extend a tourist visa more than once, but you may leave the country and return on a new tourist visa, which you can then extend. It is illegal to work on a tourist visa. See

Chapter Six on Working if you plan to seek work in Japan while on a tourist visa.

Working visas

If you have a job in Japan, with a contract and salary of at least ¥200,000 per month, then you are eligible to apply for a working visa. Someone else, such as an employer, may apply on your behalf. The employer must provide the necessary documentation. See Chapter Six on Working for information on how to apply for and renew a working visa. A working visa imposes no restrictions on your working hours and you are considered a resident of Japan. Working visas are issued for six months, one year, or three years. You are only permitted to work in the field specified on your visa.

Student visas

Student visas are available to people who wish to study at an educational institution in Japan. The school must provide the necessary documentation. Student visas are valid for three months, six months, or one year. Students may work up to four hours a day, providing they get permission from the government and prove that working will not affect their studies. See your educational institution for more information.

Permanent resident visas

Permanent residency is rarely granted to people who have been living in Japan for less than ten years, although there are some exceptions. Visit your nearest immigration office for more information on the necessary requirements and documentation. You must prove that you are capable of supporting yourself in Japan. If you have permanent residency, then there are no restrictions on your activities in Japan and no need for visa renewals.

Long-term resident visas

Long-term residency is usually given to foreign spouses of Japanese, or in cases where an employer requires you to stay for more than one year. The term of this visa status is usually limited to three years. A three-year working visa allows you to work in a specified field only, whereas long-term residency imposes no restrictions on your activities.

Dependant visas

These are issued to foreign spouses of Japanese or foreigners. They are also issued to children of foreigners. If you are not married, or the marriage is not registered in Japan (see the section on Getting Married in Chapter Four) but the father of your children is Japanese, then your child requires a dependant visa until the necessary paperwork is completed. Dependant visas are valid for three months, six months, one year, or three years. Spouses of Japanese nationals have no restrictions on their activities in Japan, whereas spouses of foreigners may not work more than twenty hours a week. In the event of a divorce, spouse visas are cancelled. See Getting Divorced in Chapter Four and Requirements in Chapter Six for more information.

Changing your visa status

You may apply at any time to change your visa status. For some changes, for example from tourist visa to working visa, you are required to leave the country and re-enter. See Finding a Job in Chapter Six for more information. For others, for example changing to spouse visa status, just notify your ward office of the change. Ask at the nearest immigration office for information on applying for a change in visa status.

Re-entry permits

Re-entry permits must be obtained in order to maintain your present visa status if you wish to leave Japan and return (for example, for a holiday or a visit home). If you do not have a re-entry permit, then your visa status will be cancelled. Re-entry permits are available from immigration offices for a few thousand yen. There are two kinds: single and multiple, and they are valid for one year or three years, depending on your visa length. A single permit allows you to leave Japan just once, a multiple one allows you to leave Japan several times. Everybody complains about having to get re-entry permits, so it's best just to get a multiple one—if you have to go home on an emergency, it will be one less thing to worry about.

Alien registration

If you have any visa other than a tourist visa, you are required to register at your local ward office. You will be issued with an 'alien registration card', which you must carry with you at all times if you are over sixteen. You will also be issued with a ward handbook, which, although most people don't realise it, is one of the most valuable resources you will find. You must report to the ward office any change in your status within fourteen days of the change. This includes changes in address (either in or outside Japan), name, nationality, visa status, employment, passport, marital status, and number of children. Should your alien registration card be lost, damaged or stolen, you must report the loss immediately. If you fail to report the above information to your ward office within fourteen days, you must write a letter of apology. Should you leave Japan permanently, you are supposed to hand in your alien registration card to the immigration officer at the airport (see Before You Go in Chapter Eight). The card must be returned to the ward office in the event its owner acquires Japanese nationality or if the owner dies (see Bereavement in Chapter Four).

Useful Japanese

visa	*biza*	dependant visa	*juuzoku biza*
visa status	*biza no zairyuu shikaku*	re-entry permit	*sai nyuukoku kyoka*
passport	*pasupooto*	single re-entry permit	*tansuu nyuukoku kyoka*
visa extension	*biza enchou*		
tourist visa	*kankou biza*	multiple re-entry	
working visa	*shuugyou biza*	permit	*fukusuu sai nyuukoku kyoka*
student visa	*gakusei biza*		
permanent visa	*eikyuu biza*	alien registration	
long-term resident visa	*chouki taizai biza*	card	*gaikokujin tourokushou*

I'd like to extend my tourist visa. .... *Kankou biza o enchou shitai no desu.*
I'd like to apply for a ... . *... o shinsei shitai no desu.*
I'd like some information on applying for a
... visa. .... *... biza no shinsei ni tsuite oshiete kudasai.*
I'd like to register my status in Japan. .... *Nihon no zairyuu shikaku o shinsei shitai no desu.*
I'd like to apply for a ... re-entry permit. .... *... sai nyuukoku kyoka o shinsei shitai no desu.*

I'd like to renew my visa. .... *Biza o koushin shitai no desu.*

I'd like to change my visa status. .... *Biza no zairyuu shikaku o henkou shitai no desu.*

I'd like to notify you of a change in my visa status. .... *Biza no zairyuu shikaku o henkou shita node oshirase shimasu.*

I'd like to make some changes in my status in Japan. .... *Zairyuu shikaku ni henkou shitai kasho ga arimasu.*

My address/name/nationality/visa status/ employment/passport/marital status/ number of children has changed. .... *Watashi no juusho/namae/kokuseki/biza zairyuu shikaku/shuugyou/pasupooto/ kon'in/kodomo no kazu ga kawarimashita.*

I've lost my alien registration card. .... *Gaikokujin tourokushou o funshitsu shimashita.*

My alien registration card has been stolen/ damaged. .... *Gaikokujin tourokushou ga nusumare mashita/orete shimaimashita.*

Please re-issue an alien registration card. .. *Gaikokujin tourokushou o saihakkou shite kudasai.*

Resources

Immigration Offices
There are nearly a hundred immigration offices throughout Japan, classified as branches, sub-offices, or main offices. For a full list, contact the Immigration Bureau.

Fukuoka 092-623-2400
Kobe 078-391-6377
Narita Airport 0476-32-6771
Osaka 06-941-0771
Sendai 022-256-6076
Tokyo: Otemachi 03-3213-8523
Tokyo: Tachikawa 042-528-7179

Hiroshima 082-221-4411
Naha 098-832-4185
Nagoya 052-951-2391
Sapporo 011-261-9211
Takamatsu 0878-22-5851
Tokyo: Shibuya 03-5458-0370
Yokohama 045-681-6801

Immigration Bureau 03-3213-8523
    http://www.moj.go.jp/ENGLISH/IB/ib-01.htm

Independent Organisations
The following provide legal services for immigration and visa processing:
AAA Legal Consultant 0423-25-8849
Emiko Miki 045-662-2226
Hiroshi Itoh Administrative Office 03-3842-0451
Mr Inomata 03-3582-7482
ILS Shimoda Office 03-3291-5562
Japan Golden Club 03-3358-8521

Nakai Immigration Service 03-5282-7654
    http://www.tokyovisa.co.jp/index.html
Onedera Administrative Office 03-3590-7511
Tokyo Administrative Office 03-3379-2251

Web Resources
Ministry of Foreign Affairs—A Guide to Japanese Visas
    http://www.mofa.go.jp/j_info/visit/visa/
Ministry of Foreign Affairs—The Working Holiday Programmes in Japan
    http://www.mofa.go.jp/j_info/visit/w_holiday/index.html
United Front Japan—Immigration Information
    http://www.ufj.gol.com/newsletter/immin.html

Emergencies

If you call the police (110) or the fire brigade or an ambulance (119 for either), you need to give your name, address, and telephone number along with the nature of the emergency and the address and telephone number at the site of the emergency.

Ambulance

Emergency transportation to a hospital is a 24-hour free service. You have to give them your health insurance information (so they can give it to the hospital and save you the trouble), so make sure it's handy at all times. Someone is also expected to 'greet' the ambulance outside, which may be impossible to do if you live alone and are totally incapacitated—one of the better reasons to establish good relationships with your neighbours. The ambulance staff will probably not speak English, but they have a manual in eleven different languages that they will use to diagnose your problem. There are also many privately owned companies listed in the telephone book that can transport non-urgent patients unable to move to their destination, or you could just call a taxi.

Preparation for emergencies

Fire extinguishers, safety helmets, flashlights, first-aid kits, and emergency food rations are easily obtainable from the 'disaster' sections of Japanese department stores. Some people keep their bathtubs full of water in case of fires. Local fire fighters may patrol the streets at times, loudly knocking two wooden batons together as a warning to be careful of fires due to dry air. Schools and companies hold fire or earthquake drills once a year. To participate in local fire or earthquake drills, contact your ward office. Some ward offices have an 'earthquake simulation room' which, although fascinating, I don't recommend visiting when your parents come to stay unless you want them to haul you back home on the plane with them.

Earthquakes

Japan hosts one tenth of the world's active volcanoes and Tokyo is located on land particularly prone to earthquakes; its last major one was in 1923 and over 140,000 people died. Major earthquakes are predicted as occurring on a seventy-year cycle, and every year a mysterious rumour circulates identifying the date of the 'big one' that is overdue for Tokyo. Some people take this so seriously that they camp out in a homemade shelter for a day (I'll admit to doing this myself during my first year), some people leave Tokyo for a few days. One psychic left Japan altogether, so convinced was he that it would hit soon.

You don't need to take such drastic action, but can take the following precautionary measures. Get some fire extinguishers and keep your bathtub filled with water—note that this is a hazard for small children. The worst damage is not caused by the earthquakes themselves, but from the fires that follow them. Switch off the gas at the mains whenever you are not using it, as gas is the biggest cause of fires during earthquakes. Secure tall furniture and, although it is difficult to avoid in the land of minimum storage space, don't put piles of heavy objects on top of furniture.

Keep the following supplies handy: food, water, a first-aid kit, a portable radio (tuned in to an English station), a flashlight, candles, matches, batteries, plastic bags, towels, soap, change for vending machines and phones, disposable dishes and cutlery, and a small portable gas stove. You could also keep a notepad and pen, because every foreigner says they're going to write a book about their experiences in Japan and you could be missing out on a whole load of material while you're stuck under all that rubble. Also keep changes of underwear handy; I suspect you'll need them immediately after the earthquake anyway. Also, one thing that really irritates me about movies is that the heroine is never menstruating when she is stranded in some bizarre situation. Keep some sanitary products and a disposal container of some sort too.

Plan beforehand where to meet and how to make contact with your friends or family in Japan. There are evacuation areas throughout Japan: make sure you know where the nearest one is.

If an earthquake happens

Put out any fires with the extinguishers or the bath water you've been keeping and switch off the gas at the mains. Find a place away from falling objects: under a doorframe, under a table or desk, or in a small room (they are stronger than large rooms) such as inside your closet or in the toilet, the latter of which will also save you a change of underwear. Open a door as soon as possible because doors often warp and cannot be opened after an earthquake. If you live in a city, resist the urge to rush outside; stay indoors instead. In a city it is safer to be inside a building rather than outside where you will be surrounded by falling broken glass and lumps of concrete. Switch on your radio or television if it is working. InterFM was established after the Kobe earthquake in 1995 when it became apparent that foreigners who didn't speak Japanese had no way of getting information.

If you are driving, you are supposed to pull over, leave the key in the ignition and abandon your car, without locking the driver's side door. Don't worry, this is Japan and your car will probably be returned to you fully intact after being taken to the car wash.

Even if there is a large earthquake, you don't have to leave your house as long as you have extinguished all fires. There will be announcements on loudspeakers in Japanese and English telling you if you have to leave your house, so just stay there until you hear them. Then walk slowly to the evacuation site.

Useful Japanese

police	*keisatsu*
police car	*patokaa*
police station/box	*keisatsusho/kooban*
car accident	*jidousha jiko*
ambulance	*kyuukyuusha*
fire	*kaji*
fire extinguisher	*shoukaki*
fire engine	*shoubousha*
health insurance	*kenkou hoken*
safety helmet	*anzenbou*
torch/flashlight	*kaichuudentou*
first-aid kit	*kyuukyuubako*

emergency food rations	*hijoushoku*
firefighter	*shouboushi*
earthquake	*jishin*
flood	*kouzui*
mudslide	*doshakuzure*
fire/earthquake drill	*hinankunren*
earthquake simulation room	*giji jishin taiken shitsu*
evacuation area	*kinkyuu hinan basho*

Call 110. (the police)	*Hyakutouban shite kudasai.*
There has been an accident.	*Jiko ga arimashita.*
I want to call an ambulance. (Call 119.)	*Kyuukyuusha o yobitai no desu ga.*
Please call an ambulance.	*Kyuukyuusha o yonde kudasai.*
My house is on fire. (Call 119.)	*Uchi ga kaji desu.*
Someone has collapsed.	*Hito ga taorete imasu.*
Someone has had a heart attack.	*Shinzou hossa desu.*
Someone is bleeding.	*Hito ga chi o nagashite imasu.*
Someone has had a stroke.	*Hossa o okoshita hito ga imasu.*
Someone is unconscious.	*Ishiki o nakushita hito ga imasu.*
Where is the disaster department? (in a department store)	*Saigai taisaku youhin no uriba wa doko desu ka.*
I'd like to visit the earthquake simulation room.	*Giji jishin taiken shitsu ni itte mitai desu.*
Where is the evacuation site?	*Kinkyuu hinanjo wa doko desu ka.*
I am injured.	*Kega o shimashita.*

Resources

Useful Numbers

Accidents/Burglaries 110	Ambulance/Fire/Rescue 119

English Language Emergency TV and Radio Broadcasts
FEN 810AM (all Japan)
FM COCOLO 76.5 (Osaka)
Fukuoka LOVE FM 76.1 (Fukuoka)
InterFM 76.1 (Tokyo)
NHK Television Channels 1 and 2, Radio 639AM (all Japan)
RADIOi 79.5FM (Aichi)

Life Saving Learning Centres
Life Saving Centre Head Office .... 03-3621-0119 (J)

Embassies

Australia	03-5232-4111	Austria	03-3451-8281
Canada	03-5412-6200	Czech Republic	03-3400-8122
Denmark	03-3496-3001	Finland	03-5447-6000
France	03-5420-8800	Germany	03-3473-0151
Greece	03-3403-0871	Hungary	03-3798-8801
India	03-3262-2391	Ireland	03-3263-0695
Italy	03-3453-5291	Jamaica	03-3435-1861
Luxemburg	03-3265-9621	Netherlands	03-5401-0411
New Zealand	03-3467-2271	Norway	03-3440-2611
Philippines	03-5562-1600	Russian Federation	03-3583-4224
Singapore	03-3586-9111	South Africa	03-3265-3366
Spain	03-3583-8531	Sri Lanka	03-3440-6911
Sweden	03-5562-5050	Switzerland	03-3473-0121
Turkey	03-3470-5131	UK	03-5211-1100
USA	03-3224-5000	Yugoslavia	03-3447-3571

Web Resources
Disaster Information System in Japan
      http://ghd.uic.net/98/ghd/sld027.htm
US State Department Emergency Services for American Citizens Abroad
      http://travel.state.gov/acs.html#emr

Safety

I feel so safe in Japan. I feel like I can walk anywhere alone at any time of night wearing whatever I like; I don't get a tight feeling in my stomach when I see a group of lads walking towards me; I don't hold my breath if I am wearing a miniskirt and walk past construction workers; and if a stranger initiates a conversation, generally I am polite and responsive. This is very different from Plymouth (UK), where I grew up, which isn't even that dangerous. I have not lost my instinct to be on guard should a situation arise, but I have never felt that I was in any serious danger in Japan.

Most Western women feel the same way:

I feel incredibly safe in Japan. We lock our front door only because neighbors and delivery people just WALK in and say HI if we don't—not from fear of criminals. I do live in the countryside, but still feel safe nearly anywhere in Tokyo when out and about.

NO COMPARISON! I'm from L.A. Now where my mom lives there are drive-by shootings. I go to visit her for a couple of weeks and can't sleep because of the helicopters flashing their lights over the houses and the firecracker sound of gunshots somewhere! Spooky, let me tell you, when I think 'I grew up there and know the neighborhood.' I don't anymore.

According to the White Paper on Police from September 1999, an average of 1,700 rapes are reported in Japan each year, which is relatively low when compared with US and UK statistics, and with a comparatively high arrest rate of 90 percent. As with any country, the statistics do not indicate unreported rapes, and one can only speculate on the number of unreported sexual harassment cases. Most Western women have at least one story of an 'incident', such as the man who cycled up behind me and grabbed my breast then cycled off, or the man who pulled up my friend's skirt then ran away without even looking at what was underneath. However upsetting and shocking these incidents undoubtedly are, they tend to be almost childish in nature and Western women rarely feel in any physical danger.

Women attribute their feeling secure to a number of factors, the most prevalent one being that to us, Japanese men are physically smaller than Western men are and tend to be less aggressive in their manner. Look at a station full of drunk salarymen at nine o'clock on any evening. They wander around like a bunch of school kids; unable to handle their alcohol, giggling in groups, oblivious to any women in the vicinity, throwing up over the edge of the platform— the image is comical rather than threatening. Compare that with a group of drunk blokes in your home country and it is easy to see why Western women feel so safe. If any comments are made, most women find unwanted attention from Japanese men irritating rather than threatening and very easy to brush off:

I did feel much safer in Japan than I usually do at home (in New Zealand). I had no fear about walking alone at night, because Japanese men are so much less aggressive than New Zealand men, and are rarely physically threatening. I was hassled occasionally, but it was annoying rather than frightening.

That is not to say that Japan is completely safe and that you should drop your guard. Due to the gentle, kind manner of most Japanese people, it can be very easy to become more trusting than you would be at home, but don't. Some Western women have had frightening experiences that lead them to question just how safe Japan is:

I've had some very scary experiences with people following me, yelling out strange things, leaving disturbing phone messages, etc., that have changed my idea of 'Japan being SO safe'. There are loads of stories of women's underwear being stolen off the laundry line or even out of the dryer. I've had more problems here than ever in the US, and I've always lived in big cities.

Regardless of how friendly, generous, and kind that new student, colleague, or client in a hostess bar may seem, it is sensible to maintain your natural awareness of potentially dangerous situations while you are in Japan. Bear in mind that you will attract a certain amount of attention simply because you look different, especially if you are blonde. Most Western women feel safe here but maintain the awareness that they cultivated as they grew up, and if you do this too you will generally be safer in Japan than you would be in your home country.

Police

Police boxes are located all over Japan and are staffed 24 hours a day, every day. In cities, you are rarely further than a five-minute run to a police box, which also adds to the sense of security felt by many people in Japan. Get to know the locations of the police boxes in your area. The best ones are the ones you stumble across down a dark alley that have just one person in them who looks like they haven't had human contact for three years, so will do anything to help you. The officers are there to protect the safety of all citizens and any crime can be reported at a police box, but most of their work seems to involve providing directions—very useful for a foreigner lost in the maze of Tokyo streets.

In any society, the police play an important role regarding how secure its citizens feel. In Japan, neither Japanese citizens nor foreigners have much confidence in the police if a major crime is committed, such as assault or rape. If you report an isolated incident involving a stalker, and you are not particularly persistent in pursuing an arrest, then the police will probably be supportive:

I live alone. I feel very safe in my new apartment, but I'm very careful about locking everything. In my last apartment I was much more laissez faire and had a man turn up in my genkan [entryway] at 2:30 a.m.—luckily, he ran when I screamed at him. I reported the man to the police and they made sure that I had a zillion phone numbers to call in case of emergency and coached me on Japanese phrases to say in an emergency. They took the incident very seriously and were very helpful.

The only crime I've experienced was having my wallet stolen and the police were SO nice and supportive, although they never found the wallet or caught the criminal. They even lent me the money to go home on the train, trusting me to pay it back when I could.

However, if there is a succession of incidents, such as a man often following you or waiting for you, or regularly groping you on the trains (more about trains later), then rarely will you be content with the attention you receive from the police. This also applies if you are insistent that the police arrest your harasser. The general attitude of the Japanese police will be something resembling that of those in our own countries twenty years ago—claims that the man is harmless, the man hasn't really done anything, and even questions regarding your attire and whether you should be out alone at night are not uncommon. One woman had this to say after being continually followed and harassed by the same man:

> *The police told me it was my fault for being out at 8:00 p.m. (I was returning from a Japanese class), and that I should take it as a compliment. They also informed me that if I defended myself in an attack and I managed to hurt the man, I would be arrested for assault. I felt helpless and unsupported. The police told me they would come to my apartment to check on me the following day, a Saturday. They never showed up and I moved out of my apartment. Although I left, I worried about other women in the area who were exposed to him. What made matters worse, the police were not interested in getting involved because I was American and he was also non-Japanese.*

If when reporting a crime you do find the police unhelpful, then keep calm. Japanese people do not respond to hysterics—intense displays of negative emotions upset the harmony that is intrinsic to Japanese culture and will result in a loss of your 'status', i.e., you will not be taken seriously. Bear this in mind when speaking to the police (or indeed to any Japanese person) and try to keep your cool, even though you may feel you are being treated outrageously. If you are not satisfied with your treatment from the police, contact the Japan Help Line or the Tokyo Bar Association, who will assist you free of charge. There is also a very friendly interpreter on hand at the Police Counselling Hotline for Foreigners (see Resources) who can assist you with any problems. The police are becoming the subject of rather a lot of bad publicity due to their attitude towards crimes against women, so things may begin to change for the better.

Other citizens

It is not just the police who turn a blind eye to harassment of this sort, but also the general public. If you are being followed, groped or assaulted, then I am sorry to say that you cannot rely on assistance from general passers-by.

It's a shame not more Japanese are willing to get involved. On more than one occasion when I have witnessed a fight or attack in Tokyo, passers-by walk past the woman getting hit, or the bleeding young man on the street. Strangely, it's often foreigners who will go call the police, or nurse the victim while help is on its way. It was a harsh and quick adjustment that fortunately most foreigners and most women don't have to take on, but it let me know very quickly how society works in Japan.

Part of Japan's idea of harmony is the reluctance to get involved with other people's problems. To 'interfere' with a crime taking place would increase the victim's duress as the victim would have increased attention directed towards them (something the Japanese generally do not seek) and they would feel a sense of obligation towards the person offering help. Again, this is very sad to Westerners, so be prepared.

Theft

Your personal and household belongings are generally safe in Japan, but if anything is stolen, then report it to the nearest police box. Purses generally turn up in Japan, usually with everything intact, including your cash. Remember to contact your bank immediately if any bank-related items have been stolen. It's always a good idea to write down your bank's name, your bank account number, and passport number somewhere other than in your purse. If your items are found and turned in to the police but are uncollected by you, then they will be sent to the local Lost and Found office after about two weeks.

The Japanese are very honest about things like this, or perhaps it's something to do with the fact that if a purse is turned in and not claimed then the honest person receives the cash within. Also, there is an unspoken rule that you give ten percent of the cash in your purse to the person who handed it in. Either way, if you find a wallet, hand it in—you'll build up your good karma and probably get some cash too.

Friends are usually pretty good in these situations. A friend of mine raised about ¥50,000 within two days just by sending out some emails about her lost purse.

The trains

For some newcomers to Japan, it may seem strange to include trains within a section on safety, although my mother tells me that the international media have picked up on this phenomenon. Most women (foreign and Japanese) have encountered a *chikan*. Pronounced chee-kan, there is no direct English translation, but 'a man who gropes women on a train' pretty much explains it. On a busy train, you may experience an unwanted hand on your boobs or bum. At first, it may be difficult to tell if it really is a chikan or if it is simply someone's briefcase, and a quick movement or glare at everyone around you will usually put a stop to it.

Again, you cannot rely on others to support you here. Other passengers will probably completely ignore what is happening, whether they have full view of the assault or you even if you scream 'chikan' at the top of your voice. If you drag the man off the train and take him to the railway police, even then you may get no help. The chikan will probably offer you some money to make you go away, which the police will probably urge you to accept. You may be asked to show mercy to this poor man who just couldn't help himself and risks losing his home, his family, and his job if you pursue your report.

Of course, groping women on trains is sexual assault and if it happens to you and you are worried about your physical safety, then take some peace of mind in the fact that the incident will probably go no further. It is your emotional and psychological well-being that you need to focus on, especially if the abuse is repeated by the same man on the same train on the same route you take every day, which has been known to happen. If it happens to you and you are confused by your feelings, you are not alone. If you don't feel comfortable in yelling at the guy, you can always carry a pin in your hand (which is what a student I once taught did).

If I were referring to this kind of assault in our home countries, my advice would be very different. But one of the aspects of living in another country is learning to choose your battles. I spent a long time thinking and talking about certain abuses of women's rights and freedoms in Japan, until I finally realised that it was not my responsibility to change things, and I didn't like the negativity that dominated my thoughts during that period. I wanted to make a difference, but I needed to channel my energy in a positive, constructive way. If you are an English teacher, one of the best things you can do is talk to your students about these issues. If you are a high school teacher like I was, then it will probably be the first time that your students have talked to an adult about their experiences with chikans (and almost every girl in your class will have had this experience). Instead of storing up your own negative feelings, allow your students to express theirs and educate them in how to empower themselves.

Domestic violence

If you are a victim of domestic violence while in Japan, then do not expect the police to take your phone calls for help or attempts to press charges seriously. At the time of writing, Japan has only just passed a law to recognise domestic violence. If you do report domestic violence to the police, then one of my translators advises you to say that a 'man' hit you, rather than a boyfriend or husband. The police consider domestic violence to be a private matter and may say that they can only do something if there is murder involved. Questions about your role in provoking his violence will be asked. You may be told that this is just a form of communication and that you should go home and be nicer to your partner, which will stop him from hitting you. Serious injuries such as multiple broken bones, stab wounds, and serious head injuries may be taken seriously if you have a witness. Most Western women who experience domestic violence while in Japan (although this is not a common occurrence) are very dissatisfied with the police:

> When I fled the apartment and reported that my husband was beating me (he was drinking heavily), they wanted to know why. When I told them that he assumed I was having an affair, they asked, "Well, are you?" Even though I said no, they had no interest in accompanying me home to get my daughter out of the apartment.

I've deliberately presented you with a bleak picture in order to prepare you for an unsupportive police reaction. However, the police are becoming increasingly concerned about their public image regarding domestic violence, and threats to go to the press may force them to give you more attention. My friend Monique was beaten by her Japanese ex-boyfriend; she reported the crime to the police and was successful. This is her story:

My ex punched me ten times. I went to the police station two days after. I told them that they had a bad reputation in dealing with domestic violence and that I wanted to be taken seriously. The police told me that it was because so many women eventually drop the charges that they didn't take complaints seriously. They told me that I would have to be tough, I may have to see my ex end up in jail, and that I had to be certain that I wouldn't drop the charges. They photographed my injuries and took ages compiling a report. I went to a Japanese lawyer who someone recommended and he told me that I could get ¥100,000 for every punch—that's the way they work it out here. I thought this was crap considering I would be left with scars on my face, so told him to go for a lot more. I said 5 million or I'd press charges, that way I reckoned I'd get half. The lawyers negotiated everything privately so I didn't even have to see my ex and eventually settled for 3.5 million. Before it goes to court it goes to the prosecutor and it was up to her whether it went on from there. She thought that my ex had paid enough and I didn't want to completely ruin his life, so I said that I would drop the charges if he paid the money. He wasn't sorry at all—he only paid it because the police threatened to come into his company and take him down to the station. He would have done anything to prevent getting a criminal record which would have stopped him being employed anywhere. He paid it to prevent loss of face. I feel kind of weird about the whole thing—I feel bad for doing that to someone, but I had to do it. I hope he's learned his lesson. My advice is to go to the police and get everything you can. I didn't have any trouble at all. The police are really trying to clean up their act towards women.

If you are a victim of domestic violence, obviously you should get yourself into a safe environment as soon as possible. If you are financially unable to do this, there are certain steps you can take and groups you can contact for help. There are many women's shelters throughout Japan, both government and non-government. The welfare department of your local ward office can help you gain access to the government-run shelters. Some of the non-government-run shelters may ask you to pay to stay there, but they all have 'emergency funds' if you cannot pay. There is a legal aid system in Japan and the Tokyo Bar Association provides free consultations once a week. To take care of your emotional well-being after an attack, some 'Survivors' groups have recently started, mainly affiliated with the women's shelters. The shelters also operate hotlines for support, and many women's centres provide free counselling. You can also contact the counsellors and therapists listed in the Mental Health section in Chapter Three of this book.

Useful Japanese

thief	*dorobou*	flasher	*roshutsu kyou*
theft	*settou*	domestic violence	*katei nai bouryoku*
stalker	*sutookaa*	police box	*kouban*
harassment	*iyagarase*	police station	*keisatsusho*
rape	*reipu*	police officer	*keisatsukan /keikan*

Stop following me.	*Tsuite konai de kudasai.*
If you come near me again I will call the police.	*Moshi kore ijou chikazuitara keisatsu o yobimasu yo.*
Go away.	*Atchi e itte.*
Don't touch me.	*Sawaranai de.*
I'm going to call the police.	*Keisatsu o yobimasu yo.*
This man is touching me. (on a train)	*Kono hito watashi ni sawatte kimashita.*
I want to report a crime.	*Tsuuhou shitai no desu ga.*
A man hit me.	*Otoko ga nagutte kimashita.*
Please help me.	*Tasukete kudasai.*
Help!	*Tasukete.*
Do you need any help?	*Douka shimashita ka.*
Are you OK?	*Daijoubu desu ka.*
Shall I call the police?	*Keisatsu o yobimashou ka.*
Please call the police.	*Keisatsu o yonde kudasai.*
Please call an ambulance.	*Kyuukyuusha o yonde kudasai.*

Resources

Legal Advice
For your nearest Bar Association contact the Tokyo office on 03-3580-0082. Your local International Association can also organise legal help. Check with your ward office.

Emiko Miki 045-662-2226
> Specialises in domestic violence, sexual harrassment, divorce, and immigration issues. Based in Yokohama, but can give you contacts in your area.

Foreigners Criminal Case 03-3591-1301
> NGO consultation for foreigners involved in criminal or civil cases.

Japan Legal Aid Association 03-3581-6941

Police
Police Counselling Hotline for Foreigners 03-3503-8484
> Will assist you with anything to do with police, emergency, and safety matters. Can also provide interpreters if you need to go to a police station and do not speak Japanese.
> http://www.npa.go.jp

Rape
Rape Crisis Centre of Tokyo .... 03-3207-3692 (J)

Women's Shelters
Contact your ward office or House of Emergency Love and Peace (HELP) on 03-3368-8855 for your nearest shelter.

Other
Back Off
> Women's self-defense programme run by Yokota Air Base.
> http://www.backoffonline.com

Navy Family Service Center 0243-9619
> Family Advocacy Program for US military personnel and families. Addresses domestic violence prevention and education, trains command leadership on key issues involving domestic violence. Assistance and treatment services are offered to both victims and perpetrators.
> http://www.cfay.navy.mil/fsc/fap/fap.htm

Web Resources
Japan Information Network—Crime Statistics
> http://jin.jcic.or.jp/stat/category_14.html

31

Getting Around

Planes

There are many airports throughout Japan that provide both international and domestic flights. Narita Airport, near Tokyo, is the world's fifth busiest international airport and the one that most foreigners use to enter and leave the country. It is actually about a two-hour journey from the centre of Tokyo, so I don't recommend using a taxi to get into the city. All of the airports have trains and buses linking them to the nearest city centre. Check at the information desks, most of which have English-speaking staff. For long-distance domestic travel, flying is not much more expensive than taking the bullet train, and usually much quicker. Many of the airports have a special baggage handling service, and will send your luggage to your destination in Japan, where it will arrive the next day. Most people don't have any problems with this, although one woman's suitcases arrived sans underwear ...

Trains

Japanese people travel further on trains than any other people in the world: over 2000km per person per year. The extensive rail network is run by Japan Railway (JR) and several private companies. It was originally built by department stores to deliver customers right to their stores, and this explains why you suddenly find yourself in a food hall when you thought you were exiting the station. Trains in Japan are clean, frequent, on time and, in Tokyo, crowded beyond belief. White-gloved station attendants are employed to push more people onto rush hour trains already packed three times above capacity. Getting a seat on these trains depends on your timing and agility. You don't need to worry about that little old lady waiting next to you getting trampled in the rush—she'll elbow her way in to get the best seat before you're even aware that the doors are open. On the subject of doors, if you're not sure when they're about to close, don't bother rushing onto the train; there'll probably be another one in a few minutes and it's not worth the agony and embarrassment of getting your head, foot, or bum stuck between them. OK, so the doors will bounce back open pretty quickly, but who wants to stand in a carriage full of people who've just witnessed that? Also, don't be surprised if in the event of your finding a seat, you become the only person to give it up to an obviously pregnant woman accompanied by six shopping bags and two spoilt kids, only to find that she gives the seat to her kids and adds their heavy schoolbags to her own load.

In the highly unlikely event of a train being late, there will be non-stop apologies over the loudspeakers, 'late' slips handed out for you to give to your employer, and a rather large bill for the family of the person who threw themselves under the train, which is basically the only reason that a train is ever late. Rail travel is not 24-hour, except on New Year's Eve when the Yamanote Line circling Tokyo runs all night. So for 364 days of the year, your social life will be dominated by catching the last train home; one good reason among many to minimise the distance between work, home, and your stomping ground (see Finding a Place in Chapter Two). There are various train passes available that can save you money, such as tickets valid for 1–3 months, 11 tickets for the price of 10, and a one-day pass valid for most subway lines in Tokyo. Most train stations and trains have signs and maps in English and Japanese. If you get confused, just say the station name to another passenger and they will ensure that you get off at the right place, providing you let them practise their English on you for the remainder of your journey. It took me two years before I noticed that many of the ticket machines had an English button, but if you can't see it either, then buy the cheapest ticket and pay the difference at the Fare Adjustment machine when you get off. Most Tokyo foreigners spend about two hours a day on trains, which is a lot less than the Japanese do. If you can beat that little old lady to a seat, then congratulate yourself. However difficult it may sound, use your train time to read, write, or study Japanese rather than to stress out about how crowded the train is or about the man sleeping on your shoulder who's drooling whiskey-sodden saliva down the only decent jacket you own.

See the section on Safety in this chapter for information about sexual harassment on trains.

Buses

Japan has an extensive network of bus routes, both local and long distance. Local buses tend to be crowded, but take much longer than trains due to the busy traffic. Although the buses are numbered, the destination signs both on and in the buses are rarely in English and this can make it difficult to identify which bus you need, never mind when you have to get off. When you get on, you usually put your money in the machine next to the driver to whom you do not need to speak (a sign will tell you the fare for all destinations) and get off the bus at the side door. With some buses, you take a ticket when you get on and pay at the front when leaving the bus—the cost depends on how far you have travelled and there is a sign indicating how much you have to pay. Some buses only stop if you press a button to inform the driver that you want to get off. If you can't understand the loudspeaker bus stop announcements, then, as with the trains, ask another passenger to help you. If this is a regular route for you, you should memorise the *kanji* on the front of the bus and become familiar with your destination as soon as possible.

For long-distance bus journeys, you need to reserve a seat at a travel agency—see the resources that follow.

Cars

Driving in Japan is not entirely the unpleasant and stressful experience that some would have you believe. In cities, yes, there are many awkward narrow roads—Tokyo's road system is based on the idea that an enemy should be suitably confused and find it impossible to walk in a straight line to the Imperial Palace. There are traffic lights at every junction, but I like to think they make your journey a slower and more enjoyable one. The speed limit in built-up areas is 50kph but rarely will you get up to that speed. Expressways have an 80kph speed limit that most people ignore; however, there are some speed traps around Japan, so take care. The Japanese are generally careful, polite drivers, quite happy to let you go first, often bowing in front of their steering wheels as you do so. Road-rage is nonexistent; you won't hear drivers screaming obscenities out the window if a 'tense' situation occurs. Gas stations provide impeccable service, cleaning everything in sight and stopping all the traffic to allow you back on the road. Although many major roads are signposted in English and Japanese, the main problem with driving in Japan is getting lost. Be sure to get a copy of the *Japan Road Atlas* and plan your route in advance. Remember that the officers at the police boxes will be happy to provide you with directions if you get lost.

Contact the Japan Automobile Federation (JAF) for an English-language brochure explaining the traffic rules. If you become a member of JAF, then you can call them during a breakdown. If you are a member of an automobile association in your home country, then you may be eligible to become a member of JAF.

The basic rules for cars and driving are: drive on the left; the driver and front passenger must wear seat belts; car seats are required for babies and small children; do not drive under the influence of alcohol; park only in designated areas or your vehicle will be removed; but most important, you cannot buy a car unless you can prove that you have somewhere to park it. Unless your apartment comes with its own parking space, you have to rent one, which can cost from ¥100 a month in rural areas, to ¥60,000 a month in the centre of Tokyo. Parking is a problem in major cities in Japan and has led to maximum usage of parking space: cars stacked on top of each other on flimsy metal frames; narrow but high-in-the-sky and deep-in-the-ground parking buildings where you park your car on a metal circle and let the rotating machinery do the rest; as well as sprawling parking lots jammed full with cars and excessive numbers of attendants with whom you leave your keys and your faith.

To drive in Japan you need both your regular driving licence and an international driving permit from your own country. However, if you are staying for longer than six months you need to apply for a Japanese driving licence from your ward office. Ownership of cars must be registered with your local ward office. Car insurance is compulsory in Japan and your ward office provides a reasonable car insurance scheme. You can apply for this at many places including banks and post offices.

When a car in Japan reaches three years old, it must undergo a thorough inspection every two years to check its roadworthiness. When it is nine years old, it must be inspected every year. Due to the cost of the inspection (about ¥150,000), most Japanese simply buy a new car, creating a surplus of unwanted secondhand cars. Private export of these cars is popular amongst foreigners; depending on your home country, this can be a lucrative sideline if you have the initial cash to spare. The laws regulating car import are different for each country, but New Zealand and Ireland have the most favourable laws due to the fact that they don't have car manufacturing industries of their own. Check with your embassy.

Car rental is approximately ¥8,000 per day and you must have an international licence.

Traffic accidents

If you are involved in a traffic accident you should call the police by phoning 110 and, if necessary, an ambulance by phoning 119. In order to avoid increased insurance premiums, most people choose to deal with accidents privately with a cash payment.

Should you choose to contact your insurance company, the police in charge of the area where you had your accident must be notified on the day of the accident because they are required to provide a certificate. You need to write down the names, ages, addresses, and phone numbers of all concerned. Take the other driver's licence plate number and driving licence number, checking the photograph to ensure it matches the driver. If your accident is with a Japanese driver, then generally you will find them incredibly polite, even if you were driving like an idiot and the accident is solely your responsibility. If the accident was your responsibility, then it is very important to help the victim in any way possible and to regularly visit them in hospital. Regardless of whether the accident was your fault or not, have a medical check afterwards even if you think your injuries are minor. You will need a doctor's certificate if any compensation issues arise later. Contact your insurance company as soon as possible after an accident. There are Traffic Accident Consultation Offices in every ward office, but take a Japanese friend with you because their ability to deal with English speakers varies.

Motorbikes

Motorbikes are popular in Japan, especially in cities, due to their obvious ability to get you through tight spots that are hopeless for cars. You need your own country's motorcycle licence and an international driving permit unless your bike is 50cc, in which case a regular car licence will suffice. Crash helmets must be worn at all times. Motorbikes tend to be small in engine capacity due to the laws preventing sale in Japan of bikes over 750cc. If you do own a bike of that capacity, there is a condition during registration that requires you to prove that you can lift it, should it fall over. Bikes of 250cc (and under) are exempt from the Japanese inspection system, so tend to be most popular. Motorbikes of 450cc and under must be registered with your ward office; bikes over 450cc must be registered with the Bureau of Traffic.

Bicycles

Bicycles seem to rule not only the roads, but also the sidewalks in Japan; no other moving object seems to have right of way over the bicycle. Cars tend to keep a respectful distance when bicycles are on the road and pedestrians leap to one side when they hear that bicycle bell. Don't do as my mother did when she visited and froze on the spot every time she heard one, but move to one side or the other immediately—believe me, you need to know this!

Many people find the dirty air in the cities worrying, and buy nose and mouth 'masks' to wear while they are cycling.

Bicycles are fairly cheap to buy and must be registered with the police upon purchase. The shop at which you buy your bicycle can do this for you, or if you buy the bicycle secondhand, then be sure to register it with the police yourself. Registering bicycles is very important in Japan, as the police tend to pay specific attention to foreigners on bicycles, checking that it is actually registered in your name. There is nothing to prevent you from picking up one of the incredibly high number of good but abandoned bicycles for yourself. Don't be tempted though: if you are caught on a bicycle not registered in your name, you won't get in any trouble, but you will be taken to the police station and you'll have to wait while the police trace the owner to check that it isn't stolen and, if it is, ask the owner if they mind your using it. If your bicycle is stolen, report it to the police immediately, although it is unlikely that you will see it again.

There are special parking zones designated for bicycles and if you leave your vehicle in a no-parking zone it may be removed, in which case you must contact the Bicycle Control Section of your ward office. You will have to pay a fee of about ¥3000, show your alien registration card or passport, and show the key for your lock. If you don't claim your bike within two months, then it will be disposed of. You can register with certain parking areas by paying a monthly fee, a one-day only fee, or by purchasing tickets sold at the parking areas and the Bicycle Control Section of your ward office. To qualify for this, your home or work must be at least 800 metres away from the nearest station.

Most wards have a 'Rent-a-Cycle Port' where you can rent bikes on a monthly basis for about ¥2000 or just for one day at about ¥200. You can also find many bicycle rental shops close to railway stations, although they tend to be more expensive.

Taxis

I love Japanese taxi drivers; they are usually polite, don't rip you off (unlike taxi drivers in just about every other country), and will often change their radio to an English station for you. If you don't mind the drivers practising their English on you, then the journey can be quite enjoyable for all concerned. Taxis can be easily found lined up near any train station, but also cruising about the roads at most times of the day or night. If the taxi exhibits a red light, then it's available, but don't try to open the doors yourself; they open and close automatically. Fares are about five times the price of trains, so can be worth it if there is a group of you and you would have had to make several rail transfers to reach your destination. Taxi drivers in Japan do not accept tips. Try not to lose patience if it seems like the driver is lost, it is often just as difficult for them to find their way around some parts of Japan as it is for you. It's best to become familiar with the area around your home and to learn some basic directions in Japanese. In Tokyo, most taxis are bright yellow, although there are some individuals operating as taxi drivers too. My advice is to only take the yellow cabs. It is notoriously difficult to find a taxi in Roppongi after about 1:00 a.m., and you may be approached by individuals offering you a lift; although most are probably genuine, don't accept their offer.

There is also the 'daiko' taxi service—providing someone to drive you and your car home if you are drunk.

Useful Japanese

bullet train	shinkansen		local train	futsuu densha
aeroplane	hikouki		express train	kyuukou densha
bus	basu		transfer (noun)	norikae
bus stop	basutei		transfer (verb)	norikaeru
train	densha		ticket	kippu

car .... *kuruma*

international driving

license .... *kokusai menkyoshou*

traffic accident .... *koutsuu jiko*

motorbike .... *baiku*

crash helmet .... *herumetto*

bicycle .... *jitensha*

How can I get to ... ? .... *... e wa douyatte ittara ii desu ka.*

I want to book a flight/seat to ... . *... e no hikouki/densha no zaseki no yoyaku o toritai no desu ga.*

When is the next flight/train/bus to ... ? .... *... e no tsugi no furaito(bin)/densha/basu wa itsu desu ka.*

I want to send my luggage to this address.

(show address) .... *Kono juusho made watashi no nimotsu o okutte kudasai.*

When will my luggage arrive? .... *Watashi no nimotsu wa itsu todokimasu ka.*

Which train/bus goes to ... ? .... *... e iku densha/basu wa dore desu ka.*

Does this train/bus go to ... ? .... *Kono densha/basu wa ... e ikimasu ka.*

Please take my seat. .... *Douzo osuwari kudasai.*

I'd like to buy a discount ticket. .... *Disukaunto chiketto o kudasai.*

Could you please tell me when we

reach ... station? (to the person sitting next

to you) .... *... eki ni tsuitara oshiete kudasaimasu ka.*

Where is the fare adjustment machine? ...... *Seisanki wa doko desu ka.*

Where is the exit of this station? .... *Kono eki no deguchi wa doko desu ka.*

Please stop falling asleep on my

shoulder. .... *Watashi no kata ni yokkakatte nemuranai de kudasai.*

Excuse me, I'm getting off now. .... *Sumimasen, orimasu.*

I'm sorry officer, I didn't realise I was going

so fast. .... *Sumimasen, son'na ni supiido o dashiteiru towa kiga tsukimasen deshita.*

Fill it up please. (fuel) .... *Mantan ni shite kudasai.*

I am lost, can you help me? .... *Michi ni mayotte shimaimashita. Tasukete moraemasu ka.*

Please send me the English version of

'Rules of the Road'. .... *Koutsuu ruuru no hon no eigo ban o okutte kudasai.*

My car has broken down. .... *Kuruma ga kowarete shimaimashita.*

I'd like to rent a parking space. .... *Chuushajou o karitai no desu ga.*

I'd like to apply for a Japanese driving

licence. .... *Nihon no unten menkyoshou ni kakikaetai no desu ga.*

I'd like to register my

car/motorbike/bicycle. .... *Watashi no kuruma/baiku/jitensha o tourokushitai no desu ga.*

I'd like to apply for car insurance. .... *Sharyou hoken o moushikomitai no desu ga.*

My car needs its biannual inspection. .... *Ni nen ni ichido no shaken ga hitsuyou desu.*

I'd like to send my car back to ... (your

home country). .... *Watashi no kuruma o ... e okurikaeshitai no desu ga.*

I'd like to rent a car/bicycle.	*Rentakaa/rentasaikuru o karitai no desu ga.*
Can we arrange compensation privately? ...	*Watashitachi de hoshoukin ni tsuite hanashiaimashou ka.*
I'd like to report a traffic accident.	*Koutsuu jiko no todokede o shitai no desu ga.*
I would like to visit you in hospital.	*Byouin ni omimai ni ikitai no desu ga.*
I left my bicycle in a no-parking zone. It was removed and I would like to collect it.	*Chuusha kinshi no basho ni jitensha o tomete shimatta node, motte ikarete shimaimashita. Dakara sore o tori ni ikanakute wa narimasen.*
I'd like to register with a bicycle parking area.	*Chuurinjou ni tourokushitai no desu ga.*
Please take me to	*... made onegaishimasu.*
Do you mind if I smoke?	*Tabako o sutte mo ii desu ka.*
About how much will it cost to go to ... ?	*... made wa ikura gurai kakarimasu ka.*
Turn right/left.	*Migi/hidari e magatte kudasai.*
Go straight.	*Massugu onegaishimasu.*
Please stop here.	*Koko de tomatte kudasai.*
I'm drunk, please drive me and my car home.	*Osake o nonde iru node, watashi no kuruma de uchi made okutte kudasai.*

Resources

General Travel Information
Japan National Tourist Organisation 03-3216-1903
   http://www.jnto.go.jp/
Japan Travel Bureau (JTB) 03-5620-9500
   http://www.jtb.co.jp/eng/index.html
Japan Travel Phone 0088-22-4800
Tourist Information Centre 03-3201-3331

Public Transport Maps and Timetables
Japan: A Bilingual Atlas
   A Kodansha Guide, Kodansha International: 1991
Japan: A Bilingual Map: A Complete Map of Japan
   Kodansha International: 1992
Japan Country Map
   Periplus Travel Maps: 1999
Japan Road Map
   International Road Map Series, Ravenstein Verlag Gmbh: 1991
JTB's Mini Timetable
   Japan Travel Bureau (JTB) Call 03-5620-9500 for a copy.
Tokyo City Atlas: A Bilingual Guide
   Kodansha International: 2000

Domestic Travel Agencies

Meitetsu World Travel Head Office 03-3552-1525
Nichinoku Tours (Tokyo only) 03-3447-5361
Nippon Express 03-5256-2351
Tokyu Tourist Head Office 03-3401-7131
Travel Experts (Tokyo only) 03-3262-9966

Websites

Japan Information—Travel and Tourism
      http://sunsite.sut.ac.jp/asia/japan/travel/
Transportation around Japan
      http://www.bergen.org/AAST/Projects/Japan/transportation.html
Transportation in Japan
      http://www.japan-guide.com/e/e627.html

Car Information

Accident Centre 0423-390-111
Car Tax Office Head Office .... 042-527-5453 (J)
Compact Car Inspection Association .... 03-3472-1561 (J)
Fundamental Traffic Rules
      http://www.pref.kanagawa.jp/police/eng/e_mes/engf1001.htm
Japan Automobile Federation (JAF) 03-5976-9777
      Publish Rules of the Road
      http://www.fia.com/tourisme/infoclub/japan.htm
Licensing Head Office .... 03-3474-1374 (J)
Motor Vehicle Inspection and Registration Guide
      http://www.motnet.go.jp/unyue/index1e.htm

English-Speaking Car Dealers and Car Dealing Information

Fahren International Sales 03-3435-8667
      Domestic Volkswagen sales.
IBC Japan
      Information on car dealers, exporters, parts.
      http://www.ibcjapan.co.jp/home.asp
Michael Lay Motors 090-3805-7141
      Export, insurance, registration, disposal, buying,
      selling, bodywork.
Naz Trading 048-798-4446
      Export only.
Nikkyo Co. Ltd. Tokyo 03-3914-8301
      http://www.nikkyo.gr.jp/
Occidental Cars 03-5768-6022
      Buying, selling, registration, insurance, servicing,
      maintenance, export.
Showa Trade Co. Ltd. 03-3453-9787
      Export used cars, international auctions.
SJS Fine Imports 090-4832-0065
      Domestic sales, export.
Spectrum
      http://www.trade.co.jp/carpricing.htm

Sundon Japan Ltd. 048-254-5585
    Motorbikes, cars, parts.
    http://www.bikelife.com
Tozai Trading (see display ad, page 45) 047-429-2960
    Export, registration, shipping, sales.
    http://www.ceres.dti.ne.jp/~tozai

Car Rental
Nippon Rent-A-Car 03-3485-7196
Toyota Rental Lease 03-3263-6321

Airports
Haneda Flight Information 03-5757-8111
Limousine Bus Reservation Centre (Tokyo only) 03-3665-7220
Narita Flight Information 0476-34-5000
Narita Terminal 1 Lost and Found 0476-32-2105
Narita Terminal 2 Lost and Found 0476-34-5220
Tokyo City Air Terminal (TCAT) General and Flight Information 03-3665-7111

Airport Websites
Airports—Japan
    http://www.thetravelsite.com/Dests/DGPac/Gjapan/airport.html
Kansai International Airport Information
    http://www.kansai-airport.or.jp/index-e.html
Komatsu Airport Information
    http://www.pref.ishikawa.jp/k_air/index_e.html
Narita Airport Customs Homepage
    http://www.narita-airport.or.jp/customs/eng/
Narita Airport Information
    http://www.narita-airport.or.jp/airport_e/index_e.html
Niigata Airport Information
    http://www.pref.niigata.jp/sec25/en/index.html

Travel Agencies for International Flights

Air and Sea Service 03-3501-3955	Air Bank Co. 03-3233-1177
Air Voyages 03-3470-3795	Beyond Travel 03-5358-3177
EIS Japan 03-3265-3421	http://www.go-beyond.co.jp
Four Seasons Travel ...03-5907-5220	Just Travel 03-3362-3441
Number One Travel 03-3770-1381	Sky World Travel 03-5954-8871
http://www.no1travel.com	STA Travel 03-5485-8380
Trizephyr 03-5431-7371	(see display ad, page 44)
Trywell International 03-3498-2926	http://www.statravel.co.jp
Will Tour 03-3239-1631	Toppan Travel 03-5403-2525

Transportation of Luggage to Airports
Also check courier services listed in **Utilities** in **Chapter Two** and **Before You Go** in **Chapter Eight**.

Air Baggage Service Co (ABC) 03-3545-1131
NTS Sky Porter 03-3590-1919

Train and Subway Information Lines

Eidan Subway	03-3837-7046	JR	03-3384-0934 (J)
JR East	03-3423-0111	Keisei Skyliner	03-3831-0131
Seibu	042-996-2888		

Train and Subway Websites

Japan Bullet Train Schedule
http://www.sfjnto.org/bullet.html
Japan Rail Pass
http://www.jreast.co.jp/jrp/
Tokyo Subway Stations
http://www.subwaynavigator.com/bin/select/english/japan/tokyo
Travel Expert on Business Insight Japan
Type in your origin and destination and the site produces several travel routes, including prices and times.
http://www.japan-magazine.com/cgi-bin/expwww/exp.cgi

Bus Information Lines

JR East Overnight Bus 03-3423-0111
JR Overnight Bus Kanto .... 03-3215-0489 (J)
Kanto Bus .... 03-3371-7116 (J)
KB Bus .... 03-3928-6011 (J)
Keio Bus .... 03-3381-0643 (J)
Keio Highway Overnight Bus Reservation Centre .... 03-5376-2222 (J)
Kokusai Kogyo Bus Tokyo and Saitama 03-3273-1126

Cycling

Paul Dorn: Cycling in Osaka, Japan
http://userwww.sfsu.edu/~pdorn/japantrip.html
Tokyo BHB—Cycling
http://jpop.hatch.co.jp/bhb/
Tokyo Cycling.com
http://www.tokyocycling.com/index2.htm

Finance

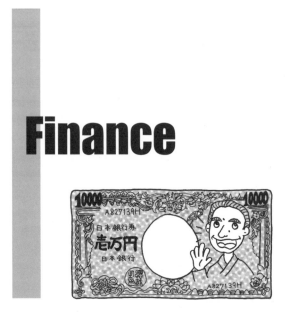

Earning

You will probably earn more in Japan than you would doing the same job at home. Some women come to Japan precisely for the financial opportunities, although most find their motivation for staying is different. I came here for adventure, but I wouldn't have gone looking for adventure if that adventure wouldn't provide the means by which I could repay my student loans. You don't have to be qualified in any specific area to get started in Japan, although obviously if you have specialist qualifications and speak Japanese, then your earning potential is much higher (see Chapter Six, Working). However, Japan has changed a lot and foreigners are not earning the same money they used to:

> *Fifteen years ago when I first came here it was more for the adventure of starting something new. After I got here I realized I could make a lot of money (back in THOSE days!) and managed to pay off my loans. Today, this simply isn't possible. The going rate for an hour private student is ¥4000, whereas in 1985 it was double that.*

So be realistic and take with a pinch of salt the comments of your friend who returned home loaded in 1990. If financial security or comfort is one of the reasons you are here, then I think you need to earn ¥250,000 a month at the absolute minimum, or you may as well be in another country. And don't expect many trips around Asia or loan repayments if you're earning that money. Here's an example of one Tokyo woman's basic monthly outgoings:

Expenses	¥
rent	90,000
bills	40,000
food	60,000
transport	30,000
misc.	30,000
ward tax	10,000
health insurance	10,000
	270,000

See Finding a Job in Chapter Six for initial costs when you arrive in Japan.

According to my research, the average monthly income for a Western woman in Japan is about ¥350,000 a month, which is enough to travel, repay debts, save, and increase your general standard of living above what you are used to at home.

Managing your money

You can open an account in any bank in Japan. Take along your alien registration card and your passport, and complete an application form. Your employer may do this for you as most employers will not employ you unless you have a bank account. I recommend opening an account with a bank that has ATMs with English instructions. This will save you the hassle of asking staff to help you every time you go in, although they will happily do so. Bank services available include savings deposits, remittances, money transfers, overseas remittances, and payment of utility bills. Post offices provide the same services. To close your account, you may need to go to the branch where you opened it. Banks and ATMs (except Citibank) are not open 24 hours a day or every day, which may come as a shock to you at first, so make sure you have enough money with you at all times. If you lose your bank card and/or bank book be aware that it will take two weeks for them to be replaced, so in the event that you lose both, you need to have some cash at home or a generous and understanding friend.

Spending

It has been said that every time you walk out of your apartment you should say goodbye to ¥5000. All the foreigners I know earn really good money yet always seem to be broke. It's not just that Japan is expensive, but you seem to spend money on things here that you wouldn't at home. You take more vacations because living in Japan is stressful or you take advantage of the fact that you are close to so many interesting countries, you go home for a wedding, you feel more aware of your appearance so you spend more on clothes or beauty products, you get drunk more often because of the alcohol-orientated environment, you take classes because you need to meet new people, you join networking groups to improve your job prospects—the list is endless. In short, you are probably earning a lot in Japan, but you will be spending a lot too, and not just in Japan:

> *I have spent all of my money on airplane tickets and graduate school tuition. When the exchange rate was ¥80 to the dollar, I went sailing in Greece. When it was ¥140 to the dollar, I went backpacking in Thailand. Ah the joys of an academic schedule! I may be broke, but I have one and a half graduate degrees and a heart full of golden memories of travelling in about a dozen different countries. I wouldn't trade it in.*

Tax

There are two types of tax that you must pay in Japan: national (income) tax and local (ward/residential) tax. (Check with your home country to see if you have to pay tax there while you are overseas.)

National tax is deducted from your salary and paid by your employer. The tax year starts on the 1st of January and ends on the 31st of

December. For your first year, twenty percent will be deducted from your salary and thereafter your tax rate depends on your income. At the beginning of each year your employer must provide you with a tax certificate that indicates your salary for the previous year and the amount of tax you paid. You must submit this certificate (or certificates if you had more than one employer for the previous year) to the tax office when you complete a tax return form. You will receive notification (in Japanese) in February and tax forms are supposed to be submitted by mid April, although, in fact, you can do this at any time of the year. The tax office has a detailed English brochure explaining how to complete the return, but they also have English-speaking staff that will help you and, at peak periods, a special office for foreigners. Note that your medical expenses may be deductible, so include them in the form. If you haven't paid enough tax for the previous year, you will be expected to settle the balance. If you have paid too much tax, you will be reimbursed within two months via your bank account. If you haven't reported your tax for several years, you can also take your tax certificates for previous years and complete those years' tax returns.

Local tax is paid for the previous year, so if you have moved house, you have to pay local tax to your previous ward. Local tax is determined by the ward and is not related to your income. Some wards are more expensive than others; expect to pay around ¥8000 a month. You will receive a ward tax bill, which you can pay monthly at post offices, banks, or at the ward office itself.

Sending money overseas

All banks send money overseas, as do major post offices, and there is a special branch of Lloyds TSB Bank Plc. in Tokyo that offers the GoLloyds service to many countries throughout the world. Banks can telegraph or airmail your money, or write cheques for you to send. Fees vary. The post office can send money overseas via postal order, cash remittance, and account transfer (although the latter method is mostly to European countries). Again, fees vary. The whole process can keep you in the bank or post office for up to one hour. I've used GoLloyds since I came to Japan and, in my opinion, it is the best way to send money overseas—it takes about three minutes. I like the convenient service and the knowledge that I can speak to another native English-speaker by telephone if I have any questions. GoLloyds will send you a transfer card that you can use in your chosen bank whenever you want to send money. All you have to enter into the ATM is the amount. GoLloyds sends you confirmation of the transaction within a few days, including the exchange rate, so you don't need to wait for confirmation from the recipient.

Saving and Investing

If you're saving money in Japan, then you might want to look into investing too. There are several companies established in Japan specifically to meet the investment needs of foreigners. Investment advisor Alison Pockett, of Magellan Tresidder Tuohy in Tokyo, often works with Western women who feel nervous about approaching investment advisors. She urges women not to hesitate to ask for advice and is available to help:

> *It's amazing how many of us feel afraid or lack the confidence to seek financial advice. Many women have said to me prior to a seminar or a personal visit to my office for advice, "you really have to speak in basic terms to me—I know nothing" or "I haven't a clue about money or investments and I don't know what questions to ask." I came to Japan in 1994 and up until that time I had met very few women who had money of their own and made their own decisions by choice. Here, we have the opportunity to save far more than if we were living and working in our home countries. It's an opportunity not to be missed.* *

A good advisor shouldn't make you feel uncomfortable for asking basic questions and should start thinking in terms of what Alison calls 'broad-minded investing', so if you don't think you are getting your needs met, don't be afraid to shop around.

* From 'Financially Independent Women Take Control' from the Female-Friendly Finance column by Alison Pockett, *Being A Broad*, July 1998.

If you get into debt in Japan

In Japan, severe financial difficulties can seem much scarier than in your home country. I don't mean being a bit strapped for cash, I mean situations where you are receiving court orders for utility bills, cannot afford to pay your rent, have fairly large loan repayments to meet, are getting threatening phone calls and visits from people you would really rather not deal with, and know your next paycheck won't even begin to make a difference. Most Westerners will never experience this, but if you do, don't panic—I have been there and, although it is scary, you can get through it.

Contact everyone to whom you owe money, including utility companies whose next bill you know you will be unable to pay. Utility companies will not cut you off providing there is ongoing communication with them, as these services are considered essential to life, including the telephone. However, if you are unable to contact them or reach a repayment agreement, this is where being a Westerner in Japan can work to your advantage. Lawsuits take years and are expensive for everyone involved. Generally, neither lawsuits nor violent means of collecting debts are resorted to in Japan. Everyone is always aware that you can leave the country at any point and that your debtors would then receive nothing. If you are dealing with Japanese people, their lack of enjoyment of confrontation will make the negotiation process less unpleasant, but do not take advantage of this. Work out a reasonable repayment scheme (reasonable for you not for them), however small, to each of your debtors and do not make promises that you cannot keep.

In order to meet those repayments you have to be incredibly disciplined: sell what you can, eat carefully but healthily as you will need your strength, don't go anywhere (remember the ¥5000 thing), do not make any long-distance phone calls home, get some extra work (don't do anything you will regret later), get as many private students as you can (they are easy to come by and provide immediate cash), and try not to get depressed (this may be the hardest of all).

Having no money in Japan will change your whole life here until you are back on your feet and you do need some guardian angels around to help you through it. Friendships can be superficial in Japan and some will disappear slowly, which may be hard to deal with, but the friends who are truly there for you will come through offering apartments to stay in, food parcels that bring tears to your eyes, surprise I'm-taking-you-out-for-dinner visits, emergency cash with no repayment terms, and genuine and much-needed shoulders to cry on.

You will be OK in the end, and you will make sure it never happens again. I got through it and you will too.

Useful Japanese

money	*okane*	national (income)		
bank	*ginkou*	tax	*shotokuzei*	
monthly salary	*gekkyuu*	local tax	*chihouzei*	
yearly income	*nenshuu*	ward tax	*kuminzei*	
hourly rate	*jikyuu*	residential tax	*juuminzei*	
bank account	*ginkou-kouza*	tax certificate	*nouzei shoumeisho*	
exchange rate	*kawase souba/reeto*	tax office	*zeimusho*	
tax	*zeikin*			

I'd like to open a bank account. .... *Kouza-kaisetu no tetsuzuki o onegaishimasu.*

I'd like to transfer some money. .... *Furikomi tetsuzuki o onegaishimasu.*

I'd like to send some money overseas. .... *Kaigai e no soukin o onegaishimasu.*

What is the exchange rate today for
yen to ... ? .... *Kyou no yen kara ... no reeto wa ikura desu ka.*

I'd like to close my bank account. .... *Ginkou-kouza o tojiru tetsuzuki o onegaishimasu.*

I have lost my bank card/book. .... *Ginkou no kaado/tsuuchou o nakushite shimaimashita.*

I'd like to complete a tax return. .... *Shotoku shinkoku no tetsuzuki o onegaishimasu.*

I'd like to complete tax returns for the past
... years too. .... *Kako ... nen bun no shotoku shinkoku no tetsuzuki o onegaishimasu.*

I'd like to pay my ward tax. .... *Kuminzei o harau tetsuzuki o onegaishimasu.*

I'm sorry but I'm having some financial
problems at the moment. .... *Moushiwake arimasen ga, genzai kinsenteki na mondai o kakaete imasu.*

I cannot pay my telephone/gas/electricity/
water bill this month. .... *Kongetsu wa denwa/gasu/denki/suidou ryoukin o haraemasen.*

I'd like to pay my telephone/gas/electricity/
water bill. .... *Denwa/gasu/denki/suidou ryoukin no shiharai tetsuzuki o onegaishimasu.*

Resources

Bank Information
Tokyo Bankers Association 03-3216-3761
     http://www.zenginkyo.or.jp

Banks with English Information Telephone Services
Asahi Bank 03-3216-0059
Bank of Tokyo 03-3240-2176
Citibank 0120-504-189
Dai-ichi Kangyo Bank 0120-860-810
Fuji Bank 03-3216-2211
Sanwa Bank Foreign Customer Service 03-3586-3328
Sumitomo Mitsui Banking Corporation 03-3282-5353
Tokyo Mitsubishi Bank 03-3240-2176

Financial Consultants for Foreigners
Banner Overseas Financial Services 03-5724-5100
Magellan Tresidder Tuohy (see display ad, page 55) 03-3582-3773
Stirling MacGuire 03-5575-3761

Sending Money Overseas
Lloyds Bank Plc (see display ad, page 54) 03-3589-7745
Post Office
     http://www.yu-cho.mpt.go.jp/goods/e_g2700.htm

Tax
AA American Tax Service 03-3485-1971
     Helps US citizens complete tax forms for the US.
Government Tax Counselling Office 03-3821-9070

Websites
Business, Taxes and Customs—National Income Tax of Japan
     Detailed explanation of Japanese income tax system and requirements for US
     nationals.
     http://ny.cgj.org/btc/btc_1.html
Guide to Sending Money Overseas from Japan
     Lists banks with whom you can send money home, plus costs. Information
     pertains to Kanagawa only, but is relevant to people living all over Japan.
     http://www.nsknet.or.jp/heartkcb/sending_money.html
International Cost of Living
     Cost of living chart for several countries including Japan.
     http://expatforum.com/Resources/icol.htm
Price Check Tokyo
     Unofficial guide to prices of goods in Tokyo.
     http://www.pricechecktokyo.com/
Universal Currency Converter
     http://www.xe.net/ucc/

53

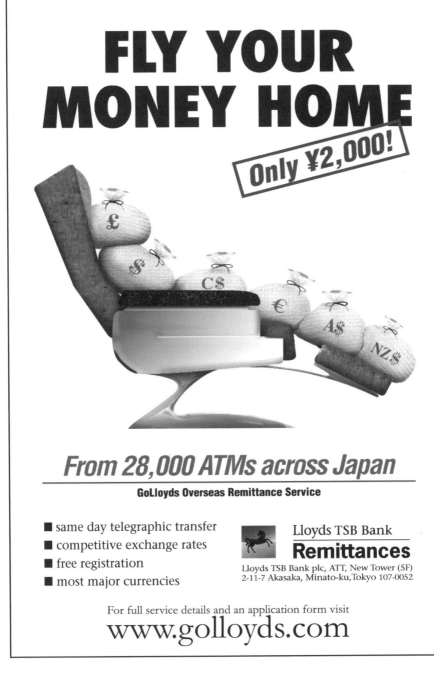

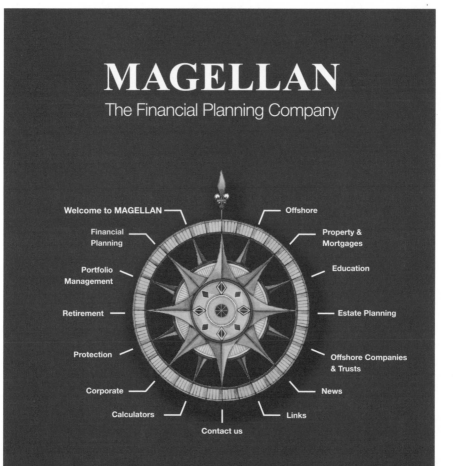

Food

Kitchens

Due to a lack of space, most kitchens in Japan contain the minimum of cooking facilities (unless you're on an 'ex-pat package' where Western style accommodation is provided). Two gas rings and a small grill are what most people have available. Depending on your perspective, this can either be incredibly stressful and limiting, or it can stimulate your creativity in finding new ways to cook and new dishes to prepare. Rice cookers, 'water-heaters' and microwaves are fairly cheap and widely available. I once managed to prepare a five-course Christmas dinner for twelve people, but I did use three different kitchens simultaneously and almost had a nervous breakdown at the end of it.

Food shopping

Whereas you may be used to visiting a huge supermarket once a month, in Japan people tend to shop every few days due to limited kitchen storage space. Fresh fruit, vegetable, fish, and meat shops can easily be found within walking distance of your home. (Elise Mori later explains why a traditional Japanese diet is so incredibly good for you and suggests several recipes to try.)

Imported food tends to be more expensive in Japan, and is available in several specialised shops and supermarkets, some ordinary supermarkets, and from mail-order stores as well. Check out the list at the end of this section for recommended stores that carry foreign and organic food.

Eating out

It may be that in your home country buying ingredients at a supermarket and cooking at home is usually much cheaper than eating out, but in Japan eating out can be only a fraction more expensive than eating at home. Many Western women find themselves able to eat out much more frequently than before they moved here. Busy schedules or jobs in several different locations often make eating out a necessity.

There are many kinds of restaurants in Japan, including 'Viking', all you can eat; 'coin', where you pay a machine and press a button to choose your dish; and regular 'sit down and order' restaurants. Service in restaurants is usually excellent, and you do not need to tip. Smoking is permitted in most restaurants.

On display outside Japanese restaurants you will often see plastic models of menu items. If you're having trouble ordering, then don't be shy; gesture for the staff to follow you outside and simply point to what you want to order. The staff won't mind. An increasing number of foreign food restaurants are available in Japan, although you may need to read *katakana* (the written form of Japanese used for 'foreign' words) in order to understand their menus. If you ask the staff what a menu item is, you may be able to understand their Japanese-English, for example, chips (UK) or fries (US) are 'furaido poteito' in Japanese.

Vegetarians beware: vegetarianism is not popular nor fully understood by most restaurants in Japan, so despite the fact that the staff may confidently tell you that your dish contains no meat, be prepared to see bits of bacon lying on top of it.

Japanese food
By Elise Mori

The traditional Japanese diet boasts much that is healthy for both men and women since it is essentially simple and uses a narrow range of indigenous produce, with an emphasis on freshness and seasonality. Even today, a typical Japanese meal consists of steamed rice, miso soup with the addition of some seaweed (and/or shellfish, daikon, mushrooms, etc.), pickles, fish, vegetables, and tofu or another soy-based product in some form or other. It is a diet based primarily on carbohydrates (rice), with sea and land vegetables secondary, followed by proteins in a distinct third place. Dishes are usually either steamed or grilled, and for as short a time as possible. Rice is readily available in three forms: polished white, unpolished, and brown. It is steamed, not boiled, so that more of the nutrients remain available. So much for simplicity, but what about freshness? Unlike the West, in Japan people don't tend go to the supermarket in their cars to stock up on the week's provisions; instead, they shop for the day's food from local greengrocers and fishmongers, which ensures that what they buy is fresh, seasonal, and by extension, healthier. People also buy from farm shops, dotted around the countryside and suburbs, where the produce couldn't get any fresher or, for that matter, more local! Some of these smallholdings use organic farming methods—look out for those with compost heaps in the corner, or ask the farmer. But it's not just what the Japanese eat that makes them so healthy, it's also what is left out of their diet that contributes to their longevity. Traditionally, no milk or milk-based products are used in Japanese food, a minimum of oil or fat is used (some notable exceptions—tempura, tendon, aburage, and chahan—are relatively late and foreign additions to the Japanese diet), meat is a rarity or is seen as a luxury, dessert is rare, and wheat-based products such as pasta and bread up until fairly recently were a novelty. All that's changing now, but there are still people, young people too, who refuse to eat *youshoku* (non-Japanese food).

Japanese food that's especially healthy for women
By Elise Mori

Seaweed/sea vegetables: One of the richest known sources of vitamins, minerals, and trace elements.

Wakame (a type of seaweed): Contains more than ten times the amount of calcium found in cow's milk. Especially good for pregnant, breast-feeding, menopausal, and post-menopausal women.

Sesame seeds: Another unbeatable source of calcium. Also giddily high in magnesium. Especially good for breastfeeding women and women who suffer from pre-menstrual tension.

Shiitake and maitake mushrooms: Incredible auto-immune boosting powers. Statistically, women have more problems with their auto-immune systems than men do.

Daikon: Contains more Vitamin C per 100g than grapefruit. Especially good for pregnant or breast-feeding women and women on the pill.

Turnip tops: Contains Vitamin A, Riboflavin (Vitamin B2), Vitamin C and Folic Acid, all in abundance. Especially important for pregnant women.

Tofu: More calcium than feta cheese, Camembert, and natural yoghurt.

Shoyu: More calcium than single cream or Savoy cabbage, more iron than oatmeal or almonds, and also contains Thiamine (Vitamin B1) and Riboflavin (B2).

Aburage (deep-fried tofu sheets): Thankfully contains more iron than pig's kidney, ox heart, and even spinach. Especially good for women of childbearing age, pregnant women, breast-feeding women, and those who have just given birth. (Pour boiling water over it first to remove the excess oil.)

Japanese green tea (Camellia sinensis): Reduces the risk of breast, skin, and other cancers. Has been credited with the ability to reduce the risk of heart disease and strokes, reduce blood sugar levels, heighten the body's ability to fight off viruses, and cope with menopause. Be aware that it's also high in caffeine.

Recipe 1: Instant Pickles

I can never get over how this recipe makes raw turnips a real pleasure to eat. They are a good complement to hot, fluffy steamed rice and salty grilled fish. Miso soup is a good addition to this menu too.

You will need: 3 white turnips with their greens still attached; 1 teaspoon salt; the juice of either half a lemon or *yuzu* (Japanese citron).

Method: Cut the greens off the turnips at the base. Wash, and throw into a pan of boiling water for all of ten seconds, then drain quickly and re-fresh in cold water. Squeeze out the water, cut into 2cm lengths, and put them in a bowl. Meanwhile, peel and trim off the top and tail of the turnip root, and slice very finely. Put the slices with the greens in the bowl, add the salt, and kneed firmly. Eventually the turnip pieces start to go floppy and release some of their water. Squeeze out as much water as you can, rinse under cold water, and refrigerate for at least an hour or until thoroughly chilled. Just before serving, squeeze the lemon or yuzu juice over them. This pickle recipe can be adapted to many other vegetables. Good ones to try are carrot, cucumber, cabbage, Chinese cabbage, or *daikon*.

Recipe 2: *Miso Shiru* (miso soup)

You will need: 3 to 4 heaped tablespoons of miso, 1 1/4 litres of water (this amount includes the 1 cup of *dashi* for Recipe 3), 1 sachet of dashi or a big pinch (use all five fingers) of *katsuobushi* flakes (put this inside a submersible strainer ball).

Method: Simmer for 4 minutes. Remove the sachet or ball and switch off the heat. (N.B.: You don't need to simmer sachet dashi.) Immerse one heaped tablespoon of miso paste in the stock and dissolve it with long chopsticks. Do this three times. Put a little of the soup in a saucer, taste it, and if you immediately think "Ahhh!" then your miso shiru is ready. If not, add another spoonful of miso. Now add a few of your favourite ingredients. I add only diced tofu and *wakame*; after all, if it ain't broke, don't fix it. Slices of aubergine (eggplant) or cucumber are also good. When reheating miso shiru, be careful not to boil it or it'll lose its flavour.

Recipe 3: Red Sea Bream

For a party of four, here's a great traditional recipe that uses *kinmedai* (red sea bream), but you can substitute almost any oily white fish.

You will need: 4 100-150g slices of kinmedai, 1 cup (230ml) dashi stock (see Recipe 2), 2 tablespoons cooking *sake*, 3 1/2 tablespoons sugar, 3 1/2 tablespoons *mirin*, 4 tablespoons *shoyu*, aluminium foil.

Method: Bring the dashi to a boil in a saucepan. Add sake and sugar. Place the fish, with skin facing up, in the pan. Ladle the stock over the fish and skim off any scum that forms. Lay crumpled aluminium foil directly over the fish, then simmer on a low heat for about 10 minutes. Serve with steamed greens, plain rice, and miso shiru (miso soup.)

Recipe 4: Noodle Broth

Here is my husband Takehiro's recipe for stock that can be used for hot or cold *soba* and *udon*. I can't begin to count the times when the near instant nature of this broth has saved me from the wrath of a starving child on an infernal summer's day. Or perhaps it was the child saved from the wrath of a starving mother? Whatever. You need never buy soba from a *konbini* again.

You will need: 200ml water, 2 tablespoons of katsuobushi flakes, 1 table-spoon of sugar, 4 tablespoons of shoyu, 4 tablespoons of mirin, a dash of cooking sake.

Method: Bring the water to the boil. Add the katsuobushi flakes. Boil gently for 4 minutes. Switch off the heat and remove the flakes from the stock using a straining spoon. Next, add the sugar, shoyu, mirin, and cooking sake. Pour into bowls and add already boiled noodles. This soup broth can be refrigerated for up to two days. Good things to add to a bowl of cold soba: grated ginger, grated daikon, finely shredded *negi* or shallots, *shishi togarashi* pepper, *aburage* cut into 1/2cm widths, mustard cress, *wasabi* paste, mustard.

Recipe 5: *Onigiri* (rice balls)

If you want to try to blend in with the Japanese, you can buy bento boxes everywhere or you can make onigiri yourself.

You will need: 6g rice per person, a handful of katsuobushi, 1 pitted and shredded *umeboshi* per person, *nori*, shoyu.

Method: Steam the rice. Stir in the katsuobushi, umeboshi, and whatever else tickles your fancy (sesame seeds or finely chopped negi, for instance). Wet your hands to stop the rice from sticking to them and form the rice into balls, triangles, or rolls. Cut nori into rectangles and dredge one side in a saucer of shoyu. Wrap the pieces around each rice shape until covered. My onigiri are still really wobbly, inauthentic shapes, but a simple pleasure indeed.

Bibliography

All you ever wanted to know about Japanese cooking, but were too drunk on sake to remember, can be found in Tokiko Suzuki's book, *The Essentials of Japanese Cooking*, published by Shufunotomo/Japan in 1995. I bought this book when I first got married (my husband is Japanese) and it has smoothed over those bumpy patches where even the fur-trimmed nightie failed. It's that good.

Useful Japanese

General

set meal .... *teishoku*
chopsticks .... *hashi*
cuisine/cooking .... *ryouri*
Japanese cooking .... *nihon-ryouri*
Chinese cooking ...... *chuuka-ryouri*
Western cooking ...... *seiyou-ryouri*

Style

raw .... *nama*
grilled .... *yaita*
boiled .... *yudeta*
stewed .... *nita*
deep fried .... *ageta*
steamed .... *mushita*
roasted .... *itta*

Meat

meat .... *niku*
beef .... *gyuuniku*
chicken .... *toriniku*
pork .... *butaniku*

Fish

fish .... *sakana*
shell fish .... *kai*
shrimp .... *ebi*
octopus .... *tako*
squid .... *ika*
tuna .... *maguro*

Rice

brown rice .... *genmai*
cooked rice .... *gohan*
white rice .... *hakumai*

Vegetables

vegetable .... *yasai*
cucumber .... *kyuuri*
potato .... *jagaimo*
onion .... *tamanegi*
tomato .... *tomato*
celery .... *serori*
corn .... *toumorokoshi*
carrot .... *ninjin*

spinach .... *hourensou*
eggplant .... *nasu*
mushroom .... *masshuruumu*
black mushroom ...... *shiitake*

Fruit

fruit .... *kudamono*
strawberry .... *ichigo*
orange .... *orenji*
tangerine .... *mikan*
grapefruit .... *gureepu furuutsu*
lemon .... *remon*
peach .... *momo*
plum .... *puramu*
pear .... *younashi*
Japanese pear .... *nashi*
grapes .... *budou*
raisins .... *hoshi budou*
apple .... *ringo*
fig .... *ichijiku*
pomegranate .... *zakuro*

Drinks

black tea .... *koocha*
Chinese-style tea ..... *oolong cha*
green tea .... *ocha*
coffee .... *koohii*
hot chocolate .... *kokoa*
milk .... *gyuunyuu*
processed milk .... *kakounyuu*
soy milk .... *tounyuu*
water .... *mizu*

Other

egg .... *tamago*
bread .... *pan*
garlic .... *nin'niku*
parsley .... *paseri*
ingredient .... *genzairyou*
flour .... *komugiko*
honey .... *hachimitsu*
oil .... *abura*
salt .... *shio*
sugar .... *satou*
spices .... *supaisu*

63

fat-free	*mushibou*		nori	laver
low-fat	*teishibou*		raamen	Chinese noodle soup
low-salt	*gen'en*		sashimi	raw fish
reduced sugar	*teitou*		shabu shabu	thinly sliced beef dipped in boiling broth
sugar-free	*mutou*			
chemical-free	*munouyaku*			
organic	*yuuki saibai*		shouyu	soy sauce
preservative	*boufuzai*		soba	buckwheat noodles
reduced chemicals	*tei-nouyaku*		sukiyaki	beef cooked in Japanese style

Japanese food

atsuage	deep fried tofu		sushi	raw fish with rice
daikon	white radish		tempura	deep-fried vegetables and fish
daizu-rui	soybean products			
dashi	Japanese soup stock		tofu	soybean curd
gyooza	Chinese dumplings		tonkatsu	deep-fried battered pork with sauce and shredded cabbage
katsuobushi	dried bonito flakes			
kaisou	seaweed			
katsudon	rice with pork cutlets		tsukemono	Japanese pickles
komezu	rice vinegar		udon	wheat flour noodles
menrui	noodles		umeboshi	sour plum
mirin	rice wine		wasabi	Japanese horseradish
miso	fermented soybean paste			
miso shiru	miso soup		yakitori	charcoal grilled chicken
nattou	fermented soybeans		yakiniku	Korean barbecue
negi	Japanese leek		yuzu	Japanese citron

Excuse me.	*Sumimasen.*
Please wait a moment.	*Mou sukoshi matte kudasai.*
What is this?	*Kore wa nan desu ka.*
I'd like this one please. (Pointing)	*Kore o kudasai.*
I'll have	*... o kudasai.*
Do you have anything without meat in it?	*Niku ga haitte inai no wa arimasu ka.*
I can't eat	*Watashi wa ... ga taberaremasen.*
I'm allergic to	*Watashi wa ... ni arerugii desu.*
What would you recommend?	*Osusume wa nan desu ka.*
Where do I pay?	*Doko de kaikei sureba ii desu ka.*
I like	*... ga suki desu.*
Thank you for this meal. (No direct translation but is said before eating)	*Itadakimasu.*
Another cup/glass please.	*Mou ippai onegaishimasu.*
Delicious.	*Oishii.*
Thank you, I enjoyed my meal. (No direct translation but is said after a meal or when leaving a restaurant)	*Gochisousama deshita.*

Resources

Check department store basements, local grocery stores, and supermarkets for foreign and health food too.

Foreign Food Shops

Al Flah Supermarket 03-3985-9784
Ikebukuro, Tokyo. Delivers throughout Japan, accepts mail orders.

Carnival Discounts 0422-22-3303
Tama Plaza, Tokyo. No delivery or mail orders.

Benten Supermarket 03-3202-2421
Shinjuku, Tokyo. Delivery within Tokyo if you spend ¥10,000,
delivery charge of ¥350, accepts mail orders.

Daiei Himonya (Head Office) .... 03-3710-1111 (J)
Stores throughout Japan. Delivery to local areas if you spend
¥30,000, delivery charge of ¥600, accepts mail orders.

Daimaru Peacock (Head Office) .... 03-5378-2107 (J)
Stores in Tokyo and Osaka. No delivery or mail orders.

Foreign Buyers Club (FBC) (see display ad, page 69) 078-857-9001
Store in Rokku Island, Kobe. Delivery throughout Japan,
delivery charges vary. Accepts mail orders.
http://www.fbcusa.com

Hallo Do Nagoya .... 052-781-5311 (J)
Higashiyamakoen, Nagoya. No delivery or mail orders.

Hanamasu Meat Pavilion 03-5628-8700
Stores in Tokyo and suburbs. No delivery or mail orders.

Hara Tokyo 03-3451-5211
Azabu Juban, Tokyo. Free delivery within Tokyo if you spend
¥5000, does not accept mail orders.

Imran Trading Company 0462-77-6844
Free delivery throughout Japan if you spend ¥10,000, mail
order only.

Kaldi Coffee Farm 0120-522-699
Stores in Aomori, Kanagawa, Shizuoka, and Tokyo. Free
delivery to local areas if you spend ¥5000, accepts mail orders.

Kinokuniya International 0422-21-7779
Stores in Kamakura, Kichijoji, Kunitachi, and Tokyo. Delivery
throughout Japan, ¥500 delivery charge, does not accept
mail orders.

Kyle's Good Finds Bakery 03-3385-8993
Nakano, Tokyo. Free delivery throughout Japan if you spend
¥10,000, accepts mail orders.

Meidi-ya (Head Office) 03-3444-6221
Stores throughout Japan. Free delivery to local areas if you
spend ¥10,000, accepts mail orders.

National Azabu Supermarket 03-3442-3181
Store in Hiroo, Tokyo. Free delivery to local areas if you spend
¥10,000, accepts mail orders.

Nissin Deli 03-3583-4586
     Azabu-Juban, Tokyo. Delivery in Minato-ku, ¥840 delivery
     charge, does not accept mail orders.

Odakyu Ox 03-3439-8111
     Stores in Kanagawa and Tokyo. No delivery or mail orders.

Pompadour Bakery 045-662-4180
     Stores in Sendai, Tokyo, and Yokohama. No delivery or
     mail orders.

Prince Delica 03-5420-5661
     Stores in Kanagawa and Tokyo. Free delivery to local areas,
     accepts mail orders.

Sanmi Discount Shop 03-3561-9891
     Ginza, Tokyo. No delivery or mail orders.

Shell Garden 03-3718-6481
     Stores throughout Japan. Delivery throughout Japan, ¥600
     delivery charge, does not accept mail orders.

Union Supermarket 045-641-8551
     Stores in Haiyama, Kamakura, and Tokyo. Free delivery to
     local areas if you spend ¥5000, accepts mail orders.

Warabe-Mura 0574-54-1355
     Mino, Gifu. Free delivery throughout Japan if you spend over
     ¥20,000, accepts mail orders.

Health and Organic Food Shops

Daichi 0424-87-7127
     Delivery throughout Japan, ¥400 delivery charge, accepts mail
     orders. Operates a membership system: ¥5000 deposit, ¥1000
     annual fee, and you must order weekly. Also have their own
     stores in Chiba and Tokyo and distribute products to stores
     throughout Japan.

F & F 9 03-3723-6412
     Stores in Kanagawa and Tokyo. Delivery to local areas,
     accepts mail orders.

Foreign Buyers Club (FBC) (see display ad, page 69) 078-857-9001
     Store in Rokku Island, Kobe. Delivery throughout Japan,
     delivery charges vary. Accepts mail orders.
     http://www.fbcusa.com

Fruity Vegeta .... 0473-50-5656 (J)
     Store in Shin-urayasu, Chiba. Delivery throughout Japan,
     ¥500–750 delivery charge, accepts mail orders.

Global Village's The Fair Trade Company Shop 03-5701-3361
     Store in Jiyugaoka, Tokyo. Organic food. Delivery throughout
     Japan, ¥800 delivery charge, does not accept mail orders.

Gruppe 03-3393-1224
     Stores throughout Japan. Macrobiotic food. No delivery, does
     not accept mail orders.

Levain Bakery 0424-81-1341
     Store in Shibazaki, Tokyo. Sugar- and egg-free bread. Delivery
     throughout Japan, ¥450 delivery charge, accepts mail orders.

Levain Bread 03-3468-9669
      Store in Yoyogi-hachimae, Tokyo. Organic bread. Delivery
      throughout Japan if you spend ¥3000, accepts mail orders.
Life Natural Food .... 0425-76-3413 (J)
      Store in Kunitachi, Tokyo. Organic food. Delivery throughout
      Japan, ¥100–500 delivery fee, accepts mail orders.
Lifely 03-3232-6527
      Stores throughout Tokyo. Organic food. Delivery throughout
      Japan, ¥600 delivery charge, free if you spend ¥10,000,
      accepts mail orders.
Nagamoto Kyodai Shokai 03-3331-3599
      Store in Nishi-ogikubo, Tokyo. Organic food. Delivery near
      Suginami-ku if you spend ¥5000, accepts mail orders.
Natural House .... 03-5469-1411 (J)
      Stores in Kansai, Kobe, Osaka, and Tokyo. Some stores
      deliver and accept mail orders.
Osawa Japan .... 03-3465-5021 (J)
      Store in Higashi-kitazawa, Tokyo. Delivery throughout Japan,
      ¥800 delivery charge, accepts mail orders.
Polan Hiroba 0428-24-7200
      Stores in Hokkaido, Nagoya, Osaka, Saitama, and Tokyo.
      Delivery throughout Japan if you spend ¥10,000, ¥400 delivery
      charge, accepts mail orders.
Rengeya 03-3326-5085
      Store in Setagaya, Tokyo. Delivery to Suginami-ku and
      Setagaya-ku, ¥200 delivery charge, accepts mail orders.
Tengu Natural Foods 0429-85-8751
      Free delivery throughout Japan if you spend ¥18,000, otherwise
      delivery charges depend on your location, mail order only.

Online Food Stores
Foreign Buyers Club (see display ad, page 69)
      http://www.fbcusa.com
Emu Store
      Australian food.
      http://www.emustore.com
Expat Stuff
      North American products.
      http://www.expatstuff.com
Mono USA
      American supermarket.
      http://www.monousa.com/eindex.html
The Global Grocer
      http://www.theglobalgrocer.com

Other
JOY Gourmet Coffees 0721-98-3265

Resources and Further Information
A Taste of Culture
>Classes on Japanese food and cooking.
>http://www.tasteofculture.com

Global Village 03-5701-3361
>Produce a guide to organic shops and natural food
>restaurants in Japan.

Tokyo Food Page
>Restaurant listings, recipes, links, guides to Japanese food.
>http://www.bento.com/tokyofood.html

Tourist Information Centre 03-3201-3331
>Produce a list of Tokyo's natural food and vegetarian restaurants.

A Dictionary of Japanese Food: Ingredients and Culture
>By Richard Hosking, Charles E Tuttle Co: 1997.
A Guide to Buying Food in Japan
>By Carolyn R. Krouse, Charles E Tuttle Co: 1986.
Food and Recipes of Japan
>By Theresa M. Beatty, Powerkids Press: 1999.
The Essentials of Japanese Cooking
>By Tokiko Suzuki, Kodansha International: 1995.
The Food of Japan: Authentic Recipes from the Land of the Rising Sun
>By Takayuki Kosaki, Periplus World Cookbooks: 1998.
What's What in Japanese Restaurants: A Guide to Ordering, Eating and Enjoying
>By Robb Satterwhite, Kodansha International: 1996.

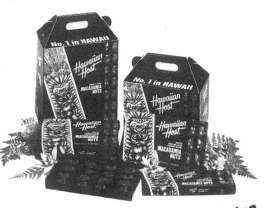

Clothes

Western women face two problems when it comes to clothing in Japan: the few clothes available that fit the Western figure, and the style crisis.

Clothes

Regarding size, Japanese women tend to be much smaller than Western women, and the majority of clothing available in Japan reflects this. All this causes difficulties for women above UK size 8 (US 6) in clothes or UK size 4 (US 5.5) in shoes, not just for practical reasons but for psychological and emotional ones too. In other words, at some point during their stay here, most Western women feel like an elephant:

> *I feel very BIG in this country and must keep in mind that it is not me, but the small Japanese around me. I am not a petite*

person by any means, but when I go back to the USA all of a sudden I feel normal or even smaller than many! A good refresher. So I keep in mind that just because I cannot find clothes or bras to fit doesn't mean that I am abnormal!

Japanese shop assistants will quite cheerfully send you off to the 'big size' or men's department for clothes, which, although done with the best intentions, doesn't do a lot for your self-esteem:

I gave up shopping the year I was sent to the 'clothes for big people' department at the top of Seibu and even then the sleeves came up to between my elbow and wrist in a pathetic no-hope way and the pant legs looked like I was waiting for a flood!

Fashionable clothes in larger sizes for women are becoming more available and clothes shops you would find at home are opening. This is probably because Japanese teenagers are now taller and curvier than the generation before them. When I first came to Japan in 1996, I couldn't find any trousers to fit over my thighs (which aren't particularly big). Four years later and I can usually find something that fits me.

Most Western women who can't find clothes in Japan, or find the prices too hefty, either do a big shop when they go home or use mail-order shopping:

I'm too tall to find pants to fit me here. I refuse to pay three times the price for Levi's, so I get them when I go to L.A. once every two years or so. Actually, I do ALL of my clothes shopping in L.A., and that amounts to very little.

If you find yourself comparing your body with those of the women around you and don't like how you feel, then you need to know that most Japanese women wish they had a figure like yours:

I was trying on a sweater and skirt set at a local Italian import place. Both pieces were stretchy, boucle sweater material, about size 10. I put them on, and of course I had to leave the dressing

71

room to see the mirror (I HATE when they do that!). The
saleswoman practically screamed "SEXY BODY!"

They admire your curves! I was once scribbling away furiously on the
board in a Japanese high school classroom, and became increasingly
aware of the commotion growing amongst my female students behind
me, which I slowly realised was being caused by the 'wobbling' of my
behind as my hand flew across the board (try waving your hand hard
in the air—unless you go to the gym every day you'll see what I mean).
Although I was mortified with embarrassment, my Japanese was good
enough to work out that they were saying how wonderful the wobble
was and they wished their bums would do the same! Just be thankful
that you don't have to go through that experience to realise that you
are admired.

Style

The second problem is the style crisis. Most Japanese women pay great
attention to their appearance (see Pampering and Beauty in this chapter)
and that includes their clothes. Designer clothes are everyday clothes,
high heels are ideal for shopping or travelling, and everything is in im-
maculate condition. In Tokyo, even high school girls carry designer bags
and purses, and there's you in your jeans, trainers, and the favourite sloppy
sweater you've had since you were nineteen. Many Western women start
comparing themselves with Japanese women, not just with respect to
size, but also style, and start to feel unattractive and frumpy:

> *I was fine at work in trousers and shirts, the problem was, out of*
> *my professional armour—in the evenings, on days off, on*
> *holidays—I felt fat, frumpy, and unfeminine. One Japanese friend*
> *told me my clothes were 'sick' (later I learnt she meant 'chic', but*
> *at the time it hurt and anyway, she was lying). It wasn't that I*
> *wanted to look like a Japanese woman, it was more that I admired*
> *the way they took care of themselves and that had begun to rub*
> *off on me. I wanted to look like myself, only more so ... ***

* From 'Dressed to Impress or Worn to Conform' by Samantha Lierens, *Being A Broad*,
August 1998.

Due to the lack of clothes that fit, the clothing issue isn't as easy to solve as the hair and beauty issues are. However, if you can find clothes that fit (and many secondhand stores carry larger sizes), you can find a range of styles that may not be available in your home countries.

Almost anything 'Made in Japan' is too small in every way, but I don't have a problem with the imported clothes, which there are plenty of. I rather like shopping here. There's so much funky, weird and wild stuff. Definitely better shoes than the States in the last few years.

Bear in mind that being in another country means that you can explore many different things, including new styles that you may not have considered at home:

Has my style changed while in T-City? You bet. Ditch the khakis, and put on the mini with sassy shoes to boot. I have enjoyed dressing up in Tokyo. No matter how crazy I want to go, I never feel outlandish compared with the Japanese girls with their matching hair and contact lens accessories.

It also means that you may try styles that you had rather you hadn't, a bit like being a teenager again when you cannot distinguish between what is fashionable and suits you, and what is neither stylish nor flattering:

I think I've been here too long, I've started to wear things that are pink and cute.

Many women found themselves feeling rather overdressed when they visited or returned to their home countries:

I made a special trip to a fashionable district and bought about $600 worth of unusual, high-fashion clothes, an unprecedented (and never since repeated) splash-out. I remember the skirts had tabs and buttons so you could adjust them to different lengths and create bustle effects. So did the jacket. They were very cleverly *designed and, of course, beautifully made. At home I wore one of the skirts once. I never wore any of the other clothes. In California they just looked ridiculous. I was probably too old for them too (late 30s). I must say, though, that I enjoyed buying them.*

I personally enjoy the freedom Japan gives me in wearing whatever I like—people think I am different just because I am a foreigner anyway. I have a crazy furry coat that resembles Cookie Monster. It's totally ridiculous I know, but I love it. I would never feel comfortable wearing it while wandering around my hometown—people would think I'd gone mad.

Shoes

Shoes can also pose a problem because of size and style. It is difficult to find anything over a UK size 5 (US 6.5), but if you ask the assistant, they may have some in the stock room. The problem is that the affordable shoes available in larger sizes tend to resemble your grandmother's. If you are a UK size 4 (US 5.5) or smaller, then you have a wide range of styles to choose from, which in your home countries you would rarely find.

When I first came in '83 it was almost impossible to find shoes for women in my size (25 cm) and, furthermore, the shoes out there were just awful looking. The styles then were only heels for women; casual shoes meant really old-fashioned canvas shoes or boots. These days, imported shoes in my size are much more common and readily available at larger stores, but still very expensive. Conversely, when my stepmother came to visit she was thrilled to be able to find so many shoes small enough to fit her. In the States she struggles to find shoes her size.

Underwear

For women whose breasts are around a 32B and who would like them to appear bigger or more shapely, Japan is heaven!

Fabulous stuff, if you're in small cup sizes (as I happen to be). I can find high quality embroidered lace, etc., here. Back in the US

I'm limited to training bras or the equivalent; here I can find cute, sexy, flirty, etc. The price is high, but I've never found a better selection for my build.

There is an abundance of bras, in an assortment of colours and styles, with a range of panties to match, and although the padding may be a little more than what you are used to, most Western women with smaller breasts are more than happy with the availability of under-wear. (Incidentally, you can also buy special padded pants called 'Hip-Up' that 'lift and separate', just to reiterate that Japanese women would like to have a big, round, curvy backside like yours!) For the rest of us, however, it is practically impossible to find a bra that will fit, especially if you don't want any padding. The sizing is not quite the same as in your home countries, so try everything on before you buy:

Underwear? Bras? Humiliation? Yes. Those tiny little panties that look so cute in the store and claim to fit hips my size, but don't. I fell for that a few times. Bras too. They say they'll fit my width around, but when I put them on feel like I'm in the grip of a Sumo wrestler.

And if you're not sure about your size, don't worry, as there may be an enthusiastic staff member ready to help you:

I'm 36C in American size. When I was struggling with the prices and the converted sizes, a representative came to help. I explained I didn't know my size. She studied my breasts, then over my sweater cupped them with her hands! I was so shocked I didn't know what to do but laugh. Holding the mold of my breasts, she searched her wares, checking to see if any cups were equal in size. She found a few and led me to the dressing room. While I was trying one bra a bit small for me, my attendant burst into the dressing area and started helping me get into the bra. She reached inside the cup area of my bra and grabbed my breast, trying to force my breast into the cup. One thing's for sure ... I memorized my bra size, 95DD; thank you very much.

Rely on friends or family to send you underwear from home or you will go crazy. Note that most panties here have a high percentage of nylon; with that and the abundant wearing of tights under trousers, I often wonder why the whole country isn't riddled with yeast infections.

There is another reason why bras are so heavily padded here—showing your nipples through your clothing is considered indecent. Don't be surprised if people blatantly stare at your braless breasts bouncing around in your T-shirt, nor should you be surprised if people actually inform you that they can see your nipples. People are not looking at you in a sexual way though, they are looking because they are shocked and wondering if you are aware that your nipples and/or bra-strap can be seen:

> *Whilst flashing your knickers to all and sundry is quite the done thing here, a flash of nipple could get you a public stoning. Although recently those see-through tops are in fashion, before whenever a bra strap slipped out of the confines of my clothing, my Japanese friends would be quite horrified, as if I had done something quite indecent. Even worse than a stray strap is a significant nipple. A Japanese friend told how while she was walking in a busy business area a most concerned gentleman took her to the side to ask apologetically if she was aware that her buds could be seen.**

To prevent everyone from becoming embarrassed by an abundance of nipples, Japan has invented 'nipple covers'; small, round pads you put over your nipples. They are available from any chemist and are very popular, especially during summer, when the padding of bikini tops may not camouflage the more 'protruding' types. Just be sure to get the *right size* :

> *We went on a group retreat to the Izu Peninsula. Beach-going was involved, so I borrowed a cotton one-piece bathing suit from*

---

* From 'Dressed to Impress or Worn to Conform' by Samantha Lierens, *Being A Broad*, August 1998.

an American friend and bought a packet of nipple covers. But when I went to put them on, I discovered they were about the size of a nickel, whereas my requirement was for something the size of a silver dollar. The damned things wouldn't stay on! To quote from my book*: "There was nothing to do but sit on the beach in a hunched position with my arms folded over my chest. The Japanese are camera-mad, so I have plenty of photographs that show me doing this. They are only slightly less embarrassing than the photographs that show me forgetting to do this." I still have these photographs. I never tried nipple covers again.

If you choose to shop in Japan, it's a welcome pleasure for smaller women who have previously had problems in their home countries:

Shopping for clothes in Japan has been great as far as finding my size. Now other Western women are struggling with the ill-fitting woes I knew in America. Except in reverse.

For average or larger Western women, it may be helpful to remember that the assistants who send you off to the men's departments are green with envy as you take your luscious, curvaceous breasts and buttocks with you!

Useful Japanese

bra	burajaa	shirt	shatsu
cardigan	kaadigan	shoes	kutsu
coat	kooto	skirt	sukaato
gloves	tebukuro	socks	kutsushita
hat	boushi	stockings	sutokkingu
jacket	jaketto	suit	suutsu
nipple covers	nippuru kabaa	sweater	seetaa
panties	pantii	tights/pantyhose	pantii-sutokkingu/pansuto
pants/trousers	zubon/pantsu		
scarf	sukaafu	t-shirt	tii-shatsu

*Too Late for the Festival: An American Salary-Woman in Japan by Rhiannon Paine, Academy Chicago: 1999.

May I try this on? .... *Shichaku shitemo ii desu ka.*
Where are the changing rooms? .... *Shichaku-shitsu wa doko desu ka.*
Do you have this in a smaller/bigger size? .. *Motto chiisai/ookii saizu wa arimasu ka.*
Do you have this in any other colours? .... *Kore no iro chigai wa arimasu ka.*
Do you have anything cheaper? .... *Mou sukoshi yasui no wa arimasu ka.*
Do you have any bras without padding? ..... *Patto nashi no bura wa arimasu ka.*
Do you stock 100% cotton underwear? .... *Hyaku paasento kotton/men no shitagi wa arimasu ka.*
I'm not sure what size I am. .... *Watashi no nihon no saizu ga wakarimasen.*
I was a sex goddess in a former life. (in response to comments about your size) ..... *Watashi no zensei wa sekushii na megami datta no yo.*
I live in ... . Where is your nearest store? .... *Watashi wa ... ni sundeimasu. Ichiban chikai shiten wa doko desu ka.*

Resources

Sizes
Clothes

Japan	9	11	13	15	17	19	21	23	25	27
US	6	8	10	12	14	16	18	20	22	24
UK	8	10	12	14	16	18	20	22	24	26
Europe	40	42	44	46	48	50	52	54	56	58

Shoes

Japan	22.5	23	23.5	24	24.5	25	25.5	26	26.5	27
US	5.5	6	6.5	7	7.5	8	8.5	9	9.5	10
UK	4	4.5	5	5.5	6	6.5	7	7.5	8	8.5
Italy	36	37	38	39	40	41	42	43	44	45

Bras (bust)

Int'l	65	70	75	80	85	90	95	100	105	110
US/UK	30	32	34	36	38	40	42	44	46	48
French	80	85	90	95	100	105	110	115	120	125

Bras (cup)

US	AA	A	B	C	D	E
Other	A	B	C	D	DD	E

Shops Stocking Larger Size Clothes

Call the listed number to find your nearest store.

Gap 03-3499-8600
Over 40 stores throughout Japan. Maximum size 15.

Isetan 03-3225-2514
Stores in Kyoto, Fuchu, and Tokyo. Maximum size 27. Foreign Customer Service 'I-Club': free membership, discounts, personal shopping assistant, translation, furniture leasing, free parking, free museum tickets.

Jusco 043-212-6110
    Over 300 stores in Japan. Maximum size 21.
Kashiwaya .... 03-3205-1960 (J)
    30 stores in Japan. Maximum size 15.
Kenzo 03-5485-9860
    Over 20 stores in Japan. Maximum size 17.
Laura Ashley .... 03-5474-2643 (J)
    50 outlets in Japan. Maximum size 15.
Marui 01 Model .... 03-3384-0101 (J)
    Over 30 stores in Tokyo and suburbs. Maximum size 21.
Odakyu Department Store .... 03-3342-1111 (J)
    Stores in Fujisawa, Machida, and Shinjuku. Maximum size 19.
Talbot's Japan .... 03-3571-2922 (J)
    40 stores in Japan. Maximum size 19.
Tobu .... 03-3981-2211 (J)
    Stores in Tokyo and suburbs. Maximum size 25.
Zara 03-5449-1718
    Stores in Chiba, Fukuoka, Osaka, Tachikawa, Tokyo, and
    Yokohama. Maximum size 15.

Shops Stocking Larger Size Shoes
(ask if you cannot see them on display)
Big Shoes Collection Ten .... 03-3369-7511 (J)
    Stores in Tokyo. Maximum size 27.
Isetan 03-3225-2514
    See above. Maximum size 27.
Washington Shoes .... 03-3572-5911 (J)
    70 stores in Osaka, Tokyo, and Tokyo suburbs. Maximum size 27.
    Not all stores carry large sizes but all can order them for you.

Catalogue and Online Clothing Information
Catalog City   http://www.catalogcity.com
Catalog Mart   http://catalog.savvy.com/
Catalog World   http://www.catalogworld.com

Mail Order Services Recommended by Western Women
Coldwater Creek   http://www.coldwater-creek.com/
Freemans   http://www.freemans.com/
LL Bean   http://www.llbean.com/
Land's End   http://www.landsend.co.uk/
J Crew   http://www.media-hype.com/jcrew/index.htm
Peruvian Connection   http://www.peruvianconnection.com/
Victoria's Secret   http://www.victoriassecret.com/

Dry Cleaning and Alterations
Hakuyosha English Information Line (throughout Japan) 03-3460-9011

Hair

Many Western women, irrespective of the amount of attention they paid to their hair at home, find themselves facing two major problems in Japan: hair condition and the search for a good stylist.

Hair changes

There are some Western women who choose to change their hair here; a new life in Japan lends itself to a certain amount of reinvention. Some women change their hair in an attempt to fit in with a more conservative work environment; some women cut off long hair because it drives them crazy in the humid summer. Glossy long hair suddenly turns into a mane of frizz; a sleek short crop becomes limp and lifeless; and in summer, whatever you have lovingly created in your air-conditioned apartment is destroyed by the time you reach the station two minutes away. You may no longer want to sneak a glance in shop windows to reassure yourself about how fantastic your hair looks (don't deny it, we all do it) when it feels like everyone else around you looks like they've just left with first prize from a Perfect Hair Competition!

My hair is one of the things that has bothered me most! I don't know what has happened to it. I seem to have less of it, it's so dry, and what I do have left I can't do anything with. But the Japanese women seem to have such perfect hair!

Hair loss, brittleness and a lack in softness seem to be common complaints amongst Western women, so I talked to hair experts Elissa and Estelle, owners of Sin Den hair salon in Tokyo.

Hair loss (also known as 'alopecia') occurs in two ways. One is the accelerated loss all over that often occurs for a few months upon arrival in Japan and the other is spot alopecia, where bald spots appear on the scalp. Both can be attributed to a combination of stress, sudden changes in diet, a lack of truly fresh fruit and vegetables, and the harshness of Japanese water.

The main reason your hair changes is due to the water in Japan being different to what you may be used to. Elissa and Estelle suggest how to combat this:

With soft water, sometimes you can get away with more alkali shampoos and styling products, but in Japan, you need all the help you can get. 'Hard' water is water with a lot of chemicals in it. In Tokyo, the water is laden particularly with chlorine, which cannot be filtered out. It can be boiled out, but this seems a bit excessive, as does rinsing the hair with mineral water. Try to keep the water not-too-hot and wash hair less often. Try rinsing only, then using conditioner to clean hair, and keep shampooing down to twice a week. Moisturising/reconstructing treatments are a huge help. Use products from reputable international companies. It's a fairly safe bet that if a company is able to make colours and perms, they know how to create products safe for damaged hair. Some examples are Redken, Sebastian, Fudge, and L'Oreal. Even the best products available are not going to produce the optimum result without advice from a professional. Get a diagnosis from a trusted stylist of what your hair really needs!! Saves you a lot of time and hassle.

Women who frequently use swimming pools suffer even more from these problems, as pools in Japan tend to have higher levels of chlorine in them than in other countries. Elissa and Estelle suggest the following:

Begin by running conditioner through your hair before you swim, to form a barrier under the cap. After you swim, rinse thoroughly. Shampoo with a gentle product for frequent use (e.g., Sebastian's Celloshampoo). Once a week you may want to use a 'clarifying shampooing treatment' (e.g., Redken Cleansing Creme). This is a product which removes any build-up of chemical or styling product from the hair. Lather it up and leave it in for a few minutes, rinse thoroughly, repeat if necessary, then condition as usual. Perhaps use a reconditioning treatment once a week if the hair is looking worn out. The easiest way to tell if the hair has a chlorine build-up is when the texture of the hair has a 'slimy' feel to it.

An increase in stress can affect the condition of your hair, and most women report higher levels of stress while living in Japan, especially upon arrival. Estelle and Elissa often see the effects of stress in their salon:

We see more incidences of alopecia, dandruff, and non-communicable scalp disorders here than ever before. These are symptoms of an unbalanced body system, not an isolated problem. Treat your whole organism first. Eat well, incorporate stress relief into your routine (e.g., yoga, exercise, getting fresh air). Remove any irritants that may be exacerbating the problem, i.e., harsh shampoo, hairspray, gel. Check out resources for specific conditions on the alternative healing pages of the internet. There is a wealth of information on healing your whole body. If all else fails, visit your doctor.

Check out the Pampering and Beauty section in this chapter and the Alternative Health section in Chapter Three for more information on stress relief.

Some women report going or noticing more grey while in Japan:

My hair started to go grey. When I arrived, as best I can remember, my hair was pretty solidly red-brown. By the time I left, 18 months later, I had pronounced light streaks.

With the average age of Western women in Japan being 33, we tend to be in Japan at a time when we would be starting to go grey anyway. Estelle and Elissa agree that stress could be an accelerating factor:

The grey issue. Hmmm ... could be simply ageing, something we are all prone to. Of course, stress increases the speed of our genetically programmed degeneration process.

Although the onset of grey hair cannot be reversed without colouring, you can rest assured that the condition of your hair will quickly return to normal when you go back to your home country:

My hair lost condition radically in Japan. I'm quite sure that it's slowly regaining condition now I'm back in the UK though!

Hair care products

Difficulty in obtaining good hair products is a common complaint, as available products are designed for Japanese hair, which is of a different texture to most Westerner's hair. Shampoos, conditioners, and hair treatments are widely available, but may not produce the best results on your hair. However, an increasing number of Japanese hair salons are now stocking Western brands of professional hair products, so search the salons. If you like to home-dye your hair, you may prefer to stock up when at home, or have a kind friend send you some, rather than rely on shop products in Japan that are generally too strong for your hair:

My friend tried dyeing her hair herself using a Japanese dye ... she chose a lovely auburn, but didn't realise that the Japanese product had bleach in it as well and she ended up with a shade closer to fire engine red. Ooops.

Like most professionals who care about hair, Estelle and Elissa urge caution when colouring your hair at home, especially in Japan:

Japanese colouring products are designed for coarse, naturally porous hair that is extremely dense with pigment. This is quite different to the colours from chemists at home, which cater to a variety of natural shades. Correcting mistakes made in the kitchen will often cost twice as much as simply going to a professional colourist in the beginning.

Which brings me to the second problem facing every Western woman at one point or another during their time in Japan.

Hairdressers

Everyone invariably has at least one horror story concerning a visit to a Japanese hairdresser, stories that are so widely shared and suitably terrifying that some Western women have never visited a hairdresser in Japan:

I have been here in Japan for over nine months and I have had my hair cut once in NYC, once in my home town in Alabama (can you believe it—I went to my MOTHER'S stylist), and, I will admit—I have taken shears to my own head more than once (mainly trimming the back where it was starting to curl around my ears, or the spiky little bangs in front that were driving me out of my mind).

One of the main complaints seems to be the Japanese hairstylist's obsession with the blow-dryer:

I live in the countryside, so getting my hair cut is always a bit scary. I have naturally curly or at least wavy hair that most don't know how to handle. They want it STRAIGHT, so spend hours blow drying it that way. And if they would stop trying to blow dry it until I look like Darth Vader, I would be happier.

which Elissa and Estelle explain:

All hairdressers are obsessed with blow-drying, however, Japanese hairdressers often will blow-dry your hair flat and straight. This is due to the aesthetic principle in Japan whereby women often feel as if they have wide or broad faces that they wish to minimise. Thus, they make their hair as flat as possible. Western women, looking for a little height on the crown or width at the top to emphasise the cheekbones, are appalled at the result. A simple miscommunication. Haircutting for Japanese clients is all about minimising thick hair, razoring, sculpting out hair freehand. Cutting foreign clients is all about constructing weight and volume in the hair using precision techniques such as graduation and controlled layering. Quite a different approach.

The second problem experienced by Western women going to Japanese hairstylists concerns unpredictable perming and colouring treatments:

Big chunks of my hair just broke off at the roots due to the strong chemicals they used. It took months for those sprouty things to grow out and lay down flat (sort of an Alfalfa action).

Japanese hairdressers messed with my perms twice. Once, there was no visible effect at all, to the effect that they permed my hair again, which left it awfully damaged.

After a few months in Japan, my blonde highlights were almost completely grown out, so I thought I would like to try and get them re-done. The hairdresser said "no problem" so I thought he had experience with highlights. Later I was to find that he had never done highlights before! He began tearing foil into small pieces and covering parts of my hair, so it seemed as if he knew what he was doing. He mixed up something in a dish that smelt like bleach and began putting it on my exposed hair. The foil didn't seem to be wrapped tightly round my hair and during the process some fell out of my hair. Well, to cut a long story short, he hadn't covered my hair properly and I ended up getting dye/bleach all over my hair. The result was that all my hair turned bright yellow! My foreign friends couldn't believe it when they saw me and it was even worse when I took a trip back to the UK. My family and friends couldn't stop laughing.

These hairdressing disasters are usually due to a lack of communication or nerves (the stylist's, not yours) and because, unless you are very, very lucky, most Japanese hairdressers are simply not trained to deal with non-Japanese hair, which lends itself to many more styles than Japanese hair does.

I had a lot of trouble getting a haircut that was at all outside the middle of the road/bland style that most Japanese were wearing at the time. I would go along armed with pictures, but still the hairdresser would alter the style, taking the unique features out of it (that I particularly wanted!) until it became ordinary.

As Estelle and Elissa mentioned, bear in mind that the Japanese have ideas about what a woman wants to look like, based on the most common Japanese woman's face shape. The diversity of Westerners' hair texture and face shape is unfamiliar to the Japanese hairdresser. Japanese hair is coarser and easier to keep 'just so' than non-Japanese hair is, but lends itself to a limited number of styles. Elissa and Estelle explain why most Japanese hairstylists are at a loss when it comes to non-Japanese hair:

Consider that most other cosmopolitan centres of the world are multicultural, so hairstylists are experienced on the full spectrum of natural hair colours and curl speeds ... black to blonde, ringlets to pin straight. Japan is still largely homogeneous. The percentage of foreigners is tiny. The chances for most hairdressers having *experience on anything other than darkest brown to black coarse hair are slim. There are certainly some enormously talented stylists here, though, and perming and straightening technology is world class, as it had been the popular service of choice until just a few years ago. Colouring hair is relatively new compared with the West, achieving popularity only in the last few years, although exploding recently (witness: *Shibuya chicks!!). Unlike most foreign hairdressing qualifications, qualification in Japan does not require a final colouring exam. Hopefully this will change soon. Our best advice is to find a stylist with whom you can easily communicate, one with a lot of experience in your type of hair.*

Western women who came to Japan in the eighties claim that it was impossible to find a stylist with experience and with whom you could communicate, but now there are several who do meet those criteria and will give you a head, shoulder and neck massage at no extra cost. A word of warning though: good hairdressers in Japan are expensive, although most Western women consider the cost well worth it.

Tips

For those who decide to go it alone and find their own hairdressers:

- Check that they speak English—fairly fluently. I've included some useful Japanese at the end of this section, but I wouldn't recommend you go unless the stylist speaks English.
- Find out where they have trained; don't bother making an appointment if they haven't trained in the West for at least some period of time.
- Ask how many of their clients are foreigners.
- When you see a Western woman with great hair, ask her for her stylist's contact number—she really won't mind, we're all in the same boat on this one.
- If it goes wrong, go to one of the recommended salons that follow; they are used to taking care of other stylists' mistakes!

*Shibuya chicks: young Japanese women with bleached blonde hair who hang out near Shibuya station in Tokyo.

Useful Japanese

hair salon .... *heaa saron/*
biyoushitsu
hairstylist .... *sutairisuto*
redder .... *motto akaku*
browner .... *motto chairo ni*
darker .... *motto koku*
lighter (in colour) ...... *motto akaruku*
make it more
straight .... *motto massugu ni*
shite

make it curlier .... *motto kaaru o*
tsukete
put a curl here .... *kono hen ni kaaru o*
tsukete
make it curl inward ... *uchimaki ni shite*
make it curl
outward .... *sotomaki ni shite*

Where did you train as a hairdresser? .... *Doko de biyoushi no benkyou o shimashita ka.*
Do you have many foreign women
clients? .... *Gaikokujin josei no okyakusama wa*
takusan imasu ka.

Have you worked with Western/black hair
before? .... *Imamade ni seiyoujin/kokujin no kami o*
tegaketa koto ga arimasu ka.

Do I need to make an appointment? .... *Yoyaku wa hitsuyou desu ka.*
I'd like my hair washed/cut/permed/
coloured/blow-dried please. .... *Shanpuu/katto/paama/karaaringu/buroo*
shite kudasai.

Do you have perming/colouring products
suitable for Western hair? .... *Gaikokujin no kaminoke ni au paama/*
karaaringu eki wa arimasu ka.

My hair is really dry/fine/greasy/damaged.
Do you have any hair care products suitable
for me? .... *Watashi no kaminoke wa totemo pasapasa*
desu/hosoi desu/aburakkoi desu/itande
imasu. Watashi no kaminoke ni atta hea kea
shouhin wa arimasu ka.

Do you have any pictures I can look at? ..... *Heaa mihon no shashin o misete kudasai.*
Can you make my hair look like this?
(indicate picture) .... *Watashi no kaminoke o kouiu fuuni shite*
morae masu ka.

Can you give me something that is low
maintenance? .... *Teire ga kantan na kamigata ni shite kudasai.*
Please cut some more over here. .... *Mou sukoshi koko o katto shite kudasai.*
Please don't talk to me while you're cutting
my hair. .... *Sumimasen ga kaminoke o kitte iru aida wa*
watashi ni hanashikakenai de kudasai.

Can you blow-dry my hair so it is fuller on
top? .... *Toppu ni boryuumu o motasete buroo shite*
kudasai.

89

My hair is naturally wavy, it won't blow-dry straight.	*Watashi no kaminoke wa weebu gakatte irunode sutoreeto ni wa buroo dekimasen.*
Please stop blow-drying my hair now.	*Buroo wa kekkou desu.*
This isn't what I asked for.	*Onegai shita no to chigau mitai desu.*
I'd like you to do it again.	*Mou ichido yarinaoshite kudasai.*
I'm not happy, I'm not going to pay for this.	*Ki ni iranai node kore dewa okane wa haraemasen.*
Thank you very much. I like what you've done.	*Arigatou gozaimasu. Totemo ki ni irimashita.*

Resources

Recommended Salons

These salons were used and recommended by the women I interviewed for this book. The salons have at least one English-speaking staff member, and at least one person who is trained in taking care of Western hair. Salons with Western staff are indicated by an asterisk (*). Prices quoted are for a shampoo, cut, and blow-dry.

Salon	Station	Telephone	Price
Beverly Hills	Harajuku, Tokyo	03-3406-0963	¥5000
Beverly Hills	Roppongi, Tokyo	03-3582-9060	¥5000
Boy	Daikanyama, Tokyo	03-3476-1256	¥6000
InterWAVE	Harajuku, Tokyo	03-3402-6773	¥7500
Panorama	Harajuku, Tokyo	03-3400-3901	¥6000–6500
*PRS	Harajuku, Tokyo	03-5413-5066	¥5500
(see display ad, page 91)			
Saras	Kagurazaka, Tokyo	03-5225-4800	¥5000
*Sin Den	Gaienmae, Tokyo	03-3405-4409	¥6000–7000
(see display ad, page 92)			
*Toni & Guy	Aoyama, Tokyo	03-3797-5790	¥5000
Watanabe Hairdressing	Harajuku, Tokyo	03-3405-1188	from ¥6000
(see display ad, page 93)			
Who Ga	Akasaka, Tokyo	03-5570-1773	¥6000
Who Ga	Hanzomon, Tokyo	03-3288-2622	¥7800
Zooto Equatorial	Roppongi, Tokyo	03-3470-2248	¥5500

The following are salons that say they can deal with non-Japanese hair, but were not visited by the women I interviewed.

Salon	Station	Telephone	Price
Ash	Daikanyama, Tokyo	03-3770-3755	¥5000–6000
Arden Yamanaka	Hibiya, Tokyo	03-3271-9316	¥3000–4000
Hayato New York	Hiroo, Tokyo	03-3406-8255	¥6500
Hayato New York	Omotesando, Tokyo	03-3498-9113	¥5000
Koetsu Salon	Ebisu, Tokyo	03-3461-3171	¥4600–5400
New Hair Story	Nogizaka, Tokyo	03-3403-6558	¥5500

Taya International ....Ginza, Tokyo .... 03-3575-9121 .... ¥4400
Taya International ....Ginza, Tokyo .... 03-5250-1183 .... ¥6000
Taya International ....Harajuku, Tokyo .... 03-5474-4510 .... ¥5500–7000
Taya International ....Roppongi, Tokyo .... 03-3505-3941 .... ¥6500
YS Park ....7 salons in Tokyo .... 03-3464-3366 .... from ¥6300

Hair Products/Treatments
Cream Bath 03-5722-2345
  Hair treatments. Ebisu, Tokyo.
Foreign Buyers Club (see display ad, page 69) 078-857-9001
  Imports and delivers shampoos, conditioners, treatments and
  colours. Delivery prices vary. Accepts mail orders.
  http://www.fbcusa.com

Pampering and Beauty

Concern with beauty and your appearance may well have been something you scoffed at or objected to in your home country. To many Western women, living in a country where packaging and presentation are valued in everything around them, time spent on their own 'packaging', or pampering as I prefer to call it, often increases. One woman claimed this new awareness and attention to be:

... a necessity to keep one's sanity ...

Some women find that they simply have more time to pamper themselves, especially single working women or non-working women whose partner's job has led to their relocation. Western women often find that their skin feels tighter and dirtier, especially in Tokyo or if they spend a lot of time on the trains. During my first six months, people actually told me that they hadn't seen clear skin like mine in Tokyo (four years later and nobody says it anymore). Many women find their skin deteriorating and begin to pay regular attention to it:

My beauty regime has changed. Partly because it has become much more of a battle to maintain my skin.

Some women find that they spend more time on their appearance because they become more aware of the changes brought about by the natural ageing process. This is mostly due to the fact that, as mentioned in the previous section, Western women are often in Japan at an age when visible signs of ageing begin to appear, although increased stress levels can also accelerate the maturing process. Pampering is a great way to decrease stress and increase mental relaxation:

I had a private student for a year who planned to go to England to study reflexology, but in the meantime was studying it at night school. She used to come to my apartment for a two-hour English lesson on Sunday mornings, then practised her new reflexology techniques on me for a whole hour! It was heaven! It always set me up for the week ahead. When she finally left Japan, I not only lost a good friend but the best pampering I ever had.

The overwhelming reason for Western women's increased awareness of their appearance in Japan is one that we just hate to admit out loud. Despite being financially independent, in positions of authority and management, and irrespective of marital status, we STILL compare ourselves to the women around us:

I have definitely started paying more attention to my appearance since coming here. In Canada, people are pretty casual, but here women are always so perfectly dressed, made-up, and taken care of, that I felt a lot of pressure to do the same.

In Japan, the women around us are usually petite, fully made-up, and considered feminine in the way that they speak, dress, and walk. Regardless of their ideas about 'femininity', most Western women go through a phase of feeling big, clumsy, and unattractive. The effects of this can really knock your confidence, especially if you are single and it comes in combination with what may be the longest period in your adult life of having sex with only yourself (see Being Single in Chapter Four).

I see myself as Amazon Woman here, although back home I'm pretty average. Women here don't have hips or busts, usually. They try their darndest to look like children as long as they are single. But I was brought up to believe that being womanly was something to be proud of. The mixed messages often leave me unsure of myself.

I lived in Japan for 18 months in 1985–86. Toward the end of my stay, I got very self-conscious about my appearance. I'm 5 feet 4 inches and weighed only 115 pounds in those days, wearing size 4–6 clothes, but in Japan I felt huge—wide hips, big breasts, big hands and feet, long nose. I was taller than all of my female colleagues and taller than most of the men. My feet (US size 8 1/2) were bigger than the feet of my male colleagues. When I sat down on a train, I felt that people were having to make extra space for my 'enormous' (36-inch) hips. My hair was another source of difference. I should add that these feelings were entirely self-generated; none of the Japanese said anything to me about my looks or made me feel uncomfortable. My feelings about my appearance grew out of a profound sense of not fitting in, not belonging. As soon as I got back to the US, they disappeared.

For some women, the other women around them do not affect how they feel about themselves:

I found it a lot easier to swank around and be proud of my appearance in Japan. I never spent a lot of time and effort on beauty treatments and pampering. I prefer to be natural.

Some (although they are in the minority) feel even less aware of their appearance here:

I actually feel less conscious of my appearance on the whole as I am going to be regarded as an 'other' regardless of how I look.

I've got to admit to succumbing to all this 'pampering' business myself. The contents of my make-up bag have increased threefold since coming to Japan and I know it's not just to do with pampering myself, although I do get some bizarre enjoyment from plastering it all on in the morning. While I am in Japan, I am the character played by that British comedienne who is always saying "Does my bum look big in this?" and don't go anywhere without being fully made-up, whereas when I am in England, I feel tiny and over made-up. When I was teaching, it didn't help when my Japanese colleagues sometimes felt obliged to comment on my appearance, which would be OK if they had used tact rather than saying "You are fat today", or "No sleep?"

Most Western women who go through a phase of suddenly feeling very negative about their appearance find a way to deal with it, then get out of it; either they remember that it is environmental and make an effort to stop comparing themselves with others, or throw themselves into it all with reckless abandon:

Within weeks of arriving in Tokyo, I shed my beloved backpack for a sleek shiny purse. Tight black clothes invaded my wardrobe. I actually wore heels on my days off. I never left the house without my shades—even on cloudy days. I gave in to peer pressure. I've given in to the beauty myth as part of my acclimatization to Tokyo life!

If you need a helping hand to deal with negative feelings about your appearance, remind yourself that you are not being stared at because you look fat, clumsy, unattractive, or dull—it's happening because you are different. Many Japanese people have never seen a Westerner except in a movie, on TV or in a magazine, and many look at you because, to them, you are like a movie star (and that includes how beautiful they think you are). Not only are you different to them, but the diversity of appearances amongst foreigners makes you even more interesting to look at. Do the make-up thing if it makes you feel better (and most women do this at least for some time), but there are probably other areas that you need to explore regarding why you feel so self-conscious about your appearance. In the short term, there are some things you can do and places you can go that will help. Pampering yourself is a treat that you may not have considered in your home country.

Useful Japanese

beauty salon	*esute*	massage	*massaaji*
manicure	*manikyua/neiru kea*	facial	*feisharu kea*
pedicure	*pedikyua*	makeover	*meiku appu*

I'd like a … .	*… o shite kudasai.*
I have dry/greasy/combination skin.	*Watashi no hada wa kansou shiteimasu/ aburappoi desu/kanso shiteiru tokoro to aburappoi tokoro ga arimasu.*
That's too strong.	*Chotto tsuyosugimasu.*
You can make it stronger.	*Motto tsuyoku shite kamaimasen.*
That's too cold.	*Tsumetai desu.*
That's too hot.	*Atsui desu.*
It hurts.	*Itai desu.*
That feels good.	*Kimochi ii desu.*

Resources

Check the department stores too, as some Western women recommended the manicure booths near the beauty departments.

Salons

Arden Yamanaka Beauty Salon 03-3271-7810
    Hibiya, Tokyo. Pedicure, manicure, electrolysis, waxing.
Boudoir (see display ad, page 100) 03-3478-5898
    Harajuku, Tokyo. Manicure, pedicure, facial, massage, waxing.
Club Boy Beau 03-5454-1231
    Yoyogi-Uehara, Tokyo. Manicure, foot care, massage.
Kojimachi Rebirth .... 03-3262-7561 (J)
    Kojimachi, Tokyo. Pampering centre.
My Boo Nail Salon 03-5428-1121
    Shibuya, Tokyo. Manicure, nail art, eyelash curl.
Nail Quick 03-5524-7517
    Salons throughout Tokyo and Yokohama. Manicure, pedicure.
Nail Station 03-5456-2530
    Salons throughout Tokyo. Manicure, pedicure, foot care.
Re-born 03-5563-0628
    Roppongi, Tokyo. Manicure, pedicure, nail art.
Sunaba Teiko Sogo Biyo Salon 03-3356-2734
    Shinjuku, Tokyo. Massage, manicure, pedicure, facial. Women
    only.
Takagi Skin Clinic 03-3462-2807
    Shibuya,Tokyo. Cancer check ups. Treatment of moles, sun-spots, freckles,
    acne and acne scars. Laser hair removal, botox, restylane also available.
Tokyo Skin Clinic 03-3585-0282
    Roppongi, Tokyo. Skin treatments, skin cancer screenings,
    skin care advice, piercing, cosmetic surgery, dermatology.
Utopia 03-3398-4126
    Ogikubo, Tokyo. Sauna, massage.
Watanabe Salon (see display ad, page 93) 03-3405-1188
    Harajuku, Tokyo. Light therapy, facial, waxing, massage,
    manicure, pedicure.

Other

Japan Kurhaus Association 03-3255-2277
    Information on health spas throughout Japan.
Japan Research Consultants 03-3845-7201
    Pay Western women to test beauty products. Call to register.

Spa and Health Resort Websites

Dave's Natural and Traditional Hot Springs of Japan
    http://www.angelfire.com/or/bonnyscotland/onsen.html
Day Spas
    http://www.spaindex.com/day/asiapacific/japan.htm
NTV Documentaries/Preserving the Natural Spas
    http://www.ntv.co.jp/prog.eng/human/prese.htm
Japan—Sightseeing
    http://newpaper.asia1.com.sg/journey/travel/japan/jpsight.html

BOUDOIR

Facials Nails Massage Waxing Tinting Body Airbrush tanning...

AUSTRALIAN OWNED AND OPERATED

Maison Kawai 101,2-25-3 Jingumae, Shibuya-KU Tokyo 150-0001
TEL 03 3478 5898 www.boudoirtokyo.com GMAP 0334785898@gmap.jp

100

Home

2

Finding a Place
Utilities
Garbage and Recycling
Pests and Pets

Finding a Place

Housing

Three-quarters of Japan is uninhabitable, mountainous land, leaving the remaining 90,000 square kilometres in which to squeeze over 125 million people. Only 13 percent of the people live in the countryside, leaving the remainder (almost certainly including you) to fight for space in the cities. This results in homes that may be much smaller than you are used to, probably without a garden and much closer to your neighbours than you may prefer.

Homes are categorised as either 'apaato' or 'manshon'. An apaato is a wooden one-floor home in a one- or two-storey building, and a manshon is a concrete one-floor home in a building with several storeys. There are also Western-style two-storey or more houses that tend to be inhabited by wealthy Japanese families or are provided by companies to foreigners on ex-pat packages. Apaatos are usually old, Japanese style, and rather quaint, although they rattle noisily at the slightest earth tremor. Manshons tend to be ugly grey buildings, with Western-style interiors (these sway gently with a tremor). There are also 'gaijin' houses, filled with foreigners who each have a small private or shared room and communal kitchen, lounge, and bathroom facilities. Many foreigners start their lives in Japan in gaijin houses.

The size specifications for apaatos and manshons are: 1K (a room and a kitchen), 1DK (a room and a kitchen/dining room), 1LDK (a room, a living room, and a kitchen/dining room). A 2LDK means the place has an extra room. Note the absence of a letter indicating a toilet, shower, or bathroom, and don't assume that the place has one or any of these. In my first two places I shared a coin shower with ten people. You can always join the local gym (see the section on Fitness in Chapter Three) in order to use their shower facilities or visit local public baths, which are very reasonably priced. In fact, I recommend visiting public baths for the experience. Not all places to live lack toilet and bathing facilities, but almost all Japanese homes have incredibly thin walls. You can hear everything your neighbours are up to and they can hear everything you are up to as well. I remember snuggling down intimately with my old boyfriend, when neighbours on the left launched into a blazing row, neighbours on the right became noisily engrossed in their own intimacy, and the guy upstairs suddenly started blasting 'Dancing Queen'. We gave up and did what most Japanese do under such conditions—started frequenting *love hotels, another type of place I recommend visiting for the experience.

*Love hotels: multi-storey buildings, often near train stations, built for couples (married or unmarried) to visit at any time of the day or night for a 'rest' or 'stay', where they can get away from their cramped homes, families (some Japanese children sleep with their parents), and nosy neighbours. Everything is designed for the utmost in privacy, the face of the attendant in the lobby is obscured, there are lit-up pictures of the vacant rooms for you to choose from, and the windows in the rooms are frosted or non-existent. Don't be shy— if you get the chance, go and visit one—they're great fun!

Prioritise

It's important to sort your priorities when looking for a place to live. City centres (especially Tokyo) are expensive, but the benefits of living close to your work will become more apparent the longer you live in Japan. Spending more than one hour a day on busy trains, carrying heavy bags, and constantly being aware of the last train home can all greatly increase the stress of living anywhere, let alone in a foreign country. You may have to pay a bit more rent, but you'll save on travel expenses and gain some peace of mind. It is worth it. My friend Cressie had a great place, but she lived outside Tokyo and travelled for an hour and a half each way (a bike ride and three trains) every time we met up for coffee or wanted to go out for the night. After three years of that she moved to Tokyo—her rent doubled, but she was happier and didn't have to disappear at 11:00 p.m., which, selfishly, I was happier about too. After two and a half years in Japan, I moved to a place within a five-minute walk of my job, and my life completely changed. No more trains and no more lugging half my belongings around in a heavy bag all day. If you can't be that close, at least live near the train line you take to work.

Many women often find that the practicalities of their home environment bring more stress than peace, and they emphasise the importance of investing in a home that is a haven from the everyday stresses of life in Japan, especially life in Tokyo:

Make sure to live in a space that you like or, at the very least, don't mind spending time in. Sanity is best maintained when you have a peaceful, orderly, and pleasant oasis to come home to at the end of the day. Invest whatever it costs to create that space, even if you don't think you spend enough time there to justify it. If you've been here for more than a few months, you should have enough money to do so by now. If you're going to be here for more than a year or so, only letting go of whatever amount of money you need to barely survive is penny-wise and pound-foolish, believe me! I have just spent a ridiculous amount of hard-earned money installing kitchen facilities and proper communications equipment in the 'drawer' I live in. Now I can control what, when, how much, and under what conditions I eat, and I can run up exorbitant phone bills calling my friends and family back home in order to have someone to talk to in English sometimes.

Guarantors

It used to be virtually impossible for foreigners to rent a place if they didn't have a Japanese guarantor, and was even very difficult for those with one. Long-timers, including those married to Japanese, have tales of putting one foot in the door of estate agents only to be met with shouts of "No foreigners!" Luckily this has changed and although in most cases you still need a guarantor, there are many agents that speak English and specifically rent to foreigners. Even some regular housing agencies now rent to foreigners providing that you have a Japanese guarantor, so it may be worth trying a local housing agency. Note that a guarantor is also a requirement for Japanese people seeking a new home.

For those on ex-pat packages or earning higher incomes, your employer may assist you with finding an apartment, or you can go to one of the posher estate agents. In many cases, your company will pay your rent, and expatriate housing is quite different from what I described above, instead verging on the luxurious.

Cost

Unique to Japan is the 'key money' system, which makes moving into a new apartment an expensive investment. Key money is between one- and three-months' rent; it is non-returnable and payable to the landlord/lady as a thank you for allowing you to pay them rent.

You will also pay a damage deposit; this can be up to three-months' rent and, theoretically, it is returned to you when you leave. The amount you receive obviously depends on how much you have trashed or cleaned your place. The reality, however, is that rarely will you see any of your deposit when you leave, regardless of how conspicuously cleaned and repaired you leave your place. I helped my Japanese friend clean her apartment when she relocated to New York and the landlord sent round these two little old ladies to check the place. No problem, we thought, we'll have the cash back before you can say "pass me the bleach". Not only did these two invent a million reasons why they weren't going to give Naomi her money, they actually tried to charge her extra! If it's important to you, then, in your presence, make the landlord/lady point out everything that needs cleaning and/or repairing when you move in and out. I'd still be surprised if you get anything back though.

The third payment you have to make will be required if you find the apartment through an agency, in which case you have to pay them the equivalent of a month's rent. Many of the agencies that deal with foreigners don't charge an agency fee, but check first. When you calculate everything, including one month's rent in advance, moving into a new apartment could cost you up to eight months' rent.

However, don't despair; if you take your time and look very carefully, you can find a fairly decent apartment without spending a fortune. My first two apartments didn't require any key money; for both places the deposit was only one month and the agencies didn't charge fees so I only had to pay the equivalent of two months' rent up front. I found my first apartment in four days and my second in just one, and while I don't advise taking the first place you find, sometimes luck will run your way. OK, so my first apartment had rats and it didn't take long before I had christened it 'Cockroach Cottage', but I was new to Tokyo and had hardly any money—it was all part of the adventure for me and provided great material for letters back home.

Your rental contract is renewed every two years when, generally, you have to pay an extra month's rent and there may be a rent increase. Check your contract for terms regarding the termination of your lease. One good thing is that Japanese law is in your favour if you are renting an apartment; if you don't pay your rent, your landlord/lady cannot evict you until after six months have gone by without payment. If, just before the end of six months, you pay one month's rent, they cannot evict you until you haven't paid for another six months ... you get the picture. Obviously, I don't recommend doing this.

Useful Japanese

guarantor	*hoshou nin*	key money	*reikin*
rent	*yachin*	agency fee	*chuukai tesuuryou*
deposit	*shikikin*	contract	*keiyaku*

I'm looking for a place to live.	*Watashi wa sumu tokoro o sagashite imasu.*
I'm looking for somewhere in ... (area).	*... ni sumu ie o sagashite imasu.*
I'm looking for somewhere on the ... line. (train line name)	*... sen ensen ni sumu ie o sagashite imasu.*
My budget is ... per month.	*Yosan wa ikkagetsu ... (yen) desu.*
Does it have a private toilet/shower/bath? ..	*Kobetsu ni toire/shawaa/ofuro wa tsuite imasu ka.*
Where is the nearest public bath?	*Ichiban chikai sentou wa doko desu ka.*
How far is the nearest station?	*Moyori eki made wa dorekurai kakarimasu ka.*
Do I need a guarantor?	*Hoshou nin wa hitsuyou desu ka.*
Do I have to pay key money/deposits?	*Reikin/shikikin o harau hitsuyou wa arimasu ka.*
Is there an agency fee?	*Chuukai tesuuryou wa arimasu ka.*
How much is the ... ?	*... wa ikura desu ka.*
Are pets allowed?	*Petto o katte mo ii desu ka.*
Is there a place to store a bicycle?	*Jitensha okiba wa arimasu ka.*
Is there a parking lot?	*Chuushajou wa arimasu ka.*
Is there a laundromat nearby?	*Chikaku ni koinrandorii wa arimasu ka.*
I'd like to renew/terminate my contract.	*Keiyaku o koushin/shuuryou shimasu.*
Sod this noise, let's go to a Love Hotel.	*Aa urusai! Rabuhoteru ni ikou.*

Resources

Apartments, Guest Houses, Gaijin Houses, or Rooms Available to Foreigners

The following have been listed because their managers speak English and long-term rent of at least six months is available, although some also rent on a daily or weekly basis. Most of these types of accommodation include all utility bills except the telephone. Agencies whose staff were rude on the telephone are not included—I thought I'd save you the stress.

Chiba

Bamboo House 03-3645-4028
       Ichikawa. Rent ¥50,000–100,000, no key money, deposit
       ¥20,000, guarantor not required.
       http://www.bamboo-house.com

Stone House 0473-22-9920
       Ichikawa. Rent ¥60,000, no key money, deposit ¥30,000,
       guarantor not required.

Kawaguchi

Dream House 048-256-3099
> Nishi Kawaguchi. Rent ¥59,000–64,000, no key money,
> deposit ¥10,000–20,000, guarantor not required.
> http://members.aol./hhhayashi/green.htm

Lily House 048-223-8205
> Kawaguchi Station. Rent ¥50,000, no key money, no deposit,
> guarantor not required.

Kyoto

ISE Dorm 075-771-0566
> Kyoto Station. Rent ¥30,000–57,000, no key money, deposit
> ¥10,000, guarantor not required.

Kyoto Green Peace 075-791-9890
> Matsudasaki. Rent ¥42,000, no key money, no deposit,
> guarantor not required.

Pension Kyoto 075-934-5010
> Kyoto City. Rent ¥120,000, no key money, no deposit,
> guarantor not required.

Takaya 075-431-5213
> Imazegawa. Rent ¥50,000, no key money, deposit ¥10,000,
> guarantor not required.

Tani House Dormitory 075-492-5489
> Tenkunjinjamae. Rent ¥54,000, no key money, no deposit,
> guarantor not required.

Toji An Guest House and Dormitory 075-691-7017
> Kyoto Station. Rent ¥40,000–45,000, no key money, no
> deposit, guarantor not required.

Uno House 075-231-7763
> Marutamachi. Rent ¥55,000, key money ¥30,000, no deposit,
> guarantor not required.

Yuraku-So 075-491-6900
> Kita Oji. Rent ¥26,000, no key money, deposit ¥15,000,
> guarantor required.

Saitama

Guest House Hanata 048-966-9533
> Kita Koshigaya. Rent ¥48,000, no key money, deposit ¥38,000,
> guarantor required.

Tokyo

ABC Guest Houses 03-3923-4240
> Oizumigakuen. Rent ¥50,000–80,000, no key money, no
> deposit, guarantor not required.

Apple Houses 0422-51-2277
> Higashi Kogane, Ogikubo. Rent ¥46,000–75,000, no key
> money, deposit ¥10,000, guarantor not required.
> http://www.applehouse.ne.jp

110

Bamboo House 03-3645-4028
  Toshima, Suginami, Shibuya, Arakawa. Rent ¥50,000–100,000,
  no key money, deposit ¥20,000, guarantor not required.
  http://www.bamboo-house.com
Crystal Village 03-3388-7625
  Nakano, Koenji. Rent ¥130,000, no key money, deposit
  ¥30,000, guarantor not required.
Dream House 048-256-3099
  Iidabashi, Waseda, Jujyo, Chofu, Nerima. Rent ¥59,000–64,000,
  no key money, deposit ¥10,000–20,000, guarantor not required.
  http://members.aol./hhhayashi/green.htm
Friendship Houses 03-3765-2288
  Nakano Sakaue, Kichijoji, Oimachi, Nippori, Iidabashi Honcho.
  Rent ¥30,000–200,000, no key money, deposit ¥30,000,
  guarantor not required.
  http://gaijinhouse.com
Hitomi Guest House 03-3558-8326
  Rent from ¥57,000, no key money, deposit ¥20,000, guarantor
  not required.
Iwata Sekisan Jimusho Inc. 03-3721-4461
  Higashi Koenji. Rent ¥80,000–180,000, no key money, deposit
  2 months rent, guarantor required.
Liberty House 03-5272-7238
  Waseda, Meijiro, Iidabashi, Nezu, Nakano Sakaue. Rent
  ¥53,000–86,000, no key money, deposit ¥10,000–half a
  month's rent, guarantor not required.
Maple House 0424-22-3126
  Hibarigaoka. Rent ¥55,000–60,000, no key money, deposit
  ¥30,000, guarantor not required.
Oak Houses 03-3979-8810
  19 houses throughout Tokyo. Rent ¥47,000–80,000, no key
  money, deposit ¥30,000, guarantor not required.
  http://www.whatsuptokyo.com
Rikko Kaikan Dormitory 03-3972-1151
  Kotakemukaihara. Rent ¥46,000, no key money, deposit
  ¥20,000, guarantor required.
  http://www.bekkoame.ne.jp/~rikkokai/index.html
Takara Foreign Students' Dormitory 03-5966-4325
  Oyama. Women only. Also available to non-students. Student
  discounts available. Rent ¥47,000–64,000, no key money,
  deposit 1 month's rent, guarantor not required.
Tokyo English Centre 0422-51-9900
  Higashi Kogane. Rent ¥55,000, no key money, no deposit,
  guarantor not required.
Tokyo Houses 03-3910-8808
  Otsuka. Rent ¥48,000, key money ¥1000, no deposit,
  guarantor not required.

U & I Guest House 03-3996-4958
>Nerima. Rent ¥50,000–125,000, no key money, deposit
>1 month's rent, guarantor sometimes required.
>http://www.home.apt.ne.jp/funu/i.house

Yokohama

Eldorado 045-903-3808
>Tama Plaza. Rent ¥48,000–59,000, no key money, deposit
>¥10,000, guarantor not required.
>http://www.imagining.to

Villa Paradiso 045-911-1184
>Tama Plaza. Rent ¥48,000, no key money, deposit ¥10,000,
>guarantor not required.

Yokohama Hillstone House 045-243-9001
>Mitsukyo. Rent ¥70,000, key money ¥3000, deposit ¥20,000,
>guarantor not required.

Real Estate Agencies for Foreigners—English Spoken

I have to say that I found it incredibly difficult to find real estate agencies outside of Tokyo who would deal with foreigners. If you find any, please send their contact information to me. I'm afraid that nearly all of what follows only operate in Tokyo, unless otherwise indicated.

Advance International Guest Houses 03-3377-7471
>Tokyo. Guest houses: rent ¥75,000–80,000, no key money,
>deposit ¥50,000, guarantor not required. Apartments: rent
>¥120,000–130,000, no key money, deposit 1 month's rent,
>no agency fee, guarantor not required.

AOI Realty 03-5464-7177
>Tokyo. Rent ¥100,000–2 million, key money 2 months' rent,
>deposit 2–6 months' rent, agency fee 1 month's rent,
>guarantor required.

Apartment Hotel Azabu Court 03-3446-8610
>Tokyo. Rent ¥230,000–700,000, no key money, deposit half a
>month's rent, no agency fee, guarantor required.
>http://www.ac.prdi.com

Family Home Co 045-201-9165
>Yokohama and Kawasaki. Rent ¥120,000, no key money,
>no deposit, no agency fee, guarantor not required.
>http://www05.u-page.so-net.ne.jp/ya2/family/index2.html

Fontana Guest Houses 03-3382-0151
>Tokyo. Guest house: rent ¥60,000–100,000, no key money,
>deposit half a month's rent, no agency fee, guarantor not
>required. Apartment: rent ¥60,000–400,000, no key money,
>deposit 1 month's rent, agency fee 1 month's rent, guarantor
>not required.

Housing Consultation Centre for Domestic and Foreign Students 03-3359-5997
>Tokyo. Students only. Rent ¥30,000–80,000, key money
>¥50,000, deposit ¥50,000, no agency fee, guarantor required.
>http://www.naigai.or.jp/

Hoyo Tokyo 03-3362-0658
    Tokyo. Rent ¥120,000–180,000, no key money, deposit
    1–2 months' rent, no agency fee, guarantor not required.

International Homes 03-3505-8611
    Tokyo and Yokohama. Rent ¥300,000–4 million, no key money,
    deposit 4 months' rent, agency fee 1 month's rent, guarantor
    sometimes required.

Kimi Information Centre 03-3986-1604
    Chiba, Kanagawa, and Tokyo. Rent ¥55,000–300,000, some
    no key money but most require 2 months' rent, deposit half a
    month's rent, agency fee 1 month's rent, guarantor required.
    http://www2.dango.ne.jp/kimi

Nichiyo 03-3728-7061
    Tokyo. Rent ¥55,000–130,000, no key money, deposit ¥20,000–
    1 month's rent, no agency fee, guarantor not required.

Nord House Corporation 03-5474-7412
    Tokyo. Rent ¥70,000–2 million, some no key money but most
    require 2 months' rent, deposit 2–3 months' rent, agency fee
    1 month's rent, guarantor usually required.
    http://www.nord.co.jp

Real Estate Systems 03-3280-0537
    Tokyo. Rent ¥40,000–1 million, key money 2 months' rent,
    deposit 3–6 months' rent, agency fee 1 month's rent,
    guarantor usually required.

Relocation House 03-5766-2300
    Tokyo. Rent from ¥120,000, key money 2 months' rent, deposit
    2 months' rent, agency fee 1 month's rent, guarantor required.
    http://www.interhouse.co.jp/

Sakura Corporation (see display ad, page 115) 03-3551-2666
    Throughout Japan. Rent ¥40,000–1.5 million, key money
    usually 2 months' rent, deposit usually 2–3 months' rent,
    agency fee 1 month's rent, guarantor sometimes required.

Sakura House 03-5330-5250
    Tokyo. Rent ¥100,000–370,000, no key money, deposit
    ¥30,000, no agency fee, guarantor not required.
    http://www.sakura-house.com/

Time Healer Inc 03-5976-5366
    Tokyo. Rent ¥73,000–200,000, some no key money, deposit
    ¥30,000–2 months' rent, agency fee 1 month's rent,
    guarantor required.
    http://www.media.ne.jp/web/thealer

Tokyo Apartment Rentals 03-3368-7558
    Tokyo. Rent ¥145,000–400,000, no key money, deposit
    1 month's rent, agency fee 1 month's rent, guarantor
    not required.
    http://www.tokyoapartment.com
    http://www.japanapartment.com

113

Tokyo House Bureau 03-3501-2496
     Tokyo and suburbs. Rent ¥90,000–400,000, key money usually
     not required, deposit 2/3 months' rent, agency fee
     1 month's rent, guarantor required.
     http://www.bekkoame.ne.jp/ha/tokyohouse
Tokyo Room Information 03-5607-5508
     Tokyo. Rent ¥50,000–75,000, no key money, deposit
     1 month's rent, no agency fee, guarantor not required.
World Student Village 03-3917-0301
     Tokyo. Available to non-students. Rent ¥85,000–100,000,
     no key money, deposit 1 month's rent, no agency fee,
     guarantor required.
     http://www.intacc.ne.jp/HP/wsv/index.html

Housing Guarantors

These companies can arrange housing guarantors for a fee.
Japan Golden Club 03-3358-8521
JOS Enterprise 03-5330-3300

Home Services

Benriyasan
     'The one who does everything!'. Check your local phone book
     for your closest benriyasan. You can use this sevice if you have
     anything that needs doing in your home.
Homeaid 03-3781-7536
Speedikleen House Cleaning Service 03-5721-8663
Tokyo Domestic Service Centre 03-3584-4769
Tokyo Maid Service 03-3291-3595
Tokyo Rex Interior Services Home Decorating 0422-49-0083

Domestic Moving

ABC Moving Service 03-3368-5995
Eddy's Moving Service 03-3393-6810
Side By Side 03-5306-3367
Nippon Express 0120-220-202

Home Exchanges

International Home Exchange Service
     http://www.intervac.com

Other Sources of Housing Information

Information Bureau of Tokyo 03-3354-0502
Japan Association for Working Holidaymakers 03-3389-0181
     http://www.mmjp.or.jp/jawhm

Web Resources

Excel Property Management Osaka
     http://excelproperty.com/
Freebell Apartments Nagoya
     http://www.freebell.co.jp/index.html

Housing in Japan Assistance Schemes in Osaka
    http://byjnet.com/INFO/About_Japan/Life/House/
Nissho Apartments
    http://mediazone.tcp-net.ad.jp/nissho/index.html
B & M Realty Nagoya
    http://www.bekkoame.ne.jp/i/bmrealty/furnished.html
Okyo Bunka Gakuen
    http://www.tokyobunka.ac.jp/dataroom/apart/index2.html

Resources and Further Information
Finding a Home in Tokyo
    Published by the American Chamber of Commerce.

Utilities

When you move into a new place, your landlord/lady, or agency if you have one, will probably take responsibility for contacting the electricity, gas, and water companies for you. If they don't, you need to contact the local branches of the above companies yourself, and inform them of the date you are moving in so they can switch everything on and organise the bills. Regarding the electricity, locate the circuit breaker and you will find a postcard that must be completed and mailed to the electricity company. The utility companies must also be contacted when you leave your apartment. If your landlord/lady does not do this, then do it yourself to avoid paying any bills belonging to the next tenant.

Find out where the main valves or switches are for the gas, water, and electricity in case you need to turn them off in the event of a problem. The electricity circuit breaker switch will turn off automatically if you blow a fuse or exceed the amount of electricity designated to your apartment—this usually happens about one second before you save that urgent report on your computer. Don't panic—switch a few machines and lights off and you can turn on the breaker switch immediately. If you find this happening often, you can increase your power supply by contacting the local electricity branch. Electricity voltage in Japan is 100 volts AC and the plugs are flat with two pins or prongs, as found in Canada and the US.

Japan's tap water is safe to drink, although it has a higher chemical content than that of Western countries and plays havoc with your hair and your teeth (see the sections on Hair in Chapter One and Dentists in Chapter Three), so who knows what it does to your insides. I drink it all the time and I don't think I'm quite as doolally as some people do. It's up to you.

Payment of utility bills

You will receive telephone, gas, water, and electricity bills separately, in Japanese, with about three weeks to pay. Reminders usually state as such in English, which is handy. Payments can be made at post offices, banks, or the relevant company's office, but most convenient are designated convenience stores, funnily enough. Look for the symbols on the backs of the bills that tell you which convenience stores accept utility bill payments. You can also arrange to make regular payments directly from your bank account, in which case you should take a bill and your bankbook to your bank. If you don't pay your bills you will receive great numbers of reminders before you are cut off. If your telephone is cut off, simply walk to the nearest convenience store, pay the bill and the phone will be reconnected by the time you get back. For other utilities, contact the local branch and they will reconnect you within a few hours. Having had severe financial difficulties during one period in Japan, I have had everything cut off at one time or another and I love the fact that it is reconnected so quickly upon payment. I continued to receive outstanding bills on my old apartment that I was unable to pay for a year after I left it. Reminders kept coming, but only the mobile phone company sent a court order about eight months later and then they were very reasonable about it.

Telephone

A new telephone line costs about ¥70,000, but you can buy a secondhand one from somebody leaving Japan for about ¥40,000–50,000. The process is basically the same whether you buy a new or used phone line, except if you are buying one from a person instead of from NTT; in this case both of you have to go to the NTT office. You need to show NTT your alien registration card or passport and another official item with your name and address on it, such as an electricity bill. There is a small subscription and installation fee. Should you move, you may transfer this phone line to a new address for a small charge.

There are several telephone companies that provide long-distance domestic calls; check them out for the most competitive rates. For international phone calls, there seem to be hundreds of new companies providing this service, and they all swear they are the cheapest. The great thing about these companies is that if you don't pay your bill, they cannot cut off your phone line, whereas NTT can if you don't pay them. Theoretically, you can work your way through the different international phone companies without paying a single yen, although of course I don't recommend this. There are also several companies operating callback systems that can greatly reduce your overseas telephone bill.

Public telephone boxes accept ¥10 and ¥100 coins, but some only accept telephone cards. Phone cards can be bought for ¥1000 or ¥5000 and are available at convenience stores and sometimes from machines right next to public phones. Not all public phones allow international calls, so look for the grey phones if you want to call outside Japan.

Mail

The post office has a really useful detailed English pamphlet explaining all services provided. Services available at your local post office include domestic, international, registered, and express mail. If registered mail or a parcel is delivered to you and you are not there to accept it, then there will be a delivery notice (all in Japanese) with a telephone number on it. In addition, the post office has a range of other services that include banking, sending money overseas, and acceptance of utility bill payments. Most post offices are open from 9:00 a.m. to 5:00 p.m., Monday through Friday, but some are open later or on weekends for undelivered mail collection and regular services. It is sensible to write all the names of your household members on your post box.

There are several companies other than the post office who will deliver parcels, often within 24 hours. Look for the green signs with a yellow dog and cat on them. These are outside many convenience stores and you often see the vans around. They provide excellent service—friendly, cheap, and efficient. You can send something by cash-on-delivery and you can even send bulky items like furniture. Some companies will pick up your parcels, but you need an extra helpful convenience store owner or a Japanese friend to give you this information. I spent three months carrying packages of 100 magazines to the convenience store to be sent out all over Japan before the owner took pity on me and a delivery guy turned up at my apartment one day. If a parcel comes when you're not there, they will leave a card with a telephone number on it. Call the number and leave your address (you should learn to say it in Japanese). They will have you on file so will understand why you are calling without your needing any more Japanese ability.

Useful Japanese

utilities	*setsubi*
bill	*seikyuusho*
electricity	*denki*
gas	*gasu*
water	*mizu/suidoo*
telephone	*denwa*
local call	*kinkyori tuuwa*
long-distance call	*chookyori tsuuwa/ denwa*
overseas call	*kokusai tsuuwa/ denwa*
callback service	*kooru bakku saabisu*
post office	*yuubinkyoku*
mail (noun)	*yuubin/tegami*
mail (verb)	*yuusou suru/okuru*
domestic mail	*kokunai yuubin*
international mail	*kokusai yuubin*
registered mail	*kakitome*
express mail	*sokutatsu*
post box	*yuubin posuto*
mail deliverer	*yuubin-haitatsu nin/ yuubin-ya san*
delivery service	*deribarii/takuhai saabisu*
cash on delivery	*daikin hikikae barai/ daibiki*

119

I have just moved into a new apartment.	*Atarashii apaato/heya ni hikkoshita bakari desu.*
I will be moving into a new apartment on [date].	*[date] ni atarashii apaato/heya ni hikkoshi masu.*
Please connect my	*... o tsunaide itadakemasu ka.*
Where is the circuit breaker in my apartment?..	*Apaato no bureikaa wa doko desu ka.*
I am leaving my apartment on [date].	*[date] ni ima no apaato kara hikkoshimasu.*
Please disconnect my	*... o hazushite itadakimasu ka.*
Where are the main valves/switches for the gas in my apartment?	*Watashi no heya no gasu no motosen wa doko desu ka.*
I would like to increase the electricity supply to my apartment.	*Watashi no heya no anpea o ookikushite hoshii no desu ga.*
I received a reminder for my ... bill, but I paid it on [date].	*... no seikyuu no tokusokujoo o uketotta no desu ga, [date] ni haratte imasu.*
I'd like to pay my ... bill.	*... no ryoukin o haraitai no desu ga.*
I'd like to arrange a direct debit for my ... bill.	*... no ryoukin no shiharai o ginkou-hikiotoshi ni shite itadakemasu ka.*
My ... has been cut off.	*... ga tomerarete shimaimashita.*
I'd like to buy a telephone line.	*Denwa-kaisen o hikitai no desu ga.*
Please send me some information.	*Shiryou o okutte itadakemasu ka.*
Where is the nearest pay phone?	*Ichiban chikai koushuu-denwa wa doko ni arimasu ka.*
I'd like to buy a phone card.	*Terehon kaado o kaitai no desu ga.*
Do you have change for the phone?	*Denwa o kaketai node ryougae shite itadakemasu ka.*
May I have your English brochure about the post office?	*Yuubinkyoku no eigo no panfuretto o itadakemasu ka.*
I'd like to send this by ... mail.	*Kore o ... (yuubin) de okutte kudasai.*
What is the cheapest way I can send this?	*Kore o okuru ichiban yasui houhou o oshiete kudasai.*
How long will it take?	*Nan-nichi gurai de touchaku shimasu ka.*
I wasn't at home to accept a parcel you delivered.	*Nimotsu o haitatsu shite itadaita toki, ie ni imasen deshita.*
I'd like to send some money overseas.	*Kaigai ni soukin shitai no desu ga.*
Please pick up some parcels I need to send.	*Okuritai nimotsu o ie made tori ni kite itadakemasu ka.*

120

Resources

Telephone Companies Providing Domestic Telephone Calls

Dai-Ni Den Den Inc (KDDI) 0077-778

      For domestic access dial 0077 before the number; for
      international access dial 0078. You need to register if you are
      dialling internationally from a cell phone.

NTT 0120-364-463

      http://www.ntt.com/index-e.html

Private Companies Renting or Selling Phone Lines

ASIST Co. Ltd. 06-6352-6465

      http://www.asist.co.jp/ISDN

GFSG... 03-5413-7341

IT Corporation 03-5337-7972

Townnet.com

      Information on buying and renting telephones from
      different companies.
      http://www.townnet.com/business/companies/phone.html

Welcome Travel & Trade 0488-45-8031

      http://pws.prserv.net/jpinet.hossain

Telephone Services

Directory Assistance 104

International Directory Assistance 0057

Japan's Telecommunications Overview

      http://www.igc.apc.org/ohdakefoundation/telecom/overview.htm

Out of Order .... 113 (J)

Speaking Clock .... 117 (J)

International Telephone Companies and Services

Dial connecting code, country code, area code (omit first 0 if there is one),
phone number.

AT & T 03-3500-2400

AT & T@phonecard 0120-633-234

      Prepaid card available at convenience stores.
      http://www.jens.co.jp

Discount-Long-Distance.com

      Lists international telephone companies.
      http://www.discount-long-distance.com/international.htm

Global Call 098-833-8555

Global One 03-5498-8111

      http://www.global-one.net

Global Telecom Solutions

      http://www.globaltelecom.org/japan.htm

International Digital Communications (IDC) 0061 0120-03-0061
      http://www.idc.co.jp/english/index.html
ICS.. 03-5470-1590
i-Tel 03-3407-8100
Japan Telecom 0041 0088-22-10-59
      http://www,japan-telecome.co.jp/index_e.html
Kallback
      http://www.kallback.com
KDD 001 0057
      http://www.kdd.co.jp/indexe.html
Liberty Telecom 053-450-3121
Orion
      Companies selling phone lines and cards.
      http://www.orions.ad.jp/c/urls/word/p/r/epaid+/telephone.html
Telematrix Callback System 03-3281-4303
UltraCall 03-3354-9532
      http://www.ultracall.co.jp
World Link Discount Telecom
      http://www.mmjp.or.jp/worldlink.ir/

Overseas Country Codes

Australia 61	Hong Kong 852	Poland 48
Austria 43	Hungary 36	Portugal 351
Belgium............ 32	India 91	Russia 7
Canada 1	Ireland 353	Singapore 65
Czech 42	Italy 39	South Africa 27
Denmark 45	Netherlands 31	Spain 34
France 33	New Zealand .. 64	Sweden 46
Germany 49	Norway 47	Switzerland 41
Greece 30	Pakistan 92	UK 44
Hawaii 1	Philippines 63	US 1

Post

Post Office Home Page
      http://www.postal.mpt.go.jp/new-eng/index.htm
Postal Service Mail 03-5472-5851
Postal Service Savings 0120-085420
Services of Post Office
      http://www.mpt.go.jp/service/index-e.html

Mailbox Services

Tokyo Voice Net System 03-3589-8008
Mail Station Ebisu 03-5469-1408

Telegrams

Domestic 115   International 0053-519

Courier Services

Baiku Kyubin 0120-378-1999
DHL Japan 03-5479-2580
Express Mail Service (EMS)
      Available at post offices.
Federal Express Japan 0120-003-200
      International only.
      http://www.fedex.com/
Hubnet Express 03-3455-6611
Nihon Baiku-bin Kyokai 0120-287-4000
Nippon Express 03-3253-1111
Overseas Courier Service (OCS) 03-5476-8123
      International only.
Sanei Kyubin 0120-006-995
Seino Transportation Co. Ltd. 03-3667-0881
Super Express Mail Centre 03-3546-1123
      Available at post offices.
Yamato Transport 03-3541-3411

Other Utilities' Customer Service Centres

Call for your nearest office.
Gas 03-5400-7564   NHK (TV) .... 0120-151-515 (J)
Water 03-5320-6427

Internet Providers and Resources

Crisscross
      http://www.crisscross.com
Global Online Japan (see display ad, page 124) 03-5334-1720
      http://www.gol.com
Internet Access Providers
      http://www.konradh.net/jp/computing/providers.html
Internet Service Providers in Japan
      http://www.imug.org/ispjapan.html
Public Internet Providers in Japan
      http://www.twics.com/~dmortell/provider.html
TWICS 03-5740-1155
      http://www.twics.com

Other

Cognigen
      Search engine for the best telephone rates.
      http://ld.gbtel.net/
Telephone book 03-3356-8511
Townpage Telephone Directory 0120-46-0815
      http://english.townpage.isp.ntt.co.jp/

Garbage and Recycling

Garbage

If there is one thing guaranteed to induce an argument with your neighbours, it is your inability to adhere to the garbage system. If your neighbours complain to your landlord/lady a lot, renewal of your apartment contract is at risk. Garbage disposal is taken very seriously here and you have to respect that. Although the rules can be difficult to follow at first, it is an excellent system.

All garbage is divided into burnable: food, paper, etc., which is collected two or three times a week; and non-burnable but not 'bulky': plastic, glass, metal, etc., which is collected once a week. Batteries are supposed to be returned to the shop from which you bought them. If you mix your garbage, then your neighbours will return the bag to your doorstep for you to sort through. I don't know if they actually know whose garbage it is. Perhaps they assume that it must be the stupid foreigners who made the mistake as I have had other people's garbage placed on my doorstep. There are collection points about every ten houses and if you live in a house rather than a shared building, you share the responsibility of sweeping the garbage area. One of your neighbours will turn up one day with a wooden clipboard in one hand and a broom in the other. This means that the collection point is your responsibility this week and you have to hand over the broom and clipboard to the person on the other side of your house after that. Garbage must be put out before 8:00 a.m. and some neighbours go berserk if you put it out the night before. It's best to watch what your neighbours do in order to determine how strict your neighbourhood is about putting garbage out the night before. Also look out for special days when bottles, cans, and paper (including newspapers) are collected separately. Don't put anything out on a non-garbage day—leave it to rot in your kitchen rather than put it out on a non-garbage day. You must put garbage out in special bags you can buy at stores or in a large plastic bin with the lid removed. Mark 'danger' on it if it contains broken glass. You must bring in the bin immediately after the garbage has been collected, so, unless you want to spend four hours waiting for the garbage to be removed, use the bags. Leaving your bin out is grounds for your neighbours to call your landlord/lady immediately. An alternative for food waste is the small 'composter' available from your ward office that, if you have one, fits on a balcony. Contact your ward office for details.

Bulky items such as furniture, bicycles, and electric appliances are collected twice a month for a fee and you must first contact your local Bulky Items Reception Centre (yes, that's its real name, check your ward office handbook). Or you can try sneaking such items in with your non-burnable garbage, which sometimes works. The Centre will tell you the collection date and the cost, which is paid by purchasing special stickers from a convenience store. Most Centres have an English-speaking member of staff. Put your name on the stickers, attach them to your items and put them outside before 8:30 a.m. on collection day. Items are repaired and recycled.

Recycling

Japanese people tend to replace items often, so you will see perfectly good televisions, stereos, and furniture outside houses or in designated areas waiting for the Bulky Items collection people the next day. Despite it being illegal, many foreigners take advantage of this and furnish their homes with such items, either for environmental or economical reasons. Just be discreet when you're rummaging through garbage outside other people's homes.

There are many secondhand and recycling shops throughout Japan, especially in certain areas of Tokyo. They have become increasingly popular with younger Japanese. Flea markets are common, although it can be difficult to make a reservation because many employ a complicated telephone reservation system, all in Japanese. My advice is to team up with a Japanese friend if you want to book a table at a flea market.

Useful Japanese

garbage	*gomi*	paper	*kami*
burnable garbage	*moeru/kanen gomi*	danger	*kiken*
non-burnable		bulky items	*sodai gomi*
garbage	*moenai/funen gomi*	recycle	*risaikuru*
plastic	*purasuchikku*	composter	*mimizu konposto*
can	*kan*		*youki*
broken glass	*ware garasu*	secondhand shop	*chuukohin ten*
bottle	*bin*	flea market	*furiimaaketto*

What day is burnable/non-burnable
garbage day? .... *Moeru/moenai gomi no hi wa itsu desu ka.*
I'd like to return my used batteries. .... *Tsukaikitta denchi o henkyaku shitai no desu ga.*

127

When can I leave bottles/cans/paper out for
recycling? .... *Risaikuru you no bin/kan/kami wa itsu
dasemasu ka.*
I'd like a composter, please. .... *Konposuto youki o kudasai.*
I have some clothes that I would like to
recycle/donate. .... *Risaikuru/kifu shitai irui ga arimasu.*
When can you collect my bulky items? .... *Sodai gomi no shuushuu wa itsu desu ka.*
I'd like to buy some bulky items garbage
stickers please. .... *Sodai gomi you no shiiru wo kudasai/kaitai
no desu.*

Resources

Contact your local ward office to find your nearest recycling centre.

Environment Organisations

Earth Day Japan Tokyo Office 03-3263-9022
    Information for Earth Day participants; newsletter and
    publications regarding environmental issues.
    http//:www.earthday-j.org
Foundation For Global Peace and Environment 03-5442-3161
    Information, events, campaign projects.
Friends of the Earth 03-3951-1081
    International environment issues.
    http://www.foejapan.org
Global Village 03-3705-0233
    Fair trade, organic food, advocacy, campaigns.
    http://www.globalvillage.or.jp
Greenpeace Japan 03-5351-5409
    Toxic, nuclear, forest, climate issues.
    http://www.greenpeace.org
Japan Environmental Exchange 0424-88-8943
    Information, projects, educational activities.
    http://www.web.kyoto-inet.or.jp/org/s-world/jee
Japan Tropical Forest Action Network (JATAN) 03-3770-6308
    Information, projects, research, campaigns.

Environment Websites

Directory of Organisations and Institutes Active in Environmental Monitoring
        http://www.gsf.de/UNEP/contents.html
Global Environment Information Centre
        http://eco-web.com/cgi-local/sfc?a=index/index.html&b=register/01627.html
Japan-Related Organisations—Environment
        http://www.bridgetojapan.org/environment.html
Japan Environment Issues
        http://student.uq.edu.au/~s337508/japanpage.html

Tokyo Flea Markets

Arai Yakushi Temple .... 03-3386-1355 (J)
Citizens Recycle Movement of Japan .... 03-3226-6800 (J)
Meiji Park 03-5228-3320
Nogi Shrine .... 03-3402-2181 (J)
Ota Recycle Movement Association .... 03-3733-3471 (J)
Salvation Army Bazaar 03-3384-3769
     Also accepts unwanted clothes donations.
Togo Shrine .... 03-3403-3591 (J)
Urawa-juku Furusato .... 03-3921-0292 (J)

Recycle Shops

Everybody .... 03-3454-2727 (J)
     Minami-Azabu, Tokyo. Clothes, accessories, bags, shoes.
Garage House .... 03-3419-6914 (J)
     Shimokitazawa, Tokyo. Women's clothes.
Garage Shop .... 03-3708-3930 (J)
     Futakotamagawa, Tokyo. Clothes.
Marushin Service .... 0425-27-4446 (J)
     Tachikawa. Anything.
Ninjin 03-3310-1739
     Asagaya, Tokyo. Women's, children's, and babies' clothes.
Recycle Centre 03-5982-4400
     Koenji, Ikebukuro, and Nerima, in Tokyo. Can deliver. Can also
     pick up your unwanted goods. Household goods and clothes.
Recycle Dream 0422-43-2269
     Mitaka. Sewing machines, generators.
Recycle Sanko 03-3706-3261
     Setagaya, Tokyo. Furniture, washing machines, TVs, videos.
Recycling Everything Attractive Possible (REAP) 03-3922-6402
     Nerima, Tokyo. Stamps and prepaid cards (phone, rail, etc.).
     Used to help print Christian literature in six Asian languages.
Vintage Kimono .... 03-3661-0641 (J)
     Kimono. Chiba, Kyoto, Saitama, Tokyo, and Yokohama.
Wave Recycle Shop 03-3353-3313
     Shops throughout Tokyo. Can also pick up your unwanted
     goods. Household goods and clothes.

Other

Council for PET Bottle Recycling
     http://www.petbottle-rec.gr.jp/english/e_gaiyo.html
Kurukuru Paper Recycle Centre .... 03-5718-7181 (J)

129

Pests and Pets

Pests

Depending on your home country, you may or may not be used to sharing your home with unidentified objects, flying or otherwise. They tend to create havoc in your life during your first summer and for some reason leave you pretty much alone thereafter. The Environmental Sanitation sections of each prefecture attempt to combat this by treating the sewage system with chemicals that kill flies and mosquitoes.

Cockroaches are also a problem, ranging in size and ability to freak you out. There is a whole range of products available in convenience stores if you are into killing them—go into any large store with a whole floor of cleaning products and so on, and they'll have an extensive display. You can try to kill each cockroach by hand, but it's a never-ending battle. My friend Alison is a Buddhist, so leaves them roaming around—I respect her beliefs, but I don't visit her apartment during the summer. If you have a major pest problem in your garden, you can rent insecticide equipment from the Sanitation Office.

I wouldn't say that it's common to find rats in apartments, but two of the four places I have lived in had them, which was more a reflection on the building than my housekeeping skills, honest. I put up with it in the first place for weeks because I could only hear them and not see them, but one day I woke up to find one sitting on my cooker. It jumped at me and ran under my bed; I could no longer rely on my avoidance tactic and moved in with a friend that day. You can get rat traps, call the Sanitation Section, or leave immediately demanding your money back from the landlord/lady. It is unlikely that they will give it to you, but if you found your place through an agency that deals with foreigners and threaten to spread the word that their places have rats, then they'll probably return your money.

Japan is host to a few types of poisonous snakes, which can be found in cities as well as the countryside, but it is rare that you will meet one. If a snake bites someone, don't try to suck the poison out, but do wrap the area tightly, keep the person still, and call an ambulance. It will help if you speak enough Japanese to describe the snake, or have a Japanese person call for you who can.

Pets

Various types of rodents tend to be the most popular pets among young Japanese due to the fact that most landlords/ladies don't allow dogs. Dogs must be vaccinated before they are 91 days old and registered with the local public health centre or a community branch office within 30 days of the vaccination. If you acquire an adult dog, it too must be registered. Dogs must be vaccinated annually. If you have brought your dog from home, then you need to show the quarantine certificate when you register it. In public they must be kept on leads at all times, yet everyone seems to ignore this law and carries them in handbags or bicycle baskets. Your dog must wear a collar with its registration and vaccination tags. You have to clear up after your dog if it defecates in the street, so save all the plastic bags you accumulate from the convenience stores or buy some special bags from your local pet shop.

Dogs in Japan tend to be impeccably groomed and accessorised with bows and frills. Ask your ward office, vet, or the owner of the nearest poodle to recommend a dog groomer.

If your dog goes missing you are on your own; official bodies deem it your responsibility. Stray dogs are taken to the local dog pound; the telephone number can be found in your ward handbook.

Tokyo encourages neutering of cats at a local vet and will contribute financially to this. If your dog or cat dies, you must tell the Public Health Centre or Community Branch Office to cancel your registration. The Refuse Collection Office will collect your pet for a fee and they will contact a pet cemetery for you to save you the trauma.

Check with your embassy about quarantine laws regarding taking pets into and out of Japan.

Useful Japanese

pest	*gaichuu*	ferret	*kenaga-itachi*
mosquito	*ka*	bird	*tori*
ant	*ari*	rabbit	*usagi*
cockroach	*gokiburi*	gerbil	*arechi-nezumi*
rat	*nezumi*	gecko	*yamori*
snake	*hebi*	dog groomer	*inu no biyoushitsu*
pet	*petto*	quarantine	*ken'eki*
dog	*inu*	pet shop	*petto shoppu*
cat	*neko*	dog pound	*hokenjo*
hamster	*hamusutaa*	vet	*juui*

What do you recommend to get rid of ... ?	*... o kuchikusuru osusume no shouhin wa nan desu ka.*
Where do you get your dog groomed?	*Anata wa dokode inu no teire o shite imasu ka.*
I'd like to get my dog groomed.	*Watashi no inu no ke no teire o shite hoshii desu.*
I'd like to vaccinate my	*Watashi no ... ni yobousesshu o ukesasetai desu.*
I'd like to register my	*Watashi no ... o touroku shitai no desu ga.*

I'd like to buy some bags to clear up after
my dog. .... *Watashi no inu no fun o shimatsusuru*
fukuro o kaitai desu.

My ... is missing. .... *Watashi no ... ga inakunarimashita.*

I'd like to have my ... neutered. .... *Watashi no ... o kyosei sasetai desu.*

My ... has died. .... *Watashi no ... ga shinimashita.*

Please cancel my ...'s registration. .... *Watashi no ... no touroku o torikeshite*
kudasai.

Please contact a pet cemetery for me. .... *Petto you no bochi to rennraku o totte*
kudasai.

Resources

Animal Protection Centre, Tokyo Metropolitan Government................... 03-3790-0861 (J)
Dobutsutachi No Kai (Group for Animals) ....Fax 042-584-4354
    Non-profit volunteer group. Low-cost veterinary services such
    as spaying and neutering of cats and dogs. Pets available for
    adoption. Throughout Japan.
Japan Animal Welfare Society 03-3409-1821
    Locations in Hokkaido, Kanagawa, Kansai, and Tokyo.
Japan Society for the Prevention of Cruelty to Animals (JSPCA) .... 03-3409-1821 (J)
Veterinary Sanitation, Tokyo Metropolitan Government .... 03-5320-4412 (J)

Websites
Animal Quarantine Service
    http://www.animal-quarantine-service.go.jp/english/index2.htm
Pet Net
    Everything a pet owner needs to know.
    http://www.pet-net.net/japan.htm

133

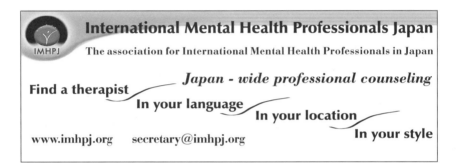

Health

3

The Health System

Finding a doctor with whom you feel comfortable can take years in your home country. In Japan, it ranks alongside finding a good hairdresser (see the Hair section in Chapter One) and meeting a partner if you're single (see the section on Being Single in Chapter Four). If you need an English-speaking doctor, or prefer a female doctor, and expect the 'personable' manner that most Western doctors have now developed, then you may feel like giving up visiting doctors here altogether. With the exceptions of abortion (see this section later in this chapter) and childbirth (see this section in Chapter Five), Western women have many criticisms of the Japanese health system, but there must be something good about it as Japanese people still have the highest life expectancy in the world, with women living on average to be 83 years old.

For peace of mind, it is sensible to bring to Japan copies of your medical records as well as any regular prescriptions, including those for eye glasses or contact lenses.

Health facilities

Japanese health facilities consist of hospitals, smaller clinics, and various services provided by public health centres; i.e., there is no GP system. Rarely is there an appointment system; you can visit a hospital any time, for any reason.

Due to the fact that hospitals are visited by people with all sorts of ailments, however minor, you can expect waits of about two hours to see a doctor. Clinics tend to be smaller and friendlier with shorter waiting times but, on the whole, your consultation with the doctor will often be less than five minutes long. Most Western women find that Japanese doctors provide insufficient medical explanations, inadequate attention, patronising attitudes, and sometimes incorrect diagnoses and prescriptions:

I have found the stereotypes to be true—that doctors in Japanese hospitals and clinics spend as little time with you as possible, that you are not encouraged to ask questions, and you are not given an explanation of the problem; you are only given mysterious prescriptions and sent on your way. I have had to wait 2 to 3 hours to spend only two minutes with a doctor.

Of most concern to Western women seems to be the lack of discussion with the doctor. Japanese people have traditionally preferred not to hear details about their illnesses and questioning the doctor is believed to show a lack of trust. Doctors in Japan are simply not used to being questioned and most cannot speak English confidently or well enough to meet your needs, so of course there will be communication problems. By all means take a Japanese friend with you to translate, but bear in mind that they may not be comfortable with questioning a doctor either. One school of thought is that the hospital experience is made deliberately unpleasant to prevent people from wanting to go or going needlessly; however, this doesn't seem to dissuade the Japanese, who visit a doctor fourteen times a year on average, compared with five times a year for Westerners.

Before you decide that these are just the opinions of foreigners imposing their judgements on a culture not their own, you should know that Japanese people are generally not happy with the quality of care they receive from their doctors either, with many complaining particularly about the long waits and short consultation times. The difference is that, for the most part, Japanese people complain privately and rarely have another system with which to compare their own. Recently, however, the government is showing signs of investigating the medical system and looking to Western doctors to learn about patient-centred medical care, so the situation may improve in the long-term future.

There are two positive aspects of the Japanese health care system that are not to be underestimated: surgery and the preventive health system. If you have a potentially serious problem or need an operation, you won't have to wait months like you might in your home country. You will generally be dealt with quickly, efficiently, and with care, including after surgery:

> *They expect you to stay in the hospital until you are recovered, as opposed to the U.S. where they'll send you home the same day because it's not covered by insurance. In California, my husband was actually sent home while he was still bleeding from major oral surgery.*

I found a lump in my breast and went to a health clinic; the English-speaking Japanese doctor immediately arranged for me to have tests with a specialist the very next day, telling the specialist to call him at home if I needed translation. It turned out to be nothing serious, but should there be later, then I feel reassured with the knowledge that I am in good hands.

Preventive medicine is popular in Japan, with schools and companies holding free and thorough annual health checks, including checks for cancer. You are also eligible to participate in these, so ensure you are notified of dates and times.

There are also several hospitals and clinics that operate under the title 'international', but be aware that this term is used lightly. It can mean that the entire staff is foreign and speak English, or that there is a doctor available who has spent some time training in another country. Foreign doctors can only practise in Japan if they have five years of medical training, have passed the national Japanese medical examination, have permanent residency, and have passed the top level of the Japanese Proficiency Test. In some cases, foreign doctors can work at a specialised foreign clinic without meeting all of the above requirements. Western women report better service from the international clinics as opposed to the international hospitals. Some international clinics are more expensive than regular Japanese hospitals or clinics and do not accept Japanese health insurance, although you may use private insurance.

Public health centres provide a variety of preventive health services that many Western women are unaware of, including general health checks, women's health checks, and a variety of cancer checks. Take advantage of them—they are quick, thorough, and often free. If you are referred to a specialist via a public health centre, then often you will not need to pay any further costs. Check with your ward office for details.

Things to take when you visit a doctor

You need to take your alien registration card and health insurance certificate (if you have one). You will be asked to complete a registration form on your first visit. If you have visited other doctors in Japan, it is your responsibility to bring copies of previous medical records with you. You will then receive a health card and be directed to various waiting rooms until you see the doctor. You should also take about ¥20,000 with you to cover any costs or in case your health insurance is one that reimburses you later. Some hospitals will actually trust your promise to pay them later if you don't have enough money with you. It is advisable to research your medical problem first and have questions ready. If you would like to visit the same doctor, check beforehand to find out when they will be on duty.

Health insurance

There is no free national health service in Japan, so be prepared to pay something for any visit to a doctor. This can be costly if you do not have insurance. All citizens are expected to be members of an insurance scheme operated via their employer, and that includes you. Citizens not eligible for employer-operated health insurance are expected to join the national health insurance scheme. This costs a few thousand yen per month during your first year in Japan and thereafter depends on your income, and can be quite expensive. National health insurance covers 70% of your hospital bills. Join at your ward office after having lived in Japan for six months. Be warned: if you decide to join the national health insurance scheme when you have been here for longer than six months, then you will be required to pay from the time you first arrived in Japan. One woman found out the hard way:

> *I was required to pay three years in back-payments (about ¥90,000), because the jerks at the conversation school where I'd been working only gave us a travel insurance policy that is no good if you stay here more than a year.*

Be warned: if you join the national health insurance scheme then you are not permitted to withdraw from the scheme until you leave Japan permanently. The only way to get out of the scheme is in the event that you move to another prefecture and don't report to that prefecture's health department.

As I mentioned before, most international hospitals and clinics do not accept national insurance, so if you prefer to see an international doctor, then arrange private health insurance. There are several companies offering private health insurance specifically for foreigners in Japan (see Resources).

You should keep your health insurance card with you at all times, in case of emergency.

Medicine

In most cases, Japanese doctors tend to prescribe just a three-day course of treatment, meaning that you have to return to the hospital to renew your prescription, thus boosting their income and your stress levels. Most Western women report that both prescription and over-the-counter medicines have less effect than similar medicines in their home countries. This is due to the medicines manufactured for Japanese people being based on a lower average body weight than those manufactured for Westerners. Many Japanese doctors love to dish out prescriptions for anything, partly because that's how they make money, but also to keep patients happy. This suits many Japanese patients just fine. I recommend bringing over-the-counter medicine with you from home. If you require specific prescription medicine such as for diabetes or haemophilia, check with your doctor regarding the documents required for taking such medication overseas.

Useful Japanese

doctor	*isha*	ankle	*ashikubi*
nurse	*kangofu*	foot	*ashi*
female doctor	*joi*	toe	*ashi no yubi*
hospital	*byouin*	ear	*mimi*
clinic	*shinryoujo*	eyes	*me*
head	*atama*	mouth	*kuchi*
throat	*nodo*	health checks	*kenkou shindan*
neck	*kubi*	health insurance	*kenkou hoken*
shoulder	*kata*	Japanese national	
arm	*ude*	health insurance	*nihon no kokumin*
elbow	*hiji*		*kenkou hoken*
wrist	*tekubi*	private health	
hand	*te*	insurance	*kojin no kenko hoken*
finger	*yubi*	medicine	*kusuri*
lower back	*koshi*	tablets	*jouzai*
chest	*mune*	painkiller	*itamidome*
breast	*kyoubu*	side-effects	*fukusayou*
stomach	*i*	prescription	*shohousen*
hip	*hippu*	pharmacy	*yakkyoku/kusuriya*
leg	*ashi*	pharmacist	*yakuzaishi*
knee	*hiza*		

I'd like to see a doctor.	*Isha ni mitemoraitai no desu.*
Is there a female doctor available?	*Joi-san ni onegai dekimasu ka.*
Do you have an English-speaking doctor?	*Eigo o hanaseru sensei/isha wa irasshaimasu ka.*
Please, can you write everything down for me. My Japanese friend can explain.	*Subete o kaite itadakemasu ka. Watashi no nihonjin no yuujin ga setsumei shitekuremasu.*
I have a pain in my	*... ga itamimasu.*
I have had this pain for ... [period of time].	*Kono itami ga ... kan tsuzuite imasu.*
I have had this before.	*Mae ni mo arimashita.*
I have never had this before.	*Kon'na keikein wa arimasen.*
I'm sorry, I don't have enough money with me right now, can I pay later?	*Sumimasen ga, ima juubun na okane ga nai node, atode haratte mo ii desu ka.*
Do you take ... insurance?	*Kono ...... hoken o tsukaitai no desu ga.*
I'd like to join the national health insurance scheme.	*Kokumin kenkou hoken ni kanyu shitai desu.*
This prescription is for only three days, can you give me a longer one?	*Kono shohousen wa mikka bun dake desu. Motto chouki ni shite moraemasu ka.*
Are there any side-effects?	*Fukusayou wa arimasu ka.*
Drink after each meal.	*Maishoku go ni nomu.*
... tablets a day.	*Ichinichi ... jou.*
Between meals.	*Shokkan.*
On an empty stomach.	*Kuufukuji ni.*

sore throat	*nodo ga itai*	haemorrhoids	*ji*
runny nose	*hanamizu ga deru*	dandruff	*fuke*
cold	*kaze*	halitosis	*koushuu*
cough	*seki*	athlete's foot	*mizumushi*
menstrual cramps	*seiritsuu*	hay fever	*kafunshou*
vaginal yeast infection	*koukuu kanjida shou*	fever	*netsu*
cystitis	*boukouen*	indigestion	*shouka furyou*
cold sores (oral)	*koushin herupesu/ tanjun houshin*	travel sickness	*norimono yoi*
		insect bites	*mushi sasare*
cold sores (genital/ herpes)	*inbu houshin/ herupesu*	dry/itchy eyes	*me no kansou/kayumi*
		excessive perspiration	*kado no hakkan*
headaches	*zutsuu*	acne	*nikibi*
sunburn	*hiyake ni yoru yakedo*	body odour	*taishuu*
excema	*shisshin*	foot odour	*ashi no akushuu*
muscle pain	*kin'niku tsuu*	spot/zit	*fukidemono*
diarrhoea	*geri*	migraine	*henzutsuu*
constipation	*benpi*	stomach ache	*fukutsuu*
		hangover	*futsukayoi*

Resources

Information Centres

Association of Medical Doctors in Asia (AMDA) 03-5285-8088
Medical information. If you call them and tell them your
problem or what kind of doctor you would like to see, they
will tell you the doctor nearest to you.
http://www.osk.3web.ne.jp/~amdack/

Foreign Nurses Association In Japan 03-5469-0966
Teach CPR and first aid; medical information brochures; 03-3370-3415
newsletter; lectures; health booths.

Fire Department Information Service for Emergency Hospitals 03-3212-2323

Kawasaki City Emergency Medical Care Information Centre 044-211-1919

Yokohama City Emergency Medical Care Information Centre 045-201-1199

Tokyo Metropolitan Health and Medical Information Centre 03-5285-8181
Medical information, introductions to English-speaking doctors,
Japanese health system and insurance explanations, available
throughout Japan. For emergency translation call 03-5285-8185.

Clinics and Hospitals

All of the following clinics and hospitals have some English-speaking doctors. With the
hospitals, it tends to depend on the department as to whether you will be treated by an
English-speaker or a female doctor, but some hospitals may call for another doctor to
help with translation. 'NHI OK' means that national health insurance is accepted.

Tokyo

Akasaka Sekiguchi Clinic International 03-3584-1727
2 Japanese doctors (one female, one male), studied in the US
and Germany. NHI OK. Akasaka.

Helios Clinic 03-3403-3272
American male doctor. Nogizaka.

Hirano Kameido Himawari Clinic 03-5609-1823
Japanese male doctor, NHI OK. Kameido.

Inoue Eye Hospital 03-3295-0911
Japanese female and male doctors, some speak English,
some studied in the US, NHI OK. Ochanomizu.

International Catholic Hospital 03-3951-1111
Japanese female and male doctors, some speak English,
some studied overseas, NHI OK. Shimo Ochiai.

International Clinic 03-3583-7831
European and American male doctors. Roppongi.

Kaijo Clinic 03-3212-7690
Japanese female and male doctors, some speak English,
many studied overseas, NHI OK. Tokyo Station.

Kamiyacho Clinic 03-3433-0343
Japanese male doctor, NHI OK. Kamiyacho.

Kanda Second Clinic 03-3402-0654
   3 Japanese female doctors, NHI OK. Roppongi.
Keio University Hospital 03-3353-1211
   Japanese doctors, a few female doctors, many speak English,
   some studied overseas, NHI OK. Shinanomachi.
King Clinic 03-3409-0764
   1 Japanese male doctor, NHI OK. Harajuku.
Koseikai Suzuki Hospital 03-3557-2001
   2 Japanese doctors (one female, one male), studied in the US,
   NHI OK. Nerima.
Kyorin University Hospital 0422-47-5511
   Japanese female and male doctors, some studied overseas
   (depends on the department), NHI OK. Mitaka.
Machiyahara Hospital 0427-95-1668
   3 Japanese male doctors speak English, NHI OK. Machida.
Mizumachi Clinic 03-3348-2181
   1 Japanese male doctor speaks English, NHI OK. Shinjuku.
Nozaki Eye Clinic 03-3461-1671
   Japanese male doctor, studied in the US, NHI OK. Shibuya.
Ogikubo Hospital 03-3399-1101
   Japanese doctors, some female, some English-speakers,
   some studied overseas (depends on the department),
   NHI OK. Ogikubo.
St. Luke's International Hospital 03-3541-5151
   Japanese doctors, some female, some speak English
   (depends on the department), NHI OK. Tsukiji.
Saiseikai Central Hospital 03-3451-8211
   Japanese doctors, some female, some speak English
   (depends on the department), NHI OK. Shiba-koen.
Sakakibara Kinen Clinic 03-3344-3313
   1 Japanese male doctor speaks English, studied in the US,
   NHI OK. Shinjuku.
Sanno Hospital 03-3402-3151
   Japanese doctors, some female doctors (depends on the
   department), NHI OK. Aoyama Itchome/Nogizaka.
Shimazu Medical Clinic 03-5430-5556
   Japanese male doctor, studied in the US, NHI OK.
   Shimokitazawa.
Shinjuku Mitsui Bldg Clinic 03-3344-3311
   Japanese doctors, some speak English, some female,
   NHI OK. Shinjuku.
Shiseikai Dani Hospital 03-3300-0366
   Japanese and Chinese doctors, 50% female, some speak
   English, some studied overseas, NHI OK. Sengawa/
   Seijogakuenmai.
Takeshita Clinic 03-3208-0833
   3 Japanese doctors (1 female), NHI OK. Takadanobaba.

Tokai University School of Medicine Tokyo Hospital 03-3370-2321
    Japanese doctors, some female, some speak English,
    NHI OK. Yoyogi.
Tokyo Adventist Hospital 03-3392-6151
    Japanese doctors, some female, some speak English, some
    studied overseas, NHI OK. Ogikubo.
Tokyo British Clinic 03-5458-6099
    1 British male doctor. Ebisu.
Tokyo Medical and Surgical Clinic 03-3436-3028
    Foreign and Japanese doctors, French female doctor.
    Kamiyacho.
Tokyo Medical University Hachioji Medical Centre 0426-65-5611
    Japanese female and male doctors, some speak English
    (depends on the department), some studied overseas,
    NHI OK. Takao.
Tokyo Women's Clinic 03-3408-6950
    Japanese female doctor. Roppongi.

Gunma
Cardiovascular Hospital of Central Japan 0272-32-7111
    Japanese doctors, some speak English, some female,
    NHI OK. Shinmaebashi.

Kanagawa
Bluff Clinic 045-641-6961
    Japanese male doctor, studied overseas, NHI OK.
    Ishikawacho.
Jujodori Clinic 0462-74-5884
    Japanese male doctor, NHI OK. Minami Rinkan.
Kobayashi International Clinic 0462-63-1380
    Japanese male and Korean-Japanese female doctors, both
    speak English, NHI OK. Yamato City.
Minatomachi Medical Centre 045-453-3673
    3 Japanese doctors (2 female), studied overseas, NHI OK.
    Kanagawa Station.

Kobe
Kobe International Hospital and Medical Services Association 078-241-2896
    British male doctor. Sannomiya.

Kyoto
Japan Baptist Hospital 075-781-5191
    Japanese doctors, some speak English, some female, some
    studied overseas, NHI OK. Sakkyo-ku.
Sakabe International Clinic 075-231-1624
    Japanese male doctor, studied in the US, NHI OK. Nakayo-ku.

145

Nagoya

Hatano Clinic 052-951-1432
Japanese doctors (one female), some speak English, some
studied overseas, NHI OK. Sakaie.

Niigata

Yukiguni Hospital 0257-77-2111
Japanese female and male doctors, some speak English,
NHI OK. Urasa.

Osaka

Gracia Hospital 0727-29-2345
Japanese doctors, some speak English, some female, some
studied overseas (depends on the department), NHI OK.
Mino City.
Otani Clinic 06-6441-1980
Japanese male doctor, NHI OK. Nishi-ku.

Sapporo

Kotoni Naika Icho-ka Clinic 011-643-5311
Japanese male doctor, NHI OK. Chuo-ku.

Vaccinations

Some clinics can also perform vaccinations, so check with your doctor.
Tokyo Quarantine Station 03-3471-7922
Japan Quarantine Association 045-671-7041

Private Health Insurance Providers

American Life Insurance Company (ALICO) Japan 03-3284-4111
Banner Japan (see display ad, page 147) 03-5724-5100
http://www.bannerjapan.com
Global Healthcare 0120-63-4419
http://www.globalalljapan.com
International Health Insurance (IHI) Danmark 03-3405-0794
Viator Healthcare 03-3825-7074

Pharmacies with English-Speaking Staff

American Pharmacy 03-3271-4035
Stock some imported products. 2 stores in Tokyo (Yurakucho
and Tachikawa).
Boots Chemist 03-5229-6590
Some imported products. 3 stores in Tokyo (Ginza, Harajuku,
Kichijoji), 1 store at Yokohama Station.
Foreign Buyers Club (FBC) (see display ad, page 69) 078-857-9001
Deliver over-the-counter American medicine and other health
products throughout Japan. Store in Rokku Island, Kobe.
http://www.fbcusa.com
Kerry Drug Store 03-3581-4511
2 locations in Tokyo (Kokaigijodomae and Kamiyacho).

Medical Dispensary 03-3434-5817
    Kamiyacho, Tokyo.
National Azabu Supermarket Pharmacy 03-3442-3495
    Will try to find the Japanese equivalent of your regular
    medicine by matching the ingredients on the package.
    Hiroo, Tokyo.
Koyasu Pharmacy 03-3401-8667
    Some staff speak English. Locations throughout Tokyo
    and suburbs.
Tanabe Pharmacy 03-5731-6620
    Staff are trained to provide a 'Western-style' service, including
    explanations of side-effects. 13 locations in Ibaraki, Tokyo,
    and Yokohama.

Resources and Further Information

If you need more information about any aspect of the health care system in Japan, then the *Japan Health Handbook* is an invaluable resource.

Japan Health Handbook
    By Meredith Enman Maruyama, Louise Picon Shimizu and Nancy Smith
    Tsurumake, Kodansha: 1998 revised edition.

International Medical Centre of Japan
    http://www.imcj.go.jp/imcj2.htm
Medical Institutes where Foreign Languages are available
    Includes the ability to search by language and area.
    http://on-top.net/cgi-bin/hospital/index.cgi
Ministry of Health and Welfare
    Includes regulations on importing medicines.
    http://www.mhw.go.jp/english/index.html
National Institute of Public Health
    http://www.iph.go.jp/indexeg.html

Dentists

Westerners often talk about the poor condition of Japanese people's teeth, compared with their own. There is not the stigma attached to 'crooked' teeth in Japan that is prevalent in the West. Tooth and gum decay is very common in Japan, and you will often find restrooms full of women brushing their teeth. Supermarkets and chemists have extensive displays of items designed to take care of your teeth and gums.

If you're not careful, you will find the condition of your own teeth rapidly deteriorating due to the water and toothpaste content, and the lack of good dentists. Water in Japan doesn't contain fluoride, but it does contain various chemicals that are not conducive to healthy teeth. Dr Nakashima, a Tokyo dentist who trained in the US, uses only bottled water for drinking and for brushing his own teeth, as well as when treating patients. He recommends that everyone should do the same. Fifty percent of the toothpastes available in Japan contain fluoride, so check before you buy. One woman recommends using supplements:

> *Without fluoride in the water here, my children have had too many cavities despite regular brushing. I would advise anyone to bring fluoride drops for their children if possible.*

Check with a doctor before using fluoride supplements.

As for dentists, Dr Nakashima urges caution when visiting dentists in Japan as their knowledge and training do not match standards in Western countries. You may find that a dentist will ask you to visit several times, yet appear to do very little work on your teeth:

> *One dentist made me come back five Saturdays in a row to do basically nothing. He spent about ten minutes the first day cleaning my teeth (which should take much longer if done properly) and then had all kinds of excuses why I needed to come back again. But every time I did, he just spent five or ten minutes poking around or polishing and never really did anything. Then he had the nerve to tell me it was time for another cleaning after five weeks! Totally money grabbing!*

Before you waste your time and money visiting a dentist, find out where they have trained. If they haven't trained overseas, then I wouldn't recommend you visiting them. If they have trained overseas, then not only will you be able to communicate with them, but you can also expect the quality of attention that you are used to at home, without the expense:

> *I've had a mind-blowingly amazing experience with a dentist here. First rate. She was far better than any dentist I had in the States. She gave me six fillings, extensive cleaning, and two root canals with crowns. Minimal pain, maximum care. As I have the national health insurance, I paid for only about 30% of the total*

job—which came to around ¥20,000. If that had been done in the US, even with insurance, I'd be paying around $1000. My dentist also gave me a great education in how to care for my teeth—taught me what I was doing wrong and so forth. I think the key to Japanese dentists is their age. The younger the better. Once they get the licence, they don't have to renew, so, usually, the fresher out of school they are, the newer their equipment is and the higher their standards.

As opposed to doctors, dentists do operate an appointment system. Most dentists accept Japanese national health insurance, but check beforehand. If you have private health insurance, check to see whether your policy covers dental treatment. National and private insurance rarely cover 'cosmetic' dental treatments such as cleaning or whitening or even a regular checkup, the latter of which will cost about ¥10,000.

Public health centres also conduct preventive dental health care—check with your ward office.

Useful Japanese

dentist .... *haisha*
tooth/teeth .... *ha*
gums .... *haguki/shiniku*
wisdom tooth .... *oyashirazu*
toothpaste .... *nerihamigaki*
fluoride .... *fusso*
to brush one's
teeth .... *ha o migaku*

to floss .... *dentaru furosu o*
tsukau
dental floss .... *furosu/itoyouji*
tooth decay .... *mushiba*
gum decay .... *shisou nourou*
teeth cleaning .... *ha no kuriiningu*

I'd like a toothpaste that contains
fluoride. .... *Fusso ga haitta nerihamigaki o kudasai.*
I have toothache. .... *Ha ga itamimasu.*
My wisdom tooth hurts. .... *Oyashirazu ga itamimasu.*
Part of my tooth fell out. .... *Ha no tsumemono ga toremashita.*
Please clean/whiten my teeth. .... *Ha no kuriininngu/hyouhaku o*
onegaishimasu.

150

Resources

All the listed dentists speak English. Fees quoted are for a regular checkup. NHI OK means that the dentist accepts national health insurance.

Tokyo
Aspen Orthodontic Clinic 0422-21-8888
      Trained in the US. ¥5000. Kichijoji.
Dr. Kaku's Office 03-5449-3308
      Trained in the US. ¥5000. Hiroo and Shinjuku.
Japan Orthodontic Centre 03-3499-2222
      Trained in the US. ¥3000. Shibuya.
Jason Wong Dental Clinic (see display ad, page 152) 03-3473-2901
      Trained in the US. ¥6000. Meguro.
Kyoritsu Dental Associates (see display ad, page 153) 03-3770-5515
      Trained in the US. ¥3000–5000. Ebisu.
Nakashima Dental Office (see display ad, page 152) 03-3479-2726
      Trained in the US. NHI OK. ¥5000. Roppongi.
Royal Dental Clinic 03-3404-0819
      Trained in the US. NHI OK. ¥5000. Roppongi.
Sanshiro Kikuchi 03-3373-1180
      Trained in Japan. NHI OK. ¥7000. Yoyogi/ Minami Shinjuku.
Shinjuku Orthodontics 03-3200-8661
      Trained in the US. ¥5000. Shinjuku.
Tanaka Dental Clinic 03-3475-1188
      Trained in the US. NHI OK. ¥2000–3000. Aoyama Itchome.
Wing Dental Clinic 03-3505-3131
      Trained in Japan. NHI OK. ¥10,000. Tameikesanno.
Yamazaki Family Dentistry 03-3418-6611
      Trained in the US. NHI OK. ¥3000. Komazawadaigaku.
Chiba
Tokyo Dental University 0473-22-0151
      Trained in Japan. NHI OK. ¥3000. Ichikawa.

Fukuoka
Chang Dental Clinic 092-526-6331
      Trained in Korea. NHI OK. Checkup fees vary. Fukuoka City.

Hokkaido
France Dental Clinic 011-251-6022
      Trained in France. NHI OK. Checkup fees vary. Sapporo.

Hyogo
Yamamoto Dental Clinic 0798-54-0863
      Trained in the UK. NHI OK. ¥3000. Nigawa.

151

Kobe

Kitano Dental Office 078-331-3522
     Trained in the US. NHI OK. ¥5000. Sannomiya.
Yamamoto Dental Clinic 078-391-2025
     Trained in the US. NHI OK. ¥5000. Chuo-ku.

Kyoto

Nakamura Dental Clinic 075-711-0242
     Trained in Japan. ¥5000. Sakyo-ku.
Suwa Dental Clinic 075-955-4118
     Trained in Japan. NHI OK. ¥3000. Hankyu Nano Okatenji.

Gynaecology

As in your home country, all Japanese hospitals have a gynaecology department. As with general visits to hospitals in Japan, expect long waits. You can also go to a smaller clinic that offers gynaecological care along with other services, but it is rare that your doctor will be a specialist. Many Western women have a full checkup every time they return to their home countries, but in the case of needing immediate gynaecological treatment, this is what you can expect.

Lack of privacy, both during discussions and examinations, seems to be the common complaint amongst Western women regarding gynaecological care. Generally, you wait in a common room for your consultation and talk to the doctor in another area off a corridor, to which any partitioning will usually be left open. You can console yourself a bit with the knowledge that it is unlikely that the people passing can understand a word you say, but my advice is don't feel intimidated—shut the door or partition yourself. For the actual examination, you go into a small adjoining 'room', undress, and get on the chair. This can feel strange because you can hear people bustling around outside and you may spend most of the time panicking that a crowd of people are about to join you. On one emergency visit, the doctor's loud English announcements of "Now I put finger/speculum/camera in vagina" throughout the examination made me feel like the entire hospital staff were being informed on the state of my examination.

The two things that are different from most Western gynaecologists' treatment rooms are the stirrups and the curtain. In my experiences in the UK, rarely had the gynaecologists used stirrups and they certainly didn't strap my ankles into them—this is common practice with Japanese gynaecologists, so be prepared. Also, when you get on the chair there is a curtain hanging down to your waist, so you cannot see the doctor's face and he (usually a he) cannot see yours. It is supposed to save the embarrassment that Japanese women are said to experience if they can see the doctor during gynaecological examinations. If the curtain disturbs you more than its absence would, don't be intimidated—push it away before you get on the chair.

Some gynaecologists seem to be trying a friendlier approach with Western women:

> *My gynaecologist is a doll—in an attempt to be 'international', he slapped the inside of one of my widely opened knees to focus my attention on the ultrasound monitor so I could get a good view of the inside of my uterus ... My favorite experience was enduring the series of gestures executed by a pharmacist to ensure that I did not take orally the vaginal suppositories prescribed for a yeast infection.*

> *I have noticed a huge change in the approach to gynaecology in my area. They now inform me so well, and have great service for sonograms* [ultrasounds] *for regular checkups AND pregnancies.*

155

You get to watch right along with the doctor and he explains what you are seeing. I like that a lot.

One doctor I visited in a women's clinic pushed the curtain away himself, making the small talk that doctors in the West generally do to help you relax. He obviously knew something about what Western women expected from a gynaecological examination. The actual examination is very quick, which you can perceive as being either a welcome relief or rather abrupt.

Some gynaecology departments also offer routine breast examinations that, although sometimes lacking in privacy, can be worth getting done while you are there:

Working in the same office as my gynaecologist is the breast guy—he does a routine ultrasound, which I have never had in the States, and can also do a mammogram at another location. No problem with the mammogram apart from the parade of technicians marching past while your breast is being squished between two plates of glass.

Also, check with your ward office as public health centres provide free breast and cervical examinations, although usually only for women over 30. If you are under 30, the ward office may make a special arrangement, or speak to your doctor who will arrange a (paid) examination.

A word of warning: in Japan, it is not uncommon for a childless woman in her late twenties or older who is suffering from gynaecological problems to be told that she has 'The Career Woman's Disease' and that she should get pregnant as soon as possible. If you are told this, then my advice is to immediately change doctors. The doctors listed in this section and The Health System should be able to provide you with the kind of service (and respect) that you would expect at home.

Sexually transmitted diseases

As in any country, you are at risk of contracting a sexually transmitted disease every time you have sex, and the best method of prevention is using condoms, which are readily available throughout Japan (see the section on Contraception in this chapter). If you suspect that you may have a sexually transmitted disease, you can visit any doctor at a regular clinic or hospital. You can get a free AIDS test at any public health centre, although some will not test foreigners. You can also get an AIDS test at hospitals and clinics, although you will have to pay for this service. This test is supposed to be anonymous, but there have been several cases of foreigners having the fact that they had an AIDS test put on their records and this information somehow got back to their employers. Irrespective of the test result, they were unofficially and rather abruptly 'deported'. To avoid this, when you get the test don't give your name and you will be allocated an identification number. My advice is to visit a foreign doctor at an international clinic to ensure confidentiality and sensitivity. You collect the results about one week later. There is usually no counselling prior to an AIDS test in Japan. If you test positive, treatment is available in Japan if you are covered by national health insurance. If you have company insurance, the details of your treatment will be reported to your company and you will probably lose your job. If you have private insurance, check that it covers AIDS treatment. There are some specialist centres in Japan; check the resources that follow.

Useful Japanese

gynaecologist	*fujinka-i*	ultrasound	*chou-onpa*
vagina	*chitsu*	cervical examination	*shikyuu no shinsatsu*
cystitis	*boukouen*	STD	*seibyou*
thrush/candida/yeast infection	*chitsuen*	condom	*kondoumu*
irregular bleeding	*fusei shukketsu*	chlamydia	*kuramijia*
irregular discharge	*orimono*	herpes	*herupesu*
irregular period	*gekkei fujun*	AIDS	*eizu*
mammogram	*chibusa no rentogen satsuei*	pubic lice	*kejirami*
		itchy	*kayui*

I'd like to see a gynaecologist. ..... *Fujinka-i ni mite moraitai desu.*
Do you have a female gynaecologist? ..... *Joi-san wa imasu ka.*
Do you have a private examination room? .. *Koshitsu no shinsatsushitsu wa arimasu ka.*
Do you mind if I close this door? ..... *Kono doa o shimete mo ii desu ka.*

Could we talk in private please? .... *Futari dake de o-hanashi dekimasu ka.*

Please could you speak more quietly? .... *Mou sukoshi shizuka ni hanashite itadakemasu ka.*

Please don't strap my legs down. .... *Watashi no ashi o shibaranaide kudasai.*

Do you mind if I move this curtain? .... *Kono kaaten o ugokashite ii desu ka.*

I'd like a breast examination. .... *Chibusa no shinsatsu o shite kudasai.*

I've found a lump in my breast. .... *Chibusa ni shikori ga arimasu.*

I'd like an AIDS test. .... *Eizu kensa o uketai desu.*

Can you guarantee confidentiality? .... *Himitsu genshu dekimasu ka.*

I don't want to use my name. .... *Hontou no namae o tsukaitaku arimasen.*

Resources

English-Speaking Gynaecologists

Note that you can also consult a doctor in one of the general clinics or hospitals listed under **The Health System** resources, or contact AMDA in the same resources. Your regular doctor may have a visiting gynaecologist or may recommend one. 'NHI OK' means that national health insurance is accepted.

Tokyo

Hayakawa Clinic 03-3666-4795
> Japanese male gynaecologist, NHI OK. Suitengumae.

Shohei Clinic 03-3393-5171
> 2 Japanese male gynaecologists, studied in the US, NHI OK. Ogikubo.

Toho Women's Clinic 03-3630-0303
> 4 Japanese female gynaecologists. Natural births. NHI OK. Kiba.

Yoda Ladies Clinic 03-3469-0828
> Japanese male gynaecologist, NHI OK. Shimokitazawa.

Kobe

Matsuoka Women's Clinic 078-582-0003
> Japanese male gynaecologist, NHI OK. Kita-ku.

Ueda Hospital 078-241-3305
> 2 Japanese female gynaecologists, NHI OK. Sannomiya.

Osaka

Nishikawa Clinic 06-6714-5218
> Japanese gynaecologists, 1 female, some speak English, NHI OK. Osaka City.

Yokohama

Isezaki Woman's Clinic 045-251-8622
> Japanese male gynaecologist, studied in the US, NHI OK. Isezakichojamachi.

Women's Health Products

Foreign Buyers Club (FBC) (see display ad, page 69) 078-857-9001
Over-the-counter American medicine for vaginal infections.
Store in Rokku Island, Kobe. Delivers throughout Japan.
http://www.fbcusa.com

AIDS Information in English

AIDS Hotline 0120-46-1995
24-hour information on testing and assistance in tracking
down partners.

AIDS Hotline 03-5259-0750
Information and care support. Branches in Nagasaki, Nagoya,
Okayama, Osaka, Sasebo, Shikoku, Shogo, Tokyo, and
Wakayama, but provide services throughout Japan.
http://member.nifty.ne.jp/jhc/

Japan Foundation for AIDS Prevention (JFAP) Support Line 03-5521-1177
Extension 2 for English information. Pre-recorded FAQs
and answers.

Shinjuku Public Health Centre 03-3369-7110
HIV testing and consultations.

Contraception

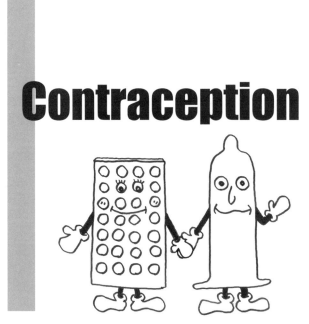

Birth control was first publicly addressed in Japan after World War II. Japan's economic situation would not support large families, so people were urged to have fewer children. During the 1990s, however, public concern increased regarding the high percentage of elderly people in Japan and the decreasing number of younger working people able to financially support them. The Japanese government panicked and started to encourage people to have more children, claiming that the Japanese race would eventually be wiped out. A new national holiday (Conjugal Day) was tentatively suggested to encourage Japanese husbands to spend more time with their wives (this was met with a mixture of contempt and ridicule by the wives). Women were urged to 'do their duty for Japan' by getting out of the boardroom (a place it has taken them longer to get into than in any other developed country) and back into the bedroom. The limited number of birth control methods available in Japan remain popular; 64 percent of married couples use contraception.

Male condom

The male condom is the most popular method of contraception in Japan, where a quarter of the world's condoms are used. Condoms are the choice for 80 percent of Japanese couples who use contraception, compared with 10 percent of Western couples. Most Western women in relationships with Japanese men say the men tend to accept responsibility for using condoms:

> *In Japan it's a man's world when it comes to contraception. Japanese men are pretty reliable about using condoms, whereas Western men leave it up to the woman.*

If your partner is Western, then Japanese condoms may be a little on the snug side. You may be tempted to giggle about this, but believe me it is a nightmare—imagine putting a rubber band around your thigh and you've got the look of agony and the loss of blood supply that basically sums up the experience. Western men are not the only ones who experience this though:

> *My first Japanese boyfriend was so big that the Japanese condoms didn't fit him. We had to buy special condoms when I went back to the States. I'm afraid I insulted my husband terribly one night, when we were first dating. I still had these big American condoms, and he knew that they were for my previous boyfriend. My husband says (I don't remember this) that I told him that the condoms would be too big for him. What an insult! Still, he married me anyway.*

It makes you question why condom manufacturers in Japan don't make different sizes. I have a theory: in an effort to eliminate the inferiority complexes that Japanese men have about the size of their penises, ALL Japanese condoms are made tiny so that EVERY Japanese man is too big for them. There is some good news though; a new brand of condoms has just been released, called 'Big Nose'. They are large sized and feature a picture of a big hooked nose on the box. In Japan, nose size is said to be indicative of penis size, which pleases Western men no end as Westerners (male and female) are considered to have large noses.

Condoms are readily available throughout Japan in chemists, supermarkets, convenience stores, specialist stores, and vending machines. As opposed to some Western countries, you have to pay for contraception in Japan, including condoms. If you object to this, get a friend at home to visit a family planning clinic, stock up for you, and mail them over. Of course, you may need a very good friend because if it is their first visit, they will be required to have a gynaecological examination as part of the initial checkup. Alternatively, stock up yourself when you visit home. Be aware that family planning clinics have a limit on the number of condoms they can issue to one person; this amount may not last you that long.

Female condom

The female condom was approved in Japan and became available from the year 2000. It is imported from UK manufacturers and sold in Taiho pharmacies. As in the UK, it is not very popular. Size does not apparently appear to be an issue.

The pill

Japan legalised the low-hormone birth control pill for contraceptive purposes in 1998. Women and doctors worldwide have been astounded that Japan was one of the last developed countries to do so. Preceding this, a high-hormone pill (high in oestrogen and with a greater possibility of side effects) was available for extremely irregular periods or for severe period pain; i.e., not for contraception. In 1997, only 200,000 women used it. At that time, prescription of the low-hormone pill was completely prohibited.

The main government argument against the availability of the pill for contraceptive use was that it would decrease the use of condoms and thus increase the spread of AIDS. In addition, publicity about the side effects of the pill has outweighed that of the benefits, leading most women to believe that the pill would give them cancer and leaving them unaware of the relative safety of the low-hormone pill. Japanese women have been denied fully comprehensive, unbiased information. Many have been reluctant to pressure the government to legalise the pill for contraception. Now that it is legal, many women are still reluctant to take it.

In other countries, statistics show that abortion rates decreased after the pill was introduced. Abortion is a lucrative means of income for some doctors in Japan and is considered a method of contraception by many. One has to question whether the reluctance of the Japanese government and health system to condone use of the pill as a contraceptive is connected to the widespread use of abortion as a method of contraception.

There are some foreign doctors in Japan who are confident about prescribing the pill. If you are already on the pill, you should take your current brand with you. Prescriptions for the pill are not covered by insurance. None of the Western women interviewed for this book got their supply from Japan, but received it from their home countries and/or stocked up when they visited home. This works if you visit your home country regularly, as there are various health checks that need to be made and it is highly unlikely that your doctor will prescribe the pill to you over the telephone. If your doctor is co-operative, then someone may collect your prescription and mail it to you, providing that they do not mail more than three months' supply in one package.

Diaphragms

Diaphragms are not popular in Japan but, again, check with a foreign doctor or a midwife if you would like to have one fitted. Western women who use a diaphragm get it fitted in their home countries and bring extra spermicide with them as it has a long shelf life. You need a prescription for spermicide from pharmacies in Japan, or you can contact the Foreign Buyers' Club who have some in stock.

IUDs

IUDs are also not popular in Japan and many doctors are not capable of fitting one. If you have an IUD fitted in your home country and experience problems whilst in Japan, visit a foreign doctor.

Withdrawal

Although some question whether this is actually a method of contraception, it is popular in Japan:

We use a combination of withdrawal and celibacy, which seems to be very common among my friends who have Japanese husbands.

The rhythm method

You should bring booklets and information on the rhythm method from the family planning clinics in your home country. In Japan, accurate information on this topic is scarce and rarely in English. A special thermometer is available at most pharmacies for taking your temperature for this method of contraception.

Emergency contraception

The availability of the 'morning-after pill' has been and still is affected by similar issues as the regular pill, although it is available. See a foreign doctor as soon as possible, because a Japanese doctor is likely to urge you to wait until you know you are pregnant, then suggest an abortion.

Useful Japanese

contraception	*hi'nin*
male condom	*dansei you kondoumu*
large size	*ookii saizu*
female condom	*josei you kondoumu*
the contraceptive pill	*hi'nin you piru*
low-hormone pill	*tei-youryou piru*
high-hormone pill	*kou-youryou piru*
diaphragm	*kakumaku*

IUD	*shikyuu nai ringu*
spermicide	*sasseishi zai*
withdrawal	*chitsugai shasei*
rhythm method	*shuuki hi'nin hou*
thermometer	*fujin taionkei*
emergency contraception (morning-after pill)....	*jigo keikou hi'nin-yaku (mooningu afutaa piru)*
side-effects	*fukusayou*

Do you stock ...? .... *... wa arimasu ka.*

This is my current brand of the pill, which I got in [your country's name]. Can I get this in Japan? .... *Kore wa ima watashi ga tsukatte iru piru no burando desu. ... de te ni iremashita. Nihon demo te ni ireru koto wa dekimasu ka.*

I'd like to be fitted for a	*Watashi ni atta ... ga hoshii no desu ga.*
I had unprotected sex and need emergency contraception.	*Hi'nin sezu ni sekkusu o shita node, ato kara nondemo kiku piru ga hoshii no desu ga.*
Please write down any possible side-effects and what I should do. My Japanese friend can explain.	*Subete no fuku sayou to, watashi wa dousureba yoi ka o kaite kudasai. Watashi no nihonjin no tomodachi ni setsumei shite moraimasu.*

Resources

Large-Size Condoms
Condomania .... 03-3797-6131 (J)
> Stores in Sendai, Tokyo, and Yokohama.

Foreign Buyers Club (FBC) (see display ad, page 69) 078-857-9001
> Store in Rokku Island, Kobe. Delivery throughout Japan.
> Delivery charges vary. Accepts mail orders.
> http://www.fbcusa.com

Female Condoms (MyFemy)
Taiho Pharmaceutical Company 03-3294-4527
> Locations throughout Japan
> http://www.taiho.co.jp/english/index.html

Spermicide and Lubricant
Foreign Buyers Club (FBC) 078-857-9001
> See above.

Further Information
Japan Family Planning Association (Tokyo) 03-3235-2694
> Mostly for single people, up to age 25. Contraception information: IUD, the pill and emergency contraception. Gynaecologist available.

Abortion

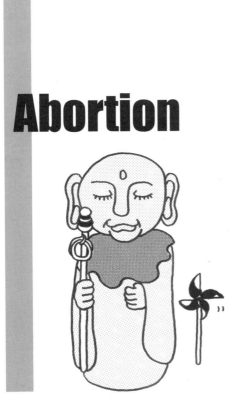

Part One

Terminating a pregnancy is a controversial issue, but it is a decision made by about 350,000 women in Japan every year, and a small percentage of them are Western women who have the added difficulty of being in a foreign country. The Western women I spoke with agreed that there were certain aspects of this experience that made it less unpleasant than they felt it would have been in their home countries.

The reasons that Western women terminate pregnancies in Japan tend to be the same as those in their home countries; that is, they are generally not Japan-related. For one reason or another, these women feel unable to raise a child at the time.

For young women, parental consent is not required; however, for all women, written consent from 'the father' is required. If this is not possible, then a male friend will suffice (officially he is the father, of course). You cannot use health insurance for an abortion, so you will need to pay about ¥120,000.

Pregnancy testing kits are available from any chemist and are pretty easy to spot. They come in pink boxes showing pictures that represent urinating on a stick and seeing the stick change colour. Some have instructions in English, but the pictorial instructions are really easy to understand. If you think you are pregnant and you know that you'd rather not be, but are unsure what to do, then confiding in a Japanese friend (male or female) will not induce the shocked reaction that you might get from some friends back home. Rather, you will receive a lot of understanding sympathy and practical advice without too much fuss or any moralistic comments.

All of the Western women I spoke with visited Japanese doctors and seemed glad that they had for this particular health issue. Upon the initial consultation, the women reported surprise at their doctors 'matter-of-fact' attitudes regarding abortion. One woman's experience:

He could speak some English and I remember that he said, "You are in pregnancy. Baby born March," and he smiled broadly. From the look on my face he could see that I was not very happy about this news, so he said, "Ah, you not happy. No problem. We abortion here."

For some women this may be the first indication that the attitude towards abortion is quite different here from that in our home countries:

When he noticed the abnormality [of the fetus]*, the doctor mentioned in a casual way that the pregnancy could be "terminated here in Japan". The obstetrician was Japanese, but had trained ... in the US for several years and was aware of the controversy surrounding abortion there. I was so stunned that I didn't have time to be upset by his mentioning abortion rather nonchalantly*

*when the problem had just moments before been discovered. Later,
I realized he was just reflecting the general attitude of Japanese
society, that if there's a problem, you get rid of it and start over.*

This matter-of-fact attitude obviously has its good and bad
points, as does the fact that there is no counselling required in Japan
before you make your 'final' decision. Counselling in our home countries can be abused by the 'counsellor' whose personal beliefs may
run counter to yours.

*As far as moralistic counselling, you don't get it from the doctor.
They asked me why and how, but we didn't go into depth regarding
alternative solutions. The shame and the weight of the act itself
were not so much of an issue, probably because it is not looked on
as a 'sin' here. You therefore aren't made to feel the pangs of
regret that you probably would in the US.*

The women I spoke to were certain about their decision; had
they not been or had they not had a close friend or partner with whom
to talk, then their feelings regarding the lack of counselling may have
been different. However, counselling regarding an unexpected and
possibly unwanted pregnancy is available at any stage of the process
through Tokyo English Life Line (TELL), who have staff specifically
trained to give counsel on unplanned pregnancies.

An anesthetic is not always used, so check beforehand. If you
are in the first three months of pregnancy, the cervix will be dilated
and the womb scraped or suctioned. Your visit may take just a few
hours. If your pregnancy is more advanced, labour will be induced and
you will need to stay overnight. Your doctor will explain the methods
in detail. All the women specifically commented on how kind and
friendly the staff were throughout the whole procedure:

*The doctor went out of his way to ensure my comfort, and to
ensure that his staff were sensitive to me as well. They all tried
their best to explain in English what was going on through the*

whole ordeal. For the hospital stay, they put me in a room with two other women who were having troubled pregnancies, not with a bunch of joyous new mothers. Since I was in the 13th or 14th week, I had to go through labour rather than have a D&C. They explained to my husband and me what was happening, and bowed to my husband's instructions to give me some general pain relief, which is not common here. The greatest kindness was the warm towel-bath the nurse gave me as I lay on the table after it was over. I felt like I didn't deserve such kindness. I think overall my experience here was much kinder than it ever would have been in the US.

The general environment of the clinics may not be intimidating:

It was quiet, serene and very comfortable. I remember lots of trees surrounding the hospital, and did not feel the atmosphere was cold or sterile like normal clinics might be.

After a termination, TELL are also available for you to talk to someone, but most women choose to address their feelings more privately whilst in Japan. The next section discusses a practice in Japan that helps many Japanese women in their grieving process, and the history and philosophy of which comforts some Western women too.

Part Two

I think this topic in particular merits specific explanation because the attitude towards abortion in Japan is quite different to that in Western countries. This often leads to outraged discussions among Westerners here who do not have the cultural or historical information necessary to make informed comments regarding a practice that evokes emotional responses in our home countries. I aim to provide this information whilst omitting my personal opinion, and to dissuade the idea that abortion is treated lightly in Japan, contrary to what some Westerners may assume.

There are several important points specific to Japan that should be kept in mind throughout explanation of this topic:

- In Japan, an unwanted child is always referred to as a 'child'; not a fetus or anything less than a fully formed, functioning child, regardless of at what stage the abortion is performed.
- Japanese children are traditionally given a high quality and quantity of love, attention, and financial support by their immediate and extended families.
- Sex is not traditionally seen by Japanese people as either a sin or as solely for the purpose of procreation; it is seen as necessary to enjoy a full life.
- The official attitude towards abortion in Japan (i.e., its legal status) has historically depended on what was regarded as best for the country as a whole, usually in terms of the number of soldiers or farm workers needed.
- Japanese women have historically been the leaders and developers of the family's and society's attitudes, methods, and rituals concerning abortion.

The ritual

Many women or couples in Japan who have terminated a pregnancy, suffered a miscarriage, or had a stillborn baby choose to honour the soul of this child through a practice called *mizuko jizo*. Mizuko means 'child of the water' and is used to refer to the soul of a child who has been returned to the gods, and Jizo is the name of the Buddhist god who protects and guides that soul on its journey to another world. The practice involves erecting a small statue of Jizo at a temple and/or establishing a private shrine at home, to which the parents offer gifts such as money and rice. Parents often give the child a Buddhist name and decorate the statue with a red bib, toys, knitted clothing, or an umbrella (for protection during the child's 'journey'). Present and future children may be introduced to their dead sibling. Temples for mizuko jizo have the aura of a slightly subdued nursery, rather than a cemetery. Most of the statues and people attending these temples are present because of a terminated pregnancy rather than a miscarriage or stillbirth. Such temples are publicly advertised and people publicly participate in the ritual.

The concept

Abortion is regarded as the parents willingly making a decision to return a child to the gods, sending a child to a temporary place until such time that it is right for the child to come into this world, either into the same family or another one. The child is returned because the parents, at the time, feel unable to provide enough love, money, or attention to this child, without it being to the detriment of their present family. Practising mizuko jizo allows the parents to provide a certain amount of attention to the child, who is regarded as a member of their family; to apologise to the child that they could not bring them up (these apologies often take written form); and to ask for forgiveness from their child for being unable to bring them up. As the statue represents both the child and the god Jizo, it also allows the parents to pray that Jizo will protect their child and grant them success in future child bearing. The availability of mizuko jizo is regarded as showing compassion for both the child and the parents. It should also be noted, however, that there is an element of fear of retribution that some temples are perceived as exploiting in their literature on mizuko jizo services: they say that parents should perform this ritual or their present family will suffer.

The history

Information about abortion in Japan dates to around the sixteenth century, when abortion and infanticide were regarded as family planning methods. It was regarded as sensible to space and select the number of children in order to preserve the quality of life for the present family, as well as to achieve a balance in the gender of children. From the sixteenth century onwards, abortion and infanticide were widely practised and tended to increase when areas were threatened with starvation or overcrowding. Religious leaders of the community were seen as understanding of the needs of individuals and families, and were asked to provide a service by which parents could honour the memories of the children whose lives they had chosen to terminate. There were no laws against abortion or infanticide and, in general, both practices were regarded as private matters not relevant to government, but that is not to say that opposition did not exist. Opposition came from a small minority and mainly from the perspective that Japanese children belonged to Japan, not to their parents, and that the gods intended Japan to be highly populated and thus a strong nation.

By the end of the Edo era (1603–1867), during which Japan was generally closed to other countries, abortion and infanticide rates had increased to sixty to seventy thousand children per year. When Japan was opened at the beginning of the Meiji era (1868–1912), abortion and infanticide were made illegal because the government felt that Japan was then open to threats from other countries and needed to expand its military. From then until the 1940s, any information regarding birth control of any kind (abortion was seen as the main method in Japan) was banned, fines were imposed for using contraception, and women were arrested and imprisoned for seeking or having backstreet abortions. Graphic material depicting aborted babies and what revenge the gods may take upon the mothers was produced and distributed by the police. Women over twenty were forbidden from working but were encouraged to fulfil their duty to Japan by producing as many children as possible, especially sons who could go to war. Families with ten or more children received free university education for all their children.

During this seventy-year period, Japanese women and their families still sought and had abortions and still required the mizuko jizo service, but obviously could not publicly participate. Also, Jizo's image changed somewhat and came to be regarded as a phallic symbol (some believe that Jizo is a Shinto god of fertility), which was actually very convenient for women who were in reality praying for their aborted child, but in public appeared to be praying for more children.

Despite the government's efforts, it wasn't until after World War II when the men returned to their homes that women actually did start having large families. The government, however, had to discourage this as Japan had no need to fill a non-existent military and the country did not have the resources to support a rapidly growing population.

So, in 1948 abortion was again legalised in case of rape or when a doctor deemed a pregnancy to be detrimental to the physical, mental, or economical well-being of the mother. But women continued to have large families, so in 1952 the law was modified, granting doctors full decision-making power regarding abortions, without requiring them to justify their decisions to any organisation.

Abortion again became the main method of birth control in Japan. By the 1970s, with the abortion rate fluctuating between two and three million a year, mizuko jizo was again very popular. Temples felt pressured to provide the service or risk losing their regular parishioners, and entrepreneurial priests set up some temples specifically for mizuko jizo. The abortion rate slightly decreased during the 1990s, but mizuko jizo remains popular. The majority of participants are middle-aged married women, possibly because they have more time than younger women do. Doctors who have performed abortions often meet and attend ceremonies together. The legislation of the pill for contraceptive purposes is still a very recent event in Japan, and it is too early to determine its effect on abortion or mizuko jizo.

Public debate regarding abortion has been minimal and mostly male-dominated in Japan. Some have suggested that the financial gain for doctors performing abortions is one reason the contraceptive pill has only just been legalised, and also why the abortion pill RU-486 isn't available. There does exist a small religious organisation called 'House of Life' that campaigns against abortion. Some people do not oppose abortion itself, but do oppose the mizuko jizo ritual as taking money from people and prolonging what they understand to be a difficult experience for the mother.

Today

Three opinions seem prevalent in Japan today:

1) birth control and abortion should be widely available and not perceived in religious terms;
2) abortion is a sin against the gods and should be illegal; and
3) abortion is a 'necessary sadness' and one should show compassion for both the unborn child and the parents.

173

Western women and mizuko jizo

The Western women that I spoke with who had had abortions whilst living in Japan were aware of mizuko jizo, but most felt that they personally didn't really need to participate, except for one woman:

My husband's mother helped us find a temple where we could offer prayers to Jizo. I had read about this practice a long time ago and sought the temple as some sort of closure to the nightmare, and because it seemed a positive outlook on such an ugly situation. There's nothing I know of in Christian practice that parallels Jizo. We sent the fetus to the crematorium and somehow it makes me feel better to know that everything was burned away, sent up to the sky, and not dropped on a garbage heap somewhere.

One woman told me about an acquaintance's reaction to photographs of the statues:

My friend and I visited the Hase Kannon temple complex. Since this was around New Year's, all the statues of Jizo had been outfitted in new little crocheted caps and bibs. Though my friend and I have never experienced pregnancy, we were moved by the gesture of celebration combined with mourning. We took many pictures. When my friend returned to the US, she was showing these pictures to an old friend, one who had suffered a miscarriage during her only pregnancy about 25 years ago. When she saw the pictures, even before my friend had a chance to explain what they were, she burst into tears. She explained how much easier it would have been for her to have dealt with her miscarriage had she had a way to express her grief in such a manner.

Many Western women who were informed about mizuko jizo, regardless of whether they had carried a child to term or not, generally felt that participating in this ritual was a nonjudgemental way of expressing grief and sorrow for both oneself and for the unborn child:

While abortion is a terribly emotional subject—no matter what your beliefs—dealing with the emotions surrounding the choice through the symbolism of the jizo is far more open and, dare I say it, healthier than the practices of most of us who come from Judeo-Christian heritage.

Useful Japanese

pregnancy .... *ninshin*	pregnancy testing
termination .... *chuuzetsu*	kit .... *ninshin kensa youhin*

I think I am pregnant. .... *Ninshin shita you na kiga shimasu.*
I would like a termination. .... *Chuuzetsu shitai desu.*
Can you write down the exact procedure?
My Japanese friend will explain it to me. ..... *Tejun o kaite itadakemasu ka. Nihonjin no yuujin ga watashi ni setsumeishite kuremasu.*
How long does it take? .... *Dono gurai jikan ga kakarimasu ka.*
Do I have to stay overnight? .... *Ippaku shinakereba narimasen ka.*

Resources

Contact your doctor, or any of the gynaecologists or women's clinics listed in **Gynaecology** to find a doctor who can perform a termination.

Resources and Further Information
Family Planning in Japanese Society: Traditional Birth Control in a Modern Urban Culture
By Samuel Coleman, Princeton University Press, 1992.
Liquid Life—Abortion and Buddhism in Japan
By William R LaFleur, Princeton University Press: 1992.
Marketing the Menacing Fetus in Japan
By Helen Hardacre, University of California Press: 1999.
The Twilight Years
By Sawako Ariyoshi, translated by Mildred Tahara, Kodansha International: 1984.

Menstruation

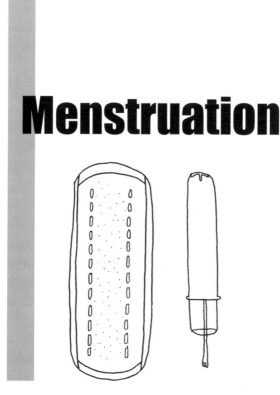

The actual Japanese term for menstruation means 'life essence' (seiri), and a Japanese girl's first period is a time of celebration. Traditionally, the family has a special meal of rice with red beans. The girl often receives gifts and thoughtful insights from the women of the community. With the decrease in the number of extended families living together, this ritual sadly seems to be on the decline.

Most Western women have no problem obtaining satisfactory sanitary products in Japan. Most bring a plentiful supply from home to use when they first arrive, until they become familiar with shopping in general. Amongst Japanese women, pads are far more popular than tampons and both can be bought from supermarkets, pharmacies, and convenience stores, as in our home countries.

Difficulties arise if you want to use washable or unbleached sanitary products. Although they are becoming increasingly popular amongst Japanese women, they are still difficult to find due to Japanese import regulations, which are determined and imposed by a group of sanitary product manufacturers. According to Jack at Tengu Natural Foods, unbleached tampons cannot be imported into Japan on account of them not being 'shiny enough'. Jack has been busy fighting the manufacturers in an attempt to import alternative sanitary products from the West. He was successful in importing 'Glad Rags', which was a welcome relief for many environment-concerned and body-conscious women:

> *I know that at the mention of 'rags' some women might feel like we're going back to the Dark Ages, but when you think about how many pads a woman will use in her lifetime, it makes sense to use a reusable product when circumstances permit. My period is fairly light, so it's a good option for me.*

Glad Rags are 100 percent unbleached organic cotton washable pads, which Jack says Japanese women have been ordering in bulk. He attributes this popularity to Japanese women having a higher awareness of dioxin contamination than their Western counterparts. Environment expert Sandra Guth explains the dioxin problem in Japan:

> *Consider how commercial pads are made—polypropylene and other synthetics are woven together, bleached, fluffed up, and a plastic sheet is slapped on the back. We wear them in intimate contact with our bodies and toss them away after one use. Where do they go? If you wisely don't flush your pad or tampon, it is likely headed for the incinerator. Japan burns almost three-quarters of its garbage, a higher proportion than any other industrialized country. Plastic packaging, nappies, and menstruation products account for much of it. When plastics and other chlorinated compounds are incinerated, dioxins form. Dioxins are readily*

absorbed and stored in the fat cells of humans. They cause cancer, skin and nervous system disorders, and liver disease. They interfere with the normal functioning of human hormones and lead to birth defects. If headlines, health lawsuits and mothers' fears are accurate indicators, then the problem of dioxins is frighteningly grim in Japan. Dioxins lurk in the soil of rice paddies. They drift through the air in ten times the amount they do in the US and parts of Europe.'*

If you feel concerned about dioxins, but uncomfortable about reusable sanitary products, then look for products that contain no plastic, either in the wrapping or in the applicator. In Japan these products have a picture of a cotton plant on the packaging. You will find sanitary disposal boxes in most toilets in Japan, including in private homes. Be sure to use the disposal boxes rather than flushing your paper and plastic waste down the toilet.

Regarding pain relief, a variety of over-the-counter medicines are available at any pharmacy at reasonable prices. If you object to taking medicine, a range of aromatherapy products is also available (see the Alternative Health section in this chapter) and, in case you didn't know—one of the best cures for menstrual cramps is an orgasm!

Useful Japanese

menstruation	*gekkei/seiri*	recyclable	*sairiyou dekiru*
sanitary products	*seiri youhin*	reusable	*saishiyou dekiru*
tampon	*tanpon*	wrapping	*rappingu*
sanitary pad	*napukin*	applicator	*apurikeetaa*
unbleached	*muhyouhaku*	menstrual cramps	*seiritsuu*
washable	*sentaku dekiru*	dioxin	*daiokishin*

Does this product contain plastic? .... *Kono seihin ni wa purasuchiikku ga fukumarete imasu ka.*

---

* 'Earthwise and On The Rag: What No One Tells Us about Menstruation' from the column Putting the Mother Back into Earth by Sandra Guth, *Being A Broad*, August 1998.

Resources

Where To Buy Environment-Friendly Sanitary Products

Foreign Buyers Club (FBC) (see display ad, page 69) 078-857-9001
      Store in Rokku Island, Kobe. Delivery throughout Japan.
      http://www.fbcusa.com

Tengu Natural Foods 0429-85-8751
      Stock Glad Rags. Mail order.
      http://www.tengufoods.com

Warabe Mura Wholefoods 0574-54-1355
      Stock Glad Rags. Mail order only.

Environment-Friendly Products Available in Regular Stores/Pharmacies

Charmsoft Bodyfit (non-applicator tampons)
Eldy by Lion (non-applicator tampons)
Shelf Sarasaty by Kobayashi (cotton panty liners)
Sofi by Unicharm (cotton panty liners)
Tampax (cardboard applicator)

Alternative Health

Alternative health treatments are very popular amongst Western women in Japan, many of whom seek them here for the first time.

Alternative versus conventional medicine

Western women seek alternative health practitioners and medicines for a variety of reasons. Alternative health is becoming more popular in our home countries, so for some it is natural to continue regardless of where they live. For others, curiosity about these medical practices increases when living in a country where such treatments are common, as reiki specialist Rosalyn Hagiwara relates:

> *Some Western women in Japan may be more likely to seek out a complementary health practitioner here rather than at home just because there is such a wealth of choice. Others may have had an interest at home, but were too busy. They find themselves in Japan with time on their hands and decide to try healing techniques based on 'Eastern philosophy'.*

Many Western women seek alternatives when faced with the conventional Japanese medical system (see the section on The Health System in this chapter) and find that complementary medicine suits their needs, as Hari Tahil, alternative health practitioner, explains:

Among the (Western) foreign community there is often a reluctance to submit to the vagaries of the Japanese medical system (few Western doctors available), and a Japanese doctor speaking English just is not enough. Especially, women are treated somewhat peremptorily and explanations can be less than forthcoming (I'm being polite here) and this, I think, is why many Western women seek alternative therapies—they don't trust the Japanese medical system and all it entails.

Lynette Airey, an acupuncture and shiatsu specialist in Tokyo, finds that Western women often prefer visiting one of Tokyo's many foreign alternative health practitioners due to the communication issue:

Women feel very comfortable talking to another Westerner who's trained in such therapies, since the very nature of these healing therapies involves a personal approach, a sense of thoroughness, and a lot of care and concern for the client.

Common health problems

Western women visit alternative health practitioners for a variety of physiological and psychological reasons:

... chronic tiredness, overall feeling of stress, severe headaches, lower-back pain, arthritic pain, serious illnesses such as kidney disease, diabetes and cancer, desire to lose weight, stomach aches, vague feeling of dissatisfaction with life, to help with recovery after an accident, or help with remaining pain from old injuries, child-related stress, stress from living in a foreign country ...
—Rosalyn

Women see me for pretty much everything. It seems to come in phases. One month it's reproductive problems, next it's being overweight, and then it's depression. Probably 'not feeling right' is the most common ailment: depression, anxiety, lack of confidence, and a host of physical complaints. —Hari

Being unable to pinpoint what is wrong, but feeling out of balance seems to be common. Living in a foreign country, a change in diet, and an increase in stress all add to a feeling of imbalance. Alternative therapies are ideal for these complaints, as they are holistic in nature and aim to return your body to a balanced state:

Exploring alternative health therapies can be not only a re-education into one's health, but a path of self-discovery about oneself emotionally and spiritually. One finds that becoming healthy is not just getting rid of the symptoms, but is a balancing of one's whole inner being. —Lynette

Some Western women wish to regain some sense of control over their life. There are so many aspects of living in Japan that promote a feeling of powerlessness: language difficulties, bureaucracy, company policies, etc. Many Western women seek methods to empower themselves, including health methods:

I do know that many women come to my reiki classes and my self-awareness retreats because they want to find ways to help themselves, rather than depending on practitioners.
—Rosalyn

For some, alternative health is also a means of pampering themselves (see the section on Pampering and Beauty in Chapter One).

Alternative health practitioners and treatments

There are many alternative health practitioners throughout Japan. Whether the practitioner speaks English or not, you will probably find their approach more personal, thorough, and enjoyable when compared with conventional doctors in Japan. There are a wide variety of treatments to choose from, including yoga, shiatsu, reiki, acupuncture, tai chi, and moxabustion. Some treatments are better than others for certain problems and, unlike conventional doctors, the practitioner will spend time discussing your specific problem. Many health practitioners have private practices at their homes, some even come to yours.

Prices tend to vary and in some cases can seem rather expensive. Expect to pay in the region of ¥10,000 for an hour's treatment, but bear in mind that a two-hour wait followed by a five-minute consultation with a conventional doctor could cost the same and leave you feeling dissatisfied. Most alternative health practitioners do not accept health insurance, so check beforehand.

Useful Japanese

See the Useful Japanese in **The Health System** in this chapter for words and phrases to describe your ailment.

alternative health	*minkan ryouhou*	moxibustion	*okyuu*
shiatsu	*shiatsu*	chiropractics	*kairopurakutikku/ seitai*
acupuncture	*hari*		
aromatherapy	*aromaserapii*	Chinese medicine	*kanpou*
massage	*massaaji/anma*	medicinal herbs	*yakusou*
yoga	*yoga*	tired	*tsukarete iru*
tai chi	*taikyokuken*	stressed	*sutoresu ga tamatte iru*
chi gong	*kikou*		
reiki	*reiki*	depressed	*ochikonde iru*

Can you come to my place for the
treatment? .... *Chiryou o shini watashi no tokoro made kite moraemasu ka.*

Do you accept health insurance? .... *Kenkou hoken wa tsukaemasu ka.*
I'm not sure what's wrong; I just don't
feel right. .... *Doushite daka wakaranai keredo, kibun ga yoku arimasen.*

Resources

English-Speaking Clinics and Practitioners
Tokyo

Akasaka Chiropractic Research Centre 03-3589-1905
Japanese male, trained in the US. Chiropractics. ¥7000 for
1 hour (first time ¥10,000). Akasaka Mitsuke.

Chinese Acupuncture Studio 03-3464-5819
Japanese male. Acupuncture. ¥4000 for 30 minutes (first time
¥2000). Shibuya.

Edward Acupuncture Clinic 03-3418-8989
British male. Acupuncture, moxibustion, anma, shiatsu.
NHI OK if referred by a doctor. ¥6000 for 1 hour 15 minutes
(first time ¥9000 for 90 minutes–2 hours). Sangenjaya.

Helios Clinic 03-3403-3272
American male. Acupuncture. ¥13,650 for 2 hours (first time
¥15,750). Nogizaka.

SUTO Healing Centre 03-3402-1654
Japanese female and male, studied in the US. Chiropractics,
energy work. Fees vary. Azabu Juban, Motoazabu.

Life Forces 03-3357-2067
Bulgarian female and British male. Holistic therapy, bodywork
(craniosacral therapy), hypno-psychotherapy, energy healing;
also teach meditation, reiki and other channeled energy
classes. ¥10,000 for 1 hour 15 minutes. Shinanomachi/Yotsuya
Sanchome.

Life Support Clinic 03-3724-7840
Japanese male. Acupuncture, herb medicine. NHI OK. Call for
prices. Jiyugaoka.

Karamiya 0422-20-8990
American female. Ayurvedic and aromatherapy massage, body
treatments, facials. ¥7000 for 1 hour.
Omotesando, Kichijoji.

Karen Crow 03-5789-4958
English female. Holistic aromatherapy massage. ¥9000 for
1 hour 15 minutes–1 hour 30 minutes (whole body), ¥5000 for
45 minutes (back, neck and shoulders). Minami Azabu.

Kimura Shiatsu Institute 03-3485-4515
Japanese male. Shiatsu (teaching and treatment). ¥5000 for
1 hour or ¥10,000 for 1 hour (home visit). Sasazuka.

Kojimachi Rebirth Clinic 03-3262-7561
Japanese female and male. Acupuncture, massage.
¥6650–7650 for 40–60 minutes. Yurakucho.

Neuromuscular Therapy (Hiroko Yanagida) 03-3584-7670
Japanese female. Neuromuscular therapy. ¥10,000 for 1 hour
(first time ¥12,000). Roppongi.

Rokubo Clinic 03-3590-5421
    Chinese male. Acupuncture, massage. ¥5000 for 30 minutes.
    Otsuka.
Rosalyn Hagiwara (see display ad, page 186) 03-3392-4681
    American female. Women's reiki workshops, relaxation, stress
    reduction, weekend self-awareness retreats, individual healing
    sessions. ¥5000 for 1 hour (individual session), call for other
    prices. Minami Asagaya/Ogikubo.
Soma Acupuncture House 03-3329-3955
    Japanese male. Acupuncture, shiatsu. ¥3000 for 1 hour (first
    time ¥4000). Shimotakaido.
Tokyo Reiki International 090-4844-8317
    Group reiki. ¥500 for 3 hours (each person receives
    20 minutes). Yotsuya.
Toyotama Harikyu Massage Clinic 03-3992-5589
    Japanese female. Acupuncture, moxabution, massage,
    shiatsu. Fees vary. Shinegota/Egota.
Uchiike Acupuncture and Chiropractics 03-5411-0115
    Japanese male. Acupuncture and chiropractics. ¥7000 for
    1 hour. Gaeinmae.

Kanagawa
Yokohama Pia City Toyo Clinic 045-212-1640
    Japanese female and male. Chinese medicine. NHI OK. ¥3000
    for 1 hour. Sakuragicho.

Kobe
Dr Ken's Physical Clinic 078-242-4600
    Chinese male. Acupuncture. NHI OK. ¥5250 for 1 hour (first
    time ¥6300). Kitano.

Kyoto
Hara Chiropractic Office 075-812-0093
    Japanese male. Chiropractics. ¥5000 for 40 minutes (first time
    ¥7000). Kyoto City.
Rikobian Shiatsu 075-491-2144
    Japanese male. Shiatsu. ¥5000 for 1 hour 30 minutes.
    Kita Oji.

Osaka
Shinsaibashi Chiropractic Centre 06-6245-6511
    Japanese male, studied in the US. Chiropractics. ¥5000 for
    15 minutes (first time ¥8000 for 15 minutes). Shinsaibashi.

Mental Health

Wherever we are in the world, for most of us there are times when life seems a bit too much to handle. I wouldn't say that living in Japan makes you crazy, but many of the Western women I know have consulted professionals for help during some period in their lives here. Depending on your home country, you may have mixed feelings about seeing a therapist; a New York friend told me that when she is at home, 'therapist' is alongside 'dentist/hairdresser/meet friend for lunch' on her daily list of things to do. When I told my English friends that I had seen a counsellor a few times, I received concerned letters telling me to come home immediately because I was the sanest person they knew and Japan must be making me lose the plot.

For the majority of Western women, it is quite natural that emotional problems surface at some point during their lives here. The problems are similar to those for which they would seek help in their own countries: relationship issues, stress, childhood-related issues, and difficulties at work, as well as problems more specific to living in Japan: loneliness, culture shock, or homesickness.

> *People often seem cold, aloof, and unfriendly. You may wonder why people tend to ignore you or treat you like you're not there. I chalk it up to big city life. As a woman you may wonder why men aren't more attentive. The Japanese style of communication can be very confusing. You may constantly feel that you've said something wrong when people don't respond to you, but that could be a language barrier or they just need lots of time (!!) to think of a response. As foreigners we all have moments of feeling lonely here; as outsiders, that we don't belong. Well, we don't. And that's important to keep in mind. No matter how comfortable you may feel at times here, you will inevitably be reminded that this is not your country. Those messages, no matter how kindly delivered, can be devastating at certain times. Be prepared.*

Culture shock often hits at around the six-month period, when the 'honeymoon' feelings slowly disappear and the reality of everyday life in Japan becomes apparent. Don't be surprised if this is accompanied by 'I-Hate-Japan Days' that turn into weeks or even months. There then follows what for some is a difficult period of readjustment, resulting in a more realistic understanding and attitude towards life in Japan. The whole process can come and go in cycles, so just when you think you've got your life in Japan sorted, the blues set in again. Being aware of this helps; I remember being in shock when my honeymoon period ended and I struggled to cope with the feelings for several months. Had I expected it to happen, I'm sure I could have coped with it a lot better. Many single Western women bury themselves in isolation in their apartments when they experience a negative phase of culture shock, but this is not advisable. Do keep in touch with friends and family from home; however, not to the point where you neglect to make new friendships in Japan. Go out, start new activities, join groups, and make friends with people in your neighbourhood as well as those you work with. However difficult it may seem at the time, look at the positive aspects of living in Japan.

Living in a different country can put a strain on relationships, long-distance or otherwise, and if the relationship breaks down, this can lead to depression and isolation:

I did not intend to seek a therapist here in Japan and was doing pretty well adjusting when I lost my girlfriend (back in the US) to another. Because I had not been here long enough to have developed any kind of network of friends, I was desperate to find a therapist to talk to.

Unresolved issues or issues of which you were previously unaware tend to arise in Japan. This is often because of the greater amount of time spent alone, either mentally or physically; for example, two hours a day on the train without something to read is a lot of thinking time. For some women, it may be the first time they spend so much time alone.

Most Westerners here seem to have several part-time jobs, often in addition to one full-time job. Consequently they spend several hours a day every day commuting all over hell to widely dispersed locations, schlepping through crowded trains and stations whilst loaded down with half their body-weight in stuff they have to carry around for the various jobs, etc. This being the case, few have the time or energy to prioritise pure social time, and again, the logistics are complicated, so just getting together with friends, unless they live in the same neighborhood, becomes a time-consuming, fatiguing ordeal. This is very isolating, and people become lonely and depressed on top of being stressed and fatigued.

I spoke to Ana Kishida and Prem Dana Takada, two clinical psychologists based in Tokyo. I asked them what they found to be the most common problems facing Western women living in Japan:

Depression, anxiety, consequences of sexual and emotional abuse, relationship problems at home and at work, difficulties balancing family and career, etc. Many women also seek therapy for personal growth. For women who left careers behind in order to follow their partners, the issues have more to do with coming to terms with their new role/identity and balancing autonomy and dependence. For unattached Western women, finding partners in Japan can sometimes be difficult. Therefore, loneliness and lack of validation of their femininity are problems unique to some of these women.

—Ana

Relationships, depression, and sexual problems. Relationship problems range from the trip home and family issues to communication, or should I say miscommunication, issues through to the anguish of affairs. Problems with depression range from dealing with the struggles of identity change that many women undergo when they move to Japan through to post-natal depression following childbirth.

—Dana

You may feel that you can cope with these problems without seeking help, but Ana suggests:

If you are overwhelmed, unable to function at home and/or at work, and are isolated without your normal support network, then professional help is indicated.

This may sound pretty straightforward, but if your life is becoming difficult for you, then it can also be difficult to recognise when you need help. My general guideline is that if feeling stressed, unhappy, or anxious starts to feel normal, then get help. In Japan, friends are sometimes too busy to notice that you are in trouble, schedules are too hectic, therapy seems expensive (generally about ¥10,000 per hour, although some operate on a sliding scale), and, if you're British, seeking psychiatric help may make you feel like you're just one step away from being locked up. But don't let these things put you off; a therapist can help you clearly identify your problems and develop strategies to deal with them. Because your problems may be specific to living in Japan, a good psychotherapist should be aware of and have experience in dealing with this.

If you prefer to solve your problems by yourself, Ana suggests:

... self-help methods aimed at reducing stress, a healthy lifestyle (exercise and diet), keeping a diary and being more self-aware, engaging in activities that are meaningful and self-enhancing ...

Mike Nendick, a former Board Member at Tokyo English Life Line, also has recommendations:

Call somebody. Expression relieves depression. Think about how you've coped if you've felt like this before. What worked then may work now. Get regular sleep, food, and exercise. If your body feels better, your mind should follow.

I found that admitting that I wasn't invincible and that I actually needed a good night's sleep really helped with my ability to cope with problems. If you live in Tokyo, it is very easy to fall into a fast paced life that includes long working days and late nights, and which contributes to the burn-out that many foreigners suffer from, along with other 'side-effects' of living in Japan. One woman points out:

I think I've had constant and unremitting emotional problems since I've been here. But exactly what are they from??!! Consuming things that have not been a part of my diet for many years, like coffee/caffeine, excessive alcohol, meat, fried foods, excessive oil, fast food, etc.? Or just life in Tokyo???

If you plan on living here for more than a year, taking care of yourself will greatly help with your ability to deal with emotional and psychological issues. There are several strategies that other Western women in Japan use to cope with their problems, without seeking psychotherapy. These include thinking about where they live (see the section on Finding a Place in Chapter Two), pampering themselves occasionally (see the section on Pampering and Beauty in Chapter One), as well as making an effort to meet new people and form close friendships, regardless of how difficult this may be at times:

Try to make more than one good friend here who speaks your language, and remember to give as well as take, even when you think you have nothing left to give. It all comes back around anyway.

I feel the best resources are good friends, and the best way to make friends is to join organizations of foreigners. I think the foreign community is pretty small here and, even though it's not necessarily a tight-knit group, when you're having a bout of the blues, every other foreigner here knows what you're going through, so talk it out with someone.

For women who are planning to come to Japan, probably the best advice is to keep an open mind, as one woman suggests:

Accept the country and all its differences. It is difficult for foreigners because we are not used to it. I am not saying there could not be great improvements made to this country, but to dwell on the negative will only cause your experience here to be less than what it could be. Seek out the differences, the culture, and the travel opportunities and enjoy them while you can.

Finally, if you do seek professional help, a word of warning. There is nothing in Japan that regulates foreigners claiming to be psychotherapists and nothing to check that they are adhering to any code of conduct. Check out a therapist's credentials carefully. If you're not sure what you're looking for, then contact International Mental Health Providers Japan. They can provide a list of psychotherapists who are fully trained and registered in their home countries. Get recommendations from friends or use those recommended by other Western women.

Useful Japanese

I have not included 'Useful Japanese' for this section due to the obvious importance of being able to communicate with a therapist without the need of a phrase book.

Resources

Helplines, Information, and Support Groups

Alcoholics Anonymous (AA) 03-3971-1471
  http://www.aatokyo.org
Japan Helpline 0120-461-997
  24-hour counselling service.
MAC and DARC Alcoholism and Drug Rehabilitation Centres 03-5685-6128
  English information available, but must be able to understand
  Japanese to participate.
Overeaters Anonymous 03-5605-9425
  Weekly meetings in Roppongi, Tokyo.   03-3423-2067
Tokyo English Life Line (TELL) (see display ad, page 196) 03-5774-0992
  Phone counselling.

Clinics, Counsellors, and Therapists
Tokyo

Allen Leroy Robinson (see display ad, page 195) 03-3407-5696
  American male and Japanese female. Biofeedback method,
  psychosomatic disorders, relationship issues, depression.
  ¥16,000 for 75–90 minutes. Shibuya.
American Psychotherapy Centre 03-3716-6624
  American male and Spanish male. Expatriate adaptation,
  depression, panic, relationship problems. ¥10,000–12,000 for
  45–50 minutes (sliding scale possible). Yutenji.
  http://www.japanpsychiatrist.com
Ana Maloyan-Kishida (see display ad, page 197) 03-3448-1272
  American female. Depression, anxiety, adjustment, women's
  growth and individuation, grief, couple counselling. Sliding
  scale for 50-minute sessions. Meguro/Shiroganedai.
Aurora Counselling Centre (see display ad, page 195) 03-5275-3638
  7 counsellors (4 Japanese, 3 foreign). ¥6000 for 50 minutes.
  Ichigaya.
  http://home.att.ne.jp/moon/aurora
Betsey M Olsen 0422-47-1824
  American female. Individual, couples, and family therapy,
  EMDR. ¥8000 for 1 hour. Mitaka/Kichijoji.
Can Do Harajuku 03-3423-2501
  2 Japanese males. Preventative medicine and counselling
  centre, addictions and eating disorders. ¥5000–7000 for
  1 hour (first time free). Harajuku.
Ikebukuro Counselling Centre 03-3980-8718
  7 English speakers, different nationalities, female and male. Also
  operate dance therapy classes, adult rehabilitation counselling,
  and group therapy. From ¥10,000 for 50 minutes. Ikebukuro.
  http://www.gol.com/hozumiclinic/counselinge.html

Inner Light Service 03-3781-5977
    Japanese male. Hypnotherapy. ¥5000 for 1 hour. Togoshi.
Jim McRae 03-3983-0582
    American male. Clinical psychologist. Individual and couple
    psychotherapy, cross-cultural counselling. ¥8000–18,000 for
    50 minutes (sliding scale based on income and negotiable).
    Omotesando and Takadanobaba.
Jo Lovell 03-3498-2158
    Australian female. Past life regression, meditation,
    relationships, grief, depression, and anxiety counselling.
    ¥10,000 per hour. Omotesando.
Jonna Douglass 03-5570-5225
    American female. Family and Jungian therapy. Fees are
    negotiable. Roppongi.
Opportunity Counseling Services (see display ad, page 196) 090-1551-9925
    American female. Motivational counselling. ¥6000 for 1 hour.
    Mutually convenient locations.
Prem Dana Takada (see display ad, page 198) 03-3491-8144
    Australian female. Individual and couples psychotherapy.
    60- to 90-minute sessions (call for fees). Meguro.
Ros Reuter.. 03-3479-9802
    British female. Child therapy, behaviour problems, adaptation
    problems, individual pschotherapy for adults. Sliding scale for
    1-hour sessions. Roppongi.
Stewart Wyndham 03-5285-2085
    British male. Holistic counselling, stress management seminars,
    meditation groups. ¥12,000 for 90 minutes (counselling, call for
    seminar and meditation prices). Takadanobaba.
Tokyo English Life Line (TELL) Community Counselling Service 03-3498-0231
    (see display ad, page 196)
    7 counsellors (female and male, from the US, Japan, Canada,
    Mexico). General mental health, cross-cultural issues,
    depression, anxiety, eating disorders, relationship issues.
    Sliding scale for 50-minute sessions, Omotesando.
    http://www.tell.gol.com
Tokyo Medical and Surgical Clinic 03-3436-3028
    Japanese female psychiatrist. ¥10,000–15,000 for 40 minutes
    (first time ¥15,000–20,000 for 1 hour). Kamiyacho.

Kanagawa

Family Service Centre 0468-21-1911
    7 Americans, female and male. For anyone connected with the
    US Dept of Defense. Free 50-minute sessions. Yokosuka.
Homecoming Educational Program 045-313-3281
    Japanese male. ¥11,340 for 1 hour (first time ¥13,650 for
    unlimited time). Addictions and eating disorders.

Osaka

Resolutions Counselling Service 0728-67-4437
> American male and Canadian female. General psychotherapy,
> anxiety, depression, personal growth, relationship issues
> especially between cross-cultural couples, Buddhist
> psychology. ¥6000 for 55 minutes (first time ¥9000 for
> 85 minutes). Hirakata-shi.
> http://www.resolutions.org

Resources and Further Information

Counselling and Support in Japan
> http://www2.gol.com/users/andrew/index.html

International Mental Health Providers Japan (IMHP)
> Information on psychotherapists and counsellors registered in their home
> countries, contact for complaints or problems with therapists (but can only take
> action if the therapist is a member). Publish a resource directory. Contact TELL
> on 03-3498-0231 or check the Website for the current telephone number.
> http://www.imhpj.org

Psychotherapy in Japan
> http://www.japanpsychiatrist.com/ryouhou.html

The Japan Experience: Coping and Beyond
> By Tazuko Shibusawa and Joy Norton, The Japan Times Ltd: 1989.

195

Tokyo English Life Line (TELL)

Tokyo English Life Line (TELL) is a multifaceted, nonprofit organization that has been serving the international and business communities since 1973. Our services include free phone counseling and information, professional face-to-face counseling, and educational workshops.

Visit http://www.telljp.com for more information.

Tokyo English Life Line
03-5774-0992
Daily 9:00AM - 11:00PM

TELL Community Counseling Service (TCCS)
English: 03-3498-0231
Japanese: 03-3498-0232
Call for appointment
Face-to-face counseling with
professional licensed therapists
on a flexible fee scale

TELL Business Office
03-3498-0261
Fax: 03-3498-0272

Life Line Services
03-3498-0246
Inquiries about Life Line and Training

Need a safe place for personal exploration?

For seeking solutions to stressful situations?

PROFESSIONAL PSYCHOLOGICAL SERVICES

ANA MALOYAN-KISHIDA, PH.D.

Clinical Psychologist

Licensed Marriage, Family & Child Therapist

Individual & Couple Therapy
Cross-cultural Counseling
Depression
Anxiety
Stress
Bereavement
Women's Individuation
Life-transitions

**For details or appointments,
please call 03-3448-1272**

Fitness

Western women usually find that fitness centres in Japan are new, clean, and well-organised, with excellent equipment and facilities, a wide range of classes, and friendly and helpful staff, many of whom speak English. Many centres also have well-maintained swimming pools and some have public baths. There are many health centres, gyms, and swimming pools (public and private) all over Japan, so it is usually quite easy for a Western woman to find one near her home.

Fitness centres in Japan are usually more expensive than those in your home country, although you'll probably find them affordable with your higher income. It's a little-known fact that some employers provide staff with fitness coupons, so check with your company:

I have two friends who get special coupons to use at Nautilus. Each time I go, I pay either ¥1050 or ¥840 (depending on which coupon I'm using). This way, I don't have to pay if I don't go, and I would have to go more than three times a week, every week, to equal what I would pay for a membership. I recommend that other women check with their employers (especially if it is a big company) to see if they can get fitness centre coupons.

Depending on the time of day, overcrowding can be a problem. It can, however, be difficult to avoid at any time because most Japanese fitness centres tend to open later in the day (around 10:00 a.m.) and close earlier (around 10:00 p.m.) than many fitness centres at home. Fitness centres are very woman-friendly, with much less testosterone floating around than you'd expect. You're also unlikely to feel intimidated by Lycra-clad model types; most people wear baggy clothes. If you are the only foreigner though, you may feel self-conscious for reasons discussed in the Pampering and Beauty and Clothes sections in Chapter One. Remember to reassure yourself—people are admiring your unique looks and your curves!

There are also many government fitness centres and swimming pools throughout Japan. They tend to be cheaper, although, of course, not quite as flash. Check your ward office brochure for details.

Useful Japanese

fitness centre	*fittonesu kurabu/ sentaa*
swimming pool	*suimingu puuru*
sauna	*sauna*
gym	*jimu*
membership fee	*kaiin-ryoukin*
monthly fee	*gekkaihi*

I'd like to join this gym. .... *Kochira no jimu ni nyuukai shitai no desu ga.*
Do you have any information in English? .... *Eigo no setsumeisho wa arimasu ka.*
What time do you open/close? .... *Nanji ni aki/shimarimasu ka.*
How much is the ... ? .... *... wa ikura desu ka.*
Do you have any special classes? .... *Nanika tokubetsuna kurasu wa arimasu ka.*
Am I eligible for any fitness centre
coupons? [to your company] .... *Shain you no fittonesu kurabu/sentaa no yuutaiken wa arimasu ka.*

200

When is the gym/pool's busiest/quietest
time? .... *Itsu ga ichiban konde/suite imasu ka.*
Do you have any hours/classes that are for
women only? .... *Josei senyou no jikantai wa arimasu ka.*
Is there anything I should bring (towel,
shoes, etc.)? .... *Motte kurubeki mono wa arimasu ka (taoru,
kutsu, nado).*
I forgot my membership card. .... *Membaa kaado o wasuremashita.*

Resources

Check at your ward office for information on public facilities in your area. Fees quoted
refer to the monthly membership fee. Some private clubs charge an annual or one-time
enrolment fee in addition to this. Check your local magazines and newspapers for sports
clubs or groups organised by individuals in your area. If there aren't any, you could
always start your own.

Fitness and Sports Centres

Big Box Seibu Sports Plaza .... 03-3208-7171 (J)
    Pool, gym, golf school. ¥12,000. Takadanobaba, Tokyo.
Central Sports .... 03-5543-1800 (J)
    Pool, aerobics, gym. Fees vary. Throughout Japan.
Club Boy Beau 03-5454-1231
    3 studios, gym, pool, golf range, saunas, jacuzzi, beauty salon.
    ¥10,000. Yoyogi-Uehara, Tokyo.
Crunch .... 03-3478-2118 (J)
    Gym, studio, sauna. ¥12,000. Omotesando, Tokyo.
Do Sports Plaza .... 03-3344-1971 (J)
    Pool, gym, sauna, tennis. ¥12,500. Shinjuku, Tokyo.
ELIX .... 03-3545-0109 (J)
    Gym, aerobics, golf, pool. ¥11,000. Musashikogane, Tokyo.
Hello Sports Plaza Gym .... 075-252-0086 (J)
    Gym, pool, aerobics, sauna, jacuzzi. ¥8000. Throughout Kobe,
    Kyoto, Nara, and Osaka.
Higashi Tokorozawa Sports Club .... 0429-44-2344 (J)
    Pool, fitness centre. ¥5000 for once a week. Higashi
    Tokorozawa, Tokyo.
Levene Sporting World .... 03-3720-4110 (J)
    Gym, aerobics. ¥6000–10,000. Throughout Osaka and Tokyo.
Nautilus Health Club .... 03-3233-1188 (J)
    Gym, pool, studio, sauna. ¥15,000. Throughout Japan.
Oak Three .... 0429-56-0093 (J)
    Pool, gym, jacuzzi. ¥9970. Saitama.
Oasis .... 03-3200-0109 (J)
    Pool, gym, aerobics, massage. ¥12,000. Throughout Osaka
    and Tokyo.

Pal .... 03-3252-6041 (J)
        Studio, aerobics, dance, karate, yoga, gym. ¥11,550. Kanda
        and Machida, both in Tokyo.

Tipness .... 03-3464-3531 (J)
        Gym, pool, aerobics. ¥11,000. Throughout Osaka and Tokyo.

Tokyo American Club 03-3583-8381
        Squash, cardiovascular room, weights, outdoor pool. Free for
        club members. Kamiyacho.
        http://www.tac-club.org

Tokyo Yoga Centre 03-3354-4701
        Individual classes, Japanese teachers, female and male.
        ¥10,000 admission, ¥18,000 for 10 1-hour lessons, ¥38,000
        for every day for 5 months. Shinjukugyoenmae, Tokyo.

Tokyo Yoga Circle 03-3582-3505
        Beginners, prenatal, and mixed levels. Fees vary. Aoyama,
        Tokyo.

United Sports Club XAX .... 03-3561-9595 (J)
        Pool, gym, aerobics, culture school. ¥4000–10,000.
        Throughout Japan except Okinawa.

YWCA Sports Centre 03-3219-2565
        Pool, studio, gym, aerobics. ¥12,000. 2 locations in Tokyo.

Other

Ski Japan
        Guide to skiing and snowboarding throughout Japan.
        http://www.skijapanguide.com

Tipness Fitness Club

Personal training in English, Yoga, Mat Pilates, Aqua-aerobics, Core Reset… and lots more weekly activities to choose from.

A one-day trial is available and will be refunded if you sign up within two weeks

- Over 40 Tipness gyms located conveniently near stations.
- No Registration fee
- Tours of the facilities are available anytime during our office hours.

Monday- Friday: 7am–11pm
Saturday: 9.30am–10 pm   Sunday and National holidays: 9.30 am–8pm
Second Sunday of every month: closed

For full details please see our website www.tipness.co.jp

Weekender is the only English free magazine with two whole pages devoted to women's issues, compiled by Being A Broad, the support network for foreign women in Japan. Recent topics covered include: being pregnant in Japan, modeling, women in politics, women entrepreneurs, making friends in Japan, buying clothes to fit, and alternative health remedies.

Weekender is published on the first and third Friday of the month and is available at major bookstores, restaurants, bars and international supermarkets. The magazine is also available at FEW meetings.

Also online at www.weekenderjapan.com

Relationships

Friendship
Being Single
Being in a Relationship
Getting Married
Getting Divorced
Bereavement

Friendship

Most Western women in cities in Japan find it easy to make initial connections with other foreigners and Japanese. Japanese people are often interested in talking to you because you are a foreigner, they want to speak English, or they just want you to feel comfortable. It is not unusual for men or women to approach you on a train, in a bar, or even in the street. As for meeting foreigners, it's easy to spot most other foreigners and many Westerners exchange greetings that sometimes develop into conversations:

> *It seems to be fairly simple to make friends in Tokyo. There are many people here from other countries who all need friends and since we all stick out in the crowds we are easy to pick out.*

Some Westerners find this rather odd, claiming that they wouldn't greet a complete stranger in their home country, so why do it here? My personal opinion is that we're not in our home countries, it takes very little effort to smile at someone, and as life can be very isolating for many foreigners in Japan, why not increase the human connection? Generally, Westerners are supportive of one another and willing to introduce you to others, for both work and friendship purposes:

People seem much more willing to meet with you here and take time to help you out. All you need is the name of a person from a common friend and a phone. Most people are happy to meet you for a coffee or lunch, to make a connection.

Compared with home I think it is much easier to make friends here. At home, a lot of people have had the same friends for years and are not interested in expanding their circle. In Tokyo, everyone needs more friends and is in the constant mode of meeting people.

There are many organisations and events in Japan, either for foreigners or foreigners and Japanese, through which one can meet new people. Check Chapter Nine: Women's Organisations, classified ads in magazines and newspapers, or join one of the many email newsletters. You could always place a classified ad yourself. Be aware though, one of the difficulties of being in any new environment is that you may find yourself hanging out with people with whom you have very little in common:

I encourage people who have just moved here to relax and really look for the type of people they enjoy spending time with. I have seen many people make a friend too quickly without really knowing the person and then there are hard feelings later when one of them discovers there is not much in common between them.

Many Western women say that it is much more difficult to form deep friendships with Japanese people:

I am very sad to say that after a total of eleven years in Japan I don't have many close Japanese friends, although I have many friendly acquaintances. I refuse to let anyone use me to practice English and the group dynamics are just too different.

207

Those that do develop friendships with Japanese women find that they are close, supportive, and loyal, and it is often those friendships they miss the most when they return to their home countries:

> *I didn't find true friendship in Japan until I met some good, stable, open, sparky Japanese women—then I felt that I had found my friends, and I'm still in touch with them now, which hardly applies to the foreigners I knew.*

It takes effort to maintain close friendships in Japan. It is rare to be living in the same neighbourhood as your close friends and most people have such busy schedules that they often find themselves booking a coffee with each other two weeks in advance, especially in Tokyo.

Most Western women find the most difficult aspect of friendships in Japan is the fact that people leave:

> *I think at first you are somewhat devastated and lonely. But after it happens so many times, you tend to accept it as a fact of living in Japan—not many foreigners here intend to stay forever. Besides, you can always stay in touch with them—their leaving doesn't mean they are dropping off the face of the earth.*

> *The difficult part is getting used to the revolving door, or people coming and going from other countries. In the two years I have been living in Tokyo, I have made three good friends here who have all since moved. However, we have managed to keep up the communication and even get together in other locations.*

To cope with this, people tend to ensure that they have a wide variety of friends and often seek 'replacement' best friends:

> *When close friends have left Japan, I have just tried to make new friends. I have gotten into the mode of always looking for people that I think I might feel like spending time with.*

Being in a foreign country provides you with the opportunity to meet all kinds and nationalities of people you may never have met in your home country. (It also gives you countless places to stay all over the world!) One woman gives some good advice with respect to friendships in Japan:

Keep an open mind and be interested in learning about others. It takes time and a lot of inner strength if you're not used to 'being alone'. But there are many interesting people—Japanese and foreign alike—that are worth getting to know. When all is said and done, it's not the nationality, gender, age, or quantity, but the quality you will look back on and be grateful for.

Useful Japanese

It is difficult and awkward to list useful phrases in Japanese for 'making friends' but the phrases at the beginning of this book should help with basic conversational Japanese.

Resources

There are hundreds of clubs, organisations, and associations through which you can meet people and many are listed throughout this book. You should also check listings in local magazines and newspapers. Most wards in Japan have an international association that helps foreigners settle into Japan, provides information, runs classes, and holds events. Check with your ward office to find your local international association. There are also many overseas' university alumni organisations in Japan. Check with your university.

Being Single

You might be tempted to skip this section. Single? What will that have to do with your life in Japan? You're a mature woman who can take a relationship or leave it. Your life in Japan won't be affected by something like whether you've got a partner or not! You are an INDEPENDENT woman!

Skip the section then—I guarantee you'll come back to it at some point during your time here.

For some women, being single in Japan can be quite a different experience to being single in their home country where they may not even think twice about it. Part of the reason that some women come to Japan is to get away from relationships in general, or a relationship in particular:

> *I am a heterosexual female who came to Japan to learn to love myself as much as I had loved the men in my life. While living in the States I had had numerous difficult relationships and even one life-threatening relationship. I wanted to understand why I had these bad relationships. I found before I could have a good relationship in love I truly had to respect and love myself.*

For others, the idea of incorporating a relationship into their lives in Japan is overwhelming. You've got enough trouble dealing with your own life in Japan, why double it by having to deal with a new partner?

> *I haven't felt like I WANT to be with anyone seriously since I came here. I feel like my life is so hectic here ... I can't imagine complicating it with a relationship. I hardly have enough time for myself.*

Being single is a matter of choice for many women, but I would say that the extent of that choice changes somewhat for many Western women in Japan. At home, there exist various circles of friends that probably evolved from school, university, jobs, friends of friends, etc. But in coming to Japan you are leaving those circles behind and starting from scratch. You're not just leaving those friends behind, you are also leaving the potential partners that introductions through those friends inevitably lead to. At home, you can safely rely on the myth that the 'Love of Your Life' is right around the corner. In Japan, the myth can become a story your Mum once read to you, but you can't quite remember the beginning, let alone the ending:

> *I feel like a female eunuch!!! I also find that I don't even get the sort of everyday compliments in Japan that I got in America to give my ego a little stroking and positive validation, so my self-esteem is a little low.*

211

Most heterosexual single Western women in Japan agree that their being single is not a matter of choice, but is due to the feeling that they cannot meet suitable partners in Japan, foreign or Japanese. There are a few women for whom meeting partners in Japan is easy:

> *I found that finding prospective partners was very easy because of the novelty/exoticness factor. For a while this was a novelty for me, but in the end the type of people I attracted were unable to provide a deep relationship, either because they were on the move (in the case of foreigners) or because we didn't share a language and culture (Japanese natives). I must say, I met some fantastic men in Japan, a wide array of them, and they were all very special. If I had stayed at home, my love life would have been dull in comparison. I had lots of romantic and dramatic experiences, but found myself being very lonely and craving a soul mate, which is a major reason why I came home.*

The overwhelming majority of heterosexual single Western women in Japan really don't like being single and find it difficult to change their status. My (Western male) friend says "You lot just don't find Japanese men attractive and Western men prefer Japanese women", which is an irritating thing to hear, but according to my research with Western women and men here, in most cases what my friend says is true. Most Western women's criteria for potential partners are not met by Japanese men, and for this we should not 'blame' Japanese men (which is an easy option), but recognise that it is because of our expectations that Japanese men do not seem attractive. At the same time, it is important to remember that even in your home country, potential partners were not everywhere just waiting for you to date them. If you are looking for a guy who is physically bigger than you, will take the initiative in the relationship physically or emotionally, will regard you on an equal level and share the same basic value system, then you are in for a tough ride wherever you are. Even more so, it seems, in Japan:

The main difference that I notice is that most Japanese men are shyer than their American counterparts and they are usually less familiar with communication skills. So if you're not willing to do the work, both communication wise and by jumping their bones first, it might not be for you.

There are Western women who adore Japanese men and this is often the key reason being single in Japan isn't an issue for them:

As I was strongly attracted to Asian men, I was very happy when I first came here. I remember thinking how many good looking men there were around me every day!

My friend Elise's feelings led her into ripping off one unsuspecting young Japanese man's underwear with her teeth only a few hours after they had met—they are now married with two children. Some Western women find Japanese men gentle, sensitive, handsome, and disinclined to dominate a relationship, which sounds pretty good now, doesn't it?

As for Western men, according to my research, most of them are in or prefer relationships with Japanese women. Many Western women aren't particularly attracted to the Western men who live here anyway:

Foreign guys are a big disappointment here. Mostly, they aren't interested in foreign women. Also, I find that many of them, after getting so much attention in Japan, start thinking that they are really great.

If you look at this statistically, there are seventy million Japanese women and fifty thousand Western women living in Japan, so it is more likely that a foreign man will be dating a Japanese woman. It's a matter of numbers. As for the attitude, unfortunately the Western men who turn into the biggest arseholes here are always the loudest, so it's their bad behaviour that sticks in your mind.

It's obviously also a matter of numbers regarding Japanese men and Western men, but the difference is that Japanese women generally meet a Western man's criteria for a partner. Japanese women tend to be very kind, generous, and thoughtful, which you will find in your friendships with Japanese women. In addition, they are generally more petite than the average Western woman, pay more attention to their appearance, have a reputation for doing more than their share of housework without complaint, and, I'm told, give frequent massages without expecting one in return. I guess that's tough for anyone to pass up, but it can be tough for you to find out that men who proudly proclaimed their feminist tendencies at home will happily abandon them over here:

Sometimes I have felt really disappointed in my foreign male friends because they seem to become so superficial (dating a woman who can barely speak a word of English because she is HOT). It is not always just a sexual or simple relationship either ... sometimes I am amazed that these relationships are so long-lasting when the communication is obviously lacking. I have often thought that perhaps communication is overrated ... look at how many of these relationships actually DO last. It can be very discouraging and confusing, to say the least.

This confusion can play a large part in Western women's negative feelings about being single, and can lead them to question their appearance, their values, and relationships in general. It can also lead to negative feelings about men in general.

Of course there are Western men who may or may not have had Japanese girlfriends here who would prefer a partner from a country and culture more similar to their own. Most heterosexual Western women say that these men make the best partners in Japan, but are difficult to come by:

I would like to be able to meet some decent foreign men, but that is like looking for a needle in a haystack ...

214

One Western man I spoke to had this to say:

> *The foreign women I met when I first came here fifteen years ago were not here for the long term and were not looking to build any kind of meaningful relationship. Nowadays, it is different. There are many more foreign women here and there are many more realistic job opportunities for them. Sometimes I wish I was fifteen years younger and single and could have a second chance at finding an American wife and be able to stay in Tokyo. For the life of me, I cannot understand why so many foreign men in Tokyo automatically rule out having a relationship with a foreign woman.*

After having met my share of arseholes at one time or another in Japan, I now know of several nice Western men who like to meet and date Western women, but they say it is difficult to meet any who don't give off don't-talk-to-me-you-bastard vibes. It's important to be open to meeting new people (as prospective partners or otherwise) in order to maintain a positive outlook and healthy attitude towards your life anywhere, not just in Japan. So if you are feeling defensive and critical, try to look for the good in the people around you. As one woman says:

> *The advice I would give to single foreign women coming to Japan is to hang in there, believe in yourself, and don't look so hard— something good will come along when you're least expecting it.*

It seems just as difficult for a lesbian to meet prospective partners in Japan. Again, it's a numbers thing, but it's also due to communication problems. Whereas you have had years and various methods by which to establish friends who are aware of and comfortable with your sexuality in your home country, it can be like coming out all over again in Japan in terms of developing a new social group and support network:

215

If I were still in New York, not only would I have more women to choose from for potential partnership, I would also have a developed circle of friends to support me. I have not been on my own in about 18 years—and the loneliness, coupled with the foreign land, has been profound. However, I am slowly meeting others of my 'kind'—and, while partnership is probably not in the offing anytime soon, just having friends to talk to, to have dinner with, and to do silly things like go bowling with has been wonderful. My advice to single lesbians coming to Japan is that there are certainly people out there who are willing to be both friends and partners.

Homophobia in Japan doesn't seem to manifest itself in quite such a violent manner as it does in some countries, but this isn't a country where being open and frank about anything is welcomed with open arms.

I've got to be honest, I really didn't enjoy my first period of 'singledom' here. Those occasional dates that don't fix but do take your mind off a broken heart just didn't happen for me after my break-up. However, I'm a firm believer in learning from every situation, regardless of how negative or painful it seems at the time. Moving to a foreign country is a conscious or subconscious decision to remove yourself from your past and the old you; to develop in new directions and learn more about yourself. The disadvantages of being single in Japan can be turned into opportunities to move towards that new you. The lonely times can be turned into times where you learn more about yourself or start new things. Japan lends itself to great opportunities. I know of a couple of women who started new businesses when they got sick of feeling sorry for themselves after break-ups: one established a movie production company and the other opened a restaurant. I started *Being A Broad* magazine after my break-up and my life completely changed. If all else fails, then take a short-term lesson from one woman:

I found a full-blown remedy by running off to Bali and hooking up with the first romantic, lovey-dovey Bali boy who laid eyes on me. After two and a half years of being ignored, I was overcome. Disgusting, isn't it?!

And a long-term lesson from another:

I hate being alone here. I hate not having someone at home to come home to. I hate it that I will probably be alone for my tenure here. But, I am TRYING to learn something from it. I am trying to build friendships. I am trying to learn that loving myself can be the best relationship.

Useful Japanese

date .... *deeto*

Would you like to go out with me for lunch/
dinner/coffee/a drink sometime? .... *Watashi to isshyo ni ranchi/shokuji/kohii/*
nomi ni ikimasen ka.
Could I have your phone number? .... *Denwa bangou o oshiete moraemasen ka.*
Are you single? .... *Dokushin desu ka.*
I'd really like to see you again. .... *Zehi mou ichido oai shitai desu.*
Thank you for the meal/drink. .... *Gochisou-sama deshita.*

Resources

Elite Introduction International Inc (see display ad, page 218) 03-5464-6371
Singles introduction agency with many members keen to meet
Western women. Free membership for Western women.
http://www.elitejapan.com

Being in a Relationship

Aside from the joys and challenges that are par for the course for any relationship, living in Japan can bring other joys and challenges for Western women and their partners, whether they come here together or meet in Japan, whether their partner is Japanese or foreign.

Coming to Japan together

If you come to Japan as a couple and your relationship remains stable amidst the mayhem of relocating, then you have the security and support of a partner—this is not to be underestimated, especially during the first few months. At the very least you have someone who is going through the same experience as you. A familiar person in an alien environment can help both of you in your adjustment period. Someone with whom to share the excitement of living in a new country, to be with at the end of what may be a busy working day, to talk to about the home and friends you have left behind (thus minimising feelings of homesickness) can help bring you closer together and enrich your experience in Japan. A word of warning though: in the absence of previous support networks, you may become each other's sole source of support during the beginning of your life in Japan. It is important to seek out activities and friendships to ease this potential dependency on one another:

> *I came here with my (foreign) fiancé. We both found it difficult to meet new friends and became increasingly dependent on each other. Living in a one-room apartment, the pressure to be there for each other became unbearable and led to our separation. We spent four months apart with no contact, during which time I was very unhappy at first but then made a lot of friends and took up an old hobby. One day I called him and we met. He had also met some new friends and was doing some new, interesting things. Anyway, the end of the story is that we got back together. I often wonder whether we might not have had those four months apart if when we first arrived we had met different people and started doing different things separately (and had a bigger apartment!), much like at home.*

Some women come to Japan as 'relocating spouses'. These women are in Japan because of their partners' jobs. For some women this may mean giving up their own job or career at least temporarily and, although they may be happy with the decision to relocate, boredom and frustration can become problems. Conflicting feelings regarding identity can arise, especially if they valued an independent lifestyle previously. Psychotherapist Ana Kishida says:

> *Usually, being involved in an outside activity is very important, something that validates the self. These women need to do a lot of*

work on building inner strength and stability, and accepting that they will feel a certain degree of loss for the things they gave up to be with their partner.

One compensation in this situation is the greater financial reward that such couples receive. Westerners sent to Japan by their companies usually receive excellent benefits, particularly in terms of salary and accommodation. The 'free' partner is therefore able to indulge herself in activities that help develop a sense of independence. The benefits of being a financially secure couple when moving to another country are not to be underestimated:

The happiest couples I see here are those couples who came together on an ex-pat package and will stay a few years. I think those ex-pat packages do a lot to insulate one from the ravages of Tokyo.

Probably most of us feel fuller pockets here than at home and enjoy spending money freely on ourselves and our partners, less on our families back home. Also, my husband and I enjoyed trips to Singapore and Thailand that we never would have taken from 'home'. But, once the kids come along you'll miss Grandma as a babysitter and your social life with your partner comes to a grinding halt unless you're able to afford very expensive babysitting services.

When a foreigner's 'Japan honeymoon' period ends (see the section on Mental Health in Chapter Three), feelings of frustration about the reality of life in Japan are common. Your partner's honeymoon period may be of a different length to yours; you may each experience different emotions. It is this period that many couples find the most challenging. Ana offers some advice:

Don't make big decisions. Understand the adjustment process and be aware of your vulnerabilities, find support to help yourself get through this period. It is important to find time to talk, learn to really be sensitive to each other's feelings, spend time on shared activities, and become involved in a common interest. Find alternative sources of support for yourself and your partner, so you do not put too much pressure on each other.

It's important to get the balance right between doing things together and separately.

If your relationship is not entirely secure, and wasn't before you came to Japan, then bear in mind that you still have old issues to resolve, as well as the above new challenges that relocation brings. Whether you are married or not, moving to another country can expose unresolved issues or give you a fresh perspective from which to see the relationship, and perhaps advance the end of it:

I knew he was wrong for me and when we came to Japan together it took three weeks for something to 'click' in me, it was like "Ah, now I see, what was I thinking?" Japan just made the break-up happen a lot quicker.

As Ana advised, it is probably best not to make big decisions during your honeymoon or readjustment period in Japan, but to wait until you feel more at ease with your life here. Your decision may still be the same, but it is likely to be made from a more stable perspective.

If your relationship withstands the challenges of relocating, and if you, your partner and the relationship grow in fulfilling ways, then you may find yourselves closer than before:

Living under unfamiliar circumstances can put a great deal of stress on a relationship. When you survive this stress, I think you come out not only as stronger people, but also as a stronger couple. You begin to understand both the good and bad in one another to greater depths, and learn to accept and support each other where needed. If we hadn't had the experience of being a couple in Japan (or any foreign country for that matter), I'm not sure our relationship would have reached such incredible depths.

Long-distance relationships

For couples attempting long-distance relationships, be aware that you and your partner will not be sharing a common experience during the duration of your stay. Frequent contact via phone, email or regular mail is important to ensure that you can share some level of understanding about your new experiences and those of your partner at home. You are more likely to change than your partner, as you will be living a completely new life. Be aware of your partner's possible difficulties in adjusting to the changes in you. See the section on Back Home in Chapter Eight for additional information about personal change and home/pre-Japan friends. If finances allow, inviting your partner into your new life (albeit temporarily) may help. One woman found that this increased her appreciation of both her girlfriend and Japan:

> My partner lives in California and, while our relationship is still relatively new, we have accepted the challenge of being on two continents. There is much joy when she is able to come to Japan. I have so much fun showing her Japan. As someone who has lived here twice (and will be here for two more years), it is so rewarding to me to see her face as she experiences some new vista, temple, custom, art, or gastronomical delight. And, in having a place for my heart, especially given the hardship of being apart, our times together here in Japan (and in the US) are so much more special, filled with thankfulness, and yes, much joy.

Insecurity

I'm reluctant to reinforce that stereotype of women being insecure and jealous, but it does appear that Japan seems to bring out those feelings, especially for women in relationships with Western men. If you are new to Japan, you may be dealing with negative feelings about your appearance (see the sections on Hair, Pampering and Beauty, and Clothes in Chapter One) and your status as a woman in what appears to be a male-orientated society, while your partner suddenly finds himself the centre of attention from female colleagues and friends:

Back home, my boyfriend was quiet and shy. I found it endearing and it fitted well with my personality, which is more outgoing. If we went out anywhere he would never leave my side. In Japan, he gets a lot of attention, he has lost all his shyness and thinks nothing of wandering off to the other side of a bar to talk to female 'friends', seemingly oblivious to the fact that I'm sitting by myself. While I'm happy that he's got more confidence, I don't like the change in our relationship.

Western women also find themselves the centre of attention in many situations; however, they are less likely to enjoy it, especially if they're battling with negative feelings about themselves. They may be more likely to see the attention for what it is—curiosity about them because they are foreign, not necessarily because they are women. Some Western men appear to love all the attention. These are often the men for whom female attention was scarce back home, so who can really blame them? What is important is to learn to deal with feelings of insecurity that lead to jealousy. Work on your feelings of insecurity instead of focusing on your jealousy. Ana suggests:

Is there something you can do to change or improve your feelings about yourself? Find a network of friends from your own country or another, and support each other and give each other accurate feedback. If you can afford it, travel to your country to put things in perspective, such as the size of your body.

Western women who meet Western men here usually do not experience a great deal of insecurity about their relationships. First, it's easy to spot the men for whom being in Japan has gone to their heads (no pun intended), so most Western women wouldn't be dating those guys. Second, chances are the men have already explored their prospects for a relationship with a Japanese woman and have decided that it's not for them so are unlikely to play around.

If you're with a Japanese man, company alcohol- and sex-related pressures that are higher for Japanese men than foreign men may need discussing:

Another challenge in Japan is recreational business such as forced heavy drinking and hostess clubs or pink clubs* (actual participation). Education and discussion helped eliminate this trouble spot. My partner doesn't drink much, so he gets to use the excuse "my girlfriend will kill me if I come home and vomit on the tatami".

This kind of pressure is nothing new for Japanese men. Despite the fact that many men find it tiring and unnecessary, many Japanese companies expect male staff to socialise together after hours. This always involves alcohol, often involves going to hostess bars, and sometimes involves going to bars that offer sexual services. Generally it is not considered immoral, and traditionally it is seen to facilitate good relationships between colleagues and any visiting clients. It is part of the culture, although it is now less common amongst younger Japanese men.

A Japan-based relationship

If you met your partner here, your relationship is based on being in Japan, which can bring a fresh perspective to your experience:

We met here in Tokyo about two years ago. We are both from the USA. Seeing both the good and bad in Japan through the eyes of another enriches your understanding and appreciation of what the country has to offer. Comparison of compiled experiences, ideas, and resulting feelings can oftentimes clear up once-held misunderstandings and open up new doors to personal growth. You both begin to see more objectively the various choices the world has to offer you. More opportunities are brought forth to accept or reject and this results in learning and growth.

The main challenge, whether your partner is Japanese or foreign, arises when you decide to leave Japan:

*Pink clubs or 'fuzokuten': bars that offer sexual services.

225

My Japanese husband's dream is to live in the US, so I think it will be very good for us when we do get back there. However, he will still have to give up quite a lot here, and it won't be easy. I think our relationship will change a bit when we are in the States, as our entire relationship and marriage have been based in Tokyo. I imagine that, in the beginning, it will be a big adjustment for my husband to make and may be quite stressful. I am confident, though, that it will be the best thing for both of us in the long run.

Two friends of mine had a successful relationship for five years in Japan, but when they began considering their future in Britain, she was English, he Irish, they ran into troublesome traditional issues concerning family and religion, both of which neither had to address in Japan.

Ana suggests:

Before leaving Japan, anticipate the possible changes that could happen; make an honest assessment of your strengths and weaknesses, your current resources; and remember any experiences you had with change in the past. Ask yourself how you and your partner will change in the new environment, what demands will be put on the relationship. Being prepared saves quite a bit of disappointment.

If you are aware of these potential problems before you leave, then you are halfway to solving them. Don't expect to replicate your life here when you move to another country. See Chapter Eight: Leaving Japan for more information.

If your partner is Japanese

At the risk of removing all the romance, there are practical joys to be had if your partner is Japanese:

226

Of course, there's the advantage of having someone fluent in the language if you are not, but it's hard not to use his language ability as a crutch. If your partner has lived outside Japan for awhile, long enough to see with 'different' eyes, the two of you can share insights into both cultures (or amusing things) that others might not notice. Your partner can show you the 'best' of everything so you don't have to spend as much time searching for it yourself. In my case, my husband showed me how to cook some of his favorite foods. I don't necessarily like all of his favorites, but some of them are delicious. Your partner can help you make professional inroads and contacts that you might not be able to make yourself, or that might take longer to find.

One American woman married to a Japanese man partly attributes the success (as opposed to the problems) of their fifteen-year marriage to their cultural and communication differences:

We have lived in both cultures—USA for five years, Japan for ten. We have NO problems, and actually because we enjoy backgrounds with different languages and cultures we AVOID lots of problems. We avoid all of these kinds of things because we assume that the other person does not know what we want or expect, and can share the joy of each other's cultures through communication. Also, because we do not share a common language and one of us is usually speaking a foreign language, we stop to listen carefully to what the other means rather than what actually came out of our mouths. In this way we hear each other better than most couples do and avoid unnecessary fights. Instead of taking a comment negatively, we stop and say "I heard you say XYZ, is that what you meant?" And 98 percent of the time it is NOT what was meant, so we can stop arguments or hurt feelings before they ever begin. And I bet a lot of couples who do share a language would not think to stop and ask that question when if in fact they did, they would learn that language is tricky and mistakes are easy to make. Wrong messages are easily delivered.

Most Western women do speak positively of the challenges in relationships with Japanese partners:

My present partner of three years is Japanese. Living in Japan can wear a Western woman ragged. You feel like it's you against the culture in many ways and it can be exhausting. Having fought so hard to achieve my place in womanhood, I could not succumb to reverting to the Japanese ideal. My boyfriend had to struggle to understand since he had always lived in Tokyo, but he has been far more sensitive than any other man I have been with.

I met my husband here, he's Japanese. I think the biggest challenge is communication. It's hard enough to communicate with the opposite sex, even in your own language. Throw in another language and a different culture and it can be a real challenge. That's not necessarily a bad thing though; it makes you work harder so you take things less for granted. It also adds a depth that same-culture relationships don't have and I particularly appreciate that. I think the most important thing for me was to be very clear from the beginning about who I was and what I wanted. Don't do something against your nature just because it fits with someone else's cultural standard of what a woman should be. That'll get old fast!

Ana offers some advice for Western women with Japanese partners:

Learn about the communication style of your Japanese partner and that of his culture. Be very honest with yourself as to whether or not you can truly accept him and live with the rules of his culture on a daily basis. Many people say they can respect the Japanese culture on an intellectual level, but when it comes to living with it on a practical level they begin to feel angry and resentful. Do not expect him to change, at least not while he lives in Japan. Pay attention to the non-verbal messages your partner is giving you. Do not minimize or rationalize any problems you are noticing now as just cultural differences. Some may be culturally explained, but others could be your partner's own personal issues. Understand your deep motives for choosing a partner from another culture.

If you came here with your Japanese partner or met him or her here, then you may have family issues to deal with: acceptance of you, living arrangements, and responsibility for taking care of elderly parents. In Japan, it is traditional for the eldest son and his wife to take care of and often live with his parents. This tradition is becoming less popular but is still very common, so you will need to discuss it and make plans.

We are very aware that the time may come when his parents' health deteriorates, and we don't know what we're going to do then. The parents do not have a good relationship with my husband's older sister, so we doubt that she would take care of them.

One of the most important things you can do to establish a good relationship with your in-laws is to learn Japanese. They will appreciate the effort and, of course, being able to communicate with them helps a lot. Western culture likes to perpetuate the idea of the nightmare mother-in-law controlling her beloved son. In Japan, many mothers have devoted their lives to their son's education and well-being to the exclusion of everything else, in some cases really spoiling them. Many Western women find this difficult to deal with, but you should try to form a bond with your mother-in-law. Just as in our own countries, if you have kids you may find her to be an adoring grandmother.

An important thing to remember is to seek support from friends in similar situations when things seem tough. This can help you gain a better perspective on any problems in your relationship. There are many foreign women currently living in Japan who are married to Japanese men and they have all been through experiences similar to yours. Although you can get this support informally, there is one group that was consistently recommended to me by Western women married to Japanese:

I would probably have gone crazy if I hadn't joined the Association of Foreign Wives of Japanese [AFWJ]. *This group has 700 members, all of whom share this same common denominator. I think it's crucial for women in committed relationships with Japanese men to get support from other women who are in the same situation.*

I have met some of my best friends through the Association of Foreign Wives of Japanese. It has been very helpful when we get together as couples, so the husbands can see that their problems are common, and there is a good camaraderie among us.

Read more about the AFWJ in Chapter Nine: Women's Organisations.

Useful Japanese

I have not included Useful Japanese for this section as it is assumed that couples have at least enough language skills to be able to communicate about their relationship.

Resources

Association of Foreign Wives of Japanese (AFWJ) 045-753-7485
      membership-sec@afwj.org
      http://home.att.ne.jp/surf/cei/AFWJ.html
      To get *Fe-mail* (newsletter of AFWJ) email
      bjnakamura@lbm.net
Marriage Encounter Programs 03-3401-2141
      Worldwide program for deepening marriage and family life and
      communication. Christian belief helps but is not necessary.
      Run by the Franciscan Chapel Centre, Tokyo.
Married in Japan
      Email support group for foreign women married to Japanese
      men. For sharing experiences and information, making friends,
      and discussion.
      http://groups.yahoo.com/group/MarriedinJapan
      tracy@mx9.ttcn.ne.jp
Tokyo Wives Email Group
      For foreign women with Japanese partners.
      http://www.egroups.com/group/TokyoWives

Getting Married

Getting married in Japan can be a great option if you want a quiet wedding with a minimum of fuss and an effective way to avoid inviting relatives who just cannot be trusted to get on with each other when forced to spend more than an hour together. It can also be a good option if you want a huge wedding with lots of attention—if your partner is Japanese, it is traditional in Japan for the groom's parents to pay for the wedding. If they are happy with their beloved marrying a foreign woman, chances are his mother will create the event of her life, even if it isn't the event of yours.

The legal requirements regarding getting married in Japan are fairly simple, whether you are marrying a foreigner or a Japanese person. If you are both foreigners, then Japanese law requires you to comply with the regulations of both your home countries. This involves going to your embassies and requesting a 'certificate of legal capacity to contract marriage', which is a document that basically states that you are eligible to marry according to the laws of your home country. You then take the certificates, your birth certificates, passports, and alien registration cards to your local ward office, where you complete the 'Marriage Notice'. This form requires both your signatures and the signatures of two witnesses over the age of 20, who don't actually need to be present providing they have signed the document beforehand. And that's it—you are married. If you are marrying a Japanese man, then you need a 'certificate of legal capacity to contract marriage' from your embassy, which you submit to the ward office in which you are registering your marriage, along with your passport and a copy of his 'Family Register'. Once these documents have been approved, you are married, without you even needing to be there. You will then be added to the bottom of your husband's family register, a practice that infuriates many Western women:

As a foreign woman, my name was always included at the bottom of his family register, not as an official part of the family. Also, as a foreigner, my name was never technically changed to his, although by custom I was 'allowed' to take his name.

You may change your visa status if you want to. For example, if you already have a working visa, then you may not wish to change your visa status; however, there are some benefits to having a spouse visa:

I didn't bother to apply for a spouse visa until almost a year after the wedding. We had no problems getting it. Now I automatically get three years every time I renew my visa, and I plan to apply for permanent residency next year. From what I have heard there is a lot of paperwork, but it's pretty unlikely that a foreign woman married to a Japanese husband will be declined permanent residency if she has resided in Japan for at least five years straight.

There are no work-related restrictions imposed on your spouse visa if you are married to a Japanese citizen, whereas if you have a spouse visa and your spouse is a foreigner, then you cannot work more than 20 hours per week.

As you can see, the whole marriage procedure is very simple and some people leave it at that:

> *I married my Japanese husband here, but there was no ceremony. We went to the city office and filled out a marriage application form. That was it! I also registered our marriage at the US Embassy. I imagine the way we married was similar to being married at City Hall or County Court in America, although there was not even a blessing by anyone in the office, just the signing of the paper.*

Some women choose to have a small informal ceremony and party, although if your partner is Japanese, his parents may not appreciate this. My friends took two friends with them when they signed the documents at the ward office, had an afternoon picnic in Inokashira Park, then a small buffet party in the evening culminating in everybody piling into a friend's bar and getting drunk, including her and her new husband. The bride and groom made speeches and there were no family members present. The most important thing to the bride and groom was that they planned and organised the whole event exactly the way they wanted. If you are two foreigners getting married, then being in Japan allows you to have your ideal wedding, not anybody else's. If you're marrying a Japanese man you may have to hurt some people's feelings in order to do what you want—not much different from at home really.

There are some women who allow their mother-in-law to plan the whole event. Your in-laws will pay for everything, which will cost them several million yen, but you may feel like it isn't your wedding. For some women, this is a small price to pay to keep the in-laws happy, especially if they are still rather concerned about the fact that you are a foreigner:

> *We got married in 1990, first by filling out the paperwork at the American Embassy then going to the nearest ward office. We had the ceremony five months later at a Shinto shrine, traditional Japanese style. It is Japanese custom that the husband's parents*

pay for the ceremony. Advice: let mother-in-law have it the way she wants it and it'll all be over soon! If you want any control over how the ceremony is done, pay for it yourself.

Of course you can choose not to have your wedding in Japan at all, as many Japanese couples are now doing, mainly due to finances. Hawaii seems to be the most popular destination. Some women choose to go back to their home country:

We drifted back to Australia for our wedding ceremony— obviously, getting married in this country would've set our financial plans back ten years! No thanks! It was cheaper for all fifteen of us to go back to Australia and have a grand wedding at the Sheraton Mirage on the Coast.

Remember to register your new married status with your ward office.

Note:
Japanese law does not recognise same-sex marriages.

Useful Japanese

marriage .... *kekkon*	spouse visa .... *haiguusha biza*
marry .... *kekkon suru*	wedding ceremony ... *kekkonshiki*
marriage notice .... *kon'in todoke*	guests .... *shoutaikyaku*
witness .... *shounin*	wedding dress .... *weddingu doresu*
husband .... *otto*	Japanese wedding
wife .... *tsuma*	kimono .... *hanayome ishou*
certificate of legal	gifts for the guests ... *hikidemono*
capacity to marry ..... *kon'in tekikaku*	wedding gift .... *kekkon iwai*
shoumeisho	marriage
family register .... *koseki touhon*	confirmation
spouse .... *haiguusha*	ceremony .... *yuinou*

Resources

Contact your embassy and ward office for the necessary registration procedures for getting married in Japan.

A Western woman's traditional Japanese wedding

Opting out of the traditional Japanese kimono (I regret that now, but it was a very sticky July day), and dressed in a black suit and simple white dress, my husband and I entered the Hakkai-san Shrine together and were seated on two very small seats. Directly behind us sat our *nakodo* (matchmakers), who were there to oversee our union. Gathered on the tatami mats behind us were our well wishers: family and friends. In front of us was the altar room: a large wooden area decorated with a big free-handing drum, an altar with sake and fruit presented to the gods on it, streamers and banners, as well as a small bamboo-made table. Beyond the small table was the altar itself upon which were the traditional three elements that symbolize the Shinto faith—a mirror, a sword, and jewels.

After we were seated, the priest entered from the side. Bedecked in a formal kimono of gold and white and wearing a tall black hat, the priest carried a large drumstick. He proceeded to sit in front of the drum and summoned the gods with a long rhythmic drumming. He then picked up a large white paper wand and, shouting loudly, shook it above our bowed heads. Thus the gods were awakened and our spirits cleansed.

Next entered three young virgins dressed in white full-sleeved tops and bright red leggings. They carried trays with sake and cups on them. We were about to take part in the San-san-kudo ritual. One virgin maiden offered us in succession three different cups of gradually larger size. Each maiden in turn poured three sips of sake into each cup. In turn my husband and I sipped from each cup three times. Upon the completion of San-san-kudo, the priest handed branches to us, and, in turn, my husband going first, we approached the small bamboo table and, bowing, placed the branch onto the table. Our nakodo and family members also offered branches in this manner.

The priest then said a few words of prayer and the ceremony ended. We were married in the eyes of the Shinto gods.

After the ceremony we went to a Japanese inn and ate, sang, drank, and listened to speeches in our honor. We had a very good time! A great memory and experience.

Getting Divorced

Divorce can be a traumatic experience wherever you are, no matter who you are married to. If you are thinking about it or are in the middle of it, there are certain issues that you should be aware of that are specific to Japan, especially if your husband is Japanese.

Foreign couples

If your partner is foreign, then the regulations regarding divorce and child custody are those of your home country, so contact your embassy (or both embassies if you are from different countries). While living here, you qualify to follow the legal requirements of your home country without ever involving the Japanese legal system (and may negotiate via lawyers if necessary). Just remember to notify your ward office of your new status and residence, if applicable.

Foreign women married to Japanese men

As for women who permanently live in Japan and are married to Japanese men, I'm afraid that your experience may be much more complicated, so much so that one legal expert I spoke to advised Western women not to get married under Japanese law:

Anybody used to being able to divorce because of 'irreconcilable differences,' as in most states in the US, would be in for a shock.

The divorce procedure for foreign women married to Japanese men is the same as for Japanese couples. There are three types of divorce: divorce with consent, divorce through mediation, and divorce through legal suit. Divorce with consent is a divorce to which you both agree. This includes agreeing not only on the fact that you both want a divorce, but also on residences, share of assets, any cash settlements, parental authority, and childcare costs. You should try your hardest to agree on these points, even if communicating has become incredibly difficult. If the process goes beyond the first stage, then you are in for a very tough time. If you can come to an agreement, then you go to your ward office where both of you sign a divorce application form and submit a divorce report along with your alien registration card. Your divorce is then granted according to Japanese law and no nasty court visits are required. Some countries will not recognise a divorce unless it has been through a court, so check with your embassy to be sure that officials in your home country will not still regard you as being married. If one of you attempts to obtain a divorce through the ward office without the other's consent, then the non-consenting partner must complete a non-acceptance of divorce report at the ward office. The report is valid for six months and must be extended thereafter.

When one person does not give consent for the divorce, major problems begin. It is extremely difficult to obtain a divorce in Japan without both parties consenting. In this situation, or if you cannot agree on the terms of the divorce, you need to apply for a divorce through mediation. You must obtain a certificate of foreign registration from your ward office and take that, along with your family register, alien registration card and passport, to a family court. You will be assigned two mediators and a judge who will listen to your testimonies (assuming that both of you turn up for the hearing). First they will try to convince you to reconcile. Failing in that, they will attempt to help you agree on divorce terms. If you both want the divorce and can agree on the terms at this stage, then your divorce will be granted.

If one partner doesn't turn up at the mediation hearing, or you disagree on the terms, or one person still does not want the divorce, then you have to take it to the next stage, which is divorce through legal suit at a district court with lawyers and translators. This method can take years and is expensive. The court will then decide whether to grant the divorce and, if so, upon which terms. Legal aid is available on a loan basis, and the loan can be repaid in instalments after the proceedings.

Regarding money paid to a spouse directly, as opposed to for childcare, it is traditional for the person who initiates the divorce to pay the other a 'compensation fee'. On average it is about two million yen. This is becoming less common in Japan as women (traditionally not the family breadwinners) are now outnumbering men in being the motivating force behind divorce. If the divorce is due to the husband having a girlfriend, then he is expected to pay this as an apology. If the divorce is due to the wife having a boyfriend, then the new man is expected to pay the 'apology' fee.

Access to and custody of children

Again, this depends on the co-operation of your partner, whose written consent you need in order to gain 'parental authority' and/or custody. This is important: although you may be granted access, do not console yourself with the idea that you will be able to live down the street from your kids and see them when you want to, because your visa status will be affected by your divorce (more later). If your partner will not give his consent, and in many cases his family will urge him not to, then it is highly unlikely that you will get parental authority or custody.

I divorced my Japanese husband here. As far as custody of our child, I needed his consent to maintain custody. There is no stipulation for joint custody on their standard form. If he hadn't signed the paper I would have had to take the case to family court, hire a translator, etc. I know of several cases of divorce in Japan, and I would say they have all gone in favor of the Japanese partner, so take it slow and easy everyone!

Japanese law usually favours the Japanese partner rather than the foreign partner regarding custody, regardless of whether your husband is out of the house for twenty hours a day, is abusive during the four hours when he is at home, has a string of affairs behind him, and is incapable of making a cup of coffee. Your chances of obtaining custody are even lower if his family live nearby or in the same house as the children. Japanese law prefers your mother-in-law be granted custody, the idea being that you will go back to your own country and never be seen or heard from again. Falling out with your mother-in-law brings about serious consequences in Japan, so get on her good side when you get married; it may make life less painful if things don't work out later down the line. I can't emphasise this enough: get your husband to grant you custody during the divorce.

I have read of several cases in which, following a divorce, the woman or foreign partner has been denied access to their children. Even where this is technically illegal, it can happen. The Japanese wife of a friend of mine 'disappeared' with their son after their divorce. My friend has not seen his son since then. Anyone considering divorce [in Japan] should take the possibility of this happening into account when trying to decide what to do and take steps to avoid it.

David Bryan Thomas, of the Children's Rights Council Japan, urges caution even if you are granted access but not custody:

Children have the right to access to both parents but there is no enforcement policy in Japan and Japanese law does not recognise parental kidnapping.

If you are having problems, then contact the Children's Rights Council Japan (see Resources).

Your visa status

If you have a spouse visa, regardless of whether your ex-husband is Japanese or foreign, once you are divorced your spouse status is cancelled. Generally, you are not expected to leave Japan until your visa expires, and this may give you time to change your visa status. If you have children by a Japanese man, and have parental authority or custody, you are allowed to apply for long-term residency at your local immigration office (see the section on Your Status in Chapter One), and your ex-husband has no influence over this. You cannot apply for long-term residency if your ex-husband is a foreigner, and unless you apply for a different visa, such as a working visa, then you have to leave Japan. If you have no children, whether your ex-husband is Japanese or foreign, you have to apply for a different visa or leave Japan. If you have an independent visa (such as a working visa), your visa status is unaffected by your divorce.

If your divorce takes a long time and you need to have your spouse visa extended in order to attend divorce proceedings but your husband will not support you in this, then you may apply for a visa extension on your own. You need to provide a letter explaining why your spouse won't help you, a report of the divorce proceedings to date, a Japanese guarantor, and, if applicable, any employment or children's education information.

A word about breaking up whether you're married or not

Separating from a long-term partner can be distressing wherever you live, all the more so in Japan for several reasons. First, you may not have the support network to help you get through it. If you do have that support network, then most foreigner's homes in Japan are too small for you to feel able to ask a friend if you can stay with them for a while until you get your new living arrangements organised. Second, depending on your financial situation, for example, if you are accompanying a partner but are not married, you may not have enough money of your own to deal with the practicalities of starting a new life in Japan. You may not even want or feel able to stay in Japan. A friend of mine often says that Western women stay with partners in Japan whom they would have left long ago if they weren't in Japan, because here the reality of leaving seems a lot scarier. I can give you the usual advice about ensuring that you are financially and socially independent, but we all know that real life doesn't always work like that. I do know that you would be surprised how supportive other women are in these situations, irrespective of how close your friendship is, and how, if you just reach out, you will find people who are willing to help you practically and emotionally. Staying in a relationship when one of you wants to leave is no way to live, whatever country or financial situation you are in.

Useful Japanese

divorce (noun)	*rikon*
divorce (verb)	*rikon suru*
divorced (adjective) ..	*rikon shita*
divorce with consent	*kyougi rikon*
divorce through mediation	*rikon choutei*
divorce through legal suit	*rikon soshou*
non-acceptance of divorce report	*rikon todoke ni goui shinai*
certificate of foreign registration	*gaikokujin touroku shoumeisho*

family register	*koseki touhon*
family court	*katei saibansho*
mediator	*chouteisha*
judge	*saibankan*
district court	*chihou saibansho*
legal aid	*houteki fujo*
divorce compensation fee	*rikon isharyo*
parental authority	*shinken*
child custody	*kodomo hogo*
long-term residency	*chouki kyojuu*

I'd like to notify you of my divorce.	*Rikon o oshirase shimasu.*
I'd like a divorce application form.	*Rikon todoke o kudasai.*
I'd like to submit a divorce report.	*Rikon todoke o teishutsu shitai.*
I'd like to hire a translator for my divorce. ...	*Rikon no tame no tsuuyaku o yatoitai desu.*
I'd like to hire a divorce lawyer.	*Rikon senmon bengoshi o yatoitai desu.*
I'd like to apply for legal aid for my divorce.	*Rikon no houteki fujo o shinsei shitai desu.*
I'd like to apply for a visa extension while my divorce is being processed.	*Rikon ga seiritsu surumade, biza no enchou o shinsei shitai desu.*

Resources

In **Chapter One**, check the Resources in **Your Status** and **Safety** for divorce lawyers.
Children's Rights Council Japan 03-5317-0357
> An advocacy group working towards getting Japan to establish an enforcement policy to allow children access to both parents. Also supports parents who are being denied access.

Bereavement

A death in Japan

It is rare for foreigners to lose a loved one in Japan, but it does happen. In addition to the emotions you have to cope with, the practical arrangements of losing someone in Japan may seem overwhelming, especially if that person was another foreigner for whom you are responsible. If your loved one was Japanese, then usually you will have a network of other Japanese to help you through the practicalities and with whom to share your grief.

First, contact the deceased's embassy and their next of kin. The embassy can arrange this notification if you do not wish to. Also contact the deceased's lawyer and employer. The funeral can be held in Japan and a funeral service company can help you with everything

242

from cremation (the usual method in Japan) to organising the burial plot. You can arrange for the ashes or the body to be sent back home. A certificate from the deceased's embassy is required to send the ashes; if you send the body, then a funeral company at home must agree to receive it.

Funeral arrangements are expensive in Japan and can cost up to a million yen. Plots are also expensive, especially near big cities. They can also cost up to a million yen, plus annual maintenance fees. Cemeteries are usually located on the outskirts of residential areas. If the deceased was enrolled in the Japanese national health insurance scheme, then the ward office can arrange the funeral and will reimburse you up to ¥70,000. Some private insurance schemes include funeral arrangements.

The death certificate and the deceased's alien registration card must be submitted to the ward office within seven days of the death. There you must complete the Notice of Death form.

You may feel like leaving Japan altogether, especially if the deceased was your foreign partner and the major reason you live here. For more information, see Chapter Eight: Leaving Japan and contact Support in Grief for aid for foreigners in Japan suffering a bereavement.

A death at home

More common seems to be losing a loved one at home, and this brings about all sorts of emotional issues related to the fact that you are not in the same country, as Cressida Howard, who lost both her parents whilst living in Japan, says:

> ... *losing someone* [while you are] *in Japan can seem like a double bereavement. Not only do you mourn the loss of a loved one, but also the absence of a tried and true support group: other family members and old friends.* *

If you're lucky, then you may have a close friend in Japan who knows you inside out, but what you feel like you really need is someone who knows you and your loved one inside out. Depending

243

on the circumstances surrounding the death, you may have had time to return to your home country (incidentally, some private insurance policies include full coverage of a sudden trip back home due to a bereavement):

> *I'd been here about seven weeks when I found out my mother had terminal cancer. In the eighteen months that followed until she died, I was able to spend nearly half that time with her. I was lucky. I didn't feel lucky, however, just scared, sad, lonely, angry, and guilty. Not necessarily in that order, and sometimes all at once.*
> —Cressida

Of all of those feelings, it is guilt that is probably strongest felt by people living overseas: guilt that you weren't there, guilt about the fact that the last time you were home you didn't spend much time with them, etc.

> *As for Guilt's favourite taunt: 'Are you sure you did enough?' a kind friend helped me knock that one on the head. "No one," he said, to comfort me and stop my hand wringing, "can do enough." Doing enough is stopping it all from happening, it's taking away the pain of the person who's suffering, and with a wave of the magic wand—The Happy Ending.*
> —Cressida

I remember Cressida saying that, in some ways, returning to Japan after the deaths of her parents was a relief. After time has been spent grieving with relatives and practical matters have been dealt with, it is common to feel the need to get on with life somehow, and living overseas helps some people to do this. Support in Grief is a fairly new organisation in Japan, founded by foreigners to help others during bereavement. Check the Resources that follow.

* All quotes from 'Let it Out, Let it Go' by Cressida Howard, *Being A Broad*, March 1998.

Useful Japanese

bereavement	*shibetsu*
death	*shi*
dead	*shinda*
funeral	*soushiki*

funeral company	*sougi gaisha/ sougisha*
cremation	*kasou*
burial plot	*ohaka o tateru tochi*
gravestone	*boseki/hakaishi*

[Name] died on [date]. .... [Name] *wa* [date] *ni nakunarimashita.*

I need to arrange a funeral. .... *Soushiki/sougi no tehai o shinakereba narimasen.*

I'd like to send the ashes home. .... *Ihai o jitaku ni okuritai desu.*

My friend has died and I have to send the body overseas. .... *Watashi no yuujin ga nakunari, itai o kaigai e okuranakute wa narimasen.*

How much will it cost? .... *Ikura kakarimasu ka.*

Resources

Support Groups
Compassionate Friends in Tokyo 03-5481-5020
    Support group for parents who have lost a child (including
    adult children).
Sudden Infant Death Syndrome 03-5465-0556
    Support for parents who've lost a child through miscarriage,
    still birth, or infant death.
Support in Grief 03-3401-2142
    Support for anyone who has lost a loved one.

Funeral Companies
International Mortuary Systems 048-261-3302
    Preparations, paperwork, shipping, liaisons with mortuaries
    in Japan.
Yokohama Mortuary Systems 044-366-4444
    Shipping, embalming, Japanese ceremonies, arrangement of
    burials in Japan.

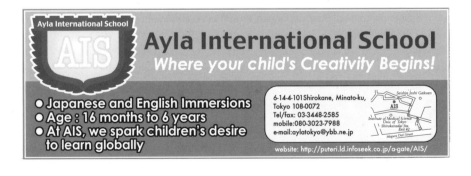

Mothers

5

Pregnancy
Childbirth
After Giving Birth
Adoption
Day Care
Schools

Pregnancy
by Judith Sullivan

Finding out that you are pregnant in a completely foreign country can be rather daunting. Rest assured that Japan is a country with all of the facilities, staff, and support necessary for you to have a healthy baby. If you choose to have your baby here, then you are in very good hands.

Confirmation

The language may be different, but the test is the same. Pregnancy tests cost about ¥1000 and can be found in all pharmacies. Some brands have an illustrated instruction sheet in simple English. Larger or international pharmacies carry imported brands. Most pregnancy tests are over ninety percent accurate and are able to confirm a pregnancy one week after a missed period. After you perform your home test you must go to a doctor to have your pregnancy confirmed. This test and checkup is not covered by Japanese health insurance, so ask the clinic or hospital how much it will be beforehand. Some private insurance schemes cover pregnancy tests; again, check beforehand. The doctor's fee and lab test can range from ¥1500 up to a staggering ¥20,000, as I unfortunately found out at a large international hospital.

Pregnancy is considered to be ten months in Japan, starting from the week of your last period.

Fertility issues

There are a number of fertility clinics for women or couples trying to conceive. English-speaking facilities and services are also available. First you should go to a regular doctor or gynaecologist (see Chapter Three: Health), who may refer you to a specialist in a hospital or fertility clinic. Western women generally find fertility specialists in Japan to be kind, caring, and very thorough:

> *I used to be very sensitive about this in my home country, but in Japan my attitude has changed. I am much more open about it now. Everyone at the clinic is so friendly and supportive. We find the clinics in Japan to be excellent.*

Check the resources that follow.

The beginning of the 'Baby Paper Chase'

As with many things in Japan, changes and events are punctuated by paperwork. When a doctor has confirmed your pregnancy, you must register this fact at your local ward or community branch office. Take your alien registration card and the Notice of Pregnancy completed by your doctor. If you didn't get this Notice from your doctor, then you must supply the following information to your ward office:

1. alien registration card;
2. estimated week of pregnancy;
3. due date; and
4. name and address of the hospital where you received confirmation of your pregnancy and the doctor's name, if possible.

You will then receive the *Mother-Child Handbook*, available in Japanese and English. The *Mother-Child Handbook* will be completed by your doctor or caregiver and is a record of your pregnancy, the birth, and your child's immunizations and physical and dental examinations. I asked for both versions: the Japanese version for the 'official' record and the English version for my own reference.

You will also receive a small new mother's handbook and an envelope filled with coupons and more information; unfortunately this is all in Japanese, so get a friend to help you go through it. The coupons entitle you to two free pregnancy checkup tests. Be sure to hold onto these and show them to your doctor—pregnancy checkups and lab tests are not covered by Japanese health insurance. The envelope also contains a Notice of Birth, to be completed and submitted to your ward office upon your baby's birth. See Childbirth, for more information.

Prenatal check-ups

In Japan, prenatal checkups are made once a month until the seventh month, twice a month until the ninth month, and once a week thereafter. Tests include urine, blood pressure, weight gain, and ultrasounds:

When I was pregnant, I liked the fact that I could get an ultrasound every visit as part of my normal prenatal care!

As I mentioned before, the coupons you receive from your ward office entitle you to two free checkups. A 'normal' pregnancy and birth are not covered by the Japanese national health insurance scheme, but complications usually are. See the next section about the financial 'gift' you receive if you have national health insurance. If you have private insurance, find out whether pregnancy checkups are covered.

250

Physical health

With regard to physical health, I suppose that being pregnant in Japan is the same as being pregnant anywhere. If you are in Tokyo it is like any other big city, but there are many parks to take advantage of. Walking is by far one of the best activities to continue throughout your pregnancy. Other great physical activities to take advantage of in Japan are maternity swimming classes, as well as maternity yoga and stretching classes. Check the resources that follow. A few mothers found that many taboos surround pregnancy and exercise or activity in Japan:

> *Some neighbors had silly ideas like driving while wearing a seatbelt is dangerous when you are pregnant. Some people thought that swimming, biking, or being active while pregnant was wrong. My mother-in-law and others insisted that I should stay at home like an invalid for the first month after birth.*

As all other literature on pregnancy will tell you, don't eat too much junk, eat a variety of fruit and vegetables, and make sure that your changing nutritional needs are met. Pay particular attention to your iron intake, as anemia in pregnancy is common. See the section on Food in Chapter One where Elise gives some great examples of Japanese food that is especially healthy for pregnant women.

Japanese doctors tend to be rather strict with regard to optimal weight gain during pregnancy:

> *My doctor said I had put on too much weight. I queried his comment, and he finally said, "Oh well, seeing your blood pressure is normal, I suppose it is okay." My thoughts exactly—so why did he say it? I was very upset.*

Weight gain anticipated for Japanese women is 7.5 to 9.5kg, while doctors in the West say anywhere between 10 to 15kg is fine. There is a commonly held medical belief that too much weight gain among pregnant mothers can cause complications during both pregnancy and birth. Japanese doctors are reluctant to perform Cesareans, and prefer natural births, which can explain their views on weight gain. Keep in mind that you know your own body best.

Maternity wear

Unless you are blessed with a petite, gamine physique a la Audrey Hepburn, you may find shopping for maternity clothes in Japanese department stores to be somewhat discouraging. You'll probably find this even if you're not pregnant (see the section on Clothes in Chapter One). If in the unlikely event you find something that fits, most Japanese maternity clothes are a no-go unless looking like an overstuffed Hello Kitty is your fashion statement. If you are not working, or your company doesn't have a strict dress code, then sweats, leggings, XL T-shirts, and sweaters from Gap stores (found throughout Japan) work great. If you are working, you may want to take your measurements and get a beloved friend or family member to pick up a few maternity wardrobe staples for you from your own country and mail them to you. Catalogue shopping is another option, as well as any resale boutiques in Japan that have sizes for Western women. Check the Resources in the section on Clothes in Chapter One for more shops that stock clothing in your size. During both of my pregnancies I managed to go back to the States, catch up with family and friends, and shop like a fiend.

Mental health

Probably one of the most important things for a foreign woman in Japan, including a mother-to-be, is to stay connected with what you consider to be your most significant support groups: friends, family back home, your partner or your spouse. Staying connected sometimes means insane international phone bills. Be sure to investigate the many long-distance discount plans and services available (see the section on Utilities in Chapter Two). Being pregnant in Japan is also a good time to make new friends with other foreign women who are in the same baby boat, so to speak. With my first pregnancy in particular, I was constantly on the phone with pregnant friends. We talked about our different symptoms, babies' names, the 'nuts and bolts' of preparations to be made and things to do, and just how we were feeling about it all. The sense of solidarity, camaraderie, and support that I gained was invaluable to me. Check the Resources that follow for support for pregnant women and mothers. Chapter Nine: Women's Organisations lists some groups and the Mental Health section in Chapter Three provides a list of recommended therapists, should you need someone to talk to.

Working outside the home/ Maternity and child care leave

If you are employed full time in Japan, there are certain laws pertaining to pregnant women and new mothers. This may depend upon your company, its resources, and your employment status. Although you work full-time hours, you may be classified as a part-time or contract worker and if so, you will be ineligible to receive the same benefits as those classified as full-time workers. If you think you are likely to become pregnant while working, you should thoroughly check your status and any conditions relating to pregnancy and childbirth before you take a job.

You must be given time off for all prenatal visits and your working hours and conditions should be adjusted to accommodate rest periods. You should not be pressured to work overtime if you do not wish to. You must be given six weeks leave before the due date and you may request eight weeks. Women carrying more than one child must be given ten weeks leave before the due date. Note that if your baby is premature, then you lose any prenatal leave not taken. If your baby is late, it is considered that you have taken some extra pregnancy leave.

After giving birth, you are not permitted to return to work for eight weeks (or six weeks with a doctor's certificate). If your baby is born prematurely, you still have to return to work eight weeks after the birth, regardless of how much maternity leave you had before the birth. Mothers and fathers are entitled to one year of child care leave from the day of the birth to the day of the child's first birthday. Guarantee of income, your job, and negotiation of details very much depend on your employer, as one woman found out:

According to my contract, because I was expecting twins, I was to be granted fourteen weeks of prenatal leave, and the [usual] eight weeks of postnatal leave. My babies were born before my prenatal leave began. When I finally had a chance to go to the office, I discovered that since my babies were born prematurely, I'd completely lost my prenatal leave. It seems that they counted it from the babies' birth, not the due date on the note from my doctor. I tried to get them to make allowances for me because my situation was special, but they wouldn't budge, probably because my situation was unprecedented and they didn't know how to deal with it. At any rate, I was forced to quit my job because I had no idea when my babies would be out of the hospital and I only had the postnatal leave remaining. Of course, things might have been different with a different boss.

If you have problems with your employer or you are not sure of your rights, check out the Resources listed in Chapter Six: Working.

Miscarriage

If you suffer a miscarriage you should go to a hospital or clinic immediately. You may be required to stay in the hospital for several days. Your uterus will be checked and possibly cleaned. Check if an anesthetic will be provided. Counselling will not be provided, as miscarriage is seen as a natural process in Japan:

I had a miscarriage and the lead-up to it was a horrible experience. The doctor didn't seem to think a miscarriage was an emotional experience, just part of nature and nothing to be upset about. I had no place private to let out my sadness and that was very hard.

The Prenatal and Infant Death Support Group can provide support and counselling (see below), or you can contact the counsellors and therapists listed in the Mental Health section in Chapter Three. One woman found the Japanese practice of mizuko jizo to help her grieve for her unborn child (see Abortion, Part Two in Chapter Three).

Useful Japanese

pregnancy	*ninshin*		prenatal checkup	*shussan mae no kenkou shindan*
pregnant	*ninshin shiteiru*		ultrasound	*chou-onpa*
pregnancy test	*ninshin kensa*		weight gain	*taijuu zoka*
fertility specialist	*funin senmon-i*		maternity wear	*ninpu fuku (mataniti)*
Notice of Pregnancy	*ninshin todoke*		prenatal leave	*ninshin kyuuka*
Mother-Child Handbook	*boshi techou*		postnatal leave	*sango kyuuka*
Notice of Birth	*shussei tsuuchi hyo*		childcare leave	*kosodate kyuuka*
coupons	*kaisuu ken*		premature	*souzan no*
			late/overdue	*bansan no*
			miscarriage	*ryuuzan*

I'd like a pregnancy test please. .... *Ninshin kensa o uketai desu.*

My last menstrual period was ... . *Watashi no saigo no gekkei wa ... deshita.*

How much is a pregnancy test? .... *Ninshin kensa niwa ikura kakari masu ka.*

I'd like to see a fertility specialist. .... *Funin senmon-i ni aitai desu.*

I'd like to register my pregnancy. .... *Watashi no ninshin o touroku shitai desu.*

Could you give me a Notice of Pregnancy please? .... *Ninshin todoke o itadakemasu ka.*

I think that the date of conception is ... . *Ninshinshita hi wa ... da to omoimasu.*

My estimated week of pregnancy is ... . *Watashi wa oyoso ninshin ... shuume desu.*

My due date is ... . *Watashi no yotei bi wa ... desu.*

I'd like a Mother-Child Handbook please. .... *Boshi techou o itadakemasu ka.*

Could I have the English and Japanese versions please? .... *Eigo ban to nihongo ban o itadakemasu ka.*

Where is the maternity wear department? .. *Ninpu fuku (mataniti) uriba wa doko desu ka.*

Do you stock Western (large) sizes? .... *Seiyou no (ookii) saizu wa oiteimasu ka.*

My baby was premature. .... *Watashi no akachan wa souzan deshita.*

My baby is/was late/overdue. .... *Watashi no akachan wa bansan deshita.*

I think I am having a miscarriage. .... *Ryuuzan suru to omoimasu.*

Resources

Information and Support

Tokyo Childbirth Education Association

Information on exercise classes, literature, and midwives.

http://www.birthintokyo.com/index.html

Tokyo Pregnancy Group

Information, meetings, and speakers; leads on to New Moms' Groups. Contact number changes as new babies are born. Check with Tokyo Medical and Surgical Clinic (03-3436-3028) for current contact number.

Tokyo with Kids
> Website with extensive resources on all aspects of having
> children in Japan, includes information for areas outside Tokyo.
> http://www.tokyowithkids.com

Fertility Specialists

Also check with your regular doctor or the women's clinics and gynaecologists listed in
Chapter Three: Health.

Hara Infertility Clinic (Tokyo) 03-3470-4211
Narita Hospital Oosu (Nagoya) 052-221-1595
Odawara Women's Clinic (Tokyo) 03-3473-1031
Sanno Clinic (Tokyo) 03-3402-3151

Maternity Exercise

Local fitness centres, public health centres, and private health clinics also have information
about maternity exercise classes in your area. If you don't live near any of the classes below,
someone at these numbers may be able to recommend a class in your area. Also check the
midwives and birthing clinics listed in the next section for class recommendations.

Anne Millar 03-3715-1568
> Irish female physiotherapist. Prenatal and postnatal
> physiotherapy, exercise, and education classes, labour
> preparation classes. Hiroo or Nakameguro, Tokyo.

Ayumi Josan'in 075-643-2163
> Yoga. Fushimi, Kyoto.

Children's Castle 03-3797-5667
> Swimming. Omotesando, Tokyo.

Japan Maternity Aerobics 03-3725-0071
> Aerobics. Jiyugaoka, Tokyo.

Tokyo Yoga Circle 03-3582-3505
> Yoga. Aoyama, Tokyo.

Maternity Wear (mail order)

JC Penney Company   http://www.jcpenney.com
La Leche League International   http://www.lalecheleague.org
Motherwear   http://www.motherwear.com

Other

Elizabeth's Pregnancy Diary
> Diary of a pregnant Western woman in Japan.
> http://www.pregnancytoday.com/diary/elizabeth/

Childbirth
by Judith Sullivan

According to the Ministry of Health, in recent years approximately one percent of the babies born in Japan were born to foreign mothers. Despite the fact that Western women are often dissatisfied with the medical system in Japan (see the section on The Health System in Chapter Three), virtually all of the thirty mothers surveyed for this chapter recounted their experience of giving birth here as a positive one. At just over three percent, Japan has one of the lowest infant mortality rates in the world, as well as one of the lowest Cesarean rates at less than ten percent.

Where to have your baby

Most Western women choose to stay in Japan to have their babies, usually for practical reasons:

It costs too much to go to the US, and also to give birth there. With one kid already, it would have been too hard to go to the US. Besides these logistical problems, I was used to my life here by the time of my second and third pregnancies. When I was pregnant with my first child, I had just moved from Tokyo to the countryside and thought I would have less anxiety and trouble if I went home to give birth.

I decided to have our twins here for many reasons: I live here, my husband lives here, I have insurance in Japan, many of my friends had given birth here so I knew what to expect, and I liked my doctor.

The birth could have taken place two weeks on either side of the expected date of arrival. We wanted my husband, who had little vacation time to spare waiting around, to be present at the happy event.

If you're unsure as to whether you should give birth in Japan or return to your home country, consider factors such as timing, your physical and psychological support network, insurance in both countries, and where you would generally feel most comfortable and stress free. Western women who have had a baby in their own country and a baby in Japan generally found their experience in Japan to be more positive:

Japan was better. The US, in retrospect, was a lot of talk about natural birth, but, as with many things, that was more hype than content. In fact, the doctor was late getting to me, and didn't give the midwife (or nurse, actually, I think) as much leeway and authority as the Japanese doctor gave the Japanese midwife. The hospital room in the US was like a hotel room, and because I chose to have the baby taken away except when I was breast-feeding her, because it was my first time, my bonding time was about zero. And they kicked me out of the hospital after 36 hours, so I had no rest time, no time to acclimatize to being a mom. It was tiring.

Absolutely, I would do it again in Japan. Motherhood, on many levels, is exalted in Japan. Many Japanese women live for the moment when they become mothers. The system is completely geared toward maximizing that experience. Be coddled for your whole first postpartem week? Or get tossed out of your hospital bed after two days? There's no comparison. However, I had a normal pregnancy and delivery. If there had been problems, I can easily imagine the difficulties that could have arisen, not only because of communication barriers, but also cultural differences regarding treatment and information.

Birth in Japan

If you decide to have your baby in Japan, there are a number of birthing options available at various kinds of hospitals and clinics. Caregivers are available to assist you with home births. Generally, labour rooms at hospitals or clinics are shared, with a curtain separating each mother. It should be noted that hospitals/clinics with shared labour rooms are reluctant to allow fathers to be present. But most allow for the father to be present at the actual birth, except in the case of a Cesarean delivery. It is important to confirm this beforehand and make your wishes known in the form of a birth plan (see below). Most hospitals or clinics specify that mother and child stay for one week following the birth, with the baby staying in a nursery. Sometimes the father is not permitted to hold the baby. Check to see if your baby can stay in your room with you.

In Japan, the general attitude towards pain relief with a normal vaginal birth is that it is not necessary. Most Japanese women do without. The debate over medicated versus painkiller-free birth remains heated amongst Western women, who are deeply divided over this issue, as witnessed during my interviews:

I genuinely believe that childbirth need not be painful if the mother is open to it and tunes into her child. I read recently that less than ten percent of women in the States have their babies without painkillers, which totally shocked me. I am left wondering why they do not think of their child more than themselves.

After thirteen hours of labor, I had an absolutely normal vaginal birth. Of course I used painkillers. One earful of the Japanese woman down the hall doing the drug-free, let-me-suffer-to-prove-my-commitment-to-being-a-good-mother version put to rest any fantasy I had that I could do without.

Pain relief is offered in most clinics and hospitals if you ask for it, but it is not given as a general matter of course.

On the financial side of things, if you have Japanese national health insurance, you will usually receive a 'gift' (¥200,000–450,000) one month after your child's birth. Medical expenses for birth in Japan can range from ¥280,000 to more than ¥800,000, depending on the way you choose to give birth. Complications are covered by national health insurance. Ironically, a Cesarean is cheaper than a vaginal birth because it is considered to be a surgical operation and is thereby covered by insurance. Check the cost with your caregiver beforehand and find out what is covered by any private health insurance you may have.

You should investigate each birthing option and choose the one that feels right for you. There are a growing number of resources to take advantage of, including online pregnancy chat groups (see the Websites listed in the previous section, Pregnancy). Ask questions. Ask yourself whether you really like or trust your doctor or caregiver. Trust your instincts and do not be afraid to switch caregivers or change birthing options if necessary. Keep a very open mind towards your options and have a viable backup plan.

Japanese caregivers traditionally prefer natural birth methods, but are trained in other methods. Check before you decide on a caregiver.

Birth at a large or international hospital

This is the option of choice if you are aware ahead of time that you have specific complications related to your pregnancy:

I loved the idea of the midwife clinics and believed in my body's ability to bring life into the world without a lot of unnecessary medical assistance. I was not afraid of the pain and I wanted to bring my child into the world in a way that I thought was best for him. After two days of contractions and what is medically referred to as an 'arrested labor', I went to a municipal hospital for the first time and the doctors there assured me, "It's a big baby, but you can have it naturally." After two more days of contractions and vomiting and back labor I was half mad from pain, exhaustion, and fear for my unborn child's well-being. I screamed hysterically for a Cesarean. My contractions started on October 11 and my 4.475kg son was born in the afternoon of October 15.

Other mothers who are relatively new to Japan feel more comfortable in a Westernized environment, where English-speaking doctors and staff are available. Large and international hospitals also usually provide the option of an epidural, while small hospitals rarely do. Midwives cannot provide epidurals.

Birth at a small or state-subsidized hospital

If you do not have problems communicating in Japanese, this is a most viable and cost-effective alternative to giving birth in a hospital that caters to foreigners. All of the facilities, medical support, and resources are there, but are not available in English.

Birth at a small neighborhood gynecological clinic

This seems to be the popular choice for Western women who have lived in Japan and have either a Japanese husband and/or relatively few problems communicating in Japanese. An obstetrician, together with one or two midwives or nurses, runs these clinics. All prenatal visits are also held there.

The clinic put me on the oft-criticized birthing table, but only at the very last minute. Until then, I was in my tatami room going through my labor with my husband and son. There wasn't the 'naming' of all the natural things your body goes through, so I was less distracted in Japan than I was in the US by what I expected to happen, what I'd read about, been told about, all the phases, etc., etc. I just did it. Like a cat.

Birth at a midwife clinic

These are similar to the neighborhood clinics, with all prenatal visits conducted there, but the primary caregiver is a licensed midwife. The main difference between midwife clinics and other clinics or hospitals is the emphasis on a natural, active birth and the belief in bringing a baby into the world with as little medical interference as possible. There are no birthing tables and women are encouraged to move around and to give birth in positions that are the most natural or comfortable for them.

Home birth

Home birth is exactly that. Giving birth in the privacy of your own home where you are most comfortable, together with the support of a midwife who visits you on occasion during a period of time before and after the baby is born, as well as attending you during the birth.

> *Giving birth here was definitely better than my first birth in Hong Kong, but only because I got what I wanted the way I wanted it. I had to make some concessions in Hong Kong as I could not have a home birth there. My Japanese midwife was also much more caring, gentle, and respectful than my English midwife in Hong Kong.*

Additionally, you are advised to have a backup medical doctor and to have prenatal checkups with that doctor. I have not met or heard from a woman who gave birth to her baby at home who hasn't raved about home birth. They are more readily encouraged after the birth of the first child, if that pregnancy and delivery were without complications.

Birth plan

After you have read all the literature on childbirth that you can possibly digest in one lifetime, have decided where and how to have your baby and which caregiver/doctor will assist you with the birth, you should write a birth plan. This plan should contain all of the above information and indicate your preferences regarding all birth procedures. Arrange for this plan to be translated into Japanese so that your doctor, midwife, and other caregivers will understand your wishes with respect to the use of medication and other hospital medical procedures.

Birth preparation classes

These classes provide information about the changes in your body and allow you to give yourself a designated time each week, together with your partner if applicable, to prepare for the birth of your baby. One of the most worthwhile benefits of a birthing class is the friends you make. Seeing the same faces each week and having the chance to share what you are feeling, thinking, and experiencing gives you a sense of solidarity, comfort, and support.

A final word from one Western mother

Trust the doctor and midwife. Don't assume there is prejudice against you as a foreigner. In this situation, women are women and babies are babies. I think in life and death we all become one. Our feelings toward our fellow human beings are more similar at times of joy and suffering than at any other time. Since birth is both joy and suffering, we can count on the empathy of a midwife or doctor of any nationality.

Useful Japanese

to give birth	*shussan*	birth preparation	
caregiver	*shussan o tetsudatte kureru hito*	classes	*shussan junbi kyoushitsu*
labour room	*bunbenshitsu*	labour pain	*jintsuu*
Cesarean delivery	*teiou sekkai*	pain/discomfort	*itami*
contractions	*shikyuu shuushuku*	breech birth	*sakago*
epidural	*kahanshin masui*	natural birth	*shizen bunben*
gynaecological		general anesthetic	*zenshin masui*
clinic	*sanfujin ka*	local anesthetic	*kyokubu masui*
midwife clinic	*josan-in*	dilation	*bouchou*
birthing table	*bunbendai*	full dilation	*shikyuu kou zenkaidai*
home birth	*jitaku shussan*		
water birth	*suichuu shussan*	placenta	*taiban*
birth plan	*shussan keikaku*	umbilical cord	*heso no o*

Is there a private birthing room? .... *Koshitsu no bunbenshitsu wa arimasu ka.*
Can the father be present? .... *Chichioya wa tachiau koto ga dekimasu ka.*
Can a friend be present? .... *Yuujin wa tachiau koto ga dekimasu ka.*
How long is the postpartum stay? .... *Sango wa dorekurai nyuuin shimasu ka.*
Will the father be permitted to hold
the baby? .... *Chichioya wa akachan o daitemo ii desu ka.*
Can my baby stay in the same room
as me? .... *Watashi no akachan wa watashi to onaji*
                                                                   heya ni tomaru koto ga dekimasu ka.
Is pain relief available? .... *Itamidome no kusuri wa arimasu ka.*
How much will it cost? .... *(Shussan hiyou wa) ikura desu ka.*
This is my first/second/third baby. .... *Kono ko wa watashi no hitorime/futarime/*
                                                                   sanninme no ko desu.
My contractions have started. .... *Shikyuu shuushuku ga hajimari mashita.*
My contractions are ... minutes apart. .... *Shikyuu shuushuku ga ... fun oki ni arimasu.*
My waters have broken. .... *Hasui shimashita.*
Can you provide an epidural if
necessary? .... *Hitsuyou nara kahanshin masui o shite*
                                                                   itadakemasu ka.
I'd like an active birth. .... *Akutibu baasu ga shitai desu.*
Are the birth preparation classes in
English? .... *Eigo de ukerareru shussan junbi kyoushitsu*
                                                                   wa arimasu ka.
Are there English-speaking staff? .... *Eigo no hanaseru sutaffu wa imasu ka.*
I want to push. .... *Rikimimasu.*

Resources

Contact your ward office for information on local services. Also, check the section on **The Health System** in **Chapter Three**, as the doctors listed there can provide you with information and recommend a clinic or midwife near you.

Information and Support
Birth Education Services in Tokyo (BEST) 03-3482-0728
　　　　Early pregnancy and birth planning, preparation for birth,
　　　　postnatal get-togethers for parents and babies.
Childbirth Education Centre (see display ad, page 265) 03-3414-7458
　　　　Classes and information. http://www.birthinjapan.com
Japanese Nursing Association 03-3400-8344
　　　　Provides introductions to midwives throughout Japan.
Kyoto Birth Network 075-881-6385
　　　　Monthly gatherings, support, library, introductions to doctors
　　　　and midwives in Kyoto.
Nagoya Foreign Mothers' Group 052-802-7047
　　　　Midwife introductions, support, friendship, equipment
　　　　sharing, classes.
　　　　http://www.top-ip.or.jp/~lorna/mothers

Tokyo Childbirth Education Association
> Information, literature, support, introductions to midwives and doctors. Website includes many interesting articles about giving birth in Japan.
> http://www.birthintokyo.com/index.html

Tokyo Twins Group 03-3465-3880
> Phone support and information.

Midwives and Clinics with English-Speaking Staff

Aqua Birth House 03-3427-1314
> Active, water, and home births. Chitosefunabashi, Tokyo.

Aquariel 075-752-1634
> Introduce midwives, home births, mothers' classes. Kansai.

Ayumi Josan'in 075-643-2163
> Active births. Fushimi, Kyoto.

Baby Healthy 0297-58-3708
> All birth styles. Tsukaba, Ibaragi.

Fun Josan'in 03-3313-5658
> All birth styles. Suginami-ku, Tokyo.

Toyoshimasan Fujinkan 03-3313-5658
> Free style, active births. Nishi-Ogikubo, Tokyo.

Other Clinics and Hospitals with English-Speaking Staff

Aiiku Hospital 03-3473-8321
> Natural births. Minato-ku, Tokyo.

Gynaecological and Maternity Hospital 072-831-1666
> Natural births. Hirokata City, Osaka.

St Barnabas Hospital 06-6779-1600
> Natural, Lamaze births. Osaka City, Osaka.

Tanaka Maternity Clinic 078-851-2284
> Natural, Keiser births, others possible. Kobe City, Hyogo.

Tokyo Maternity Clinic 03-3403-1861
> Natural births. Sendagaya, Tokyo.

Ueda Maternity Clinic 078-241-3305
> Natural births, but painkillers available. Sannomiya, Kobe.

After Giving Birth
by Judith Sullivan

Breast-feeding

Breast-feeding, as you will read in virtually every piece of literature dedicated to raising a baby, is most beneficial because it provides newborns with antibodies that fight germs and makes them strong. Breast-feeding is highly esteemed and upheld in Japan. Medical systems avidly encourage it. Part of a midwife, nurse, or caregiver's job upon the birth of your baby is to help you with breast-feeding by showing you how to massage your breasts to stimulate milk production, keeping an eye on your progress:

My milk didn't come in until my last day. Until then, every nurse in the ward was kept 'abreast' of my situation; uniformed strangers kept popping around corners asking me how I was doing and giving me advice on how to massage my breasts to get the milk flowing. I felt very supported.

However, some Western women who have their babies in a hospital find the feeding system to be too rigid and exhausting:

Every time I went in to nurse I had to put on a face mask, wash my hands, get the baby, change diapers and write down if there was pee and/or poo, weigh the baby and write down the weight, wash hands again, then breast-feed, then weigh the baby to see how much it drank, then report to the nurse who would make a bottle of milk corresponding to the amount of breast milk the baby had drunk. Then I had to give the baby the bottle and try to feed it as much as I could. I disagreed with this system, but then found out that if I didn't give bottles, the nurses would give them when I wasn't there, so I did it myself. The whole thing was ridiculous, and with twins! I was in the nursery all the time and never got enough rest.

Whilst another new mom had to fend off the advances of a powdered milk proffering midwife:

One of the midwives insisted pretty strongly that I feed my son powdered milk on the schedule suggested by the manufacturer. I couldn't really blame the midwife; she must have been in her late sixties or older, so she's of the Western Medicine Is Best school.

One of the ironies in Japanese society is that whilst breast-feeding is emphatically endorsed, the act of breast-feeding in public is not encouraged and sometimes frowned upon. I breast-fed in ladies' rooms or in a quiet, secluded place with a towel or blanket.

Back to the paperwork

Following the birth of your baby, there are several documents that must be completed:

- If you gave birth in a clinic or hospital, you will have been issued a birth certificate. If you gave birth at home, your doctor will give you a birth certificate during your checkup.
- Report the birth at your local ward office within 14 days by completing a 'Declaration of Birth', which is available from the ward office. Your baby must also be named by this time.
- Also submit the 'Notice of Birth' that is in the envelope you receive when you notify your ward office of your pregnancy. This allows you a free home visit from a licensed midwife to check on you and your baby, and to answer any questions you may have. There is no guarantee that your midwife will speak English.
- If you are not married to a Japanese national, you must apply for an alien registration card for your child at your ward office within sixty days of birth.
- If you are not married to a Japanese national, you must apply for a dependant's visa for your child, via the Japanese immigration office.
- If you have Japanese national health insurance, your child will receive all general healthcare free of charge (including doctors' visits, physical exams, and immunizations, but excluding medicine) until the age of six. Visit the child welfare/healthcare section at your ward office and ask for an application for a free healthcare card. Depending on your income, children of single parents with Japanese national health insurance receive free healthcare until the age of eighteen.
- Notify your embassy of the birth.

Your general well-being

It is now more important than ever to stay connected. It is vital to maintain relationships with people you love and with whom you can easily communicate and reach out to. Maintain the relationships you developed with women from your birth preparation classes—they understand what you are going through. Groups for new foreign mothers are becoming more popular; check the resources that follow.

Don't strive for perfection. Admit it if you need a helping hand and reach out there to take one if it's offered. Many Western mothers in Japan are juggling the same daily activities that our counterparts back home are, but doing it in a foreign country adds to the stress. If you have Japanese in-laws, they may have urged you to stay inside and rest for the first month after childbirth and been a great source of support. If you have a good relationship with them, they will often be supportive throughout your child's infant years. There are reasonably priced services available to help you with babysitting or domestic work. Time for yourself is crucial to your mental health.

Something resembling a schedule is quite good for you and your kids. It helps to punctuate the days and gives everyone something to look forward to. There are so many wonderful local places to explore in Japan. I am a single mom with a three-year-old, a five-year-old, and a full-time job outside of my home, so my time with my kids is not nearly as much as I would like it to be. I try to make the most of every moment with them. We have little rituals: on Wednesday nights we go to an udon noodle restaurant, on Fridays they get to buy one treat from the convenience store, and on Sunday mornings we have pancakes and go to the park.

One of the best things about raising kids in Japan is that it is a safe place to live.

Useful Japanese

breast-feeding	*ju'nyuu*	Declaration/	
breast	*mune*	Registration of	
breast milk	*bonyuu*	Birth	*shussan/shussei todoke*
nipples	*chikubi*		
powdered milk	*konamiruku*	Notice of Birth	*shussei shoumei*
birth certificate	*shussan shoumeisho*	babysitter	*bebii shittaa*
		home-help	*otetsudai-san*

269

Where can I breast-feed my baby? .... *Doko de ju'nyuu dekimasu ka.*

I'd like to report the birth of my baby. .... *Shussan no todoke o dashitai no desu ga.*

My baby's name is ... . *Watashi no akachan no namae wa ... desu.*

I'd like to apply for an alien registration card
for my baby. .... *Watashi no akachan no gaikokujin*
tourokushou o moushikomitai no desu ga.

I'd like to apply for a dependant's visa for
my baby. .... *Watashi no akachan no kazoku taizai biza o*
shinsei shitai no desu ga.

I'd like to apply for an infant medical care
cetificate for my child. .... *Nyuuyouji iryousho no shinsei o shitai no*
desu ga.

Resources

Breast-feeding

La Leche League International 03-3394-4359
 Telephone support, monthly meetings, support groups   03-3410-6554
 throughout Japan.
 http://www.lalecheleague.org/

Viva Mamma 03-3643-0081
 Telephone support.

Babysitting and Home Help

Homeaid 03-3781-7536
 Maid service, cleaning, babysitting. Tokyo.

Japan Babysitter Service 03-3423-1251
 Babysitting. Tokyo.

Poppins Service 03-3447-2100
 Babysitting. Most areas in Japan.
 http://www.poppins.co.jp

Potpourri Kikaku 03-3630-1828
 Babysitting. Chiba, Saitama, Tokyo, Yokohama.

Mothering Centre 03-5272-3245
 Postpartum care, daily household tasks, bathing, childcare
 and breast-feeding advice, elder siblings' care, babysitting,
 housekeeping. Membership scheme: ¥10,000–30,000
 one-time fee. All Japan.

Tokyo Domestic Service Centre 03-3584-4769
 Babysitting, home help. Tokyo.

Tokyo Maid Service 03-3291-3595
 Babysitting, home help. Tokyo.

Playgroups

For more playgroups, contact your doctor, midwife, or any of the general 'Mothers' resources in this chapter.

Chiba English Playgroup 043-233-8253
Chiba.

Franciscan Chapel Centre Co-operative Playgroup 03-3401-2141
Parent-run co-operative playgroup. ¥5000 per month, ¥10,000 registration fee. Roppongi, Tokyo.

Kichijoji International Playgroup 070-5723-8330
Kichijoji, Tokyo.

General Support

EOS Family (ESSC) 03-3723-0565
Q&A service for mothers. Fukuoka, Hiroshima, Nagoya, Osaka, Tokyo.

Mothers Group in Kansai
Japanese mothers interested in cultural exchange with foreign mothers. Willing to help with foreigners' problems. Kansai. dkku@livedoor.com

Resources and Further Information

Japan for Kids: The Ultimate Guide for Parents and Their Children
By Diane Wiltshire and Jeanne Huey, Kodansha: 2000, revised edition. (Contact authors directly at Japan4kids@aol.com)

Field of Mugi
For English-speaking working mothers.
http://www.mugi.com/en/

Kids Web Japan
http://www.jinjapan.org/kidsweb/

Tokyo with Kids
http://www.tokyowithkids.com

TOHO Women's Clinic
5-3-7 Kiba, Koto-ku, Tokyo 〒135-0042
tel: 03-3630-0322 fax: 03-3630-1206 URL: http://www.toho-clinic.or.jp
I minute on foot from Kiba Station Sawamibashi Exit (Tozai Line)

Taking care of all your health needs:
gynecology, childbirth, skin care, general check-ups,
and well-woman consulting for all ages.
Experienced female doctors treating women from over twenty countries.

Adoption

Adopting a child in Japan can be easier than in your home country. Japanese people are reluctant to adopt regardless of the child's nationality, but especially if there is any doubt that the child is not one hundred percent Japanese. Most of the children are of mixed nationality, often Japanese-Filipino, and most adoptive parents in Japan are European or North American. Most children adopted in Japan are adopted when they are babies, within five to ten days of birth, with the whole process beginning well before the birth. Adoption is still very much a taboo subject in Japan.

There are two methods of adoption: through your ward office and through an agency. The process is the same for all foreign women, regardless of whether their partner is foreign or Japanese. There is a lot of paperwork, so it is easier if you speak and read Japanese. The ward office or agency can help you with this. Adoptions usually take between six months and one year, although in rare cases it can take longer—it is recommended that you be in Japan for at least two years.

Adopting through the ward office

You can apply at your ward office to be a 'foster parent with intent to adopt'. There will be a lot of paperwork and plenty of interviews, but no specific requirements such as marital status or religion. Most children adopted through the ward office system are no longer babies, and will have spent much of their lives in state orphanages. Brett Cocreham is in the process of adopting a child through the ward office:

> *Foster care usually leads to adoption, especially if you have built up a relationship with your local children's home. The homes organise homestay weekends, where a child stays with a family. We had a boy come to stay with us on weekends for a couple of years before we applied to be foster parents. The head of the children's home is working with our ward office to help us with the adoption. The birth mother can refuse to sign the papers for various reasons, including if you are a foreigner, which is the problem that we are facing right now.*

Adopting through an agency

There are several English-speaking organisations specifically established to help you adopt a child. These organisations are non-profit and rely on church funding or individual donations. Each organisation has its own criteria regarding whether they can help you adopt, but if they can't, then they will refer you to another organisation that can. Before they agree to help you, they will ask you about your marital status and how long you intend to live in Japan. Some organisations will not work with unmarried couples, lesbian couples, or single women. The organisation will interview you and any children you already have, and inquire about the potential grandparents' views on your adopting a child who is of a different race from your own. The cost depends on the organisation, but it is usually around ¥100,000, which covers the home visits and completion of paperwork.

The adoption organisations try to place children very quickly to avoid the baby being placed in an orphanage. Ricky Gordon of Loving Decisions, an adoption organisation in Japan, explains that:

As ruthless as it may sound, this is because orphanages are funded according to the number of children they have, and orphanages are reluctant to lose their funding. Ninety percent of these children are never adopted compared to the fifteen percent of children in US orphanages that are never adopted.

Children placed in Japanese orphanages are state-educated until age 16 when they have to leave the orphanage, and Ricky says they often end up living or working with the Japanese Mafia.

Final approval

An approved adoption in Japan cannot take place until the laws of the parents' home countries have been adhered to. This varies from country to country, and in the US, from state to state. An adoption agency can help you through this process. In some cases, the laws of the home country are complicated and can cause problems. Most adoption agencies in Japan cite the UK authorities as being the most problematic, because they don't favour adoptions taking place between children and parents of different nationalities.

After a child is placed, the family then goes to the Japanese family court to make a formal application. A Japanese social worker will be assigned to the family, and it may be necessary to find an interpreter. The court has to approve the adoption after the child has been placed, but it is rare that approval is not granted.

Regarding the child's nationality, if a child is deemed 'officially abandoned in Japan', then they will be given Japanese nationality. However, if it is suspected that one of the biological parents is not Japanese, then the child is given no nationality and is a 'stateless citizen'. In this situation, the child has no legal right to be in Japan, but no legal right to leave Japan. Once an adoption has been approved for two years, the family can apply for the child's citizenship to be officially granted, so the child can be taken overseas as a full family member.

Useful Japanese

adoption .... *youshi-engumi*
to adopt .... *youshi o toru*
adoption agency ...... *youshi-engumi*
                        assenjo
family court .... *katei saibansho*

social worker .... *soosharu waakaa /*
                                 shakai fukushi
                                 shidouin
stateless citizen .... *kokuseki no nai*
                                 shimin

I'd like some information about adopting
a child. .... *Youshi-engumi ni tsuite oshiete itadakitai no
desu ga.*
I am married/single/living with my partner. .. *Watashi wa kekkon shiteimasu/dokushin
desu/paatonaa to doukyo shiteimasu.*
We are a lesbian couple. .... *Watashitachi wa dooseiaisha desu.*
How much will it cost? .... *Hiyou wa dorekurai kakarimasu ka.*
I'd like to adopt a baby/child/teenager. .... *Nyuuyouji/kodomo/tiin-eijaa o youshi ni
shitai no desu.*
I need an interpreter for an adoption
procedure at court. .... *Saiban de youshi-engumi no tetsuzuki no
tame ni tsuuyaku ga hitsuyou desu.*

Resources

Agencies and Information
International Family Service 03-5377-1347
       International adoption, liaise with foreign agencies. No
       restrictions on the length of time new parents must stay in
       Japan. Single women are accepted. No religious specification.
       Serves all Japan and other countries.
Loving Decisions 0476-29-1816
       Christian agency. Priority is given to married, Japanese, and
       Christian couples, but they do place children with other
       families. Can help start the process of 'international' adoption
       where the couple do not plan to stay in Japan permanently.
       Serves all Japan.
Japan International Social Service Agency 03-3760-3471
       Must plan to stay in Japan for at least 3 years. No religious
       specification. Prefer a married couple, but unmarried couples
       or single women are accepted. Serves all Japan.

Support
Adoptive Parents Support Group 03-3264-4347
Bong and Brett Cocreham 0436-98-0480
       Foreign couple who have been through Japanese foster and
       adoption procedures and are willing to give advice to others.

Day Care
by Judith Sullivan

There is a commonly held belief that there is not yet a viable infrastructure in place to support the needs of the growing numbers of working women in Japan. From my own experience, what has been put into place is absolutely phenomenal, it's just that more of these facilities are needed to meet the growing number of working mothers. The other Western working moms I have spoken to seem to have the same opinion. What follows applies to the Japanese public day care system. For private or international day care centers, check the resources that follow and contact the school directly.

Environment

The children's primary caregivers are all licensed nursery school teachers. Any part-time staff are usually student teachers. The staff includes a full-time nurse and a full-time dietician who plans all of the children's meals. The children are divided into groups according to age and there is usually a ratio of one teacher per two or three children. Activities are well organized, and generally include music, drawing, free play, gardening, and outdoor play:

> *Staff encourage kids to play outside A LOT. The food they serve is very good, highly nutritious, and varied. There is a lot of freedom for the kids: they can play with toys inside, work on crafts, read books, or play outside. The teachers take them for walks around the neighborhood and occasionally on a field trip to the library or someplace nearby. There is very little turnover among the staff. My kids had the same teachers for two years in a row, which is very healthy for the kids' need to bond.*

The daycare centers are well lit, brightly decorated, and clean. At naptime all the children sleep on their own little futons, using their own sheets, which you must wash at home once a week.

Rules and regulations

Unless you are intrinsically an anally retentive person, you will find the rules, regulations, and preparation tasks a bit frustrating. Labels must be sewn onto your kid's sheets and elastic must be sewn around a towel for the top part of their futon. There are bags for everything: the pool, dirty clothes, sheets, notebooks, the hand towel, and shoes. Preparation tasks for children under two years of age are mind bending and include taking your child's temperature every day. If your child's temperature is over 37.9 they must stay at home. For me, the craziest daily practice is that everyone locks the yard gate in the regulation two places even though hordes of people are coming and going and picking up their kids. It's enough to make even Mary Poppins cringe. I choose to look at the anal retentiveness and compulsively regimented style like this: I have amazing affordable day care and dedicated loving individuals who truly care about my kids and are helping me raise them to the best of their ability. I can go to work each day knowing that my kids are in great hands. If I have to abide by a few tiresome rules, then so be it. It is a small price to pay.

Cost

This is based on your household's total annual income. It is quite affordable. I am a single mother who works full time and I have two kids in full time day care from 8:00 a.m. to 6:00 p.m., five days a week. I pay a total of ¥39,000 a month, and this includes lunches and snacks.

How to apply for public day care

Go to the child welfare and care services division at your ward office. If you know that you will be working following the birth of your child, I recommend that you apply as soon as you are physically able. Complete the application forms ahead of time. Day care classes begin in April and your infant must be six months old by April 1.

If you're married, then both parents must work full time for you to be eligible. Welcome to the Catch-22 of 'If you don't have a job, you can't get day care; if you don't have day care ...' Applicants are chosen according to their need: single mothers and those with no backup support systems have priority.

Useful Japanese

day care .... *takujisho*	public/private .... *kouritsu/shiritsu no*

Do any of the staff speak English? .... *Eigo ga hanaseru sutaffu wa imasu ka.*
How much will it cost? .... *Ikura desu ka.*
What does that include? .... *Sore niwa donna mono ga fukumarete imasu ka.*
I'd like to apply for public day care for
my child. .... *Watashi no kodomo no tame no takujisho ni moushikomi tai no desu ga.*
I am a single mother. .... *Watashi wa shinguru mazaa desu.*
I work full time. .... *Watashi wa shuujitsu hataraite imasu.*
My husband and I both work full time. .... *Watashi no shujin mo watashi mo shuujitsu hataraite imasu.*

My child is ... months/years old. .... *Watashi no kodomo wa ... kagetsu/sai desu.*
Is there a waiting list? .... *Jyunban machi no touroku risuto wa*
arimasu ka.
Which day care centres are closest to my
neighbourhood? .... *Watashi no ie kara ichiban chikai takujisho*
wa doko desu ka.
What are the opening hours? .... *Nan ji kara nan ji made aite imasu ka.*

Resources

Also check with hotels in your area; many operate day care facilities. Costs vary
considerably.

International or Private Day Care

Children's Hall 03-3409-6361
Shibuya, Tokyo. Accepts children aged 2–18 years, open
9:00 a.m.–5:00 p.m.
Entente Child Care Room 078-858-0655
Rokko Island, Kobe. Accepts children aged 3 months–10 years,
open 9:00 a.m.–5:00 p.m.
EOS Social Service Club (ESSC) 03-3723-1122
Throughout Japan. No age restrictions, opening hours vary.
Technically not a day care centre nor a babysitting service, but
a membership club that provides a 'second home' for children.
Counselling for parents also available.
Kids World 0120-00-1537
21 locations in Japan. Accepts children aged 1–10 years, open
9:00 a.m.–7:00 p.m.
National Children's Castle 03-3797-5666
Shibuya/Omotesando, Tokyo. Accepts children from 3 years,
open 12:30 p.m.–5:30 p.m.
St Alban's Weekday Nursery Program 03-3431-8534
Kamiyacho, Tokyo. Accepts children aged 2–4 years, open
9:00 a.m.–2:00 p.m.
St Marian International Nursery 03-3461-1050
Ebisu, Tokyo. Accepts children aged 45 days–6 years, open
8:00 a.m.–9:00 p.m., but longer can be arranged.
Tokyo Kids Club 03-3440-6816
Hiroo, Tokyo. Accepts children aged 3–12 years, open
10:00 a.m.–5:00 p.m.

Schools

Japanese schools

The Japanese education system consists of public (free or with some minimum costs, depending on your income) and private (fees must be paid) schools. Both types are based on three years of pre-school (ages 3–6), six years of elementary education (ages 6–12), three years of junior high education (ages 12–15), and three years of senior high education (ages 15–18). Only elementary and junior high school education is compulsory in Japan, although most Japanese children attend pre-school and continue formal education until the age of 18. The Japanese school year begins in April and ends in March. Children of foreign residents are eligible to enter both public and private Japanese schools. The following information pertains to public schools. For private schools, contact the schools directly.

Public elementary and junior high schools notify Japanese parents automatically when their child has reached school age, informing the parents of the child's designated school. Foreign residents, however, need to apply at their ward office, where their child must undergo a health examination. For public senior high schools, a child must have completed a total of nine years of school education, in or outside Japan. Public high schools hold entrance examinations in February, in Japanese, covering Japanese, social studies, mathematics, science, and English. There are a few public 'international' schools that have a different mandate and philosophy to other public Japanese high schools, with the curriculi tending to focus on languages and 'international understanding'. Students are mostly Japanese, but many are returnee and foreign students.

The Japanese education system values academic success and social conformity. Japan has an incredible literacy rate of 99.7 percent and 37 percent of school children go on to universities or other forms of higher education at age eighteen. Learning styles focus on the memorisation and understanding of facts and information, and students are not encouraged to question ideas or to express or develop opinions. As a result, Japan produces students who far outdo Western students academically, but individuality and creativity tend to suffer. The individual's responsibility to the group is greatly encouraged, as is the importance of group spirit, with students taking great pride in their schools and actively participating in a wide range of extra-curricular activities. The group is assigned more importance than the individual, which also contributes to a lack of individuality and independent thinking. Western parents often object to this:

As the years go by, [schools] *expect more and more conformity from the kids, they stress group activities, and input from the parents is not encouraged. That is what led me to finally take my daughter out of school after fourth grade. And in order to keep 'harmony', no matter how bright or how dull a student is, they all work at the same level. There are a lot of positive things happening in schools, it's not all bad news, but the positive things don't*

281

outweigh the negative, and you have to factor in your own child's personality in choosing how to educate them.

Classes are of mixed ability, with up to forty students per class. The teacher's role is primarily one of imparting information and discipline. That is not to say that teachers do not care for the welfare of their students; on the contrary, teachers will show concern as soon as a 'problem' arises and parents are usually encouraged to participate in the search for a solution to a child's problem. Teachers are well respected by students, parents, and society on the whole; they expect high academic and behavioural standards and usually get them. Although each school has an element of choice, generally the curriculum set by the Ministry of Education does not encourage a broad and unbiased understanding of the world.

Bullying and academic pressure take their toll on many Japanese students, with several suicides each year. Although the instances of school problems and juvenile crime are low in comparison with many Western countries, the Ministry of Education is concerned with the increase in juvenile crime and is examining different methods of education. Following the success of the new public 'international' schools, a few 'experimental' ideas are slowly being introduced to Japanese schools.

International schools

There are many international schools throughout Japan where the students are mostly children of foreigners, although some Japanese attend. Many international schools take children from elementary through to senior high. Class sizes are small, usually around fifteen students per class, and the curriculum may be based on a number of curricula from other countries. Fees are high and if your company has relocated you, then they usually pay at least part of the cost, if not all of it. If you can afford it, or if your company is paying, the quality of education is generally thought to be very good and what you would expect from a school at home. The main objection from foreign parents is the lack of education about Japan:

Many of my American friends send their children to an international school's preschool. I have a problem with that— they are not getting any exposure to the country in which they are actually living—there is almost no Japanese spoken.

Some international schools have more 'international' curriculi than others, so check carefully. Contact the international schools directly for information about admissions.

Alternative schools

There are some 'alternative' schools, such as Montessori, in Japan. Class sizes vary and each school has its own admissions policy, fee system, and ethos. Again, contact the schools directly.

Home schooling

Given the choice between a fairly regimented Japanese school system or an expensive international school, home schooling is becoming increasingly popular amongst foreign families:

There is so much time wasted at school. If you know anything about the way companies are run here, you can picture the way schools operate. Wasted time in meetings, boring lectures, busywork, getting kids to settle down and be on task together. I found home schooling to be the only viable option for us and am amazed at the demand for alternatives among the foreign community.

If you have the time and patience, there is a wealth of information and resources available on the Internet, including one new Website dedicated solely to foreigners home schooling in Japan.

Special needs

If your child has learning difficulties, there are some organisations and individuals in Japan that can provide assessment and recommendations, as well as educational and emotional support. As to whether a school can accommodate your child's specific needs, this very much

283

depends on the school. Japanese schools usually cannot provide for children with learning difficulties.

> *I'm sorry to say this, but if your child has a learning disability or Attention Deficit Disorder (ADD)/Attention Deficit Hyperactivity Disorder (ADHD) and is going to one of the schools for foreigners, don't assume that the problem will be detected and remedied. (If your child is at a Japanese school, I understand that LD, as it is called, is a dismissive catch-all for an array of emotional, developmental, and academic difficulties.) From my own experience with two schools in Japan and anecdotal reports from parents at other schools, there is, generally speaking, a surprising lack of knowledge and/or action in the areas of learning disabilities and ADD/ADHD.**

Check the Resources that follow for specialists who can test, support, and provide special education for children with learning difficulties.

Japanese schools are usually not 'disability-friendly'. Check with your ward office before they assign you a school or, if your child will be attending an international school, discuss your child's specific needs when enquiring about admissions.

Useful Japanese

international school ..	*intaanashonaru sukuuru*
alternative school	*shin-hooshiki gakkou*
home schooling	*jitaku gakushuu*
public school	*kouritsu gakkou*
private school	*shiritsu gakkou*
elementary school	*shou gakkou*
junior high school	*chuu gakkou*
senior high school	*koutou gakkou/ koukou*
entrance examination	*nyuugaku-shiken/ nyuushi*

I'd like my child to attend a public school. ... *Watashi no kodomo o kouritsu (gakkou) ni nyuugaku sasetai no desu ga.*

I'd like some admissions information. .... *Nyuugaku no shiryou o itadakemasu ka.*

---

*From 'When One Size Does Not Fit All: Learning Differences Abroad' by Margaret Stawowy, *Being A Broad*, July 1998.

284

My child has completed (number of years)
years of school education inside/outside
Japan. .... *Watashi no kodomo wa nihon kokunai/*
kokugai de ... nen-sei made gakkou-kyouiku
o oeteimasu.

Do you have many foreign students? .... *Gaikokuseki no seeto/jidou wa ooi desu ka.*
My child has learning difficulties. .... *Watashi no kodomo wa gakushuu nouryoku*
ni mondai ga arimasu.
My child has physical disabilities. .... *Watashi no kodomo wa shintaiteki na*
shougai ga arimasu.

Can you accommodate my child's specific
needs? .... *Watashi no kodomo no youbou ni*
kotaeraremasu ka.

Resources

International Schools

ABC International School (see display ad, page 292) 03-5791-4358
Nishi Azabu, Tokyo. Accepts children aged 10 months–4 1/2
years. Ethos: 'All learning through fun', art, music, movement,
Japanese, English. Fees: ¥120,000–630,000 per semester.
http://www2.gol.com/users/abcintl

American Embassy Preschool 03-3224-6796
Roppongi/Akasaka/Tameikesanno, Tokyo. Accepts children
aged 12 months–5 years. Ethos: to meet the needs and
promote the physical, social, emotional, and cognitive
development of young children, leading towards the growth of
a happy, intelligent child. Fees: ¥380,000–860,000 per year
plus ¥35,000 registration fee.

American School in Japan (ASIJ) 0422-34-5300
Tama Station, Tokyo. Accepts children aged 3–17 years. Ethos:
developing compassionate, inquisitive learners prepared for
global responsibility. Fees: ¥1,900,000 per year.
http://www.asij.ac.jp

AMICI International School 03-5454-9066
Komabatodaimae, Tokyo. Accepts children aged 2–5 years.
Ethos: English and Japanese international curriculum.
Fees: ¥1,300,000 per year (5 days per week).
http://www.amicischool.com

Aoba Japan International School (see display ad, page 295) 03-3335-6620
Suginami-ku, Tokyo. Accepts children aged 4 1/2–5 years.
Ethos: international curriculum and teachers. Call for fees.
http://www.ajis.co.jp

Aoba Japan International School Meguro Campus 03-3461-1442
Shinsen, Tokyo. Accepts children aged 2 1/2–6 years.
Ethos: see above. Fees: ¥1,600,000 per year.

British School in Japan 03-5467-4321
    Shibuya, Tokyo. Accepts children aged 3–13 years. Ethos: to
    provide a high quality British education within a caring and
    stimulating environment. Fees: ¥1,215,000–1,880,000 per year
    plus ¥560,000 maintenance, registration, and enrolment fees.
    http://www.bst.ac.jp
Canadian Academy 078-857-0100
    Rokku Island, Kobe. Accepts children aged 4–17 years.
    Ethos: based on the American education system.
    Fees: ¥1,072,000–1,458,000 per year.
    http://www.canacad.ac.jp
Children's House 03-3710-1160
    Meguro, Tokyo. Accepts children aged 3–4 years. Ethos: child-
    centred, thematic curriculum. Fees: ¥150,000 per year.
    http://www.tokyois.com
Child's Play (see display ad, page 292) 03-3460-8841
    Yoyogi-Uehara, Tokyo. Accepts children aged 18 months–
    4 years. Ethos: arts and crafts, learning through play, more
    academic curriculum for older children. Fees: ¥700,000–
    1,300,000 for a full-time program; part-time programs
    also available.
Christian Academy in Japan (CAJ) 0424-71-0022
    Higashi-Kurume, Tokyo. Accepts children aged 5–19 years.
    Ethos: Christian education for the children of missionaries.
    Fees: ¥910,000–1,380,000 per year.
    http://www.caj.or.jp
Evergreen Home International Preschool 0423-73-8166
    Nagayama, Tokyo. Accepts children aged 2 1/2–6 years. Ethos:
    international, students differentiated according to English
    ability, based on the American education system. Fees: once a
    week, ¥19,500 per month; twice a week, ¥35,500 per month;
    three times a week, ¥51,000 per month; four times a week,
    ¥62,700 per month.
Fukuoka International School 092-841-7601
    Momochi, Fukuoka. Accepts children aged 3–19 years.
    Ethos: American-based curriculum with an emphasis on
    nurturing, critical thinking skills, problem solving capacity, and a
    respect for diversity within an international perspective. Provides
    a college preparatory education for students who wish to go to
    American and Canadian universities. Fees: ¥600,000–1,600,000.
    http://www.worldwide.edu/japan/fukuoka
Gregg International School 03-3725-6495
    Jiyugaoka, Tokyo. Accepts children aged 2–7 years. Ethos: based
    on the American education system. Fees: ¥1,000,000 per year.
    http://www.gis-j.com
Hiroo International Kindergarten 03-3451-8477
    Azabu Juban, Tokyo. Accepts children aged 18 months–
    5 years. Ethos: based on individual stages of development in a
    safe, loving, nurturing atmosphere. Fees: ¥30,000–150,000
    per month plus ¥100,000 registration fee.

Hiroshima International School 082-843-4111
    Fukawanaka, Hiroshima. Accepts children aged 3–14 years.
    Ethos: international curriculum, enquiry-based education,
    friendly atmosphere. Fees: ¥1,850,000 per year, tuition
    assistance program available and dependent on income.
    http://www.hiroshima-is.ac.jp
Hokkaido International School 011-816-5000
    Sumikawa, Sapporo. Accepts children aged 3–17 years. Ethos:
    based on the American system. Fees: ¥490,000–880,000 per
    year, ¥200,000 entrance fee, ¥200,000 material and
    maintenance fee.
    http://www.his.ac.jp
International School of the Sacred Heart 03-3400-3951
    Hiroo, Tokyo. Accepts children aged 3 1/2–18 years.
    Ethos: Catholic school, but Catholicism is not stressed.
    Fees: ¥1,070,000–1,900,000 per year
    http://www.iac.co.jp~issh3
Junior Athletic Club (JAC) International Pre-Kindergarten 03-3445-6326
    (see display ad page 293)
    Hiroo, Tokyo. Accepts children aged 18 months–5 years.
    Ethos: encouraging respect for self and others, ambition,
    independence, responsibility, imagination, reasoning skills,
    originality, and self-expression. Fees: registration ¥70,000,
    tuition ¥32,000–160,000 per month.
Jun International Preschool (see display ad, page 296) 03-3334-8326
    Mitakadai, Tokyo. Accepts children aged 18 months–6 years.
    Ethos: a home atmosphere for small children. Fees: ¥95,000 per
    month (5 days per week).
K. International School (see display ad, page 294) 03-5632-8714
    Koto-ku, Tokyo. Accepts children aged 3–14 years.
    Ethos: enquiry-based approach; aims to make students into
    open-minded, caring people who are thinkers, communicators,
    and risk takers. Fees: ¥700,000–900,000 per year.
    http://www.kist.ed.jp
Kids World Preschool 0120-00-1537
    Over 30 schools in Japan. Accepts children aged 2–3 years.
    Ethos: music, movement, free play, the development of
    international minds. Fees: ¥55,000 per month plus ¥40,000
    enrolment fee.
    http://www.pigeon.co.jp
Kiwi Kids 0476-29-1816
    Narita, Chiba. Accepts children aged 3–5 years.
    Ethos: provision of an English educational environment
    within a Christian philosophy. Fees: ¥420,000 per month
    plus ¥30,000 entrance fee.
Komazawa Park International Preschool 03-5707-0979
    Setagaya-ku, Tokyo. Accepts children aged 2 1/2–6 years.
    Ethos: promotion of healthy development among children,
    focuses on healthy emotional development rather than
    academics. Fees: ¥1,108,380 per year.
    http://www.nn.iij4u.or.jp/~kpip/

Kyoto International School 075-451-1022
    Imadegawa, Kyoto. Accepts children aged 3–14 years.
    Ethos: education of the children of Kyoto's international
    community with an international curriculum and environment.
    Fees: ¥725,000–1,150,000 per year.
    http://www.kyoto-is.org
Marist Brothers International School 078-732-6266
    Suma, Kobe. Accepts children aged 3–19 years. Ethos: to
    provide a well-rounded education based on Catholic values, to
    stress the individuality and potential of each student, to
    prepare students for a future in a global society.
    Fees: ¥1,165,000–1,240,000 per year.
Maya International Preschool 078-842-6883
    Hankyu Rokko, Kobe. Accepts children aged 3–5 years. Ethos:
    find the individual in the child in an academic
    atmosphere. Fees: ¥285,000–295,000 per semester plus
    ¥60,000 enrolment fee.
Nagoya International School 052-736-2025
    Owari Asahi/Kozoji, Nagoya. Accepts children aged
    3–19 years. Ethos: based on the American education system.
    Fees: ¥1,200,000–1,380,000 per year.
    http://www.nisjapan.net
Nishimachi International School 03-3451-5520
    Azabu-Juban/Hiroo, Tokyo. Accepts children aged 5–15 years.
    Ethos: a dual language program for the international
    community. Fees: ¥1,872,000 per year.
    http://www.nishimachi.ac.jp
Osaka International School 0727-27-5050
    Mino-shi, Osaka. Accepts children aged 4–18 years.
    Ethos: providing an education in an international school while
    working closely together with the host country's culture.
    Fees: ¥1,050,000–1,550,000 per year.
Pacific International School 03-5481-9425
    Gakugeidaigaku, Tokyo. Accepts children aged 2 1/2–6 years.
    Ethos: based on the American education system. Fees: about
    ¥1,000,000 per year.
PAL International School (see display ad page 293) 03-5770-8166
    Roppongi/Hiroo, Tokyo. Accepts children aged 18 months–
    5 years. Ethos: free-style play, outings, crafts, music and
    movement, languages. Fees: ¥63,000–135,000 per month.
    http://www.pal-school.com
Peter Pan International Preschool 078-857-9626
    Island Centre, Kobe. Accepts children aged 2–4 years.
    Ethos: Montessori method. Fees: ¥18,000–36,000 per month.
Roly Poly Preschool 078-843-8101
    2 schools: Nishinomiya/Rokko, Kobe. Accepts children aged 20
    months–4 years. Ethos: Japanese/English international
    community. Fees: ¥650 per hour.

St Mary's International School (see display ad, page 293) 03-3709-3411
    Futakotamagawa/Kaminoge, Tokyo. Accepts children aged 5–18
    years. Ethos: similar to the American system, with an interna-
    tional curriculum, boys only. Fees: about ¥1,950,000 per year.
    http://www.smistokyo.com

St Maur International School 045-641-5751
    Yamate, Yokohama. Accepts children aged 2 1/2–18 years.
    Ethos: Catholic-based, but all religions accepted. Fees:
    ¥860,000–1,780,000 per year plus ¥280,000 enrolment fee.
    http://www.stmaur.ac.jp

St Michael's International School 078-231-8885
    Chuo-ku, Kobe. Accepts children aged 3–11 years.
    Ethos: British curriculum. Fees: ¥850,000–920,000 per year
    plus ¥150,000 enrolment fee.

Santa Maria School 03-3904-0509
    Nerima Takanodai/Iogi, Tokyo. Accepts children aged
    4–12 years. Ethos: American education system.
    Fees: ¥520,000–550,000 per year.

Shirogane International School 03-3442-1941
    Shirokanedai/Hiroo/Meguro, Tokyo. Accepts children aged 2–5
    years. Ethos: to provide a stimulating environment for children
    of all nations to learn and grow together. Fees: ¥1,050,000 per
    year, ¥100,000 general fee, ¥100,000 registration fee.

Tohoku International School 022-348-2467
    Aoba-ku, Miyagi. Accepts children aged 5–18 years. Ethos: to
    provide a quality education for the purpose of entering English
    speaking universities; international curriculum, based on the
    American system. Call for fees.
    http://TohokuIS.webjump.com

Tokyo International School (TIS) 03-3710-1160
    Meguro, Tokyo. Accepts children aged 3–11 years. Planning to
    expand to include older children. Ethos: international theme-
    based curriculum; non-religious. Fees: ¥1,300,000–1,600,000
    per year plus ¥675,000 registration and maintenance fees.
    http://www.tokyois.com

Tokyo Union Church Preschool 03-3400-1579
    Omotesando/Harajuku, Tokyo. Accepts children aged
    3–5 years. Ethos: learning through play. Fees: ¥678,000–
    1,615,000 per year, ¥110,000 one-time registration fee,
    ¥35,000–70,000 per year facility development fee.
    http://www.2.gol.com/users/tuc

Unida International School 03-3443-6850
    Ebisu, Tokyo and Hiroo, Tokyo. Accepts children aged 2–6
    years. Ethos: providing a creative atmosphere to encourage
    each child's individuality. Fees: ¥1,386,000 per year (full time).
    http://www.unida.co.jp

Willowbrook International School (see display ad, page 293) 03-5474-8334
    Nishi Azabu, Tokyo. Accepts children aged 22 months–
    5 years. Ethos: hands-on creative activities, interpersonal
    skills, emotional intelligence. Fees: About ¥1,500,000 per year.

YMCA International Open-Minded School (YIOS) 03-3635-1023
(see display ad, page 294)
Toyocho, Tokyo. Accepts children aged 4–12 years.
Ethos: American system, English with Japanese support,
strong academic programme with a Christian base.
Fees: About ¥1,000,000 per year, all inclusive.
http://www.ymcajapan.org/tokyo/yios

Alternative Schools
Ai International School 03-5419-9821
Minato-ku, Tokyo. Accepts children aged 15 months–6 years.
Ethos: international environment, enhancement of ethnic and
cultural diversity, based on the National Association for the
Education of Young Children criteria and the Montessori
method. Fees: ¥160,000–330,000 per semester.
American World International 03-5758-3858
5 schools in Tokyo. Accepts children aged 20 months–6 years.
Ethos: hands on, similar to Montessori, each child is allowed to
grow at their own rate, teacher's role is to assist. Fees:
¥1,100,000–1,400,000 per year, registration ¥70,000.
Little People Montessori School 090-1204-2565
Yoga, Tokyo. Accepts children aged 2–4 years.
Ethos: teaching children to help themselves, developing
enquiring minds, building confidence. Fees: ¥895,000–
1,135,000 per year plus ¥10,000 registration fee.
http://www.montessorijapan.com/littlep.html
Maria's Babies Society 03-3404-3468
Gaeinmae, Tokyo. Accepts children aged 7 months–6 years.
Ethos: British education system and Montessori method.
Fees: from ¥255,000 per month.
Rainbow International Preschool 03-3406-4320
Hiroo/Ebisu, Tokyo. Accepts children aged 18 months–6 years.
Ethos: Montessori method. Call for fees.
http://www.rainbowschool.co.jp
Seisen International School 03-3704-2661
Yoga, Tokyo. Accepts children aged 3–18 years. Ethos:
Montessori method. Fees: ¥1,020,000–1,900,000 per year.
http://www.seisen.com
Sunshine Montessori School 03-3452-4244
Minami Azabu, Tokyo. Accepts children aged 2–5 years. Ethos:
developing independence through child-centred activities.
Fees: ¥1,190,000–1,450,000 per year.
http://www.montessorijapan.com/sunshine.html

Home Schooling
Home Schooling in Japan (see display ad, page 292) 03-3993-4276
Support and networking for English-speaking people who
home school or supplement their child's education at home.
http://www2.gol.com/users/milkat

Special Needs

Educational and Developmental Intervention Services (EDIS) 042-552-2511
> All US bases in Japan. Pediatric psychologists, social workers, occupational therapists, physical therapists, speech and language pathologists. For children of the American military and government and affiliated organisations. Call any base and ask for EDIS to see if your child qualifies, or call the number above and ask for extension 59993.

Institute of Psychoanalytic Systems 03-3760-3631
> Meguro, Tokyo. Psychotherapy, play therapy.

International School Support Services (ISSS) 03-3710-2330
> School psychologist, remedial programs, individual education plans, tutorial services, educational and psychological evaluations, school consultations, educational consultations, child and adolescent therapy, distance learning.
> http://www.tokyois.com/isss

Japan Down Syndrome Network Homepage
> http://infofarm.affrc.go.jp/~momotani/dowj1-e.html

Knowing Is Doing Something (KIDS) 03-3787-6255
> Shinagawa-ku, Tokyo. Supporting children with special needs.
> http://www.bekkoame.or.jp/~suzuki-k/

Parent Support Group for Children with Learning Differences 045-942-5373
> Yamate, Yokohama. Support for children with a diagnosed learning disability. Meets in Yokohama, but telephone support available throughout Japan. Affiliated with Yokohama International School.

Ros Reuter 03-3479-9802
> Roppongi, Tokyo. Child therapy, behaviour and adaptation problems.

Support Group for Parents of Children with Special Needs 042-464-0401
> Various locations in Tokyo. Meetings, information.

Tokyo International Learning Community (TILC) 0422-31-9611
> Mitaka-shi, Tokyo. Educational services especially for children with developmental delays and disabilities and their families. Saturday learning disabilities program to support students in their regular schools.

Resources and Further Information

Educational Advisory Office 03-3580-2901
> Provides information about schools in Japan.

International School Website Registry
> http://web66.coled.umn.edu/schools/Maps/Japan.html

International Schools in Japan Directory
> http://www.jmarket.com/isij/

Ministry of Education
> http://www.monbu-go.jp

291

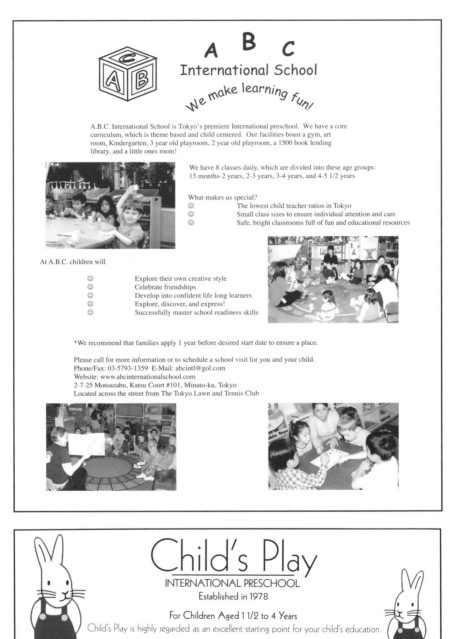

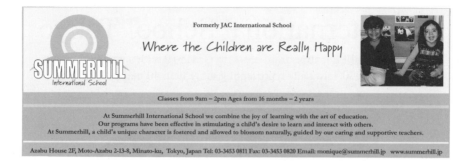

293

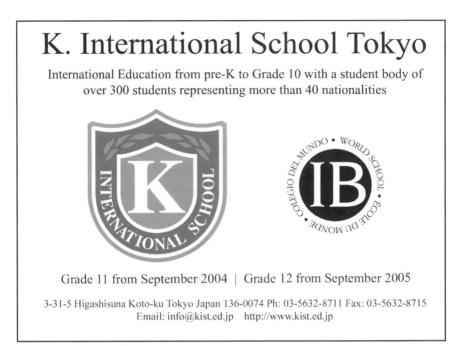

JUN INTERNATIONAL PRESCHOOL

4-25-9 Kugayama Suginami-ku Tokyo 168-0082
Tel/Fax:03-3334-8326 E-mail: jun385@dream.com
http://www.32.ocn.ne.jp/~jun_i_preschool/index.html

A happy child is a relaxed child, and a relaxed child is a receptive one

Jun International Preschool is a nurturing, home-like environment where children thrive and develop at their own pace. We believe that a happy child is a relaxed child, and that a relaxed child is a receptive one. Every child is different, and we strive to find the best way for each individual to absorb our English atmosphere. This includes everything from finding a playmate for a shy toddler to talking about space travel to a group of 8-year-olds.

A good ratio of teachers to children is adopted to give each child the attention they need.

At Jun International Preschool, children learn through play and various activities, thus enhancing not only their social skills but also their ability to express themselves and interact with children of various nationalities and backgrounds using the English language. In particular, through playing and sharing with others in a multi-age classroom, younger and older children can develop together. Jun International Preschool aims to provide an atmosphere which fosters your child's self-esteem, confidence and social skills, preparing him or her for whatever educational and social circumstances may arise in the future.

Features
All classes are conducted in English
A good student / teacher ratio (3-4 to 1 teacher)
Application can be made at any time of the year
Flexible schedule
Make-up lessons
Discount for siblings

Afternoon classes are relatively short but involve a variety of activities. We make extensive use of flashcards, letter cards and tiles for vocabulary expansion. They can be used in an endless variety of ways, from simple repetition, to guessing games and description exercises for more advanced students. Where possible, students are encouraged to make sentences, however short, and to begin to express themselves. They also learn to link familiar vocabulary with spelling, and ultimately reading and writing. Naturally, the aim is verbal communication, but reading is such a valuable learning tool that it cannot be neglected, so we try to include a little paperwork. This may range from letter and word recognition to simple comprehension exercises. Finally as soon as the student is ready, we introduce one-to-one reading practice.

Discover why T.I.S. has become the top choice for many families in Tokyo.

To nurture confident, open-minded, independently thinking, well-balanced inquirers for global responsibility.

Preschool — Middle School
Located in Minato-ku

Telephone # (81-3) 5484-1160
e-mail: tis@tokyois.com
Web site: www.tokyois.com

Working

6

Jobs Available

Whatever you did or would like to do in your home country, chances are good that you can do it in Japan too. Western women work as lawyers, accountants, teachers, sales executives, actors, etc. There are plenty of jobs available for foreigners and competition is fairly low. Certain professions, such as medical professions, require Japanese licensing, but the skills, experience, and qualifications you already have may lead to an interesting diversion that you may have never considered. Check the interviews with Western women in Japan that follow, to find out about a wide range of options you may want to explore.

Working in a Japanese company

Many of the interviews that follow are with women who work for Japanese companies. The Japanese work ethic is quite different to the Western work ethic and, much like the education system in Japan, the group is considered more important than the individual. For this reason you will find Japanese workers frequently working unpaid overtime and rarely taking their allocated paid vacation time. Japanese workers say they would feel guilty if their colleagues had to do extra work to compensate for their absence. Praise goes to the department rather than the individual, as does blame if something goes wrong, so you can see the benefits to a foreign worker for whom faux pas are inevitable. Meetings and discussions tend to be lengthy, and decisions seem to take forever to make. Japan is slow to change, but some companies show signs of attempting to incorporate Western work ethics with their own, partly in an effort to improve communications between global companies, partly because of their fascination with Western ideas. For you, however, the experience can be frustrating. Many Japanese companies are staffed by 'office ladies': female graduates in their twenties whose job basically consists of menial tasks such as photocopying and coffee-making until they get married and leave the world of employment. This can be frustrating for a Western woman to see, but you are generally not expected to be the same nor will you be treated the same.

In a Japanese company, you may find your colleagues to be rather wary of you, especially if you are the only foreigner working there. You may feel that you are left out from decision-making processes or other issues affecting your role in the company. Part of the 'compromise' in living in another country is learning how to deal with such problems, which may not even seem like problems to your colleagues. Confrontational approaches do not work with the Japanese, and you should not expect issues to be resolved overnight. Part of the reason that you may feel you are not taken seriously is more to do with you as a foreigner, rather than with you as a woman, and there is always the underlying assumption that your role in the company is temporary. Most Japanese workers stay at the same company from the day they graduate from university to the day they retire, slowly working themselves up the ranks. You are probably going to be there for just a few years. If you are patient, tolerant, open-minded, and willing to communicate in a calm way, then you may find working for a Japanese company to be a great learning experience.

The 'English industry'

Many jobs reflect Japan's need for native English speakers and for assistance in the globalisation of Japan. These jobs include English teachers, business consultants, copywriters, and translators. Many people with absolutely no experience in these fields often find themselves working at high schools, for publications, or successful companies. See the section on English Teaching in this chapter for more specific information about teaching in Japan.

Following is a series of case studies of women working throughout Japan, covering a wide variety of employment fields. It is interesting to see how many of these women are working in positions unrelated to their professional backgrounds, showing how working in Japan can vastly expand your field of experience. It is also interesting to see how many of these women have spent some time teaching English, either when they first arrived in Japan, or later to supplement their income. Many of the responses give a good idea of the general lifestyle in Japan, as well as working environments, so even if you have the perfect job, I'm sure you'll find the case studies worth reading.

Accounting

Name	Amy Mickelson
Nationality	American
Age	34
Qualifications	BA degree in accounting and psychology
Job title	Senior financial systems analyst
Employer	Boston Scientific Japan
Working hours	9:00 a.m. to 6:00 or 7:00 p.m.
Salary	¥8.5 million per year
Time in this job	6 months

Job description

I analyze our current financial processes and reporting, and try to streamline them to make our reporting more timely, accurate, and efficient.

General requirements

Financial background; high SAP computer system experience; Access, Powerplay, and Excel experience.

Japanese requirement

Not very necessary. Most of the people in the office speak a little English and I speak a little Japanese, so we manage pretty well. Occasionally there are meetings in Japanese that I cannot understand, so I give my thoughts to an assistant who translates them into Japanese. She does the same for the minutes of the meetings.

General conditions

Newer office building in Shinjuku, smoking only in break room, very small work space on one desk, no partitions equals no privacy at all, friendly work people at my level, a little hostile at the levels above me.

How she found this job

By begging and pleading and driving all the managers crazy. Before I came to Japan, I worked in the international finance area of Boston Scientific Scimed in Minneapolis, Minnesota. When I found out I was moving to Japan with my husband, I got in touch with everyone I knew in our international offices trying to find a connection in the Japan office. I finally hooked up with someone who needed a person to work on a tax project in Japan for six months. I started that project in July 1998 and completed it in December 1998. From December until May, I came into the office once a week to say hello, go out to lunch, and find out where they were with getting me another position. They were always too busy to work out the details of my position. Finally, this position became available and it was perfect for me. The Japanese managers were very hesitant, but with a big (!!) push from the US home office I now have a job that I like very much and am qualified for. The managers here are becoming less and less hostile.

Differences and similarities with this job at home

The use of technology is the greatest difference. In America everyone is so interested in making their job easier and more efficient. They take advantage of as many new financial package systems as they can, and try and keep up on the new technology. Here in Japan, where I thought the technology would be more advanced than the US, many processes are still done manually or on spreadsheets. My job has been very easy because I can introduce a very simple macro system and everyone thinks I am a genius. Change is very slow in coming and there is a lot of resistance to it. Another difference is that in the US, the accounting world is making a big effort to minimize accounting time to give more time for financial analysis. Because no effort toward higher efficiency is being made here, being an accountant is still many people's main function. There is no time for analysis work.

Best thing

The exposure to Japanese people and a lifestyle that I would not have without this job. This is what I came to Japan for and I have not been disappointed. I have made many Japanese friends who have helped me along the way: taken me to restaurants I would have been very intimidated to try; introduced me to new food, which I usually will try at least once; helped me with my Japanese; talked to me about their families, their lives, what they do on the weekends, where they go after work. I love it!

Worst thing

The inflexibility. Office hours are from 9:00 a.m. to 6:00 p.m. Lunch is from noon to 1:00 p.m. There are very few exceptions. I tried to lengthen my lunch hour by half an hour a couple times a week so I could work out and I was told that would be very difficult. The last two companies I worked for were very flexible. You could make your own hours as long as your work was completed correctly and on time.

Interesting stories

I am boring, nothing too exciting has happened to me yet.

Issues affecting her as a woman

I haven't had any issues. I have had a really great experience.

Advice

Be flexible, don't be too direct and try to keep your sense of humor. Even though I work for an American company, the work environment is not the same as in the States. Results are accomplished much more slowly and with a lot more steps and meetings than I am accustomed to. Half-hour meetings are used to discuss information that could be sent out in a short e-mail. If you don't get too caught up in it or take it too seriously, it can be rather amusing. Before a deadline, I find it very frustrating. It's just a different way of dealing with issues. I like to jump in and push ahead, where my Japanese counterparts appear to want to be more comfortable with the situation the entire way through the issue. I am not sure which way works better.

Recommended resources

Try to meet as many foreigners as possible. The network seems to be fairly small. In the past year that I have been here I have met two people who are headhunters in Tokyo.

Acting

Name	Colleen Lanki
Nationality	Canadian
Age	34
Qualifications	BFA Theatre Performance, Canadian Actors' Equity and ACTRA member.
Job title	Actor
Employer	Various
Working hours	Vary from 0 to 18 hours a day
Salary	Varies—from ¥250,000 to ¥700,000 a month
Time in this job	Full time for 12 years.

Job description

I teach movement at a Japanese acting school, do voice acting/narration and what they call 'modelling', which is really acting for commercials and 'character' print work.

Japanese requirement

Not necessary ... but it helps.

How she found this job

Connections, introductions. For modelling and narration, through agencies. I sent my photos, resumes, and voice demo tapes to all the agencies I could.

Differences and similarities with this job at home

You can have as many agents as you want here. It's a juggle, but you need to have more than one to get enough work, unless you are working under contract. There is way less competition for this work as a foreigner, especially if you are a professional actor.

Best thing

Fun, usually great people, the money, the flexibility.

Worst thing

The instability. The occasional manic pace and schedules. Narration: bad scripts with bad English that you have to say! Modelling: same shit as in America—the competition factor, eyeing each other in the waiting room.

Advice

Narration/modelling: come with a visa and a bank account, have a demo tape and a resume prepared, keep calling and faxing everyone, bring a book of photos of your other work (main types for women: mothers/business or career women/office ladies, and if you do character or comic stuff ... that too). Acting and acting teaching: be here for a long time, do your own work as a theatre artist, get to know other actors and directors, see plays, study, get your resume, as well as excerpts from any reviews you've had, translated into Japanese.

Administration

Name	Gabi Kimura
Nationality	German
Age	31
Qualifications	4-year degree from a German university in Japanese language and economics
Job title	Executive Assistant
Employer	TUV Rheinland Japan Ltd (100 percent subsidiary of TUV Rheinland/Berlin-Brandenburg, Germany)
Working hours	Monday to Friday, 9:00 a.m. to 6:00 p.m.
Salary	¥6 million per year
Time in this job	4 years

Job description

Support the local director (correspondence, business trips, translations), support foreign employees (housing, medical), office administration (printed materials, buy furniture, office layout changes/moves), HR (finding, hiring, training new employees), homepage (set up and updates, programming is outsourced), parties and special events (*hanami*, company trips, Xmas parties), special projects (research on establishing a foreign office, company brochure)

General requirements

Fluent English and Japanese, German a plus; good organisational skills; team work; common sense; and flexibility.

Japanese requirement

Absolutely necessary.

How she found this job

Was advertised in the *Japan Times*.

Best thing

Variety and new challenges.

Worst thing

Few advancement possibilities.

Advice

Learn Japanese, tread softly, make the Japanese staff your friends—you'll need them, try to combine foreign efficiency with Japanese tact, and be friendly but don't let people walk all over you.

Other jobs done in Japan

I worked for nine months in the Hilton Hotel in Nagoya as a waitress.

Advertising

Name	Anonymous
Qualifications	BA, JLI certificate
Job title	Senior Account Executive
Employer	Large Japanese advertising company
Working hours	9:30 a.m. to 5:30 p.m. (if you play it right, you leave when you want to, not after the boss has left!)
Salary	Better than I would be paid back home.
Time in this job	2 years (too long)

Job description

Handling two large international clients.

General requirements

Japanese, previous sales experience a plus.

Japanese requirement

If you want to survive, it's very necessary!

General conditions

Fairly crazy environment, the majority of my co-workers are here because of some connection they have, or because they are the son or daughter of someone important. Don't get me wrong, there are the odd Todai, Waseda graduates that are here due to their merits. For the most part, my colleagues are too shy to talk to me (well that's the excuse I have used for being snubbed most of the time); any work comes from the boss. Anyone would think I had horns sticking out of my head. It really makes me wonder how these people got into sales. Shouldn't they be good communicators? But as each day goes by I learn something new and exciting and, sometimes, something odd and surprising. Live and learn, as they say.

How she found this job

Foreigner connection ... 'When in Rome, do as the Romans do!'

Best thing

I work my own schedule, no one breathing down my neck. The freedom and flexibility.

Worst thing

The fact that I am not Japanese means I get left on the sidelines a lot of the time.

Interesting stories

I received a brilliant letter from a boss some odd years ago regarding ... wait for this ... the 'volume of my perfume'. It's a beauty! The number of times I have been tempted to send it to the press is uncountable. It goes like this:

"Dear xxx,

Very personal matter, but reported that everyone had been in trouble many months with your perfume; they say it's hard to breathe and feel dizzy because it's so strong. As you might know well, recently a tendency of Japanese life-style is gradually changing into less-fragrance life, so not only shampoo/rinse but also cosmetics are becoming less-fragrance. Therefore, everyone here is also not exception, and then they feel too strong about this case. So kindly reduce the volume of your perfume if you don't mind. I use to handle 'perfume Christian Dior' as a client, and so am knowledged about this line. So, I understand how to use it and meaning which sometimes appeal personal identity and image-building. But, just for your information according to a comment of Christian Dior's international marketing director, the best way to use perfume is that to apply slightly on some hidden portion of clothes, then after that person left if there remains a slight fragrance to remind of that person, that'll be the best. That's we call 'nokori ga' remaining fragrance, that's a elegance.

Thanks, xxxx"

Ahh, well yes I do mind. And, like any other normal foreigner would do, after a little investigation I found the old lady who sat in accounts to be the culprit. My next action, of course, was to arrive nice and early the next day and spray her little desk with a little 'opium'. Did she ever complain again? Oh no—it's all in good fun—you have to laugh at it. Really.

Issues affecting her as a woman

Yes of course, like any company that has a long history behind it, the traditional mentality of a male-dominated work place still persists. As a foreign female, I don't see me making a big career out of this. Having said so, my previous job in PR had me in the limelight.

Advice

Don't even think about working for a Japanese advertising company ... seriously. If you are keen to work in advertising in Japan I strongly urge you to find work in a 'gaishikei' (foreign) advertising agency. The opportunities are not there for foreigners on the Japanese side. You will be assigned to anything and everything related to English, which yes, has its advantages, but if you're looking for a career you'll have to look elsewhere. Of course, I speak from personal experience, but I also know a handful of other foreigners in the same situation as myself. I also strongly suggest you study Japanese. Speaking the language can get you into almost any predicament ... I mean Japanese company. Never judge a book by its cover! Talk to as many people as you can before making the decision to join a Japanese company. Get the nitty gritty beforehand.

Other jobs done in Japan

Part-time English teacher and I worked in public relations.

Art

Name	Julia Weston
Nationality	British
Age	29
Qualifications	HND Design, BA Hons Illustration, PGCE Art and Design
Job title	Illustrator
Employer	Various publishers
Working hours	Depends on the deadline—usually the deadlines are very tight and I end up working all night ... work is often unpredictable!
Salary	Illustrations can be used for ¥20,000 upwards depending on the use.
Time in this job	9 years, on and off

Job description
Freelance illustrator/artist

General requirements
Tenacity, good portfolio, some previous published work is helpful.

Japanese requirement
If you want to make it big in Japan, you definitely need Japanese!

General conditions
Illustrators can work at home, so any space is okay. Recently, access to phone, fax, computer, etc., is necessary.

How she found this job
Through taking my portfolio around and having exhibitions.

Differences and similarities with this job at home
There's more money to be made in Japan, and also as a foreigner the work style is different.

Best thing
It's great to be able to do something I like and get paid for it!

Worst thing
It's very unpredictable (that's why I'm also teaching to bring in a regular salary).

Advice
Go for it—the only way for people to know about you is through showing your stuff.

Recommended resources
Try exhibiting. There are free spaces, like Heaven's Door, which you can find in the *Tokyo Classified*.

Banking

Name	Sharona Kitahara
Nationality	American
Age	35
Qualifications	Previous experience in sales, banking, and 2 years LAN support experience
Job title	Japan Branch Manager
Employer	Microbank Software Inc
Working hours	Usually 9:00 a.m. to 7:00 p.m., plus evening conference calls lasting up to midnight.
Time in this job	Over 3 years

Job description

I run the Japanese branch of a US-based banking software company. I perform all sales, marketing, management, and administrative roles for the Tokyo branch. I am responsible for sales to all financial organizations in Japan and Korea, and I am also the Global Japan Accounts Manager, overseeing activity around the world with Japanese financial organizations. I travel quite often, up to once or twice a month, for 3 to 14 days at a time. I usually travel around Asia, but sometimes go to Europe or the US on business.

Japanese requirement

It has helped me to expand the business we are doing both locally and overseas with Japanese institutions. Although my predecessors spoke beginning or intermediate Japanese, I was hired in part because I speak nearly fluently. I believe our sales and profits have grown as a direct result of my knowledge and understanding of Japanese language and corporate culture.

General conditions

Up to the present time, the Japan Branch has been a one-person organization. This means mostly phone contact with my colleagues overseas, and a lot of time alone. We are now expanding by adding two more people.

How she found this job

I got this job from my predecessor, who happened to be a friend of mine. I had only known her about six months, and at that time, I really wanted to return to the US. When she first suggested that I take over for her, I strongly refused. Over a series of dinner meetings for the next two weeks, sometimes with my husband and sometimes without, she essentially sold me the job. She had correctly identified that it was not Japan that I was frustrated with, but rather my lifestyle (I was living in a 2DK behind my Japanese in-laws' house, with no private space of my own) and my job (I felt under-used and not respected in the hard work I was doing). My husband, a recruitment consultant, was in favor of my taking the job, and I must say, it is the best move I have ever made.

Differences and similarities with this job at home

I have not done this work anywhere else, so I am guessing when I say that it must be a lot easier in a Western country, where you don't have the language, cultural, or sexual issues, and where you also don't have the *'ringi' process to hold up every sale for a year or more.

Best thing

The perks, such as frequent travel and a good income.

Worst thing

The stress from: a) working alone, b) dealing with difficult and demanding customers, and c) having high sales targets to meet.

Issues affecting her as a woman

It is difficult for a woman to be respected when dealing with the older Japanese men in Japanese banks. In that way, it is actually easier to be a foreign woman than a native Japanese, I believe. See below for more details.

Advice

For a woman working in a) software and b) banking, it is not easy dealing with Japanese bankers. I suggest that anyone wanting to go into this work be fluent in Japanese, have an in-depth understanding of the Japanese corporate culture, and have a bottomless sense of humor about sexual harassment. For English teachers wanting to branch out, I first suggest learning some Japanese. Even if you don't speak it well, you can get English-language editing jobs in big international corporations, but you must speak some Japanese. If someone has other kinds of work skills from their home country, try to use those here, if possible. Teaching English can be a trap, as future employers don't often look kindly on you. I recommend almost any other kind of work. Take your resume to a recruitment firm, and see what they come up with.

Recommended resources

On Monday the *Japan Times* has job listings, but I never had any success with it. Networking is the best option—talk to others who work in the industry.

Other jobs done in Japan

Prior to this job, I worked for a large headhunting firm. Prior to that, I worked for a Japanese bank and a huge Japanese printing company, and my first job in Japan was as an editor in a Japanese translation and interpretation firm. I had two or three private English students during my first couple of years in Japan, and I also taught classes once a week at a Japanese insurance company for about a year. The teaching work was to supplement my income.

* 'Ringi' is the process of circulating plans and memos from department to department to gain approval.

311

Bartending

Name	Anonymous
Nationality	British
Age	27
Qualifications	8 GCSEs
Working hours	Variable—evenings until late
Salary	¥1000 per hour
Time in this job	3 months

General requirements

Smart appearance; punctuality; friendly, outgoing manner; ability to work independently and as part of a team; able to work evenings with flexibility.

Japanese requirement

Not necessary. It is my feeling that the Japanese customers enjoy hearing me speak English—their source of entertainment perhaps! A real English person! I think the foreign customers like me speaking English as they can connect and remember they are English speakers. If they have spoken Japanese all day, they can connect back to their 'roots' for a time. It's important to be able to say "I've had a shit day" without explaining the word 'shit' several times—kind of loses the impact!

How she found this job

Through a friend.

Differences and similarities with this job at home

Only in terms of legislation, i.e., hygiene and fire regulations.

Best thing

Meeting such varied, interesting people.

Interesting stories

I was not prepared for the attention and flattery I received (sounds narcissistic but it's true!). At first I enjoyed it—who wouldn't—but I soon became quite fed up with it. Getting into this thinking is not good for you, you can start building resentment. It helped me to be aware of some cultural differences, i.e., appearances are very important in Japan—you don't see a Japanese woman nipping to the shops for some fags in her slippers without makeup on—although I did and thoroughly enjoyed it! What I'm saying is that Japan is very different from Western countries and getting an insight into it helped me maintain my temper sometimes.

Advice

I found it most valuable to be able to connect with other Western women. I very often found myself feeling isolated, although there were milliions of people around me. This was quite unexpected for me, and talking with others with equal or similar experiences was very helpful.

Business Consulting

Name	Susan L. Benton
Nationality	American
Age	43
Qualifications	MBA in Management Information Systems, Certificate in Commercial Lending, 15 years banking experience, mainframe programming experience, project leader
Job title	Regional Manager, Asia Pacific Region; Senior Manager Tokyo ERS Office
Employer	Deloitte Touche Tohmatsu
Working hours	Officially 9:30 a.m. to 5:30 p.m.; unofficially—whatever it takes.
Time in this job	In Japan: 15 months. Length of time with DTT: 5 1/2 years.

Job description

Senior Manager Tokyo ERS Office: Provide consulting and IT auditing services for Tokyo Office clients. Regional Manager: Coordinate practice development (new clients, quality assurance reviews, training) throughout Asia Pacific region.

General requirements

Consulting experience—practical business management experience—practical technology experience

Japanese requirement

I am limited to English-speaking clients: I could be MUCH more effective if I were truly bilingual.

How she found this job

Direct transfer from the US.

Differences and similarities with this job at home

In the US, I have much more autonomy and MUCH more responsibility at my level. My US level functions approximately two levels higher than the equivalent title here in Japan. Much of the technology is similar, though there are still more mainframe shops here in Japan. The US has embraced distributed processing (usually UNIX) to a greater extent.

Best thing

The travel and the ability to network with peers from all over the world. I have truly become a global citizen. Oh, definitely rooted in US ideology, but much more sensitive than my US peers to the myriad different cultures here in Asia.

Worst thing

Here in Japan I am still hampered by the 'if a nail sticks out, hammer it down' mentality. Not that I get hammered down so much; because I am a foreigner, I get away with a lot, but my colleagues are SOOOO timid about acting in an entrepreneurial way.

313

Interesting stories

Well, since I have an undergraduate degree in music (voice), I have made great friends with my colleagues at work through karaoke!

Issues affecting her as a woman

My regional boss asked me this, and I replied that I felt that I was hampered more by the fact that I was a foreigner (and thus frozen out of a lot) than by the fact that I am a woman. There are more and more females in the accounting and computing fields.

Advice

LEARN THE LANGUAGE AS MUCH AS POSSIBLE! Also, since the Japanese like certificates, some sort of certification like Microsoft's CNE (Certified Network Engineer) or the CISA (Certified Information Systems Auditor) is helpful to have after your name on the meishi.

Recommended resources

Foreign Executive Women, for sure, and then the professional groups available depending upon your background.

Career Guidance

Name	Gretchen Shinoda
Qualifications	MA Career Counselling
Employer	International University of Japan

Job description

I help those graduating from IUJ in their job and internship search in Japan and Asia. I work on networking of IUJ Alumni, and I also work with the foreign students at IUJ to make their lives here as enjoyable as possible. TOOOO many jobs!

How she found this job

I am a graduate of IUJ and after 5 years in DC I was invited back by the newly appointed president to help with campus life issues. I was appointed to career counselling and alumni relations work after arrival.

Differences and similarities with this job at home

Counselling is NOT understood here. Having an MA in career counselling is a totally foreign idea. Internships are not a common practice in Japan. You name it, I have a challenge.

Advice

I am really a pioneer in Career Counselling in Japan—it does not exist here as a profession like in the US. No real advice to offer—but connections into whatever job you go for are crucial. Networking, personal contact, introductions, and an EARLY start are vital.

Other jobs done in Japan

English teaching (privately), and editing and publishing for IUJ's research institute (part-time).

Communications

Name	Lydia Nagai
Nationality	Canadian
Age	26
Qualifications	Bachelor of Arts, knowledge of HTML, Photoshop, and other design-related programs (all self-taught by the way!)
Job title	Communications Manager
Employer	Alberta Japan Office (trade and investment office for Alberta Government)
Working hours	Monday to Friday, 9:00 a.m. to 5:30 p.m., 37.5 hours a week
Time in this job	3 months

Job description

Website design and update, researching Japanese market for Alberta businesses and vice versa, speech writing, writing a bimonthly newsletter on trade and investment in Alberta, English editing

General requirements

HTML, advanced knowledge of computers, native English speaker, intermediate/upper level Japanese

Japanese requirement

Our office environment is English, but they prefer people who can function in Japanese.

General conditions

It's a government office of a Canadian province so it's smoke-free, big, and relaxed. There are only 10 employees altogether—eight Japanese and two Canadians, so it's like a big family.

How she found this job

The way it happened was quite funny because a friend of mine sent me an email saying that the Alberta Japan Office was looking for someone. It sounded really good, but I didn't get off my butt and didn't bother to apply. Then, about four months later, I needed a photo of a particular man for the Tokyo Canadian Club newsletter, for which I volunteer to write. The man was the founder of the Tokyo Canadian Club and he had recently passed away. I was directed to the Alberta Japan Office, which was also established by the same man. When I was there, the office administrator asked me how I liked my current job and mentioned that they were looking for a communications manager ... the same position that my friend had mentioned to me four months earlier. Apparently, the temporary person was getting ready to leave. It all kind of fell into my lap—just the way I like things to happen!

Best thing

Nice office, no killer hours.

Worst thing

It's an English speaking environment, so my Japanese is not improving.

Interesting stories

Once I got an email from Douglas Coupland, the famous Canadian author of 'Generation X'. Apparently he's into design and he wanted to know how he could ship to Japan a huge chair that he had designed (it didn't fit Fed-Ex standards).

Advice

Learn Japanese, it opens a lot of doors, volunteer for projects—it's good experience and it just may lead you to a job! All my experience for my current job came through learning while volunteering and through a few workshops. Coming over here with specific skills helps you to get a job faster, but the beauty of Japan is that you can also start from ground zero in a field that you are interested in.

Recommended resources

There is a women's computer group based in Tokyo called Digital Eve Japan that was a tremendous help for learning HTML from the very start and also with other computer-related issues. They have a mailing list—you can ask any computer-related question and someone will respond. People also post job openings and questions on other topics as well. They have workshops and events throughout the year.

Other jobs done in Japan

I worked for a Japanese MP who had a great sense of humor. He was always trying to set me up and once he even lent me his driver and car for a lunch date. I also taught English. I had a lovely private student who was 78 years old—she started studying English when she was 72.

Compliance

Name   Cheryl Rodriguez
Job title   Compliance Officer

Job description

There are regulations and laws that a financial company must abide by in order to maintain a licence to conduct business here. I select transactions, documents, etc., to test whether we are in compliance with the applicable regulations and laws. Very much like 'internal audit'.

How she found this job

I was working for the same company in London, and began working here in Tokyo on various projects. The nature of the projects evolved into my current compliance position.

Issues affecting her as a woman

Let's just say I feel as though as a foreign WOMAN, I face ongoing obstacles rather than creative challenges.

Advice

Go for it! In my experience, there are not many Japanese who 1) have the experience and initiative, 2) can look at the big picture, or 3) are outgoing, all of which are key qualities in compliance people. Much of the other key criteria (knowledge of regulations/finance/auditing) is often learned on the job or through training provided by the company. We are beginning to see an increase in the number of jobs, but not the number of people. If you have a legal background (studies, worked in law office or are a lawyer), or an auditing/CPA background and Japanese capabilities, you may be able to get an entry-level position (or higher) within a foreign company and move up the ladder. If you don't want to teach English, then explore. There are sooooo many opportunities out there, you can either take a risk and try it while teaching part time, or completely change fields. It requires patience, but there are many opportunities, especially if you have skills such as creativity, initiative, decision making, communication, etc. (read: basic common skills). The opportunities SEEM to be there, but it is growing difficult as more and more foreigners speak Japanese. Patience, and getting involved in women's groups will help. It's amazing how many jobs are out there, and they are not always advertised.

Recommended resources

I have recently discovered Japan Compliance Officers Association, which has just started up and offers exams on Compliance (in Japanese). In the past, I have relied on Foreign Executive Women (found a useful contact) and Women in Finance (for useful information on finance issues and some general contacts).

Other jobs done in Japan

Teaching English.

Cross-Cultural Training

Name	Meriah Hudson
Nationality	American
Age	26
Qualifications	BA (Education); MA (International Management, concentration in HR Development and Training); Japanese Proficiency, Level 2
Job title	Communications Specialist
Employer	Phoenix Associates
Working hours	Anywhere from 5 hours a week to 40.
Salary	Base: ¥280,000 per month. ¥4000 per hour overtime. Rounds out to about ¥330,000–400,000 per month.
Time in this job	8 months

Job description
According to client needs, I train from anything linguistic to job-specific. I also conduct adjustment programs for staff (in-house).

General requirements
BA; business experience, training in related field.

Japanese requirement
Not necessary, but like most other jobs in Japan, it's helpful to have.

General conditions
We often go to the clients' offices—that means a lot of traveling. We also train at our offices, but that is rarer. It can be hard work because our hours often revolve around when the client is available, so we can easily be working from 8:00 a.m. to 8:00 p.m. Tiring. Other than that, it's great. Lots of diversity, lots of different subjects. It's not boring.

How she found this job
The *Japan Times*.

Best thing
Client diversity. Diversity in training subjects.

Worst thing
The traveling required between offices.

Issues affecting her as a woman
None. I think it's BETTER to be a woman in my work—most of the clients are male and they seem to enjoy having a woman trainer more than a male trainer.

Other jobs done in Japan
English teaching, translating, modeling, ICC teaching.

Customer Service

Name	Karen Sieg
Nationality	American
Age	41
Qualifications	BS Mechanical Engineering
Job title	Coordinator of Foreign Customer Service
Employer	Sanwa Bank
Working hours	8:40 a.m. to 5:00 p.m., Monday to Friday, with one hour for lunch.
Salary	Less than ten million yen a year, but more than five! Not great, but not bad; I can live on it and save some too.
Time in this job	10 years

Job description

Basically I am a liaison between English-speaking customers and the Japanese staff. I assist foreigners with any banking needs they have in Japan.

General requirements

A college degree in any subject (for the visa), Japanese language ability, and lots of patience!

Japanese requirement

Absolutely necessary because that's the whole point: you are here to help people that aren't Japanese speakers.

General conditions

Actually it is really nice here because the bank is small, there's not a lot of people, there is a cafeteria/lounge room, they pay for my rent and transportation, and they give me lunch money. I think the general working conditions are excellent.

How she found this job

I was actually a customer here and used the Foreign Customer Service. I spent three months, full time, looking for a job and I interviewed for this position with the bank, then decided to go to language school. A year and a half later I was looking for work again and contacted the bank. I wrote a letter, but the person who interviewed me had been transferred to California. The staff forwarded my letter to him and he forwarded it to personnel. It arrived the same day that my predecessor handed in her notice. All luck!

Differences and similarities with this job at home

I don't know. I used to work with IBM as an engineer, which was very different. I now enjoy dealing with clientele as opposed to computers.

Best thing

It gives me a chance to meet a lot of different people with different jobs, purposes for being in Japan, etc. Also, they just kind of leave me on my own so, within the structure of the rules of the company, I have a lot of autonomy, which I like.

Worst thing

I don't get to take much vacation. This is very Japanese—they give me 20 days a year, but I'm never allowed to take it.

Interesting stories

In general the thing that I find most interesting is the dating situation. The company hires female staff who they think will be good marriage material for the male employees. They are then encouraged to date within the company, as the company hopes that this will be less distracting for the male employees and that if they get married, the wives will understand the pressures of their husbands' work. Another thing I find interesting relates to the company trips. We go away for the weekend to 'bond' and there are all these older married men and single young girls. It is all so innocent, but in the States no one would stand for that! "Bye Honey, I'm off for the weekend to get drunk with a bunch of single young women", "Oh, OK dear, have a good time." Nothing, as far as I can tell, has ever happened. Another funny thing related to the weekend trips is that at the beginning of each regular working day the other female staff and I all get changed together at work (we all wear uniforms). The girls all go through such contortions not to let you see their bra or slip, yet on these weekends we all sit in a bath together naked!

Issues affecting her as a woman

None, because this position is unique. There isn't anyone else in the whole bank that does this. It is not gender-specific—I am just a foreigner doing a special service. I don't feel like there are any of those issues in my work.

Advice

Learn as much Japanese as you can; talk to everyone; never give up—anybody can be a potential contact. Jobs don't just come from classified listings.

Recommended resources

Association of Women in Finance.

Other jobs done in Japan

Very brief English teaching and a three-week job as cosmetics promotions staff.

Dancing

Name	Shauna Stewart
Nationality	Canadian
Age	22
Qualifications	1999 Honours Graduate of the Theatre-Dance Program at Ryerson Polytechnic University in Toronto, Ontario, Canada. Trained in ballet, tap, jazz, voice, and acting.
Job title	Performer (Sometimes when you say that you are a 'dancer' people think that you mean 'stripper'. I am not a stripper, so I find that 'performer' works better.)
Working hours	4–6 shows a day, five days a week. Day shows are about a half hour long, and evening shows are about an hour. I am usually at work for six and a half-hours.
Salary	About ¥3.6 million per year
Time in this job	1 year

Job description

When I first arrived we went into rehearsal for about a month, eight hours a day, learning choreography and songs for the shows that I am in. Now I come in to work, put my makeup and fake eyelashes on, warm up my body and my voice for about forty minutes, and then do the shows. Each show involves three costume changes (we have dressers to help us), we wear a wig, and dance in character shoes. Each show will run for either a half-hour or an hour and the time in between each show is to be used how we wish. My job is to ENTERTAIN, to make people happy, and to impress them. I sing, dance, and act for this job; one wouldn't always use each of these mediums, but this contract requires all three.

General requirements

You need to be trained in dance with performance experience. The audition involved learning a jazz combination in a room full of over one hundred people. The choreographer taught the choreography, we 'ran it' a couple of times and then we were split into groups of four so that the staff could see us. The first cut was made after this; we were put into groups again and asked to do the combination once or twice more. More cuts were made and those left were taught a ballet combination. More cuts were made and then we were taught choreography specific to the show that we would be performing in. You also have to be over 18 years of age.

Japanese requirement

Hardly necessary at all.

General conditions

At this particular venue the conditions are wonderful—this isn't typical of a performance job, but I have been very fortunate.

How she found this job

While I was at Ryerson a friend of mine mentioned that she was going to this audition and asked if I would like to join her. I did and I got it! There was an audition tour that went to a number of places all over the States and to Canada (I auditioned in Toronto).

Differences and similarities with this job at home

Things are a little better here because, unlike at home, they provide accommodation for us. Everything here is completely set up for us.

Best thing

The fact that it got me here. Travel fascinates me and I can't think of a better way to do it. My schedule allows me to get out and see Japan as well as to get involved in many activities. I take Japanese, Aikido, and singing lessons; I volunteer, and organise talent shows.

Worst thing

This particular job does not lend itself to much in the way of creative input as all the choreography is already set. That is not true of this industry as a whole, but I am currently working in the commercial sector so I can expect more money but less room for creativity and contribution. The injuries can be frightening as well—this career can only go on for so long and you have to be very intelligent in how you treat your body, your 'instrument' as is so often said.

Interesting stories

Being foreigners in Japan I think that we all feel special and that we are stared at—sometimes with my job it goes even further with people wanting my autograph! I've signed blown up pictures of myself on occasion, which is pretty flattering.

Issues affecting her as a woman

Being a performer, there are the ever-present physical appearance issues, whether it be concerning body weight, how attractive one is, and so on. However, I do not believe that being a dancer gives an individual an eating disorder. I believe that there are certain qualities in a person that draws them to the performing arts and that some of those qualities could lead a person to self-destruction if they are so predisposed.

Advice

BE CAREFUL!!! I am lucky because I know that my company is legit. It is affiliated with an American company, so I don't have to be concerned about some of the things I have heard about here. Most of the foreigners who work at my company were hired in North America, very rarely are they hired while in Japan. The best thing to do would be to take lessons in the areas that you are interested in. Go to dance studios, take the classes that are offered, get to know the people who are in the industry already. Don't try to find work out of a classified ad unless you are interested in stripping or the other services they offer. Take singing lessons; teachers have often found jobs themselves and are willing to get you in touch with people. Go to performances and talk with the performers and the choreographer, find out where they take classes and start taking them at the same places they do.

Design

Name	Anonymous
Nationality	American
Age	31
Qualifications	Art scholarships, BA, minor in Japanese, minor in Fine Arts. I received a scholarship to study art in Japan.
Job title	Art Director
Working hours	I'm paid to work from 9:00 a.m. to 6:00 p.m., but usually I get there early, stay late, and don't take lunch. It's probably a ten-hour day.
Salary	¥6.5 million per year (not much) and half my (private) health insurance. I also get a bonus based on how much they think I'm worth, they pay for courses and networking meetings I attend. They sent me to the States for a course as well. They also give me software and hardware whenever I need it. There are a lot of perks, so the salary is actually higher and I'm benefitting in terms of my professional development.
Time in this job	6 months

Job description
Update the website daily; control all visuals that come through the office or are going to the press; design, photography, video, and print management; responsible for outsourcing; and oversee a couple of people.

General requirements
Some HTML knowledge; fluency with PageMaker, Photoshop, and Illustrator (be a super expert to the point where you can teach people); and writing experience.

Japanese requirement
More necessary than it was in my previous job. My coworkers are completely bilingual. I'm probably the least bilingual in the office.

General conditions
Excellent, extremely high profile, amazing networking possibilities, a lot of respect.

How she found this job
They found me. A friend referred me, I wasn't interested, and they pursued me.

Differences and similarities with this job at home
I would say for exposure, networking, and high profile, it's more than I would get in the United States. There's not such an intensely focused group in any city I can think of. If I were at home I might be working with other designers, but here I'm working with CEOs. The money isn't as good as at home. I would be making a six-figure salary doing this kind of work at home. Considering I have only about six years' experience and the position

I'm in, I'm very lucky. The competition is not as ferocious here—there are only a handful of other foreign women designers. I don't know that many foreign men.

Best thing

The combination of people I work with and the quality of work I get to do. I mean, it's not like designing flyers for a bar or café—it's a different sphere altogether.

Worst thing

I could use an assistant! I'm their first designer and they're beginning to realize how much they need one. I have about twenty projects on at one time.

Interesting stories

Besides being sent off to the States? That was a dream come true for me. In my last job I had to beg for software. It was a terrible place to work.

Issues affecting her as a woman

I am the only foreign woman in the office. There's one female manager. Most of the managers are men. I brought it up with my boss, so I'm not worried about it. They treat me so well—it's in their best interest to keep treating me well anyway!

Advice

If you haven't already got a portfolio, do some jobs for free—and create a portfolio of what you would do if you could, one for Nike, for example. You have to put in a lot of money to buy equipment. At some point you have to stop doing work for free because you get burned out and have to get your money back.

Recommended resources

I found my first job in a newspaper. Make a kick-ass resume—I sent out a hundred. Go through the English Yellow Pages and target whatever kind of company you are interested in. Once you get out there and get the jobs, people notice you and you get others. The Forum for Corporate Communications (FCC) is really good for networking.

Other jobs done in Japan

I've taught junior high and university. At junior high when I got engaged they dropped my salary—they said I would need more time at home and there was no discussion about it. I taught myself design from scratch during the part-time university work.

325

Editing

Name	Kristen Elsby
Nationality	New Zealander
Age	30
Qualifications	BA (Art History/Social Anthropology), Post Graduate Diploma of Arts (Art Curatorship/Museum Management)
Job title	Editor/Dissemination Coordinator
Employer	United Nations University/Institute of Advanced Studies
Working hours	Usually 9:30 a.m. to 5:30 p.m., Monday to Friday
Salary	¥4.2 million per year
Time in this job	8 months

Job description

Manage production of public information materials; coordinate dissemination of all materials through print and electronic media; coordinate maintenance of Website (English and Japanese); develop strategies to improve editorial and dissemination processes; day-to-day management of editorial and dissemination development.

General requirements

Native English speaker; strong information distribution/dissemination, editing background.

Japanese requirement

Not necessary, but helpful.

General conditions

30 days annual leave, 10 national holidays, 7 days sick leave, tax-free salary

How she found this job

In the *Japan Times*.

Best thing

A flexible environment with a lot of responsibility; results-oriented work style; and an organisational philosophy that focuses on the advancement of cutting edge ideas of global concern—a job that actually feels meaningful!

Worst thing

Because it's a university, sometimes decision-making processes are very long and drawn out (there can be a lot of red tape to overcome).

Issues affecting her as a woman

Extreme imbalance between male and female faculty staff, i.e., approximately 80 percent male, 20 percent female.

Recommended resources

SWET (Society of Writers, Editors and Translators), FEW (Foreign Executive Women), and Digital Eve Japan.

326

Education Consulting

Name	June Wai
Nationality	American
Age	26
Qualifications	BA in psychology/education, currently MA candidate in TESOL
Job title	Foreign Consultant (FC)
Employer	Yokohama Municipal Board of Education, Education Center
Working hours	8:45 a.m. to 5:00 p.m., Monday to Friday
Salary	¥4.8 million per year
Time in this job	6 months

Job description

Prepare, conduct and evaluate weekly training seminars, assist in producing weekly listening programs (on tape), assist in producing activity plans/materials for JHS and SHS classes, assist in educational research, observe and teach ES/JHS/SHS classes.

General requirements

2+ years experience teaching in Japanese public schools, teacher training experience, conversational Japanese

Japanese requirement

Not necessary for the job's main responsibilities and not needed for anything else besides answering phones and doing administrative stuff with the main Japanese-staffed office.

How she found this job

It was advertised in the *Japan Times*, Monday edition.

Differences and similarities with this job at home

Differences: (1) Qualifications for my current job in Japan seem easier to meet. (2) What's hot now in Japan, in terms of educational trends/theory, feels 'imported' from what was in vogue in the U.S. decades ago. (3) As my job-related resources are mostly from abroad, or are in Japanese, English-language resources I need for my job are relatively harder to access. (4) The salary for a young thing like me probably is much better in Japan than what I could be earning back in the U.S., I think. Not sure, because I've never looked into this kind of job back home. Similarities: educational resources are limited due to budget cuts.

Best thing

The responsibilities—I feel like I'm actually contributing something.

Worst thing

Being asked to clean the office fish tank. But, luckily, no one tried to coerce me to do it after I ever so graciously declined.

Interesting stories

Well, one that I can remember has to do with what I consider a form of sexual harassment (offensive pictures). Maybe I'm imposing my own American definition of sexual harassment on an Australian colleague, but American, Australian or Japanese, the kind of picture I'm referring to would be considered out-of-place in an education office by most people, not just by me.

Issues affecting her as a woman

See above.

Advice

Whenever possible, raise awareness about human rights (not just women's rights); educate students, teachers, administrators, etc. If the scope is limited to 'women's rights' fewer people feel involved. Human rights pull in more supporters. Just a reminder, rather than advice: Sex discrimination doesn't come from Japanese men only, or even from Japanese women. Don't let it shock you when foreign men and women (whom you might think 'should know better') show prejudice also.

Recommended resources

Deborah Tannen's publications (although I would recommend them to anybody working in any field, anywhere), The Ministry of Education's web site, any Internet-based job listings (Ohayo-sensei, ELT News, etc.).

Other jobs done in Japan

Before starting work at the Yokohama BOE, I was on the Japan Exchange and Teaching (JET) Program (as an Assistant Language Teacher). I taught English in senior high, junior high, and elementary schools in Saitama Prefecture. I also worked at a similar education center job, doing pretty much the same stuff I do now (training teachers) in Saitama. I also did some private English tutoring and community class teaching. I guess my work has always centered on education. Very boring, huh? I wish I could say I was something exciting like a 'T-shirt slogan proofreader' or 'tissuepack pusher'.

Fashion

Name	Lisa George
Nationality	British
Qualifications	12 years in Fashion, retail and production combined
Job title	Visual Merchandiser or Window Dresser
Employer	Various
Salary	One client at present, ¥3,720,000 per annum
Time in this job	2 months

Job description

To organise the J & M Davidson collection within various shops and concessions in central Tokyo, ensuring that mannequins, window displays, and interior shop displays are in keeping with the look for the season. To schedule, tally cost, and design and make props window for the company's own mixed brand shop in Nishi Azabu. Proofread faxes Monday through Friday via email.

General requirements

Understanding of British and European labels.

Japanese requirement

None.

General conditions

Work mostly alone except when merchandising. Work from home.

How she found this job

Initially advertised in National Azabu Supermarket some three years ago.

Best thing

Being my own boss and working from home.

Worst thing

Not being taken seriously. Having to change and redraft ideas for the windows three or four times due to changed minds and delayed deliveries.

Interesting stories

This is a story about a bully, fear, and tradition. I used to work full time as a nonregular member of staff within a fashion company—who shall remain nameless. In general, the staff were a fashion orientated bunch who took a certain pride in their appearance, wearing the latest designs and hair styles. While working there I was included in the various customary parties. An annual occurrence is the 'shinnyu shain' party, to welcome graduates and others who recently commenced work. On one such occasion, we gathered at Bamboo in Omotesando. The layout of the restaurant is not exactly party friendly, with rooms and coves dividing the people. The freshmen were giving their speeches during a buffet style supper, and everyone was quietly listening to the new voices introducing themselves and

329

the intermittent whining of the PA system. The President arrived late, was supplied with food and drink, and quickly immersed himself in the party by downing rapidly several small glasses of beer. While wandering amongst his staff, he located a group of young men engaged in a discussion. Furious that they were ignoring the newcomers' speeches, the President insisted they stand—which they did. They offered excuses, but the President flew into a rage and hit two of the young men: one with a slap across the head and the other with a blow to the chest. The latter offered words of apology, only to have the scruff of his collar grabbed and, while a fury of words sprang from the President's lips, he pushed the young man in question backwards. Then backing away, he issued the order that they involve themselves. The President resumed milling amongst staff, redder in the face now, not only for the beer but for his temper too. The soiree was held on a Friday night. Returning to work on Monday morning with apology letters in hand and in fear of losing their jobs, the young men arrived with their formerly long and fashionable hair cut off; one to a moderate length and the other shaved to the scalp. This is an old Japanese custom used to show shame—a shocking contrast to the company's modern business and to the era in which we live. In both Japanese and Western society this is grounds for a law suit. A case of physical abuse would not be treated lightly. Obviously, this never became a court case. Instead, these young men were led to believe that they had done something so wrong that they deserved the treatment they had received.

Issues affecting her as a woman
Often not taken seriously because I am female.

Advice
Find a job before you arrive here. I was extremely lucky to find a job in my field. I know of people who had jobs and lost them—they could not find another one in this area. An understanding of the Japanese market is crucial—this takes a lot of time. Unfortunately, it is one of the fastest markets to reach saturation point. In just fifty years a sweeping change in apparel has occurred in Japan—and don't forget that this is a very fickle area. If you work for an older company, be warned that you will have problems making changes without at least half a dozen meetings over a period of six months or more. It may cause frustration, but be patient and be positive, and resist begin too forceful. You will get there.

Recommended resources
Your embassy, *Tokyo Classified*, and the *Japan Times*.

Other jobs done in Japan
English correspondent; babysitter of children, dogs, and fish.

Financial Planning

Name   Louise Crabtree
Nationality   British
Age   26
Qualifications   BSC (Combined) Honours, currently studying for CIFA exam
Job title   Financial Consultant
Employer   Stirling Macguire Asset Management
Working hours   Variable—though generally I work nine- to ten-hour days and
                      occasional weekends.
Salary   Approximately ¥10–12 million per year
Time in this job   18 months

Job description

Mainly involves developing a client base and servicing existing clients, as well as researching investment companies and their products.

General requirements

Personality and character are more sought after than qualifications, although they are of course a factor. A high level of professionalism and integrity is also imperative.

Japanese requirement

Unnecessary, as our business focuses solely on foreign expatriates and local hires living in Japan.

General conditions

Salary is commission-based, working hours and holidays flexible. Company sponsors external training/courses as well as parties and overseas trips. Atmosphere is relaxed and friendly with monthly incentives and competitions.

How she found this job

A friend who was working for Stirling Macguire at the time recommended me.

Differences and similarities with this job at home

I've never worked in the UK in this field of work, although associates and mutual friends say the conditions are very different. They tell me that the working day is more structured, as is the salary, so there's less flexibility and consequently holidays are few and far between, so the work here is much more attractive.

Best thing

For me, there are a great number of things that I like—the flexible hours (I can work when I like), as well as the holidays (so far this year I've taken around nine weeks holiday!), the salary (which I determine), and also the great people that I work with (honest and ethical people are quite difficult to find in this field). I guess, though, if I had to choose one thing it would be the value and reward I get from helping people to plan their financial goals and solve their financial problems. It's a great and indescribable feeling to know that, no matter how small your contribution, you helped change a person's or couples' future lifestyle through simple financial planning.

Worst thing

Without trying to make my job look too perfect (!), I have to say there isn't really any 'bad' thing as such. I could mention the clients that make but don't honour their appointments or having to run around Tokyo all day when it's freezing cold, but I don't really think that's so terrible. I will say that at the start of my job, with no business or clients, I had to resort to cold-calling people, which I didn't enjoy at all. Fortunately, thanks to my clients out there, my business is created solely from referrals from those who've benefited from my services and recommended me to others, so basically I love my job!!

Interesting stories

The only thing that comes immediately to mind are our company parties, but I think such information should remain confidential!

Issues affecting her as a woman

Being female in this area has its advantages and disadvantages. On the one hand, some clients won't take the work you're doing seriously, so you can spend hours traveling to see a client and meeting with them and then you wonder why they don't go ahead. However, I've found in these scenarios that with time and experience this gradually changes, especially if your manner and dress exudes professionalism and if you are able to control the direction of the meeting from the outset. On the other hand, being female brings alongside a stereotype of trust and honesty (of course this is true!!); many clients often prefer having a female advising and managing their investments. Generally, I would say being a woman has worked more as a plus than a minus.

Advice

This field is still male-orientated, but there is so much potential in it for women. Having a job that's commission-only can be daunting for some at first, as it can take two to three months before you see any kind of salary, so be prepared for this. Some of these jobs, however, do offer a fixed salary and fixed hours, so it depends on your comfort zone. Personally, the freedom and high earning potential is attractive to me, so if you are self-motivated and self-disciplined and have confidence in your ability, then go for it! This job suits a person with a strong and confident personality, one who's resourceful, a good listener, and great communicator. Being organized and well prepared are also pluses, but I have yet to achieve perfection in those areas!

Recommended resources

Keep your eye on adverts in the English media and don't be afraid to call up and ask for an interview.

Other jobs done in Japan

I've done some teaching, as well as working for a nutrition company in sales and marketing.

332

Government

Name	Marion Tschernutter
Nationality	Austrian
Age	30
Qualifications	Masters Degree in Philosophy
Job title	No specific title (assistant would be closest)
Employer	Austrian Trade Commission/Austrian Embassy Commercial Section
Working hours	40 hours per week plus overtime
Salary	About ¥5.4 million per year
Time in this job	18 months

Job description

Marketing, press-related work, organisation of events and trade fairs, daily inquiries

General requirements

Japanese language ability, German, English, organisational skills

Japanese requirement

Necessary

General conditions

Good working environment, not a typical Japanese environment due to the fact that many colleagues are Austrians.

How she found this job

Through word of mouth and through the community.

Best thing

Meeting interesting people, opportunity to speak Japanese, good salary, long holidays, relation to home country.

Worst thing

No business trips.

Issues affecting her as a woman

Due to the fact that I am an employee of the Embassy, it makes it much easier to approach people here in Japan. Compared to my former job, where I was working as a woman in a small, unknown company, it is now a piece of cake to deal with Japanese business people/men.

Advice

Keep in touch with your embassies and trade boards and try to study the language.

Other jobs done in Japan

Worked for a small company doing advertisement for Japanese ski resorts.

Headhunting

Name	Veronica
Nationality	Singaporean
Age	30
Qualifications	BA
Job title	Consultant
Working hours	9:00 a.m. to 5:30 p.m. (but often have to work longer hours)
Salary	¥3.3 million per year, with commissions
Time in this job	3 months

Job description
Headhunting bilingual Japanese people with good work experience.

General requirements
A basic degree, self-motivation, a desire to make money and meet people.

Japanese requirement
A basic level would be good.

General conditions
Multicultural work environment.

How she found this job
Through a friend of a friend.

Differences and similarities with this job at home
A huge difference! In my country most people would jump at a chance to talk to a headhunter. But in Japan, headhunting is made more difficult as the labour mobility is very low and most Japanese people still cling to the concept of lifetime employment. However, I do find this changing somewhat as the economy evolves and many companies are forced to restructure and downsize.

Interesting stories
Culture differences—I met a Japanese lady secretary in her late twenties who told me that her company is going to close down in six months' time and, therefore, she had to look for another job. I tried to help her by telling her of a job opening at a more stable Japanese company. However, her colleagues tried to convince her to stay on for another six months to help them pack the office and make arrangements, etc. I told her that she had to now take care of herself as the company and colleagues were unable to do so. (In other words, don't be a sucker!) After all, the job opening may not be there six months' down the road. However, she told me that she wanted to stay to help her co-workers out! I didn't know whether to laugh or cry!

Advice
Be aggressive and have a desire to earn lots of money.

334

Hospitality

Name	Deborah Gardiner
Nationality	New Zealander
Age	29. I worked at this job when I was 25.
Qualifications	BA degree, intermediate Japanese, writing skills
Job title	Guest Relations Officer
Employer	Fuji Royal Plaza Hotel
Working hours	40-hour week
Salary	¥1.8 million a year plus a free apartment
Time in this job	6 months

General requirements

It was a joke, as initially I spoke no Japanese. But after six months on the job, hanging out with a gaggle of Japanese receptionists, I became pretty good. I was on the front desk doing phones, greeting wedding banquet guests, and looking after the foreign guests.

Japanese requirement

I was able to learn on the job.

General conditions

Rough, because I was the only foreign female on the team. The hotel manager was a sweetie and protected me from most of the abuse that would have been thrown at me otherwise. I felt that I was ostracized because of my imperfect language, but also because I was a white FEMALE. The Western guys were desirable objects. The women wanted to date them.

How she found this job

Through a recruitment agency.

Best thing

Offered me an amazing opportunity to observe Japanese work conditions as an insider. I was also able to learn Japanese for free.

Advice

Develop a thick outer skin. Go into the work not expecting it to be anything like what you do at home. The office culture in Japan is nothing like what you experience in the West. Different things are considered rude. People will want to know your business. If you have a male roommate, they will insist that he is your lover. Read about other women's experiences on working in Japan so you have an understanding before going in.

Other jobs done in Japan

Brief stints at hostessing, teaching, waitressing, and art modeling. Personal assistant for one year. Freelance writer for two years.

Information Technology

Name	Anonymous
Qualifications	BA in Political Science, some Japanese language skills, 4+ years of computer related experience—producing Websites for various clients
Working hours	9:00 a.m. to 6:00 p.m., generally some overtime
Salary	¥4+ million a year, benefits and options (lower than in my previous position with the same company—let's just say I don't do it for the money)
Time in this job	3 years

Job description

Everything from producing rich media banners to translating/rewriting press releases, arranging barter deals with other companies, arranging giveaways, making forms, providing tech support for co-workers, and localizing content from US headquarters.

General requirements

Computer/net savvy, able to write in English, basic Japanese—reading and listening, knowledge of the business

Japanese requirement

Not completely necessary, but very helpful and you gain respect from your Japanese co-workers.

General conditions

Generally good. Casual work atmosphere. Suit not required!

How she found this job

On the Net. It wasn't posted, but I sent my resume anyway.

Best thing

Boundless opportunities to learn new things and make contacts with new people.

Worst thing

Sometimes difficult to focus on a particular thing. My previous position at this same company became very difficult for me when I got a nasty boss. Management was more concerned with keeping the peace than preserving justice.

Interesting stories

The VP of our company is a woman. After several years of organizing the giri chocolate gift giving for Valentine's Days—for which the women received nothing on White Day*— she decided to collect the money and donate it to UNICEF in the men's honor. We still have the thank you plaque in our office. Previously I worked in Silicon Valley. I did very well there, mostly because I complained a lot and improved things. I got promoted to head of my department after six months because I corresponded directly with the president by email and he liked my ideas. Here, however, it doesn't work that way. The same tactics ended up backfiring on me. Even constructive criticism is often viewed as disruptive to the natural order of things. Being right and smart are not qualifications to try changing things. Keeping the peace is valued over being correct or efficient.

Issues affecting her as a woman

In my previous position at this company it was horrible. My boss was a misogynist and there wasn't anything I could do about it. However, my coworkers have been very supportive. The lack of foreign women in my company can sometimes make me lonely, but most of the time it's not so bad.

Advice

The Internet business here is way behind the point that it's at in the US and other countries. Learn the trends there. Learn about Japan in general. Learn some Japanese. Take responsibility for training yourself. Training tends to be poor in Japan. Definitely spring for your own computer so you can get to know its ins and outs. Share your skills and information with others—it will only serve to strengthen your own skills and you'll make friends, too.

Recommended resources

Read whatever you can about the business. Keep up to date. Join mailing lists and groups to get support. Take lessons, study.

Other jobs done in Japan

I've had my own company unofficially for a while. Basically, it involves creating Websites for companies, consulting, and sometimes training. It's a great way to meet people. I also do a lot of volunteer work for various organizations.

*White Day: Valentine's Day in Japan is celebrated by women giving chocolate to men. Most of these gifts are '*giri-choco*' or 'obligation chocolate' given to male colleagues or bosses. Women give more expensive or handmade chocolate to their loved ones. On White Day in March, the men are 'supposed' to give chocolate gifts to the women from whom they had received chocolate previously. So don't go crazy when your boyfriend/ husband returns home on February 14th with armfuls of chocolate—it's all *giri*, contrary to what he would like to believe!

337

Investment Trading

Name	Anonymous
Nationality	British
Age	26
Qualifications	Maths degree
Job title	Equity Trader
Working hours	Monday to Friday, 7:45 a.m. to 6:30 p.m. approximately
Salary	About ¥18 million a year plus benefits (e.g., housing allowance) and annual bonus of around ¥9 million.
Time in this job	3 1/2 years of which six months have been in Japan

Job description
Trading Japanese equities.

General requirements
Good maths; good written English; a few years experience.

Japanese requirement
It's not necessary.

How she found this job
I was offered the move to Japan six months ago and took it.

Differences and similarities with this job at home
It's the same because I'm working for a Western company. The only obvious difference is that client nights out in Japan virtually ALWAYS end up in strip clubs. I usually don't even go to the first part of the nights out—mostly I am not invited—but when I do show up there comes a point when I can tell they are trying to lose me and it's very uncomfortable.

Best thing
Money; opportunities to travel such as this one to Japan; and it's pretty interesting, challenging stuff most of the time.

Issues affecting her as a woman
Apart from the above, I think if I was a guy I would get more invites for lunch and stuff. It's kind of the same in London, some men don't necessarily feel at ease inviting a woman for lunch on a friendly basis. Out here there are fewer women in my field and this makes it even trickier. Hence it does get lonely and you really have to get out and do the inviting.

Advice
Think about it long and hard—it's a very demanding job. Qualifications are not so important, as long as you're numerate and clued up. The best place to learn is on the job. The difficult thing is getting IN to the job because there's high competition. Apply to as many places as possible.

Law

Name	Anonymous
Nationality	American
Age	31
Qualifications	BA, JD, Master of public policy, member of California and District of Columbia bar associations
Job title	FLA (foreign legal advisor)
Employer	Anderson Mori
Working hours	Long
Salary	Depends upon whether hours billed result in bonus payments
Time in this job	1 year

Job description
Draft agreements, correspondence, general transactional work.

General requirements
Member of the bar in a foreign jurisdiction. It helps to speak Japanese, but it isn't a job requirement.

Japanese requirement
Socially, it improves the day-to-day environment. To do the job? Not necessary, but useful.

How she found this job
Shotgun. I sent out resumes to law firms in Tokyo.

Differences and similarities with this job at home
I worked in a large government agency prior to coming to Japan. The most striking difference between working in a government agency and working in a Japanese law firm is primarily the absolute lack of diversity in terms of who is in charge (not even one woman partner), and the most striking similarity is the layers of consultation, review and, often, paralysis.

Best thing
I do not speak Japanese and I am in Japan through chance, not any desire to learn the language or adapt to a very repressive and sexist culture. Yet I am able to work in a professional job in English.

Advice
Work for an American or British law firm.

Recommended resources
The Foreign Women Lawyers' Association has monthly meetings (except during the summer) and is a good place to network and find out about jobs and work environments.

Other jobs done in Japan
Editing and a brief stint in conference planning.

Marketing

Name	Sherry Greenfield
Nationality	American
Age	32
Qualifications	BS Biomedical Engineering, MBA
Job title	Group Product Manager
Employer	Boston Scientific
Working hours	9:00 a.m. to 5:30 p.m. and about 20 more hours a week
Salary	¥8.5 million per year
Time in this job	2 months (15 months at this company)

Job description
Responsible for 2 major product lines (angioplasty products), with 3 staff reports.

General requirements
Marketing and sales experience, Japanese language, medical field experience

Japanese requirement
Intermediate to advanced level.

General conditions
Very technical, fast paced, cutting edge of medicine.

How she found this job
Internet ad for Japanese job fair in the US.

Differences and similarities with this job at home
Very similar.

Best things
People, salary, travel.

Worst thing
Long hours.

Issues affecting her as a woman
Good field for women, though still heavily male dominated.

Advice
Excellent area for women to work in; get sales experience first.

Other jobs done in Japan
Medical device sales, previous medical device product marketing, English teaching, translation company DTP.

Media: Film

Name	Anonymous
Nationality	Canadian
Age	29—always.
Qualifications	B.Arch., B.E.S., Software Training, 4 years experience before coming to latest job
Job title	Supervising Animator/Dynamagician
Employer	The Annex
Working hours	Noon till 9:00 p.m., typically. At deadlines—noon till the sun rises again, then some sleep, then do it again.
Salary	¥7 million per year
Time in this job	18 months

Job description

To design systems for animating characters, training staff to use them, animating or keyframing for the film itself.

Japanese requirement

Pretty necessary. This was a director role, so I had to be able to communicate with the minions. And you will find (as anywhere where you are not fluent in the local language) that you will miss out on opportunities if you don't speak fluently.

General conditions

Exciting, challenging, creative, fun, tiring, and in the end fulfilling.

How she found this job

Met someone who worked for a company doing this project as a special project and was coerced into joining the team and extending my planned stay in Japan.

Differences and similarities with this job at home

In most fields in Japan, women are underrepresented and those who are there have to fight to be heard. The tendency is strong in this country to disqualify a woman's point of view, at least until they look pissed off about it and are threatening to do something about it, or speaking very loudly! In my home country (North America in general) women are strongly represented in this field, with many holding managerial positions. Still a little underrepresented in the computer animation part of the industry in general though. At least at the big companies. Women are often running smaller companies. Another difference in the computer animation industry is that until now the tendency has been for one animator to do all aspects of a scene, and many companies still run this way. The larger ones, however, are starting to switch over to dividing work according to specialities in order to compete with the American system better and just run things better.

Best thing

It's fun and something I want to spend a long time doing.

341

Worst thing

Deadlines are harrowing—but usually there is a break after a tough one.

Interesting stories

Usually there is a production baby or two associated with a project that takes any length of time and runs under such intense schedules of togetherness. Life goes on despite the deadlines. One situation was kind of funny, because the affected party was nervous to let the foreigners know of her condition. She wasn't married (still a rare situation in Japan) and she didn't want us to think poorly of her I guess(?!), and so she chose not to reveal the secret and instead spent her time in the office frequently wrapped in blankets to disguise the fact. I'm not sure why she thought we might disapprove (as if our opinion mattered!), but it is probably typical of a culture that practises, accepts, and I think encourages for mental health reasons, that individuals have both a public face and a very different private face.

Issues affecting her as a woman

In Japan, it's just tougher being a woman with a career that you want to advance here. I was fortunate to be working with three other foreigners in directorial positions, so didn't have the problem there. But I did notice that I developed a permanently pissed off attitude when dealing with Japanese men in the industry. Due to language difficulties or being of the female persuasion or probably both, I constantly felt passed over when it came time for project and personal promotion. And men do expect me to be timid and respectful before driven and ambitious. Hard for many Western women to adopt this attitude.

Advice

It is a growing field here, especially if you are doing computer animation, so is a good place to look for opportunity if you are starting out in the field. But you must speak Japanese in order to be happy working in this industry, so either come with the skills or come committed to spending a steady first few months studying only the language to get you going.

Other jobs done in Japan

Always animation.

Media: Magazines

Name	Jessie Bell
Qualifications	BA in History from the University of Colorado (US) and a JD from Brooklyn Law School (US). Nothing relevant.
Job title	Managing Editor
Working hours	I'm usually in the office from 9-ish to 6-ish, but there's a lot of 'after hours' work required.
Salary	¥5.16 million per year
Time in this job	1 1/2 years as ME, 1 year as assistant editor

Job description

Responsible for all editorial (i.e., non-advertising) content of the magazine. Specific duties include managing staff (in-house) plus a pool of over seventy contributors, as well as organizing interns and volunteers. Responsible for monthly editorial budget; editing all content with the assistance of one other editor, which includes commissioning writers, photographers, and other contributors; scheduling editorial and ensuring that it is received in a timely manner; accepting new material, rejecting inappropriate material, sending letters of acceptance or rejection accordingly; giving proper credit to both writing and photographs; formatting and subediting (most of our material comes by email); checking facts; making phone calls; proofreading; working with writers; requesting rewrites; requesting images; organizing and acquiring photographs; taking photographs for articles; checking proofs for layout, design, and corrections; manage upcoming editorial schedule; providing updates to publisher and sales department; scheduling vacations, replacements, etc.; responsible for hiring and firing in the editorial department; maintaining editorial library; and in my 'free time' writing articles for the magazine.

Japanese requirement

In the beginning, when I was assistant editor and we didn't have a Japanese-speaking editorial assistant, I was responsible for all the fact-checking, interview arranging, translations, etc., that required Japanese. I use very little of it now on the job (bilingual editorial assistant!), but it's still necessary to understand it. Since a lot of what we cover is Japan-related, if I didn't have an understanding of the background, culture and some language ability, many of the articles submitted would be fairly incomprehensible and thus difficult to adequately edit.

How she found this job

Luck and the proverbial 'being in the right place at the right time'. I started out in a very low-level position at the publication and then moved wherever a job opening presented itself, all the while continuing to do the original work. At one point I told my superior that I thought I was being underused, and could I do some work on the editorial side. She agreed, and I slowly carved a niche for myself where before there was no such position.

343

Best things

The people I work with. By that I mean the people immediately surrounding me, not the higher-ups or the sales department. On those days when I'm ready to throw it all in and quit, I don't, because I realize I'd be leaving them in the lurch. I also like the fact (very important in Japan!) that I can wear whatever I want and that if I have nothing to do (not that that's ever happened!) I can take off.

Worst things

Understaffing and lack of positive feedback and/or respect from the top. Unprofessional working environment. Badly maintained equipment means we have to work harder. Having to beg for raises rather than being rewarded on a regular basis.

Interesting stories

The cops have been to our office on more than one occasion due to fights (real physical ones with blood and bruises and all) in the office between people (who shall go unnamed!) who work here. The working environment is pretty, er, 'cozy' and sometimes the tension gets really out of hand! One night I had sex on the office floor with an editor visiting from an out of town magazine. Sharing notes and all, you could say.

Issues affecting her as a woman

I got asked out on a date once during an interview with an athlete. In the end I canceled because I really didn't want to go out with him. My brother still won't forgive me; he says I 'owe him' an athlete! I think, although I'm not entirely sure, that one of our designers fights me on stuff where he wouldn't with a man. We're always at each other's throats. This is only speculation, though; I don't really have any way of testing it. It could be that the tension comes from my having once been assistant editor, and thus 'below' him, and am now 'above' him.

Advice

I don't know that I would give different advice to males and females. To me this seems to be a beautifully gender-neutral job. And since I've never done this job anywhere but Japan, I can't really say what someone might need to know that's peculiar to working in Japan.

Recommended resources

There are LOTS of English-language magazines out these days and they will be your best resource. Contact people there (by mail or email!) and talk to them, not just about looking for work, but to let them get to know you. These types of jobs are rarely advertised. Become a member of and attend SWET (Society of Writers, Editors and Translators) meetings. Take any shit job offered at a publication you're really interested in and let people know you're interested in doing more; but whatever job it is you were hired for, do it to the best of your ability.

Other jobs done in Japan

I've been here forever so the list is long: teacher's aide at a nursery/kindergarten, TV work, English teaching, waitress, typist, dog walker, lawyer, I ran my own catering business, proofreader, transcriber ...

Media: Newspapers

Name	Jayne A. Hitchcock
Nationality	American
Age	41
Qualifications	Author of 6 books, over 20 years of writing experience
Job title	Assistant Editor
Employer	Japan Update
Working hours	Very flexible
Time in this job	3 years

Job description

Write feature articles, mostly out in the field.

General requirements

Previous writing samples.

Japanese requirement

None, but I knew the basics and could get by in interviews.

How she found this job

I sent my resume to every English-language newspaper in Okinawa, Japan.

Differences and similarities with this job at home

Big difference! I had no contract in Okinawa and each article was never one set price. In the USA, I always have a contract and am quoted a firm price for each article I write.

Best thing

Writing articles about the culture and meeting all the wonderful people I interviewed.

Worst thing

Haggling with the bookkeeper about my pay each month.

Issues affecting her as a woman

At the first press conference I had to attend, I was shoved out of the way by the predominantly male Japanese and Okinawan reporters. I was trying to be polite and found that didn't work—reporters are reporters everywhere. So at the next press conference, I shoved my way to the front, and since I stood a few heads taller than most of the men, they didn't bother me. After that, I never had a problem.

Advice

Know when to be polite and when to be persistent. Read the publications you're interested in working for well and ask a lot of questions if you're called in for an interview.

Other jobs done in Japan

I taught English to a small group of women.

345

Media: Publishing

Name	Bella Katz
Nationality	New Zealander
Age	25
Qualifications	BA in English Literature
Job title	Publicity Manager
Employer	Tuttle Publishing
Working hours	10:00 a.m. to 4:00 p.m., Monday to Friday
Salary	¥3.24 million per year
Time in this job	10 months

Job description
Establishing contacts with media for the purpose of promoting Tuttle titles.

General requirements
Creativity, fearlessness, contacts, communication skills, ability to think outside the box.

Japanese requirement
It would have helped, but was not necessary since our books were in English.

How she found this job
By learning as much as possible about Tuttle and approaching them for opportunities.

Differences and similarities with this job at home
It seemed a little easier to break into this industry in Japan because the turnover of people was a lot higher. Also, you have a bit of an 'I'm indestructible' feeling and tend to pursue situations you wouldn't necessarily pursue at home.

Best thing
The fantastic people that I met in the media industry.

Worst thing
The one and a half hour commute in each direction.

Advice
Know your stuff, and know where you fit into the company before you go there.

Other jobs done in Japan
Writing, editing, teaching.

Media: Radio

Name	Anonymous
Nationality	North American
Qualifications	BA in Languages and Education/courses in radio and TV/ Method Acting training/photography coursework
Job title	Announcer
Working hours	Mostly afternoons and late into the night
Salary	Very good
Time in this job	9 years

Job description
Narrating live news and doing other freelance narrations.

General requirements
Some background in media or voice work; a good on-air presence.

Japanese requirement
Not really necessary, although in the studio Japanese is helpful in terms of understanding a director's instructions and in terms of following live broadcasts.

General conditions
OK, but need more light and fresh air.

How she found this job
This is a complicated story. I took a big risk and moved from education into broadcasting with only basic training. I started out in educational radio and made a slow transition to news and other forms of narration. I have essentially groomed myself on the job. For about five years I was also doing some teaching to supplement my income, as narrating was not full time. During that time, I met my American acting teacher, which opened up a whole different world in terms of communicating on an emotional level. Japan has afforded me the opportunity to explore myself in different ways as a communicator and for that I am grateful, hard as the ascent may have been. Branching into broadcasting was very difficult in the beginning!

Differences and similarities with this job at home
I think most network broadcasters back home do that exclusively. Freelance narrators do the commercial work. Also, there is more of a market for bilingual programming here.

Best thing
I enjoy working with my voice; interesting jobs.

Worst thing
Late hours; socially somewhat isolating for single women.

Advice
Get some voice or media training and put together a sharp looking demo and resume.

Media: Television

Name	Anonymous
Nationality	Australian
Age	27
Qualifications	BA in French and Japanese
Job title	Television News Anchor
Working hours	Ten hours a day, five days a week
Salary	¥8 million a year plus annual bonuses subject to performance
Time in this job	Nearly 2 years

Job description
Writing, producing, and presenting business and world news programs.

General requirements
Experience as a TV or radio presenter; business knowledge preferred but not absolutely necessary as you can learn on the job; journalism degree not required. The main thing is that you've had hands on experience as a presenter either in TV or radio.

Japanese requirement
It used to be policy that you had to speak Japanese, but they have recently changed that. Now it is helpful but not necessary.

General conditions
Free food—actually this is a big bonus, although the idea was that they could keep you at your desk as long as possible without you having to leave the office to get food; hard work—you don't often get a break; a lot of flexibility in terms of moving up the ranks; lots of opportunities—there are so few media-trained professionals in Japan.

How she found this job
I applied from Australia and found it through word of mouth. My company regularly puts ads in the *Japan Times* and advertises widely throughout the world and on the web.

Differences and similarities with this job at home
Longer working hours (which is pretty standard for Japan); and certain perks like excellent medical benefits, bonuses, free food, etc., that you wouldn't get to such an extent in Australia.

Best thing
You achieve something on a daily basis, you never have to take work home with you, every day you feel as if you have put out a good product that is helping people, and there's no stress apart from the intense working hours.

Worst thing
The repetitive boredom of it—being on a project would be more exciting. Being an anchor really means you are anchored there on the spot—you just sit in the studio all day. People think it looks so glamorous, but it's much more exciting to be a reporter. Oh, and the free food makes you very fat!

Interesting stories

I want to definitely say that the free food is a work hazard. Everyone puts on about three kilos in their first three months.

Issues affecting her as a woman

None at all. Actually I've found that working for a foreign company under American jurisdiction means that there aren't any problems in this area. In many cases in companies like this the bosses are foreign and female. I don't think being a woman has been any detriment whatsoever.

Advice

Without a doubt look for a company that has foreign management. In my old company the management was Japanese and the glass ceiling was extremely low. As a woman, I would never work for a Japanese boss, no matter how nice they were.

Recommended resources

Surf the web—go to the sites of the big companies and they should all have job opportunities listed. Word of mouth is very important—get to know people in the industry. The turnover is very high, particularly in Tokyo.

Other jobs done in Japan

I worked for local government as a coordinator of international relations.

Modeling

Name	Meriah Hudson
Nationality	American
Age	26
Job title	Model
Employer	Kondo Model
Working hours	About 5 a day
Salary	¥10,000 per hour
Time in this job	1 year

Job description
Model. I specialized in eye modeling. And that means working with a lot of makeup, modeling new colours. I would also occasionally do kimono modeling.

General requirements
Caucasian, with big blue eyes.

Japanese requirement
Not necessary, but extremely helpful.

General conditions
Pretty fun. I would go to the photo studio, get made up, then shoot. The people were great and fun to be around. It got hot, and it made me hate makeup for a while, though. For the kimono modeling, I would go to the modeling centre, get done up, then walk on down the catwalk. That wasn't so much fun. There was a high stress level due to built-up tension.

How she found this job
Through a friend of mine that studied makeup. Her school was looking for a model for the students to do their 'final exam' on. One thing led to another.

Best thing
Seeing the completed photos and marveling at how different they were from the real, everyday me. Makeup is amazing.

Worst thing
All the makeup. The heat from the lights. And in the case of the kimono modeling, the stress.

Interesting stories
None. Other than the fact that I looked like a freak with all that makeup on. In real light, I mean. Under the studio lights, I looked amazingly gorgeous.

Other jobs done in Japan
English teaching, translating, ICC training, corporate training.

Music

Name	Donna Burke
Nationality	Australian
Age	35
Qualifications	Bachelor of Education in Drama and Media Studies
Job title	Singer
Employer	Various
Working hours	All the time—when I'm not outside working I'm in my home working on the computer scheduling, rehearsing, emailing, burning demo CDs, and promoting my CD.
Salary	Now, after three years in the business, it's ¥14.4 million a year.

Job description

I earn half of my income from singing and half from narration and acting. Every day is different. Regarding the singing, I do studio session singing for children's CDs, TVCMs, and Eurobeat para para dance remixes. I also sing live at corporate parties, events, and weddings. I'm in a traditional Irish band and a jazz trio, and have made a CD with an acoustic guitarist that I'm promoting through the internet and at performances. I spend a lot of time on the computer keeping monthly records of jobs and payments. I continually send my demo CD out to new clients.

General requirements

Number one: you have to possess the necessary talent. Number two: you have to be punctual, pleasant to work with, confident of your skills in the studio and live, and be able to change your image to what the client needs.

Japanese requirement

Not very necessary—most agencies have a bilingual assistant who goes on jobs with you.

General conditions

Very good.

How she found this job

I met someone when I first came to Tokyo through the *Tokyo Classified* who needed singers for weddings. Then I started getting event jobs and recording work. After about six months I made a narration demo and contacted agencies that other singers and narrators told me about. After that I still kept trying to find new agencies by doing mass fax-outs. The secret is to have a fantastic demo, a resume in Japanese and English and to always be available to work—a Catch-22 when you're first getting started—if you're still working the day job, you just can't cut it. You have to starve for six to twelve months while you establish yourself.

Differences and similarities with this job at home

The work is more varied. Back home you would only have one or two agents, but here you have to register with about one hundred, which means making lots more demos and resumes. Here you rarely get residuals—it's usually a buyout and the money is less in Japan for TVCMs—but overall you can make a lot.

Best thing

The variety—every week is different. Also, if I don't like a particular client or job I can just say no. I love getting paid to do my hobby and I love being able to take holidays whenever I want.

Worst thing

Not getting paid during holidays!

Issues affecting her as a woman

I get work based on how I look—I have a clean non-threatening image and not having blonde hair and big boobs can work in my favour! For corporate parties and events I have to look the part—the client is buying my image to make a statement and I try to find out what they want me to wear so I can fit their image as best I can.

Advice

Make sure you have a great demo, be punctual, keep records of all your jobs and clients, and be as professional as you can be.

Recommended resources

The best thing is to meet other people in the industry, give them your demo tape, and ask them to help introduce you—go to where there is live music and ask around for other singers.

Nursing

Name	Anonymous
Nationality	American
Age	45
Qualifications	BS in Nursing, RN licence
Job title	School Nurse
Employer	International School
Working hours	Part time, 10 days a month, from 9:30 a.m to 4:00 p.m.
Salary	About ¥20,000 a day
Time in this job	7 months

Job description

Same as it would be in the States. Take care of the health records for each child, making sure they are complete. Take care of simple injuries that occur at school and help parents to arrange for care in a hospital, etc., if it is necessary. Do simple student health screenings (vision, hearing, etc.) and notify parents if there is a problem. Participate as a member of the Emergency Disaster Team in the event of a earthquake or other natural disaster (help with training of members, etc.). Teach health in the classroom. Accompany students on week-long ski trip to take care of medical problems.

General requirements

In general, an RN licence, and probably a BS in Nursing, but exceptions may be made depending on personal qualifications.

Japanese requirement

Not absolutely necessary, but I think that being a semi-fluent Japanese speaker helped me to get the job. Not all of our parents speak English well, and prefer to ask questions in Japanese. It also helps when you call the hospitals. Also, an understanding of how the Japanese health care system works is necessary.

General conditions

A great place to work!! The kids are relatively healthy and, for the most part, the other teachers, parents, and administrators are very supportive.

How she found this job

Through being a member of the Foreign Nurses Association in Japan (FNAJ). In Tokyo, the association seems to act as a clearing house for the few nursing-related jobs that are available.

Differences and similarities with this job at home

Quite similar I believe.

Advice

In order to work as a nurse in Japan, it is necessary to pass the Japanese Nursing Licensing Exam. Even if you are fluent in spoken Japanese, I think that it would be very difficult to pass a written test, and I know of only one foreigner who has done it (although I am sure there are more—this woman is Korean, and she actually went to nursing school here). I know of three other positions where foreigner nurses have worked here. One is doing drug testing, taking urine samples from sailors on ships that put into port in Japan. The work is erratic, but it is a good way to get to know Japan because you are asked to go to various ports around the country. Another possible position would be with a foreign drug company, working as a consultant when they are introducing a new drug. This also is not a steady job, but depends on the requests that the company receives to go around to different hospitals to give lectures. The third job is actually a nursing professor at one of the universities. This is usually a combination of teaching medical English along with a content course (usually nursing research). A Master's, at least, would be necessary. If you have some special expertise (for example, working on a transplant team or as an IV therapy nurse), you may want to contact drug companies before you come to Japan, to see if they have any need for a nursing consultant. Otherwise, you just need to be patient while you make personal contacts after you get here. It would be great to have some kind of TESOL training since one of the easiest jobs to get (and probably the best paying) is to teach medical English to nurses and doctors. Be flexible and, for your professional growth, try to keep up with new information by subscribing to your favorite journal. Various members have also started writing here (newspaper columns with health care advice, books on nursing or the health care system, etc.).

Recommended resources
Foreign Nurses Association in Japan (as mentioned above) and the *Japan Health Handbook* for information about the Japanese health care system.

Pharmaceuticals

Name	Anne Egros
Nationality	French
Age	36
Qualifications	PharmD (Doctor in Pharmaceutical Sciences), MSc in Computer Sciences
Job title	Science and Technology Information Manager
Employer	Nihon L'Oreal
Working hours	Flexible
Time in this job	3 years

General requirements

Scientific knowledge, communication and business skills, and knowledge management.

Japanese requirement

Basic (level 4) if you can afford to pay a good technical translator (as in my case) and hire a nice French guy fluent in Japanese (I got him after two years). Otherwise, YOU MUST READ and SPEAK technical Japanese fluently.

General conditions

No apartment. Japanese pension plan and insurance, commuting fees paid.

How she found this job

I asked L'Oreal HQ in France if I could follow my husband.

Best thing

Freedom, learning, networking, self-management.

Issues affecting her as a woman

I am the wife of my husband and treated as such because it is a French CIE.

Advice

Look for every type of job, be positive, open your eyes, and listen. Make it your homework to know the industry/company you target, build your network, surf the Internet, and practise your interview skills. Don't expect to find THE JOB at the beginning. FIND ANY KIND OF JOB FIRST! Master search information through the Internet and in databases.

Other jobs done in Japan

I just quit this one and I am now a Regional Business Manager for Asia-Pacific for a Chemical CIE. I found it on my own, and I am not anymore just the wife of my husband (in addition, I doubled my income!).

Psychotherapy

Name	Nancy Jeltsch Yamada
Nationality	American
Age	49
Qualifications	MA (in Comparative Culture); MSW (Master of Social Work); LCSW (Licensed Certified Social Worker, Massachusetts
Job title	Psychotherapist/Counselor
Employer	Tokyo English Life Line (TELL) Community Counseling Service, International Christian University (ICU) Counseling Center
Working hours	Up to twenty hours a week
Salary	¥6000 per hour at TCCS; unpaid at ICU (my contribution to one of my alma maters)
Time in this job	2 1/2 years (7 years in the field)

Job description

At TCCS: providing psychotherapy and counseling to adult individuals and couples, primarily in the foreign community; community presentations on subjects like depression; training presentations for Life Line counselors. At ICU: providing counseling and therapy for ICU students.

General requirements

Although Japan has no licensing requirements for therapists, at TCCS it is necessary to have a master's degree in a related field and to be licensed to practise in one's country of education.

Japanese requirement

Depends on whom you want to work with. At TCCS, there are some situations in which I use Japanese; for example, when one spouse is Japanese and prefers using Japanese. At ICU I do the majority of my work in Japanese with regular students, because the exchange students have their own counselor.

General conditions

At TCCS: an intake worker receives calls from prospective clients and assigns them to therapists according to client preferences in gender, language, nationality, day, and location (main office or satellite) and therapists' areas of expertise and preferred client population. The main office has several rooms available, and therapists share these, usually on different days of the week. TCCS offers clients a sliding fee scale based on income, and therapists receive ¥6000 per hour, whatever the fee. Therapists use satellite offices in several downtown churches, generally part of one day per week, if they agree to work without the support of the office staff. Therapists are on one-year renewable contracts that forbid private practice or seeing prospective TCCS clients elsewhere. At ICU: students either make appointments or drop in; counselors share session rooms according to need and meet together in an office for consultations. Because of my special status, I don't know about the contracts of others there.

How she found this job

I was a volunteer telephone counselor at TELL first and then applied to work as a clinician; I am a graduate (MA) of ICU and approached the Counseling Center through people I know there.

Differences and similarities with this job at home

Therapy is unregulated and unrecognized in Japan, and this presents both advantages and disadvantages. The benefits of this are: (almost) no managed care/insurance companies to deal with and no government oversight or meddling. Other differences on the plus side are the tremendous variety of clients, in terms of background, and the constant opportunity to work with intercultural issues intersecting personal issues. Drawbacks are that there is little in the way of support or networking with other professionals such as prescribing psychiatrists trained in methods acceptable to us; little cooperation from hospitals and the police in emergencies; little government financial support for our non-profit organization; fundraising difficulties; lack of understanding and respect; only a small client base in the foreign community; and a lack of priority for counseling and therapy. Group therapy, popular in the US, is next to impossible to organize in the spread-out and transient Tokyo community. Clients are often forced to leave therapy before they would otherwise, for employment and visa reasons. There is competition from untrained/unlicensed people calling themselves 'therapists'.

Best thing

Feeling that I am doing something useful.

Worst thing

Hearing about all the horrible ways people treat each other.

Interesting stories

Sorry, all my work is completely confidential.

Issues affecting her as a woman

I work for TCCS at a rather isolated satellite office in one of the churches downtown and, for safety reasons, our intake worker does not schedule first appointments for men when there will be no one else in the church.

Advice

I would advise her to be well qualified as a psychotherapist by having completed at least a master's degree in a program that includes clinical internships and to have a licence to practise, especially if she hopes to participate in the growing market. She should not expect to be able to support herself with this type of work alone—she will need a second income of some kind. She should be flexible in the kinds of clients she is willing to see, taking care not to work outside her areas of training.

Recommended resources

Contact International Mental Health Providers Japan (IMHPJ).

Other jobs done in Japan

University English teacher, editor, conducting orientations for newcomers.

Relocation

Name	Anonymous
Nationality	British
Age	39
Qualifications	BSc (Hons) PGCEA, ADM, RM, RN
Job title	Relocation Consultant
Working hours	20 hours per week
Salary	¥2.4 million per annum
Time in this job	8 months

Job description

Sell orientation programs to corporate clients.

Japanese requirement

A little basic helps.

General conditions

Good.

How she found this job

Through Foreign Executive Women (FEW).

Best thing

The great people I work with. Enjoy going out to other companies to see what is happening. It stimulates my brain.

Worst thing

The money is awful!

Advice

You can do anything if you put your mind to it. Think what you want to do and go for it. Network, network, and network. Don't be frightened to ask people for leads. Follow them up and use the name of the person who referred you.

Other jobs done in Japan

Taught English. I also do a lot of work fundraising for a charity I am very fond of. I think there is not enough emphasis on the skills that you gain working in a charity, which will enhance your time in a country and look good on your resume.

Research

Name	Kim Binsted
Nationality	Dual Canadian and American
Age	29
Qualifications	PhD in Artificial Intelligence, BSc in Physics
Job title	Associate Researcher in Artificial Intelligence
Employer	Currently Sony Computer Science Laboratories, but I'm just about to leave Sony to start my own company in Tokyo.
Working hours	Flexible and variable. I generally arrive late and leave late, but that's my choice. If there's an imminent deadline, or if I'm really excited about something, I could stay all night.
Salary	¥8 million per year
Time in this job	Just over 2 years.

Job description

I do research on expressive communication and responsive entertainment, from a human-computer interaction standpoint. I spend my time writing papers, programming, fiddling around with equipment, giving talks, and going to conferences.

General requirements

Researchers at Sony CSL generally have PhDs in their field, and an established reputation in the research community.

Japanese requirement

Not necessary, but I do miss a lot of subtle things. For example, many of the visiting researchers' talks are in Japanese and, although I get the gist, I don't understand enough to feel comfortable asking technical questions.

General conditions

This lab is very 'Western academic' in its style: hours are flexible and dress is casual. We have largish offices and a comfortable workspace. The official language of the lab is English; meetings are conducted in English or Japanese, depending on who is present. Most of the researchers are Japanese.

How she found this job

I was recruited at a conference by other researchers at the lab. It has an excellent international reputation.

Differences and similarities with this job at home

There aren't many industrial basic research labs in the world, so it's hard to compare, but I believe that working conditions, salary, etc., are similar.

Best thing

Well-funded freedom. There are no constraints on our research, and we don't have to spend our time seeking funding or teaching students.

Worst thing

The isolation. The lab is set up so that we work very much on our own. Also, because of language barriers, I find it hard to build collaborations with other researchers inside or outside of Sony.

Interesting stories

The week I started, I went for a meeting with the president of the lab. It was quite intimidating, with lots of suits in attendance, and I was on my best behaviour. While cards were being exchanged, a woman came in to serve tea. I ignored her, trying to concentrate on the important people I was meeting. As she was about to leave, the boss gestured at her and said "Oh, and I'd like you to meet X-chan, one of our top researchers." I was so embarassed. It was bad enough that she was taken away from her research to make tea for me; even worse that I, a female colleague, didn't even acknowledge her presence! I haven't faced any sexism at work myself, but I do have a cute story. I used my air miles to make a flight reservation over the phone, then went down to the airline office to pick up the tickets. The guy behind the counter pulled up my file on the computer, checked the details, checked my passport, looked at me and said, "Everything is in order. However, I'm afraid you're going to have to get Dr. Binsted to sign this form before we can give you the ticket." I just burst out laughing. The reasoning this guy had to do to get around the idea that "Dr Binsted" could be a woman was incredible! He had to a) assume that Dr Binsted was buying a ticket for someone else; b) assume that this other person had exactly the same name as Dr Kim Binsted (remember, he had my passport); and c) maintain both of these assumptions whilst looking at my file, which undoubtedly contains a lot of information about me, including my gender. He was properly mortified when I explained his mistake, so I couldn't get angry!

Issues affecting her as a woman

There aren't many. I do get a bit bummed out when, at off-site meetings, all the guys head off to one onsen room to socialize, and I go to another all by myself. However, this doesn't happen often, and isn't a big deal anyway. There is one thing: my colleagues and boss get very nervous when I show negative emotion, especially frustration. I think they might be afraid I'm going to burst into tears or something! Again, though, it doesn't happen often.

Advice

Most of my advice would be about being a foreign woman in Japan in general, rather than in the workplace.

Other jobs done in Japan

English teacher, six years ago (after my undergraduate degree). Narrator, occasionally. Improv comedian, regularly (but it doesn't really pay).

Secretarial

Name	Anonymous
Nationality	British
Age	28
Qualifications	BA Oriental Studies, MA International Relations
Job title	Secretary
Employer	Japanese politician
Working hours	9:00 a.m. to 5:30 p.m., but this varies
Salary	¥3.6 million a year tax-free, free apartment
Time in this job	4 months

Job description

Deal with any correspondence from embassies and journalists, and provide the politician with updates of Western press.

General requirements

Female Japanese-speaking graduate of Oxbridge (fairly specific!).

General conditions

Hardly ever see the politician himself. Very sexist, hierarchical office of six people.

How she found this job

I was contacted by the Japanese Embassy in London.

Differences and similarities with this job at home

I am not expected to do anything in my job in Japan, whereas I can't see anyone employing me to do nothing in the UK.

Best thing

Free apartment in Akasaka, weekends off.

Worst thing

Everything else.

Interesting stories

I don't have a contract, and I get paid cash in hand. I have nothing to prove I work here, or am getting paid, which makes me wonder how many other things slip through the auditing net ...

Issues affecting her as a woman

I have been told to stop wearing perfume as it may offend older Japanese visitors, and was told to come in early to clean the office with the other female secretary. Women are not allowed to use the toilet in my office; we have to use the one in the lobby.

Recommended resources

The Accidental Office Lady and *Working for a Japanese Company* have helped me understand that I am not alone in what I am going through.

Teaching*

Name	Lisette Schiltmans
Nationality	Dutch
Age	31
Qualifications	Masters in Sports Policy and Management
Job title	Teacher: Physical Education and Photography
Employer	International School of the Sacred Heart
Working hours	8:00 a.m. to 4:00 p.m. and after school
Salary	¥4.8 million a year.
Time in this job	18 months

Job description
Teach physical education at middle school and high school levels and coach at least two special sports every school year. Teach photography as an option class to middle school.

General requirements
BA degree or higher.

Japanese requirement
Not necessary.

General conditions
Good.

How she found this job
Went to an ECIS job fair in London.

Differences and similarities with this job at home
Similarities: content of the subjects, environment of international schools, colleagues. Differences: the fact that you are more dependent on your colleagues in a way, because it is harder to socialize with people from Japan due to the language differences.

Best thing
The kids and their energy.

Advice
If you like teaching, this is a very good country to teach in.

Recommended resources
Organization of International Schools, direct approach to schools via Internet.

Other jobs done in Japan
I have been taking pictures for a Dutch newspaper and have done a lot of other artwork.

* For information on English Teaching, see the following section.

Translation

Name	Judith Sullivan
Nationality	American
Age	35
Qualifications	Bachelor's degree in Political Science and Economics from UCLA; fluent in spoken Japanese
Job title	Senior Account Executive
Employer	Dentsu Inc
Working hours	Monday to Friday 9:00 a.m. to 5:00 p.m.
Salary	¥7.8 million a year
Time in this job	4 years

Job description

Planning, preparation, and execution of media- and non-media-related communication activities for multinational clients. Preparation of presentation materials; translation of storyboards and ad copy from Japanese into English for foreign clients; speech writing; press releases; and correspondence.

General requirements

Ability to understand Japanese, understanding of the Japanese corporate climate, understanding or experience in advertising and/or public relations, writing ability, strong communication skills. Some computer skills. Patience. Flexibility.

Japanese requirement

If I did not speak and understand Japanese I could not do my job.

General conditions

In some ways it is a typically loud chaotic messy Japanese company with phones ringing all the time and papers all over the place, although there are quite a few people in my section who speak English very well, so there is more of an international feel to it. Large Japanese companies are infamous for not being able to incorporate and use the talents of foreign staff successfully. If I were working in a foreign firm, my scope of responsibilities would undoubtedly be much greater, but so, probably, would my working hours. As a single mom with two small kids in Tokyo, I would say that this is the perfect job for me right now. I have a lot of respect for my two main bosses and I like the people that I work with.

How she found this job

This is what I call 'My Bed Story'. When I had my first child I had to leave my previous company (JAL) and was more or less unemployed for five months. I was barely scratching out a living. I had to deal with the Catch-22 'if you don't have childcare you can't get a job, if you don't have a job you can't get childcare' tail-chasing maze of craziness. It was a very hard time for me. During this time, I was reading through the *Tokyo Classified*. For some reason I focussed on an ad for a sayonara sale and I was overwhelmed with the feeling that they had something that I truly needed. I was SO curious and filled with conviction, that I schlepped my baby four trains all the way across town to see what they were selling. It turned out that the American guy was leaving Dentsu. I was then struck with the lightning inspiration that if I bought his bed, somehow, some way, I would get his job. Don't ask me to explain the logic of this because I can't. My insurance money from Nico's birth had just come in. I have always been a rather high risk-high return kind of person, so I threw caution to the winds, threw my insurance money down on the crap table, rolled the dice, and bought a bed so big that it took up my whole shitty, hole-in-the-wall, cave apartment. Call it intuition. Or call it luck. Or call it fate. Forty-five people applied and I got it. Needless to say, I moved into a new apartment, and I still have the bed.

Best thing
Very good time versus income ratio. Pleasant colleagues. Fairly stress free. Fairly flexible and understanding with regard to my child-raising responsibilities. Two bosses whom I truly admire and respect. Getting paid to write. Having my ideas and opinions taken seriously. If I need to take work home, the hours I spend working at home I am able to take off from work.

Worst thing
There is a woman in administration who is ready to crucify me if I am ninety seconds late. I don't think she really likes foreigners. Some how, some way, I have to make peace with her. Another thing about my job that I really don't like are the imposed limitations with regard to contributing and having responsibility. I don't feel that I am working to my potential. But as I mentioned earlier, there are trade-offs and my kids are much much more important to me than my work at this point in my life.

Issues affecting her as a woman
I feel that some issues affect me as a mother in my work because of my divided responsibilities, but generally I feel that I get treated with a lot of respect.

Advice
Learn the language. Enjoy what you do. Be flexible. Have a sense of humour. Be open to possibilities. Follow your instincts. Be willing to stick your neck out and buy a bed if you have to.

Recommended resources
Foreign Executive Women and International Women In Communications are good resources for women who want to network and find employment and career advice.

Other jobs done in Japan
English teaching, PR writing and editing for Japan Airlines.

English Teaching

Teaching English is a popular work choice for many foreigners because jobs are fairly easy to find, pay well (¥2000–10,000 per hour), and do not require Japanese ability. For many teaching positions, all that is required is a degree (in any subject) and a positive disposition. Conversation schools and lounges recruit throughout the year, and private students are fairly easy to find at any time. To teach English at an elementary school, high school, or university, you usually need a teaching qualification and/or experience.

Conversation schools

There are thousands of English conversation schools throughout Japan, which are always looking for teachers. Classes are small, usually with a maximum of five students, and training is usually provided. Don't worry if there isn't any training, nor if you have never taught before. These conversation schools are designed to provide a Japanese person with the opportunity to speak English to native speakers, something that is lacking in the Japanese education system. Textbooks are provided, but the extent to which you are required to use them varies from school to school. Generally, if you have an outgoing manner and can encourage people to talk, then you can teach in a conversation school. Professional teachers may find the more 'relaxed' atmosphere to be frustrating, and often prefer to seek employment in high schools or universities.

Teaching in a conversation school can be a great way to gain experience working in Japan and to learn about the culture (often the students want to teach you about their culture as much as they want to be taught about yours). If you have long-term plans to stay in Japan but would ultimately like to pursue another career, it can also be a very good way to establish yourself.

Many of these schools recruit overseas, so contact their head offices in your country. To apply within Japan, simply send your CV to the schools and then follow up with the occasional phone call or a

365

visit; even if they are not recruiting at that time, they will keep your file on record because the turnover of English teachers at conversation schools is high.

Conversation lounges

There are also many conversation lounges throughout Japan that, while they don't pay as well as conversation schools (usually around ¥1000 per hour), can be good places to meet other foreigners as well as Japanese. In many conversation schools, socialising with students isn't encouraged and in some cases is forbidden, whereas conversation lounges actively encourage socialising. There may be board or card games as opposed to textbooks, and the conversation is more realistic than at conversation schools. Working at a conversation lounge, even for only a few hours a week, can be a good way to learn about Japanese culture and have certain aspects of life here explained to you. They tend to be small and friendly, and because other native English speakers are usually present, the pressure isn't always on you to 'entertain' the students. Apply as for conversation schools.

Private students

Private students are also fairly easy to find and if you do a good job with one student, chances are they will introduce several friends to you. Students just want the chance to speak English to a native speaker, so textbooks may be optional. There are several places where you can advertise that you are looking for students, including newspapers, magazines, the Internet, and local noticeboards; some are free. Most people charge ¥2500–5000 per hour for private students and usually meet in a coffee shop or at home (yours or theirs). Obviously you must exercise caution before you go to a stranger's home or invite them to yours. The kinds of students looking for private teachers vary; some are genuinely keen to speak and improve their English, some are single mid-thirtyish men who just want to gaze at a beautiful Western woman (you) and practise the phrase "Do you know Love Hotels?" as often as possible.

Japanese education system: elementary schools, high schools, and universities

Professional teachers tend to look for jobs within the formal Japanese education system. It is preferable that you have teaching experience and a teaching qualification, but all you actually need to apply is a university degree. Recommendations from teachers presently working at the school will help a lot. For part-time teachers, pay is ¥6500–10,000 per class (usually fifty-minute classes). For full-time teachers, pay is on a monthly basis, usually around ¥350,000 and you will also be paid during the holidays (about four months a year). You may be assigned to one school, or have to travel between several schools throughout the week. Classes tend to be large, often up to forty students in a class, but you won't have to deal with the discipline problems that you would expect in a school at home; the Japanese teachers deal with what few discipline problems there are. Most high school teachers are Assistant English or Language Teachers (AETs or ALTs), which means that they 'team-teach' with a Japanese English teacher. Depending on your school, team-teaching can be a bit of a joke, really; the Japanese teacher runs the lesson and you stand in the corner waiting for the teacher to ask you to read something in English, which is actually more tiring than your having to conduct the entire lesson. It can also be frustrating if you were a teacher in your home country and are used to organising the whole class. It helps if you can develop a good relationship with your team-teacher and slowly convince them that you can be of more 'use' to them. As soon as that trust is established, they will allow you to take a more active role.

Teaching in this kind of school generally provides a good income, a secure job, and experience that is to your advantage if you decide to continue your profession when you leave Japan. Be aware though, recently the government has been decreasing budgets allocated to public schools, and often the first area to receive these cuts is the Foreign Language Department. This may mean a sudden cut in pay or hours, or loss of what was once a very secure job for Westerners in Japan. Private schools appear to be unaffected.

The Japan Exchange and Teaching (JET) Program

JET recruits thousands of teachers (JETs) from overseas every year, mostly new university graduates. As with most foreigners who are hired overseas, relocation details are taken care of by the employer, including flight and accommodation. The salary is about ¥300,000 per month, of which a lot can be saved if you are posted to the countryside. Teaching is based in one or several Japanese schools in your area and the position is usually that of Assistant Language Teacher. Many Westerners start life in Japan as JETs and then move on to a major city and a different kind of work. JETs usually stay in the program for two years and often become fairly fluent in Japanese (through necessity, if nothing else). Because most JETs are placed in the countryside, they cite loneliness and isolation as being difficult to cope with. To apply, you must have a degree and be under 35 years old. Contact the Japanese Embassy in your home country for application procedures.

Female frustration with English teaching

When teaching English, Western women often feel frustrated in ways that they may not feel in other jobs in Japan. In addition to the feeling that sometimes they are not taken seriously because they are a foreigner, they also feel that they are not taken seriously because they are female, especially when compared with the foreign male teachers:

> *I believe people's underlying stereotypes of foreign males and females, as well as their underlying (and their overt) ideas about what is appropriate behaviour for women and men ... affect the interactions of the English teacher with the students and staff at the school. For example, in my job there are five foreign English teachers who rotate amongst five schools. The reactions and tasks given to the women teachers vary considerably from those given to the male teachers (i.e., women teachers are expected to conform to Japanese social standards more so than the men). All foreigners here are subject to some degree of harassment, but I believe women are far more prone to it.*

It can be frustrating if you are serious about teaching, yet seem unable to make progress with and get little feedback or even interest from your students:

> *Teaching English at a women's college is a very different experience for men and women. Teaching at companies, I felt that I had the advantage of immediate attention from the primarily male students, but might not have been taken as seriously as the male teachers were. At a women's college, the males have the testosterone advantage, regardless of the level of sexual attractiveness as rated from a Western perspective. But in addition, I feel that the male teachers have, as a rule, lower expectations of the female students. They feel no pressure to prod the students in terms of academic achievement. The female teachers tend to push the students harder and become, as a whole, less popular for doing so, especially with the marginally motivated students.*

If you find yourself in a school where attitudes from staff or students towards women begin to spoil your experience in Japan, one woman offers this advice:

> *As women teachers in particular, as opposed to all English teachers in general, I would say be tolerant of your students' blatant use of their sexuality to get what they want. Be aware that in Japan women have fewer choices and therefore depend on their sexuality to ensure them a comfortable life by depending on men, and maybe that's the way they want it to be.*

Depending on your point of view, you may want to look for another school as soon as possible. A difficult working environment can be tolerated for only so long, and even if you don't think that such issues would bother you, according to the vast majority of women I interviewed, a working environment that does not show respect for all members involved does take its toll. When you first arrive, it may be difficult to know how to get out of your job, but think about it; you got this job, you now have experience, a visa, a regular income, and a lot less naivety. Think about the kind of job you could get with all that behind you. Don't be tempted to think that just because your school has sponsored your visa you have to stay with them.

Gender issues in the English language classroom

Gender issues seem to be increasingly incorporated into educational institutions in both the curriculum and the general ethos in our own countries. For some teachers, particularly women teachers, this is an important aspect of their educational philosophy. Western women often wish to include this in their classroom practice while teaching English in Japan. If women's education is of specific interest and importance to you, don't assume that it is assigned the same status by your school—check out your prospective employers' ideas and beliefs before you accept a job.

If your school is open to discussing 'controversial' topics such as women's issues, depending on your class, you will find a mixed reaction:

Of course I have brought women's issues into the classroom— they are pertinent to most debates and discussions. I have been particularly interested in finding out how hostesses and strippers are viewed (many students respect hostesses), and what people think of high school girls and the way they dress and get involved in selling sex (male students often like it, although there is a lot of outrage among older students both male and female). I tend to introduce controversial topics as a production activity. These sorts of issues are excellent for practising debating, listening, and interrupting skills.

I teach at a women's junior college and they haven't the faintest clue about women's issues, except for the fact that 'brand goods are so expensive, what's a woman to do?' The older women at the language school are a bit more open, I'd say. They realize the raw deal they've been given and have more interest in changing the status quo.

In a few cases, where I've had private classes with women students only, I've found that those with advanced levels of English are more open to asking questions and discussing women's issues such as harassment and what to do when you're harassed, or about sex and menstruation. I don't think those same issues [are] open to male teachers.

Students I taught were not particularly interested in women's issues, but they were mainly lower-level learners. I find language ability often corresponds with capacity to take on challenging issues. In other cases, students who were interested in women's issues were already well informed about them. It's not that they don't know how they stand in the world; it's that they aren't worried about these issues, or just don't want anything controversial in the classroom, or feel we don't understand Japanese society (which is partly true) and therefore what we try to teach doesn't necessarily apply to them.

If gender issues are important to you and your classroom, then find out how receptive your school will be to this before you take the job. You have to fit in with your school's philosophy and there really isn't any reason why we should be imposing our beliefs where they are not welcomed. Find somewhere that welcomes them. Talk to other teachers there. Ask the management about their educational philosophy and get examples of where this is implemented. Observe the way students behave around their male teachers. If you are single, do they ask you if you are getting married soon (as part of the interview, as opposed to general conversation)? It's worth finding out this information if women's education is important to you. Check out the Resources that follow for some recommended teaching materials.

Teachers are role models, so, even if your school doesn't welcome women's issues in the classroom, there will be many opportunities for you to send messages to your students about what it means to be a woman, as well as opportunities outside the classroom to discuss women's issues in a less overt manner.

As an assistant teacher, I have very little say over what is done in the classroom. I do my best teaching outside the classroom, via discussions with the students about my culture, their culture, things in the news. I try to present myself as a model of an independent and self-sufficient woman, and I talk about women I admire, in hopes of broadening the students' perspectives.

You are inspiring your students just by showing them that you are a woman working in a country that is not her own, whether you are single, married, with or without kids, the message is undeniably one of empowerment. One of the major places Western women are doing this, openly or otherwise, is in the English classroom.

Following are some interviews with women who have worked in various capacities teaching English in Japan.

Conversation Schools

Name	Melanie Lang
Nationality	British
Age	26
Qualifications	BA Honours degree French, Spanish and English Language and Linguistics
Job title	Assistant Trainer and EFL Instructor
Working hours	There are three shifts available (10:00 a.m. to 5.40 p.m., 11.40 a.m. to 7.20 p.m., and 1.20 p.m. to 9.00 p.m.).
Salary	Base salary of ¥260,000 per month in the first year (an extra ¥5000 if you have a teaching certificate), increasing by ¥10,000 each year.
Time in this job	1 year, 9 months

Job description

Lessons are forty minutes long and you teach eight a day if you're full time, with five minutes to comment on how each class did, and another five minutes to prepare for your next lesson. There are a maximum of three students per class and they are all in ability levels that are decided by how well they can say fixed phrases and the level of grammar they know. Basically, you're there to entertain as much as actually teach, because they're paying students so you have to do whatever they ask. The advantages are that it's easy, there is no preparation time required after work or at home, and it becomes so repetitive that you can even do it with a banging Asahi hangover! The disadvantages are that if you really expect to teach something meaningful and natural, it's almost impossible.

General requirements

No teaching experience necessary, only a first degree in any subject, although there are plenty of better jobs out there if you have a TEFL, TESOL, or two years experience teaching abroad.

Japanese requirement

Not necessary at all because you are only permitted to use English.

General conditions

Compared with lots of other teaching jobs in Japan, the working conditions aren't great but are improving. Somebody from the company meets you at the airport and takes you to your apartment. Teachers pay all their own housing and insurance costs, although housing in a private apartment or guesthouse is offered (up to and over a one-hour train ride away). You get ten days' paid holiday per year and the schools are generally very flexible about when you take these. However, all national holidays, including Golden Week and Obon are normal working days. Teachers pay for flights to and from Japan, and there is no completion bonus. There are opportunities for promotion if you put yourself forward.

How she found this job

It was advertised in the *Independent* newspaper in the UK.

Differences and similarities with this job at home

There are SO many differences. In Japan the students are generally harder to get information from; they are more reticent and immature/naïve. The hours are also longer in Japan and a longer travel time is expected. The national curriculum doesn't prepare students for speaking English, but their grammar may be better than yours!

Best thing

Very easy to catch on to and easy to do. Schools are very flexible about swapping shifts with other teachers and giving holiday requests. Apartments are available and rents are reasonable, so if you're new to Japan you don't have the added worry of finding a place to live. There is very little pressure from your job because it's so easy. There is no preparation time outside of school.

Worst thing

The frustration at not actually teaching very much! The fact that the students are paying means that you have to do what the students want rather than what you as a teacher think they need; the fact that promotions are handed out to those who have been there longer rather than to those with ability or to those who produce results. You can be instantly sacked for socialising with students.

Issues affecting her as a woman

In my company, women were almost always asked to perform demonstration lessons for men and vice versa!

Advice

Consider what you want out of your time in Japan. If you only want to spend a year there, maybe earn some money, and value having an easy, low-preparation-time job with a very flexible schedule, then a conversation school is a good option. If you are serious about a career teaching English and want to follow a real curriculum, look elsewhere. Also be prepared for working with Japanese colleagues, because their work ethic is very different.

Recommended resources

Look on the Internet for EFL jobs in Japan (Dave's EFL Café, for example), and keep an eye on the magazines in Japan such as *Tokyo Classified*, *Tokyo Journal*, etc.

Other jobs done in Japan

Teaching private English classes at home through agencies.

High Schools

Name	Yvonne Blomer
Nationality	Canadian
Age	29
Qualifications	TESL and TEFL certificates, university degree in Linguistics/Anthropology
Job title	ALT/English Teacher
Employer	Kyushu International Girl's University High School
Working hours	16 to 18 teaching hours per week, plus preparation
Salary	¥4500 per hour of actual teaching
Time in this job	1 year

Job description

Teach, plan lessons, create exams and correct them, help with English play, and help with special seminars.

Japanese requirement

Not necessary at all, though other teachers like it if you can communicate. There are two other foreign language teachers (American) at the school.

General conditions

Very good—heated classrooms.

How she found this job

From a friend who left the position.

Differences and similarities with this job at home

At home I am responsible for teaching all aspects of English; in Japan I am usually responsible for making it fun, for teaching oral communication.

Best thing

The students.

Worst thing

Feeling of being left out of things because I am a foreign woman.

Issues affecting her as a woman

In my first year in Japan I worked in the JET program. The school was not at all interested in having a female teacher. I taught eight classes a week there and the rest of the time I was very much ignored. My second year was much more rewarding.

Advice

Try it out at home first—through volunteering—and talk to people who are doing it or who have done it.

Other jobs done in Japan

I freelance wrote for some small press magazines.

JET Program

Name	Rosemary de Fremery
Nationality	American
Age	23
Qualifications	BA in English Literature
Job title	Assistant Language Teacher (ALT)
Employer	Shizuoka Prefectural Board of Education
Working hours	40 hours a week
Salary	¥3 million a year
Time in this job	18 months

Job description

Teach Oral Communication and Foreign Affairs courses to second- and third-year high school students at one high school in rural Shizuoka prefecture.

General requirements

Must be a native English speaker, have a BA, and be under 35 years old.

Japanese requirement

Usually, JET program participants don't have to speak much Japanese. In my particular situation, it's very useful, if not essential. I teach at a low-level school where the students don't speak much English and even the best ones often speak to me in Japanese during class. When I first arrived and did not speak Japanese, I felt there was practically nothing I could do since I couldn't communicate with the students or understand them. Since then, I've been taking private lessons and have learned a lot. That helped enormously in my classes as well as in the office, where I talk with all sorts of teachers—not just English teachers. I can't recommend it enough—studying Japanese eases much of the stress of life in Japan, especially if you're in a rural, isolated area.

General conditions

Good—I have a very comfortable working environment and my co-workers are outgoing and friendly.

How she found this job

My teacher handed out information packets to everyone in my Japanese literature class at college and I asked him about it.

Differences and similarities with this job at home

The office situation seems very similar in many ways. But the approach towards education is rather different, with the model method being one in which the teacher stands on a platform and lectures the students for the duration of the period. It's very, very difficult to get the students to participate. However, slowly that's starting to change and as I've learned to relate to my students better, I've been able to establish more of a rapport with them and get them to participate in class. However, there is a barrier and as an Assistant

Language Teacher I often have to rely on the talents and leadership of my partner. There is no failsafe way to design a lesson plan that the kids will love since it's not just my influence that's guiding them.

Best things

Constant opportunities to learn and socialize. Since I'm teaching many different classes with different teachers, there's a lot of social and intellectual stimulation, as well as variety, and it gives me a chance to learn a lot about Japan, the students, and their interests.

Worst thing

I live in the boonies and I am the only native English speaker here. Cultural isolation can make me depressed and I have to actively seek out other foreign friends in order to keep from getting down. I like to have a good balance between my foreign and Japanese friends—too much of one or the other is not a good thing. As for the work situation, I don't like feeling like a junior teacher, especially when the teachers themselves are often deferring to me and not providing any guidance of their own. It's difficult to know what's expected of me and how I can improve my job performance.

Interesting stories

I was asked to sing a duet with my team-teaching partner for the seniors' farewell ceremony before graduation. Interesting, since he can't sing but loves to anyway.

Issues affecting her as a woman

The men are rather timid around me, and I generally have much closer relationships with the women since they seem to find me more approachable. I think there's a fear that, since I'm an American woman, I'll accuse someone of sexual harassment. I get that a lot at parties. If someone compliments me, they become very afraid that I'll take offense. Everyone's standards are different where that's concerned, but in my eyes I've been treated well and the only thing I regret is not being able to get to know my male co-workers a little better.

Advice

I would say do it, but be aware that you're going to have to carve out a life for yourself outside of work and make sure your personal priorities are clear. It's easy to get swept up in all sorts of activities here, whether it be outings with other foreigners or with your Japanese friends. Find the balance that works for you, and don't be hard on yourself when you get wiped out. I'm satisfied with my life here and I would definitely recommend coming here. It certainly has given me a different outlook on American culture and caused me to take a closer look at the society from which I came.

Recommended resources

Subscribe to the JET-L electronic mailing list. Read up on Japanese culture and etiquette. Also, learn Japanese. Every little bit helps, no matter how small.

Small Children

Name	Anonymous
Nationality	Australian
Age	38
Qualifications	Diploma of Arts and Graduate Diploma in Teaching
Job title	Children's English Tutor
Working hours	Usually from about 2:30 p.m. until 6:00 p.m., five days a week
Time in this job	About 5 years.

Job description

Present the children's curriculum in an enjoyable, entertaining, and interesting way. Give level checks once a year. Organise and run children's Christmas and Halloween parties. Monitor children's progress and adapt my lessons accordingly. Give demonstration lessons to prospective students and mothers. Give demonstration lessons for training to other teachers. Comment on and provide input for curriculum development.

General requirements

Patience and a sense of humour. I think they're the main ones!

Japanese requirement

None.

General conditions

Classes are either at private homes or in community rooms. I have a Japanese assistant and no more than eight children in a class. When I teach two-year-old kids there are no more than six in a class and they're accompanied by their mothers or fathers. Kids are from ages 2 to 12.

How she found this job

One of my friends had applied for it and introduced me.

Differences and similarities with this job at home

You wouldn't probably be teaching two year olds at home. You may or may not have an assistant. You would probably have larger classes at home. You would probably have more discipline problems at home, and I guess you might be asked to do more counselling there as well.

Best thing

I get to have fun! When you teach adults, adults know they have to behave and this can be boring. Children don't operate the same way, so if it's been a rainy weekend or if it's windy or if they've just had sports day their whole mood changes, and your classroom changes as well, your activities change. I teach in many different schools so I get to be in different rooms, not just stuck in one office. I get to know some Japanese women in their houses who are not the kind of people I would normally come across.

Worst thing

I spend a lot of time travelling and I find twenty Christmas parties in one week to be stressful!

Issues affecting her as a woman

None really. It's very much a woman's world. The fathers rarely get involved in the activities.

Advice

If you enjoy children's company or if you enjoy working by yourself it's a good opportunity. It's a change from doing adult teaching, and it's very much a different skill, but the down side is that your language is never fully utilised. It's kind of a challenge to find other ways to communicate.

Recommended resources

Sensible shoes! There are a number of schools now who are targeting the children's market, so search out those companies and chat with them. As for classroom resources: simple sets of flash cards, some very simple children's English storybooks. Our company uses the 'Finding Out' series. As many songs as possible. Make up simple games like snakes and ladders and bingo, any kind of game that could be used to target language. Oh, and a singing voice is helpful, but optional.

Other jobs done in Japan

I have taught adults English. I've worked as a high school teacher and I've also worked as a tutor to some university students.

Universities

Name	May Leong
Nationality	US citizen
Age	36 (at the time that I worked in Japan)
Qualifications	Master's degree in English and teaching experience
Job title	Visiting Professor
Employer	International University of Japan
Working hours	9:00 a.m. to 5:00 p.m.
Salary	¥6.5 million a year
Time in this job	4 years

Job description

Designed and taught a special course for graduate students incorporating company creation/job interview simulation, the Internet as a business tool, problem-solving cross-cultural issues, and written and oral business communication skills. Designed, coordinated, and taught Communication and Text Skills courses. Managed Summer Colloquium Series for Visiting Faculty. Launched multi-university international email writing project. Taught cross-cultural communication, presentation, and reading skills to Japanese business executives in management training program. Led workshop session as part of short-term program for multinational VPs and CEOs. Designed and taught communicative speaking and writing techniques for Japanese high school English teachers.

General requirements

Master's degree and experience in teaching.

Japanese requirement

Not necessary; however, being able to speak Japanese is a definite bonus and also helps with adapting to the culture.

General conditions

Located three hours north of Tokyo. Small classes of graduate students (ten to fourteen).

How she found this job

Through a professional organization's newsletter—TESOL (Teachers of English to Speakers of Other Languages).

Differences and similarities with this job at home

Educators generally get more respect and pay in Japan—at least at the university level.

Best thing

I met many interesting students and colleagues from around the world and got to know the Japanese culture.

Worst thing

The problems I encountered due to cultural differences.

Interesting stories

Since we lived in the countryside north of Japan in 'snow country', we experienced living where the snow was typically higher than two metres. It was fun having to ski out of our second story bedroom window in order to shovel our front door clear of the snow. Also, even though it snows a lot in Niigata-ken, it is not that cold. The snow removal system is a water sprinkler system. So imagine driving on the roads in the winter with water sprinkling down the middle and creating rivers on the road. Where I grew up in New York City, you could get shot (figuratively speaking) for pouring water on the snow because it would immediately freeze over. So this was a new experience for us.

Issues affecting her as a woman

Being Asian, there were many times when I was mistaken for being a Japanese woman—which I really didn't mind at all. What happened was that sometimes I was treated very well because I was a female Asian foreigner (people could forgive my mistakes) and other times I was judged more harshly because of my gender and race. Also, people would constantly walk up to me and ask me what my husband teaches. I'd answer that he doesn't teach, I do. Some of my male Japanese students worried that my husband wasn't working. So finally I told them that he was a student (which was true after the first year as he worked on his master's degree via the Internet).

Advice

Create a good support system and network with people—colleagues, neighbors, and students. Being in a 'sensei' position carries a lot of responsibilities and expectations; it also gives you an interesting opening in terms of relationships with people. Also, there will be times when you need to come across as someone who is strong and focused, as someone who knows her stuff. So never doubt your own skills or knowledge.

Recommended resources

Definitely join different organizations—TESOL, SIETAR (Society of Intercultural Education, Training and Research), Foreign Executive Women, Digital Eve Japan. The advantage is that you'll get to meet both Japanese and non-Japanese members in a very supportive community.

Other jobs done in Japan

Working mom! Being a working mom involves a lot of challenges—what do to when your child is sick, scheduling pick up and drop off time, getting to know your child's schoolmates and their families. It's almost a full-time job in and of itself!! I also later worked as a freelance Curriculum Designer Consultant and later on as VP of Online Development for a small translation company.

Mizushobai

Mizushobai directly translates as 'the water trade', as traditionally this work was done on riverbanks, but it is now used to refer to work that involves alcohol. Hostess bars, 'exotic' dancing, strip clubs, and the sex trade are classified as mizushobai. Some Western women choose to work in this area while in Japan, but, for obvious reasons, information can be difficult to get. Regular bars are also considered to be part of mizushobai.

Hostess bars are lounge-like bars where mostly Japanese men pay ridiculous amounts of money to be entertained for the evening by a hostess. Depending on the club, this entertainment can involve an attractive, attentive woman sitting with the men, pouring their drinks, lighting their cigarettes, and singing karaoke with them, the purpose being to allow the men to relax after a hard day at the office. For some bars it doesn't go any further than that. For many Western women it can be an interesting way to practise Japanese, get an insight into Japanese culture, and make some contacts that may lead to other work (many of these men are very influential people, including politicians and company presidents). Some bars have a dress code, which is usually 'something bright and feminine', some may require just lingerie, some are topless, and some include strip shows. Some hostesses are expected to 'encourage' their regular customers to take them out for dinner prior to going to the club. All clubs expect you to drink. Long-time hostesses find that the alcohol, late nights, and emotional stress take their toll, but for the short term it can be OK. Hostesses usually earn between ¥2500–6000 per hour plus extras, and strippers can earn about ¥100,000 a night. See the interview that follows for more details about working as a hostess or stripper.

Some Western women work in the sex industry in Japan, and for most Western women this is a matter of choice as opposed to necessity or force. If you work as a hostess or even as a private English teacher, there may come a time when a Japanese man takes a shine to you and makes a suggestion in a way that you can choose to ignore or pursue at your own risk. In Japan, sexual activity is not as influenced by Judeo-Christian morals as it might be in our home countries. Paid sex with an acquaintance is considered quite different to paid sex with a 'street prostitute'. Alternatively, there are some clubs called 'health', 'fashion', or 'pink' clubs that employ women to provide sexual services that range from erotic massages to oral sex, for which the women are paid about ¥5000 an hour. It is not uncommon for these places to be frequented by a group of salarymen who whilst drinking over the table are being relieved under the table, although why anyone would want their colleagues watching them having an orgasm is beyond me ... sometimes the Japanese group ethic goes a bit too far. There are a few 'escort' agencies that employ Western women, but they are not highly publicised, and you are expected to have sex for about ¥30,000 an hour. For many Western women, the fact that they are not in their home country means that they can disassociate themselves from the work as soon as they leave Japan. If you choose to work in the sex industry in Japan, then please take all the precautions you would in your home country. It is actually illegal to have sex for money in Japan, but it tends to be one of those laws that most people ignore.

Following is an interview with a woman who has worked in the mizushobai industry. This interview is particularly lengthy; I feel that accurate information about this industry is difficult to come by, and, if you plan to work in mizushobai, then you probably need even more information than if you were going to work in a more 'respectable' field.

Hostessing and Stripping

Name	Anonymous
Nationality	American
Age	Now 25; 22–23 when I was hostessing and then stripping
Qualifications	Ivy League BA (obviously was not relevant to this particular field of work)
Job title	'Talent'
Employer	Various
Working hours	8:00 p.m. to 3:00 a.m., more or less for both jobs.
Salary	Varies enormously. Hostessing: I got ¥280,000 a month in a country town (plus free lodgings); no tips. Stripping: ¥400,000 plus in Yokohama. The basic salary in Yokohama was still between ¥250,000 and ¥300,000, and lodgings were NOT included, but the tips were incredible. You would think it was a bad night if you didn't get at least one ¥10,000 note down your cleavage. I didn't go all out for tips. If you're totally shameless you can get ¥100,000 in tips in one night.
Time in this job	Six months: two stints of three months in each job. I left the country in between so as not to overstay my visa. ALL Western hostesses and dancers work illegally on tourist visas, as far as I know.

Job description

Hostessing (although some of this is also relevant to stripping): flirting for cash, not to put too fine a point on it. The hard sell is important: if it looks like the clients are leaving, you have to go all kittenish to get them to stay on, and if they're being tight and not drinking enough, you complain that you're thirsty and make them buy you drinks. Some of the girls would get drunk or buzzed night in and night out, but it was totally acceptable to stick to oolong cha, as I did. You are also a waitress. You have to pour the client's drinks, light his cigarettes, and applaud his karaoke numbers. If he's too shy to sing by himself, you have to sing with him, or just accompany him onto the stage. Stripping: when I started doing it, I found that it was actually easier than hostessing. You don't have to talk to anyone when you're on stage! You would have two or three 'sets' a night, each consisting of two or three songs. It's your basic writhe around a pole, legs in the air, twirl your bra around your head type of thing. You didn't have to take your thong off if you didn't want to—some of the girls did it as their finale, but not me.

General requirements

For both jobs: being acceptable looking. Being a Playmate-style knockout like one girl I knew was actually a disadvantage as it made it difficult for clients to relate to her on any kind of human level. Deep reserves of patience are essential.

384

Japanese requirement

Not. That said, I soon realized it would be a tremendous advantage, got myself a set of language learning books, and practised on the clients. They thought this was cute.

General conditions

Hostessing: no different from going out clubbing six nights a week and talking to a lot of guys you don't particularly like. Stripping: no different from sticking on a CD and getting down in your bedroom. Or if you did private dances (which I avoided like the plague), then it's no different from sitting on Grandpa's lap, in an alternate world dominated by Nabokov family values.

How she found this job

I was in London. I answered an advertisement for hostessing and went for an interview. I did the stripping after I wised up to the fact that there was a whole lot more money to be made if I sussed out the job opportunities for myself.

Differences and similarities with this job at home

There is no such thing as hostessing in the US, except at bars catering to Japanese or Korean expats, and I would NEVER DREAM of stripping anywhere except Japan because I have the impression that almost all strippers in the US are also prostitutes. I suppose I ought to state right here that there was NO prostitution. Some girls dated and slept with their favorite clients, and got presents, but that's slightly different. The difference is that you're not explicitly selling sex. In the US that's ALL you're selling. I wouldn't DREAM of going NEAR it.

Best thing

The other girls. I've never had such laughs in my life. We developed a fantastic camaraderie. NOTE: This was much more true in the countryside club than in Yokohama. I find that bitchiness and competition among women increase in proportion to the cash up for grabs.

Worst thing

Where to begin? Pervy old men. Fat ugly yakuza bruisers who had to be treated like princes. Cockroaches in the dressing room. Having to put on Cinderella dresses and sing 'Imagine' at show time (that was in the countryside town). No, actually, the worst thing was when you would get a nice, handsome client. You would start liking him. He'd become a regular. You would go out to dinner with him on your day off. Perhaps you'd get the illusion that you were friends, or more. But you would be WRONG. There is no possibility of sincerity when the very currency of relationships, talk, laughter, and touches is for sale. Even if a hostess and client become involved outside work, it's impossible for the man to stop fearing that she's still selling herself, and impossible for the girl to get out of her head the notion that he sees her as a commodity. That was what put me off in the end, actually. The realization that the debasing of social interactions into TRANS-ACTIONS is completely poisonous to our souls. It's the ultimate triumph of materialism. Another downside for some of the girls was that they got completely put off Japan, or if they weren't put off Japan altogether, they were put off Japanese men. Understandably so, right? But you have to remember that maybe a majority of the guys at hostess bars are only there because their boss dragged them along, or because they have a brief to spend a certain amount of money on some visiting corporate type.

Interesting stories

When I was working in the countryside, the regulars provided most of our laughs. We had our resident Elvis impersonator who would come twice a week and sing Elvis songs all night. He always wanted me to sing with him because I supposedly had an American accent, but he sounded a hell of a lot more like Elvis than I did! We also had the Enka Witch, an old lady friend of Papa san who would come and, you guessed it, sing enka all night while lifting her skirt and kicking out her legs like a Toulouse-Lautrec chorus girl. It was also interesting to be taken to the host club in a nearby town where the boyfriend of one of the Filipinos with whom we worked was working. All the hosts were Filipino or Malaysian. (In Tokyo, hosts tend to be black guys.) The clientele are mostly middle-aged women. Oh my God, you would not think Japanese housewives could behave like that!

Issues affecting her as a woman

See above.

Advice

Regarding safety, you just have to exercise common sense and know how to carry yourself. If a girl agrees to meet a client outside the club, she's taking a risk. You have to know how to calculate that risk and sort out the creeps from the basically normal guys. The danger is that a girl will let herself get so blinded by cash lust that she goes out with a guy even though she's not sure about him, because he has promised he'll buy her jewellery or designer clothes or something. If you're working in metropolitan Tokyo, a lot of it is just big city smarts. Before coming to Japan I had lived in New York City for years, so I have a pretty good nose for iffy situations. Some girls have been more sheltered, and I don't think they should be hostessing at all, let alone in Tokyo. They just fall for a smile and a line; it's sad to see.

Other jobs done in Japan

I'm now working as an English teacher (private lessons). I have some of the same problems with the social interaction as transaction thing, but it's a good deal less fake, because you don't have to pretend you like your students if you don't: you can just retreat into sensei mode.

Finding a Job

Before you get to Japan

If the company that you work for at home has connections with Japan—a branch, subsidiary company, or 'sister' company—ensure that your superiors know that you are keen to go to Japan. Many of your colleagues would also probably like the opportunity to go to Japan, so the competition will be high and you may need to be patient. It's even possible that you will be sent elsewhere overseas. Alternatively, you can search for a job yourself; many Japanese and foreign companies operating in Japan recruit overseas. Recruiting overseas attracts more applicants than recruiting in Japan, so again the competition will be high. Check out magazines, newspapers, and the Internet. The great advantage to securing your job before you get to Japan is that your employer will organise practically everything: visa, flight, accommodation, insurance, Japanese lessons (probably), a relocation allowance, child care/education arrangements if applicable, and a car too.

After first arriving in Japan

If you rather enjoy taking financial and emotional risks, then you can turn up in Japan and look for a job whilst on a tourist visa. This option is not for the faint-hearted; it's stressful, but incredibly exciting and challenging! You need stamina, a constant positive mental attitude, persistence, and money.

You need enough stamina to look for a job while you are looking for accommodation, rushing around on trains, and getting over jet lag. You need a constant positive mental attitude to be friendly to all the people you are meeting who may well lead you to the perfect job (more on networking later). You need persistence because you will spend a lot of time on the phone following up job leads. You need money for your flight, accommodation, food, and expenses until you get paid, which may be about a month after you start your job. Remember that in most cases you will be unable to start working until you have the right visa. You need enough money to keep yourself going for about three months, but bring as much as you can. The following is a budget for people who would like to find a job upon arrival in Japan, but have restricted finances.

	Time Until Payday	
	3 Months	1 Month
Flight	¥120,000	¥120,000
Accommodation (incl. deposit)	200,000	100,000
Food	90,000	30,000
Other expenses	90,000	30,000
	¥500,000	¥280,000

If you know that you are coming to Japan to look for work, then you may be tempted to call the Japanese embassy in your home country to ask them for information about finding work here. Don't bother. They will emphatically tell you that it is impossible and illegal for you to look for work in Japan without a working visa. Ignore them. Just get a 90-day return ticket with a changeable return date and come to Japan on a tourist visa. You don't have to apply for a tourist visa—it will be stamped in your passport upon arrival in Japan. The immigration officer will ask you why you are visiting Japan. Under no circumstances must you tell them that you are looking for work—it is legal for you to look for work in Japan without a working visa, but it is not encouraged. You are likely to be refused entry into the country if you tell them you are looking for work. Tell them that you are travelling; this is another reason why it is important to have enough money with you—they may want to see it. It is also highly unlikely that you will be allowed into Japan without a return ticket.

When you arrive, and have found somewhere to stay (just get a base at first, you can find a better place later), start looking for work immediately. It is scary how quickly money goes in Japan, so the sooner you secure some income the better. Magazines, newspapers, people you meet on the street, the resources below; all are potential leads to jobs. You need a job that will provide you with a visa, but if you can't find one right away, look for some private English students or other sources of income that do not require a visa. Meanwhile, continue your search for visa sponsorship. The more money you have when you arrive, the less pressure you will be under. When you've secured that visa sponsorship and have returned from Korea with that lovely red working visa stamp in your passport, you can relax and, if this job doesn't meet your professional needs, take your time in securing a job that does.

After being in Japan for some time

You may find that the job you originally chose just isn't for you, and may want to look for alternatives in Japan, especially if you have been teaching English. There is a wide range of jobs available, so don't feel like you have to stay in a job you hate. If you have been here for some time, then you have probably acquired some Japanese by osmosis, if nothing else; a bit more effort in that department and your job options will increase. For all people looking for work in Japan, networking is an important skill to develop. After you have been in Japan for some time, you probably will have developed an extensive network without even realising it.

Networking

Networking is probably the most influential factor in determining your success in securing a job in Japan, whether you have just arrived or have been living here for years. Forget that First Class Honours degree from Oxford, your fluent ability in Japanese, and ten years experience in your chosen field—if you don't have the ability to let people know who you are and what you are looking for, then your opportunities are far fewer. It can be a difficult skill to develop at first, especially if you are by nature rather reserved, but Japan is a great place to develop your networking ability. Remember that every foreigner here has been in your situation, and Western women are particularly keen to connect with and support one another. There are many organisations in Japan specifically dedicated to promoting networking in the foreign and Japanese communities, and many are exclusively for women. Check out Chapter Nine: Women's Organisations. I can't emphasise enough the value of joining Foreign Executive Women, which has two groups in Japan. Don't let the name put you off; it is a very welcoming organisation for all foreign women in Japan, irrespective of 'executive' status. Whether you are a teacher, a businesswoman, or are taking time out from working for some reason, you will find a great network of women willing to support each other.

The exchange of business cards is fast and furious but friendly in Japan, so, even if you don't have a job title to include, get some printed with just your name and contact details on them. Follow up with everyone you meet, even if it is just to say that it was good to meet them—email is perfect for this. And you never know what friendships may emerge from the exchange of a business card.

Visas

You cannot legally work in Japan without a working visa. There are some jobs or means of generating income that do not require a visa, but they tend to be illegal. It is also illegal for someone to employ you if you have a tourist visa. Australia, Canada, and (just recently) the UK have reciprocal working holiday visa arrangements with Japan. Check in your home country to see if you are eligible. Foreign women who are married to foreign men and have spouse visas may work up to twenty hours a week. There are no working restrictions on foreign women who are married to Japanese men and have spouse visas.

To obtain a working visa in Japan, your employer has to 'sponsor' you, i.e., submit several documents to the Japanese immigration authorities, including your contract, your qualifications, and company details. It is a little-publicised fact that you can submit these documents yourself and apply for your own visa, as long as you can prove that your income exceeds ¥200,000 (not ¥250,000, contrary to popular belief) per month, although obviously you need your employer's co-operation. Another little-publicised fact is that you can obtain a visa by combining several different jobs: you need the documents for each employer and the total amount of income must exceed ¥200,000 per month. Just submitting the documents does not make it instantly legal for you to work, although some companies will allow you to, claiming that you are merely 'training'. If there is evidence that they have paid you during this period, then they (not you) face prosecution. It can take up to two months for your visa application to be processed and, if it is successful, your employer (or you if you submitted it yourself) will receive notification that your Certificate of Eligibility is ready for collection. The certificate must now be taken to a Japanese embassy in any country (it doesn't have to be the one in your home country), where it will be stamped. You then submit the certificate when you enter Japan and receive a working visa stamp in your passport. Most first-time visas are for one year. If you are really unlucky, then you will receive a six-month visa. In 1999 a three-year working visa was introduced, which some foreigners receive upon renewal, usually if they have been working at the same company for the three years previously. Renewal involves submitting the same documents to the immigration authorities, and waiting for confirmation and a new stamp in your passport. You don't need to visit a Japanese embassy outside Japan to have your visa renewed, but can do this at your local immigration office. If you change jobs during the year preceding your renewal, in addition to the usual documents, you are also supposed to submit a copy of your letter of resignation, although the immigration officers are not always strict about this.

If you come to Japan on a tourist visa and acquire employment, then you need to leave the country to visit a Japanese embassy to get your passport stamped. Most foreigners in this situation fly to Korea, submit the certificate with their passport on the day they arrive, collect them the following morning, and fly back to Japan that afternoon. Just take more than enough money and don't forget about the airport tax in Korea.

Japanese ability

It is entirely possible to get a good job in Japan without speaking Japanese. Some employers even forbid you from speaking Japanese at work, especially if you are teaching English. If you do speak Japanese, however, your job opportunities greatly increase. Some employers will arrange Japanese lessons for you, all at their expense, especially if you have been recruited from overseas. It's common sense that some basic Japanese ability will smooth relationships with colleagues.

Qualifications

It is highly unlikely that you will find legal work in Japan without a degree or equivalent qualification. This requirement is more to satisfy immigration officials than your employers. For some jobs your qualifications must be in a specialist subject and experience is required, although this is not always necessary.

Useful Japanese

work (verb)	*hataraku*	working visa	*shuurou biza*
job	*shigoto*	networking	*nettowaaku*
part time	*paato*	university degree	*gakushi*
full time	*furu-taimu/seishain*	Master's degree	*shuushi*
temporary	*ichijiteki na*	graduate school	*daigakuin*
get a permanent job	*teishoku ni tsuku*		

I'm looking for a job.	*Shigoto o sagashite imasu.*
I'd like to apply for the position of	*... no shokushu ni oubo shitai desu.*
Did you receive my resume?	*Watashi no rirekisho o uketoraremashita ka.*
What are the working hours?	*Shuugyo jikan wa nanji kara nanji made desu ka.*
Can you provide a working visa for me?	*Shuurou biza o teikyou shite itadakemasu ka.*
What is the hourly rate / monthly salary?	*Jikan kyu / gekkyuu wa donokurai desu ka.*
I'd like to apply for a working visa.	*Shuurou biza o shinsei shitai desu.*
Here is my business card.	*Watashi no meishi o douzo.*

Resources

See the resources in **Your Status** in **Chapter One** for more information about visas.

Information and Job Listings

Industrial Employment Stabilisation Centre 03-3836-1090
  All types of jobs, for people of Japanese descent only.
Interac 03-3234-7857
    Place teachers of foreign languages throughout Japan.
    http://www.interac.co.jp/recruit
Japan AIDS Prevention Awareness Network 03-3928-9057
    Educational materials for schools, video library, lesson   052-806-5534
    plans, speakers, presentations. Serves all Japan.
    http://www.japanetwork.gol.com
Japan Association for Language Teaching (JALT) 03-3837-1630
    Magazine, monthly meetings throughout Japan,
    annual conference.
    http://www.jalt.org
Japan Association for Working Holidaymakers 03-3389-0181
    Mostly English teaching in Tokyo, Osaka, and Kyushu.
    http://www.mmjp.or.jp/jawhm
Kimi Information Centre 03-3986-1604
    Mostly English teaching in Tokyo.
    http://www2.dango.ne.jp/kimi

Tokyo Student Living Guidance Office 03-3951-9103
    Part-time jobs for students. Computers, moving, cleaning,
    washing dishes.
    http://www.naigai.or.jp

Asia-Jobs
    Information technology jobs.
    http://www.asia-links.com/asia-jobs/
Asia-Net
    All types of jobs.
    http://www.asia-net.com
Association of Canadian Teachers in Japan
    http://www.tesl.ca/japan/
Clubnet2000
    Information about hostessing.
    http://members.tripod.com/~clubnet2000/
ELT News: The Web Site for English Teachers in Japan
    http://www.eltnews.com/eltnews.shtml
ESL Japan—a site dedicated to English as a Second Language
    http://www.esljapan.com/teachers/before.htm
Gender Awareness in Language Teaching (GALE)
    Research, develop materials, raise awareness, provide discrimination
    information, networking, discussion.
    http://www2.gol.com/users/ath/gale
Japan Exchange and Teaching (JET) Programme
    http://www.mofa.go.jp/j_info/visit/jet/index.html
JET Alumni Association (JETAA)
    http://www.jet.org/
Japan Times Monday edition
    All types of jobs.
    http://www.japantimes.co.jp/
Jobs in Japan
    All types of jobs.
    http://www.jobsinjapan.com/
Ohayo Sensei
    English-language related jobs.
    http://www.ohayosensei.com/
Teaching English in Japan
    http://eisv01.lancs.ac.uk/staff/visitors/kenji/kitao/tejk.htm
Teaching English in Japan (Embassy of Japan in the UK)
    http://www.embjapan.org.uk/ed_teach.html
The Working Holiday Programme in Japan (Ministry of Foreign Affairs Website)
    http://www.mofa.go.jp/j_info/visit/w_holiday/index.html
Tokyo Classified JobFinder (every Friday)
    All types of jobs.
    http://www.tokyoclassified.com/tokyojobsemployment/1.2.inc.htm
Women Educators and Language Learners (WELL)
    Networking, support, information, raise consciousness, improve conditions, guard
    against sexism in materials, directory, newsletter, presentations, workshops.
    http://www.miyazaki-mic.ac.jp/faculty/kisbell/well/well.html

Recruitment Companies Accepting Foreigners

ABA Secretarial Recruitment 03-3221-1331
    Secretarial, accountancy, marketing, personnel. Usually
    require Japanese ability. Tokyo.

Associates in Career Enhancement (ACE) Japan Inc 03-3503-2251
    Banks, securities. Some Japanese is helpful. Worldwide.

Alex Tsukada International Ltd (Boyden) 03-3478-5477
    Executive. Japanese ability preferred. All Japan.

Borgnan Human Development Institute 03-3989-8151
    All fields. Japanese ability necessary. Tokyo.
    http://www.hdi.co.jp

East West Consulting 03-3222-5531
    All fields. Japanese ability necessary. Worldwide.
    http://www.ewc.co.jp

Executive Consultants International Inc 03-5570-7272
    IT, manufacturing, fashion, automotive. Japanese ability
    necessary. All Japan.

Executive Search International Inc 03-3479-0918
    All fields. Some need Japanese ability. All Japan.
    http://www.esijpn.com/

First Position (see display ad, page 399) 03-5363-7936
    All fields. Some need Japanese ability. All Japan.

Heidrick and Struggles Japan Ltd 03-3500-5310
    Executives in all fields. Usually need Japanese. All Japan.
    http://www.heidrick.com

International Computer Professionals Associates (IPA) 03-5325-3218
    Financial, IT, engineering, senior management. Must speak
    Japanese. All Japan.
    http://www.icpa.com

International Contracting Corp (ICC) 03-3583-1223
    All fields. Japanese ability necessary. Tokyo and Kanto.

International Management Consulting Agency (IMCA) 03-5512-4711
    Management level, also secretarial, sales, real estate.
    Most need Japanese ability. All Japan and worldwide.
    http://www.imca.co.jp/index-e.html or
    http://www.imca.america.com

InterSearch Japan—Wouters and Associates Consulting 03-3423-7491
    All fields. Japanese ability preferred. All Japan.
    http://www2.gol.com/users/wouters

IXSUS Inc 03-3486-3695
    All fields. Japanese ability necessary. Tokyo.
    http://www.ixsus.co.jp

Korn/Ferry International Japan 03-3211-6851
    Advanced technology, financial services, consumer goods.
    Usually need Japanese. Mainly Tokyo.
    http://www.kornferry.com

Office Automation (OA) Consultants Co Ltd 03-3496-9443
    All fields. Japanese ability necessary. Tokyo.

Plaxel Co 03-5721-6484
    Executive. Japanese ability preferred. Mainly Tokyo.
    http://www.plaxel.com

Ray and Berndtson 03-5211-8411
     Senior executive level. Most need Japanese ability. Mostly Tokyo.
     http://www.rayberndtson.com
Robert Walters 03-5405-1921
     Finance, IT, commerce. Sometimes need Japanese ability. Tokyo.
     http://www.robertwalters.com
Staff Japan Corporation 0120-303-701
     All fields. Japanese ability necessary. Tokyo, Yokohama,
     Osaka, Kobe, Kyushu.
Stanton Chase International 03-5408-1400
     Executive. Japanese ability usually needed. All Japan
     and worldwide.
     http://www.stantonchase.co.jp
Technical Management Search Institute 03-3512-2601
     Consulting. Japanese ability necessary. All Japan.
     http://www.tmng.co.jp
Technics in Management Transfer Inc 03-3221-1011
     Computers, cosmetics. Japanese ability usually needed.
     Mostly Tokyo.
Tokyo Executive Search Co. Ltd. 03-3230-1881
     All fields. Japanese ability necessary. All Japan.
     http://www.tesco.co.jp
Top Research Corporation 03-3502-1371
     All fields. Japanese ability necessary. Tokyo.
Veritas International 03-3440-8404
     All fields. Most need Japanese. Mostly Tokyo.
     http://www.veritas-int.com
Wall Street Associates (WSA) Group 03-5288-5157
     IT, legal and compliance, banking. Japanese ability often
     needed. Tokyo.
     http://www.wsagroup.com
Wimnys International Inc 03-5276-3171
     Executive. Japanese ability often needed. All Japan.

Temporary Staff Agencies
Adecco Career Staff 03-3470-9300
     Clerical, secretarial, IT. Japanese ability necessary. All Japan.
International Business Service (IBS) Co Ltd 045-663-1557
     Personal assistant, secretarial. Bilingual preferred. Mostly Tokyo.
JAL Business Service Co Ltd 03-3459-0011
     Travel agents, airline staff. Japanese ability necessary. All Japan.
Network of Creative Brains As Soon As Possible International Inc 0120-864-450
     Secretarial, translation, trading, interpreting. Japanese ability
     necessary. Mostly Tokyo.
     http://www.ncbasp.com
Staff Service Co Ltd 03-3288-5601
     Office. Japanese ability necessary. Mostly Tokyo.

Temporary Services 092-472-0032
        Modelling, acting, TV. Japanese ability necessary. Fukuoka,
        Oita, Kagoshima, Hiroshima, Nagasaki.
        http://www2.tiki.ne.jp
Trajal Staff Kyushu Inc 092-262-1800
        Counter staff. Japanese ability necessary. Kyushu.

Networking Organisations and Professional Support

Check with your university alumni to see if there are any members in Japan who would be willing to help you with jobseeking.

Foreign Correspondents Club of Japan 03-3211-3161
        For journalists. Bar, lounge, access to press luncheons/
        conferences. Tokyo.
        http://www.fccj.or.jp
Foreign Executive Women (FEW) 090-7216-5171
        Networking organisation to help foreign women fulfill their
        potential, regardless of professional status.
        http://www.few.gol.com
Foreign Executive Women (FEW) Kansai 06-6441-2581
        As above but for Kansai region.
Foreign Nurses Association of Japan (FNAJ) 03-5469-0966
Japan Interpreter's Association 03-3209-4741
        Examination assistance, licensing and proficiency
        examinations, seminars.
Oak Associates 03-5472-7077
        Career consulting.

Association for Women in Finance (IWF)
        http://www.noriko.com/awftokyo.html
Digital Eve Japan
        For women in computers. Formerly Japan Webgrrls.
        http://www.digitalevejapan.org
Foreign Press Centre
        For journalists. Press information, tours, meetings.
        http://www.nttls.co.jp/fpc
Foreign Women Lawyers Association (FWLA)
        http://www2.gol.com/users/fwla
Forum for Corporate Communications (FCC)
        http://www.fcc.gol.com
Institution of Engineers of Ireland
        http://www.geocities.com/ieijapan/index.html
International Women in Communications
        http://www.iwic.gol.com
Kaisha Society
        Support for foreigners working in Japanese companies.
        http://www.kaisha.gol.com
Roppongi Bar Association International Legal Network
        http://www.rbalawnet.com

Society of Writers, Editors and Translators (SWET)
>Publish a style guide for writing about Japan: *Japan Style Sheet*,
>Stone Bridge Press: 1998 (revised edition).
>swet@infopage.net
>http://www.infopage.net/swet

Young Professionals Association
>patrick@twics.com

Resume Services

Kimi Information Centre 03-3986-1604
>Self-service. Ikebukuro, Tokyo.
>http://www2.dango.ne.jp/kimi

Kinkos
>Self-service. 24 locations in Tokyo, Nagoya, Osaka, Fukuoka.
>http://www.kinkos.co.jp

Others

American Chamber of Commerce Resume Posting Service 03-3433-7304
>http://www.accj.or.jp

Resources and Further Reading

Guide to Jobs in Japan
>By James C Gibbs, Global Village Media Co Ltd: 1998.

Learning to Bow: An American Teacher in a Japanese School
>By Bruce S Feiler, Ticknor and Fields: 1991.

Make a Mil-Yen: Teaching English in Japan
>By Don Best, Stone Bridge Press: 1998.

Office Ladies and Salaried Men: Power, Gender, and Work in Japanese Companies
>By Yuko Ogasawara, University of California Press: 1998.

Teaching English in Japan
>By Jerry O'Sullivan, NTC Publishing Group: 1995.

The Accidental Office Lady
>By Laura I Kriska, Charles E Tuttle Publishing: 1997. By the first female
>American trainee in Tokyo's Honda Headquarters.

Too Late for the Festival: An American Salary-Woman in Japan
>By Rhiannon Paine, Academy Chicago Pub: 1999.

Translate or Communicate: English As a Foreign Language in Japanese Schools
>By George Moore and Judith Lamie, Nova Science Publishers, Inc: 1997.

Western Women Working in Japan
>By Nancy K Napier and Sully Taylor, Quorum Books: 1995.

Working for a Japanese Company: Insights into the Multicultural Workplace
>By Robert M March, Kodansha International: 1992.

Working in Japan
>By Jonathan Hayter, How To Books Ltd: 1996.Trajal Staff Kyushu Inc.

Broad-Minded Business

Visit the only company in Japan that specializes in helping women find jobs!

Broad-Minded Business realizes that it can be difficult for foreign women living in Japan. Many come as "Relocating Partners" and find it difficult to continue the career they had at home. In addition, cultural and language differences pose as another obstacle to finding a challenging and fulfilling position.

We are the only job information and placement service in Japan specializing in helping internationally-minded women, having branched from Being A Broad. Candidates of all backgrounds, experience levels, and language abilities are encouraged to contact us. All of our clients are international firms committed to providing an environment in which women can thrive. In addition to our weekly job posting email, candidates can also take advantage of our resume editing and make-over services, and career exploration consultations.

To view current job openings, visit *www.being-a-broad.com/bmb.html.*

To apply for a position, please email: *jobs@broadmindedbusiness.com.*

For all other inquiries, contact: *info@broadmindedbusiness.com.*

Broad-Minded Business
Job Information and
placement service for women
Chuo Iikura Bldg 7A, 3-4-11 Azabudai
Minato-ku, Tokyo 106-0041
Tel: (03) 5549-2038
Fax: (03) 5549-2039
www.being-a-broad.com/bmb.html

Labour Laws and Disputes

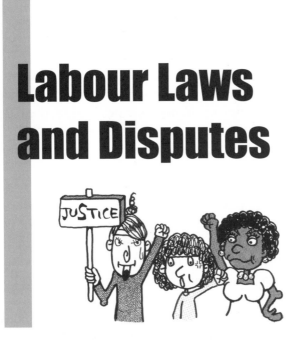

Laws

As in your home country, there are many laws regulating employment standards in Japan. These laws govern areas such as trade unions, work-related accidents, insurance, equal opportunities, safety, and maternity and child-care leave. (See the section on Pregnancy in Chapter Five for details about maternity and child-care leave.) All employment laws in Japan apply equally to foreigners and Japanese nationals. However, as with so many things in Japan, you may get the impression that these are laws on paper only, that they are not strictly enforced and that employers aren't penalised if the laws are not adhered to. There tends to be a 'shoganai' (nothing can be done) attitude amongst Japanese and foreigners alike regarding this.

Your employer must provide you with a contract, the period of which cannot exceed one year. By law, this contract is supposed to be detailed. It should include information relating to your pay, hours, safety, dismissal procedures, holidays, etc.; however, in practise, some contracts contain only the most basic information. The employer must also provide a copy of the company rules, and you are within your rights to request an English translation of it. Your employer must pay you in cash. This money must be paid directly to you (bank transfer is the most common method) at least once a month on a specified date. Full-time employees are eligible for certain company benefits such as sick leave, holiday leave, company insurance schemes, and reimbursement of transportation costs. Benefits for part-time employees and contract workers vary. Check your contract carefully to be sure about your status within the company.

It is rare for Western women to be the subject of sexual harassment at work, as the Japanese tend to be rather wary of their Western women colleagues. The concept of sexual harassment is known in Japan, but sometimes treated with a mixture of nerves and amusement with respect to Western women. Many find that after receiving a compliment from a Japanese male colleague, the question "Is that seku hara?" often follows, and is one reason why compliments are not often paid. If you find yourself the subject of sexual harassment, then take the basic steps of which we are advised in our home countries—firmly state that the comments/behaviour are unacceptable and keep a journal of all that transpires—then speak to your employer. If action is not taken and the harassment continues, get legal advice.

Disputes

If you have a problem with your employer, contact the Tokyo Bar Association; they can provide you with free legal counselling. There are also several private lawyers who can advise and represent you during any negotiations. Be aware that court cases are rarely resorted to in Japan; most people settle disputes privately.

Unions

To form a union you need four members at your place of work. There are also some regional and national unions that represent certain sectors of the foreign community that are ideal for self-employed individuals or for people who are the only foreigners at their company and would like some support. Your union can become an affiliate of the National Union of General Workers, which will then support and advise you, as well as negotiate on your behalf.

Take note!

Some employers may request your passport, telling you that it is for 'safekeeping'. This may happen if you are brought to Japan to work in the entertainment industry as a dancer or hostess and will be staying in accommodation provided by your employer. Under no circumstances should you hand over your passport. Apart from the fact that a foreigner is expected to have their passport on their person at all times, if there is a problem with your work and you wish to terminate your contract, it may be difficult to get your passport back. My friend found this out when she was brought over from the UK as a dancer, discovered that the working conditions weren't quite what she was led to believe, and then couldn't get back her passport in order to leave the country. She had to finish her three-month contract because they refused to return her passport, which was locked in the hotel safe. This is a rare situation, but one to be aware of if you are entering the entertainment industry.

Useful Japanese

law	*houritsu*	employment	
labour law	*roudouhou*	contract	*koyou keiyaku*
trade union	*roudoukumiai*	company rules	*shuugyou kisoku*
work-related		sick leave	*byouki kyuuka*
accident	*gyoumujou no jiko*	holiday leave	*kyuujitsu kyuuka*
work accident		transportation	
insurance	*rousai hoken*	allowance	*koutsuu/tsuukin teate*
equal employment		part-time employee	*hijoukin kinmusha /*
opportunities	*byoudou na koyou no*		*paato taimaa*
	kikai	full-time employee	*joukinsha/joukin*
equal opportunities		temporary staff (sent	
(for both sexes)	*danjo koyou no kikai*	from an agency)	*hakenshain*
	kintou	contract worker	*keiyaku shain*
safety at work	*shigoto no anzensei*	sexual harassment	*sekuhara*
maternity leave	*shussan kyuuka*	labour dispute	*roushi funsou*
child-care leave	*ikuji kyuuka*	lawyer	*bengoshi*

403

I'd like an English version of the company rules.	*Shuugyou kisoku no eigoban ga hoshii desu.*
I'd like to report a case of sexual harassment.	*Sekuhara no kokuhatsu o shitai desu.*
I need some legal advice about a problem at work.	*Shigotojou no koto de houritsu soudan o uketai desu.*
I will keep my passport with me.	*Pasupooto wa watashi no temoto ni oite okimasu.*

Resources

Many unions are linked, so if you cannot find one in your area then another union may be able to provide an introduction. Also check your ward handbook for your local Labour Standards Office.

Unions with English-Speaking Staff

Amagasaki Mukougawa Union 066-481-2341
    All fields. Hyogo.
Berlitz Teachers Union 03-3434-0669
    http://www.twics.com/~rpl/
Foreigners' Labour Union (FLU) 03-3963-2715
    All fields. Tokyo and Kanto.
National Union of General Workers (Tokyo South Branch Office) 03-3434-0669
    All fields. Mid, West, and South Tokyo; branches
    throughout Japan.
    http://www.twics.com/~maxim/nambu/eng/nugwts-top-e-fs.html
Zentoitsu Workers Union (All United) 03-3836-9061
    All fields. All Japan.

Nova Union of Teachers
    http://www.asahi-net.or.jp/~fs5c-kprw/nut.html
Tokyo Foreign Language College Teachers' Union (TFLCTU)
    http://www.twics.com/~maxim/tflctu-top.html
University Teachers' Union
    http://www.net-ibaraki.ne.jp/aboys/utu/
Japanese Trade Union Confederation
    All fields. All Japan.
    http://www.jtuc-rengo.org/
Kanto Foreign Language Teachers' Union
    http://www.twics.com/~maxim/ktuf/ktuf-top.html
National Confederation of Trade Unions
    All fields. All Japan.
    http://www.iijnet.or.jp/c-pro/union/aa_e/index_e.html

Legal Advice
Also see the resources in the sections on **Safety** and **Your Status** in **Chapter One**.

Information Centre for Legal Affairs 03-3581-2201
03-3581-2206
Japan Legal Aid Association 03-3581-6941
Yokohama Bar Association Consultation Service for Foreigners 045-201-1881

Organisations and Support
Hand-In-Hand Chiba 043-224-2154
Assistance with unpaid salary, labour accidents, and other
work-related problems.
Industrial Employment Stability Centre 03-3836-1090
For people of Japanese descent.
International Movement Against All Forms of Discrimination and
Racism (IMADR) 03-3586-7447
Work towards eliminating discrimination against ethnic
minorities, indigenous peoples, people with disabilities,
migrant workers, and other groups subject to discrimination.
http://www.imadr.org
Japan Association for Working Holidaymakers 03-3389-0181
http://www.mmjp.or.jp/jawhm
Kalabaw-No-Kai (Association in Kotobuki for Solidarity with
Foreign Migrant Workers) 045-662-5699
Counselling on labour problems.
http://www.jca.ax.apc.org/kalabaw
Kanagawa Occupational Safety and Health Centre 045-573-4289
Counselling and assistance in negotiations with employers and
government labour agencies.
Lawyers Association for Foreign Laborers' Rights 03-3305-0555
Provide consultative services to foreigners regarding social,
labour, visa, and other problems.
National Network in Solidarity with Migrant Workers 03-3207-7801
Works against discrimination and exploitation of foreign workers.
http://www.jca.ax.apc.org/migrant-net/
Solidarity Center for Migrants of Yokohama Diocese 044-549-7678
Provides counselling and assistance to foreign workers in
obtaining legal, medical, and other general information.

Resources and Further Reading
Manual for Migrants
By the Catholic Diocese of Yokohama Solidarity Centre for Migrants: 1997.
Phone 044-549-7678 for a copy.
The New Observer
Monthly newsletter of the National Union of General Workers.
Phone 03-3434-0669 for a copy.
http://www.twics.com/~anzu/index.html

Running Your Own Business

An increasing number of Western women in Japan are running their own businesses. Some of these businesses are fairly large, incorporated companies that are successful enough to provide a secure income and a visa. Most are part-time, small, home-based businesses with no official status. Japan can be a great place to start a business like this because fairly high incomes from other work (especially English teaching with flexible hours) can help to fund your venture, as well as provide a visa and security in times of difficulty. Whether you decide to keep your job or plunge into running your own business full time, as in your home country, expect to be working just about every hour possible. Many women who would never have considered themselves 'entrepreneurs' often find themselves creating their own businesses in Japan.

Reasons for starting a company are similar to what you would expect in your home country: frustration at working for someone else, a desire for more creativity and independence, or a lack of promotion potential. Being a foreigner in Japan sometimes allows you to see a niche that no one else may have noticed. In a few cases, Western women have accumulated enough money during their time here to give them the freedom to start their own businesses, without worrying about a regular income. Many of these female entrepreneurs have Japanese husbands, which eliminates the visa problem.

Smaller businesses that generate less than ¥3 million a year don't need to be incorporated formally in Japan. In fact, most Japanese lawyers say that a business doesn't need to be incorporated unless it generates a profit of ¥10 million a year. But small businesses do need to file tax returns every March. In this situation, hire a Japanese accountant to prepare all documents necessary for the tax office or hope that a friendly tax officer will assist you in completing the forms. You may include personal expenses as business expenses—your accountant or tax officer will help you through this process.

There are three types of 'formal' businesses in Japan, each one requiring a different amount of 'start-up capital', which actually only has to sit in the bank for a week. There are several business consultants/lawyers who can help you through this process, including lending you the money needed just to get through the paperwork. The whole process is detailed and lengthy and you do need a Japanese lawyer to do this for you, so check the list at the end of this section. In some cases you will need to change your visa status to one that allows you to run a company in Japan. This process is complicated and there are several conditions you must satisfy. The conditions include: hiring a certain number of full-time Japanese staff whose salaries (including insurance and pensions) you must guarantee, proving that your business is needed in Japan, and providing evidence of generated income. It's rather a Catch-22 situation because you are not allowed to operate as a business in Japan until you meet these criteria, yet you have to operate as a business for one year in order to prove that you can meet the criteria.

Regarding start-up capital, most Western women let their businesses start slowly, and allow the income generated to determine the rate of growth. Work out how much money you will need to get started; in most cases having enough to cover printing costs for business cards and publicity material and the fees for some networking meetings is sufficient. Depending on the nature of your business, you may require a more substantial amount of money, and if you are not in a position to use your own money, then you need to look for investors or approach a bank. Japanese banks will extend low-interest loans for business purposes to foreigners, but getting the bank to agree to the loan is a long and difficult process. You will need a Japanese guarantor and must provide a detailed explanation (in Japanese) of why you need the money. It is best to tell them that you want to buy a computer or a car; although you still need the Japanese guarantor, this will make the process easier. If you don't want to go to the banks, then you need to find investors or people who will simply lend you the money. It is best to develop your relationships with Japanese acquaintances, either on a purely business basis or as friends. They will not only have a vested interest in seeing your business succeed, but will also help you navigate your way through any paperwork or inevitable Japan-related issues. These relationships will take time to develop, so be patient.

I have already mentioned the importance of networking (see Finding a Job in this chapter) and this goes double if you are running your own business. Even if the people that you meet are unable or unwilling to provide financial support, they will help you with advice and spread the word about your business. Join all the groups that you can and don't be reserved about promoting yourself. Check out Chapter Nine: Women's Organisations.

Running your own business in Japan can be a big step in making your life here very complicated and very exciting. It is also a good way to gain insight into the 'business' side of Japan. Although Western women are not subject to the same discrimination that Japanese women are, they still report having trouble getting some Japanese people to take them seriously. You need to surround yourself with positive people, and for skills that you don't have, develop contacts with those who do. Having said all that, there is something to be said for not knowing everything about doing business in Japan. You can become a great innovator in finding ways to 'do the impossible'.

Following are case studies of women who run or who have run their own businesses in Japan. The types of businesses vary from small, home-based businesses to a large, fully established corporation.

Freelance, home-based small business

Name	Julie A. Yamamoto
Company name	No business name
Nature of business	Freelance medical editing
Working hours	Variable, depending on demand

When, why, and how did you start your own business?

I had been doing freelance medical editing for about ten years before I arrived in Japan, and had even done some work for Japanese before coming here. It started as an outgrowth of previous full-time work as a medical editor for universities. I simply pull clients with me when I move to other geographic locations and rely on regular mail and email to obtain the work and communicate with clients. Since my overhead and setup is pretty simple—a computer, a fax, and a phone—it's easy to move around.

Did you need investors or did you use your own money to start?

No need for investors or much start-up capital, only the cost of a computer, printer, fax, second phone line, and general office furniture and supplies to set up a home office.

Are you reaping the financial and emotional benefits of your business yet?

I'm not bringing in big bucks at this point because I'm working only a small number of hours. I'm the primary caretaker of my daughter, and have a second child on the way. For now, my husband is the primary wage earner. The extra money is nice, since anything I bring in is almost pure profit. One of the reasons I keep the business going, even at a minimal level, is for the psychological benefits. It's the only intellectual stimulation I get right now, and the only thing that I can truly call my own. Besides that, I've got some long-term clients I really want to keep doing work for, and I do intend eventually to build the business back up after the children are in school.

Do you have another job?

I teach English part time to adults and school-age kids. This is a continuation of the teaching I did before coming here. Before I started as an editor, I was teaching college English classes full time. That work would have burned me out quickly, and I had the chance to switch to editing full time, so I made the jump. I miss the contact with students, though, and take opportunities to teach, formally and informally, whenever they appear.

What do you think are the differences in running a business in Japan when compared with your home country?

Running my freelance business here is just about the same as running it back home. The setup is the same, a home computer and other necessities to do the work, though the clients here still seem to want me to do the editing by hand on a hard copy of the manuscript rather than in the disk file itself.

410

What kind of visa do you have?

I have a spouse visa since my husband is Japanese.

What has been (or is) the most difficult aspect of running your own business?

The biggest challenge is pulling in clients for my editing. I know there's a great need for my work because many scientists are trying to publish in English-language journals and English is the language of science and medicine. Unfortunately, it seems to take a LONG time to make connections here, and to convince people to use my services once they learn about me. There are some translation and editing companies that charge high rates to do some of the work I can do for less. I do some work for one of them that is located in a different city (we use regular mail, and I edit in pencil on hard copy—the old-fashioned way). Since budgets in the medical school nearby are tight, anyone hiring me has to pay me directly, which discourages some people from contacting me. If their departments covered the expense, they might be more willing. But even when I find clients, most need my services only occasionally, so I'd have to have an enormous clientele to produce full-time income.

Is there anything that makes running your own business easier here?

Something that helps is the word-of-mouth contact I get through my husband, who works at the med school and tries to find clients for me.

What are your plans for the future?

I will continue the editing business indefinitely, and hope to make some strong connections that I can carry back home to the States with me when we leave Japan in about a year.

Any issues specifically relating to being a foreign woman?

I have noticed that many of my editing clients (who are all men) seem surprised when they discover that I am a smart person who knows what she's doing. I get the feeling that they're not used to dealing with smart women in professional settings (often true back in the States too). It does seem to be an advantage to be a foreign woman in these situations. My 'foreign-ness' seems to put us on a more equal footing than the clients have with Japanese women. And because of this, I can get away with challenging them; for example, questioning some of the content in their manuscripts, or, in the case of my teaching, asking slightly disturbing questions that make them think in new ways.

Advice

I haven't been here long enough to know what the overall business environment is like, and I'm lucky in that I work for myself and follow my own rules. Everything would depend on what the business is and what that particular business environment is like here. If it's something you can do well on your own, and there's a need for your services, you can probably do well. But I suspect it takes much longer here to get a solid business going than in other places. Word of mouth still seems very relevant and a very good way to advertise, but that takes a long time to bring in customers or clients.

Multi-level marketing business

Name	Antoinette Price
Company name	Not applicable
Nature of business	Nu Skin multi-level marketing business
Working hours	I decide, so each week is different. Anywhere from 10 to 30.

When, why, and how did you start your own business?

I was working in the nine-to-five flog at Dentsu advertising and realized that I was trading time for money and I had basically no control of my life. I have always wanted to do something myself and I like the idea of being my own boss. In MLM (multi-level marketing) you choose who you want to work with. If you don't like someone you don't present the business to them. You make your own schedule. This business is open so it is very international. For example, I could be lying on the beach in Italy on holiday, talk to the person next to me, and they could get involved—my business goes into another country overnight with no cost on my part. The working hours and the place of work are totally for me to decide. I like the variety in my work environment and also who I work with. I like meeting new people and this is a people-based business. I wanted to create permanent income, i.e., if I don't go to work I still get paid (royalty income). I have this *inter vivos* 'retirement fund' that I can use now while I have energy and ideas, rather than flogging all my life and saving like crazy for retirement when I am sixty and clapped out. It's not a career, it's a financial opportunity. Once the money is there for me to do all the other things I want to do, I don't want to kick back and be a couch potato. I want to do what I want to do, where I want and when I want! I don't feel that the conventional world can offer me both time and money simultaneously, so that is why I started.

What were the initial start-up costs?

I started about two years ago with about a ¥50,000 initial investment, and all I did was sign a very simple contract as an Australian distributor so I am not actually registered here. The contract states that I may do this business in a legal fashion or be a product user. That is, it does not specify ways that I have to do it. The actual contract cost $35.00 Australian in addition to the ¥50,000 for the products I bought, but you don't have to spend that much on products. It is a business that is meant to help, not hinder, finances, so initial costs vary. Investors are not needed.

Are you reaping the financial and emotional benefits of your business yet?

I am receiving an income but it is still in the building phase. I believe I will reap the emotional benefits in the future. I am in different countries, which gives me flexibility. I am not tied to Japan, so I can continue wherever I want. It is not like a conventional job where money comes at the end of the month for sure. It takes time to build groups of consumers and find people who can see the big picture, but then any business takes a few years to really become established. I have nothing to lose and everything to gain. I feel that I am creating my freedom and that makes me happy. The thought of having to work for someone else until retirement makes me feel awful!

Do you have another job?

I am working freelance from home. I work with a Japanese company that sends me editing from various projects and sometimes German, French, and Italian translations. I also tutor from home.

What do you think are the differences in running a business in Japan when compared with your home country?

I don't believe that the men here always take a female business woman seriously, let alone a foreign one!

What kind of visa do you have?

I have a work visa and am just in the process of renewal. I have used sponsors, I have never sponsored myself.

What has been (or is) the most difficult aspect of running your own business?

Above, I explained that MLM it is not like the conventional business world (that is why I love it!). So the difficulties are more on being self-motivated all the time and not slacking off. I am not exactly going to sit there and tell myself off for not spending time on my business! The language has posed a problem. I am compromised in my ability to present really well. I have to simplify the English or rely on someone to present for me in Japanese unless the person I am talking to is really fluent in English. Otherwise, the nature of this business is easy: no accounting and no overhead except the usual phone, fax, and Internet use to communicate with people. It is not expensive and the initial investment is not a lot either. In this industry this is the ripest market, maybe a Japanese person in their own element wouldn't have my problems. Japan is responsible for two thirds of the world's direct sales market, so this is where it is happening in the network marketing industry. This is a plus for being here as opposed to anywhere else.

What are your plans for the future?

I will go home and carry on my business over there.

Any issues specifically relating to being a foreign woman?

Yeah, but I am not going to answer this question or I will never stop!

Recommended resources

It depends on the kind of business. There are niches to be found here in many areas: consulting, importing, etc. I would say suss it out really well and have a good fallback or an alternative for your financial security because, after all, this is the most expensive country in the world. Also have some really good totally bilingual Japanese friends—so helpful for documentation and general communication or the establishment of a conventional company here.

Informal company

Name	Colleen Lanki
Company name	Kee Company
Nature of business	Theatre company—creating and producing shows.
Working hours	Depends on whether there's a show happening. Otherwise it is my own decision. I probably spend a few hours on the company a day: writing proposals, phoning, etc.

When, why, and how did you start your own business?

I was a professional actor in Canada. I came here and wanted to do a show on a particular theme I was interested in. I wanted to work collectively with Japanese actors, so clarified my idea and approached actors I knew and wanted to work with. We started work and through introductions and because of the commitment and energy of that cast the show was a success. I then decided to try to do another show—same style, different theme—and got another collective together. Basically, the tasks involved were finding spaces (performance and rehearsal), creation of publicity material, gathering of staff, and then getting enough audience to pay for it all. Everything was done in Japanese and English as we were looking for an audience made up of both Japanese and non-Japanese. All of us have other jobs—acting teachers, translators, narrators, etc.

What were the initial start-up costs?

The first show cost ¥400,000 to do. We were given free rehearsal and almost free performance space. This is rare. The second show cost ¥800,000. The average would be more like ¥1,000,000.

Did you need investors or did you use your own money to start?

I put the money up myself. Some (very little) came from advertising in the program and flyer. I found advertisers through friends, the Canadian Embassy, and the phone book.

How easy do you think it is to find investors in Japan?

Not easy. You need personal introductions. There are foundations and arts grants for multicultural work, but you must apply well over a year in advance usually.

Are you reaping the financial and emotional benefits of your business yet?

Absolutely no financial benefits. I lose money in lost time on other work every time I do a show. Emotional benefits—huge. There is a great satisfaction in doing your own work as a performing artist. Indirectly, starting this company has allowed me to make connections with many artists and arts organizations here. It has allowed me to tour Australia and Canada with our first show, given me access to international festivals and arts groups, and has even been instrumental in my being invited to a conference in California. So the benefits have been extraordinary.

Do you have another job?

Acting instructor, narration and voice-over work, TV acting, and modeling.

What do you think are the differences in running a business in Japan when compared with your home country?

I'll speak only for theatre companies. In Japan there is no 'incorporation' and no 'board of directors'. The small companies are run either collectively or by a single person, but each project is a bit like a collective in that usually the actors pay 'noruma'—they each buy a number of tickets and then sell them to their friends. Actors are not paid for their work. I have run Kee Company on a project-to-project basis in what is called in Canada an 'equity co-op'. That is, I put up the money for the space and staff, etc. A core group becomes the 'co-operative members' and helps with production tasks as much as they can. If there is any profit it is split between the members equally. I do not have 'noruma'.

What kind of visa do you have?

Artist under contract. Not easy to get. I am sponsored by the place I teach acting and had to give the immigration office my contract and a heap of information to prove that I am a professional artist.

What has been (or is) the most difficult aspect of running your own business?

Language barriers. Unspoken 'things I should have done'. Matters of etiquette that come as a surprise at the last minute. Things will go along in a familiar manner and suddenly it is not at all familiar. It is deceiving!

Is there anything that makes running your own business easier here?

I am a foreigner and often get more attention because I am doing something very few foreigners are doing here. People are willing to help me out and forgive my mistakes.

What are your plans for the future?

A small show that I will hopefully take on tour to other places in Asia. I would like to continue to work with other groups and artists in Asia and eventually move back to Canada and bring those artists there in the form of an Asian arts festival and/or workshop series.

Any issues specifically relating to being a foreign woman?

Not only about being a woman, but people don't say no directly. They often say "maybe" and then leave you waiting for a call that they will not make anyway. If you need an answer, you can accept the "maybe, I'll call you back on it" answer, but say politely that you really must have an answer by a certain date, and if they don't call you by then you have to accept that the answer is no.

Newly-formed company

Name	Pamela Takeshige
Company name	System Design Soken
Nature of business	Database design, Web design, translation, DTP, import
Working hours	9:30 a.m. to 7:00 p.m.

When, why, and how did you start your own business?

Actually, I started my first business with another ex-pat in 1991 because I wanted to do DTP. I wanted to be my own boss and I felt that I could better meet the needs of clients by being independent. And I loved the DTP world. But, as we all know, the Internet has arrived. I want to be a part of this interesting opportunity. With my new company, I decided I wanted to do more Web-based work. I think this is where the future is and I want to be a part of it!

What were the initial start-up costs?

I bought a company for ¥200,000, but I have already spent more than ¥1 million on hardware and office setup.

Did you need investors or did you use your own money to start?

I do not have any investors. I have used only my own money.

How easy do you think it is to find investors in Japan?

I think it depends on your business plan, but I feel it would not be easy.

How helpful have the Japanese banks been to you?

In all my years in business in Japan, I knew it would be hard to get a loan from a Japanese bank, so I have never tried. I have no loans nor have I ever had a loan. But there are other institutions that will lend money to small companies—and I may go to them for a loan for my import business. I have heard of one case where a non-Japanese woman got a ¥3 million loan with no trouble. I have also heard of a case where a non-Japanese man had to make his Japanese wife the head of the company in order to get the loan, but they did get the loan in the end.

Are you reaping the financial and emotional benefits of your business yet?

I have just started the business, so it is too early to tell, but I do enjoy the work very much, so emotionally I am very happy and fulfilled.

Do you have another job?

No.

What did you do before starting your own business?

I was the head of the Editorial Department of Linguaphone Japan.

What do you think are the differences in running a business in Japan when compared with your home country?

Business 'customs' are different here. It is important to learn what they are and to try to follow them. I place a great deal of importance on forming close relationships with suppliers and with other companies that work together with me on a project. The close personal relationship that many Japanese prize when doing business takes a lot of work to develop and keep in good form—but when you have it, it can be one of your most important business assets.

What kind of visa do you have?

I have a spouse visa.

What kind of challenges have you overcome regarding running your own business?

Being small with a small budget means less advertising. Also, being small means that some companies are nervous about working with me. I have a family, so I cannot spend all of my time at work—still, my hours are long.

What has been (or is) the most difficult aspect of running your own business?

Connecting with the people who need the services I can provide is my biggest challenge. I need help with sales, but I cannot afford to hire someone right now.

Is there anything that makes running your own business easier here?

I don't feel there is any special thing that makes it easier.

What are your plans for the future?

I want to start some kind of Internet-related sales activities.

Any issues specifically relating to being a foreign woman?

You have to be confident in what you want to do. Most people treat me fairly, I believe.

Advice

If you have a good idea, go for it. But don't do something that is not right for you. And don't compromise your goals. That is the beginning of the end. You may have to scale down what you can try to do because of limited time or money, but keeping a clear hold on your goals is most important.

Internet-based business

Name	Sharlene Oyagi
Company name	Azabu Online Admissions Consulting
	http://www.azabuonline.com
Nature of business	Online admissions counselling and educational services for Japanese students applying to US universities, graduate, business, and law schools.
Working hours	Whenever I want—based on the Web. I work every day, but have flexible hours.

When, why, and how did you start your own business?

I started in April 1999 because I hated commuting on Tokyo trains and I saw an underserved market in my field. I outlined the core services I thought the market needed (and that could be done over the Internet), put up a Website, and learned as I went along.

What were the initial start-up costs?

Minimal—a host server (¥4000 per month) and payment to part-time staff. My 'expense' is mostly in investing time to promote the site and research where and how to promote it.

Did you need investors or did you use your own money to start?

I did not need much money to start, but hope to get investors for expansion and long-term growth once the business is established.

How easy do you think it is to find investors in Japan?

Hard, but getting easier with the new trend toward supporting and encouraging start-ups (to mimic the US).

How helpful have the Japanese banks been to you?

I haven't used them to borrow money, but options for business accounts are pretty good.

Are you reaping the financial and emotional benefits of your business yet?

Yes—with very little initial investment and being Web-based (no office rent, etc.), I immediately began to profit and still have great profit margins considering the work hours and expenses. Seeing my business grow well beyond my network of referrals in my first year has rewarded me, and I have gained footholds outside of Tokyo.

Do you have another job?

No, but I also study Japanese semi full time.

What did you do before starting your own business?

I was the program director at a big test prep company (in Chicago and Tokyo), doing the same work (advising foreign students on business and grad school admissions), but also managing and training staff, and designing and teaching classes.

418

What do you think are the differences in running a business in Japan when compared with your home country?

It would be far easier to grow and get investors in the US, as well as get outside advice on how to grow, manage, and promote a new business. In Japan, however, there are not really any obstacles if you are willing to do it yourself.

What kind of visa do you have?

Spouse.

What kind of challenges have you overcome regarding running your own business?

Simply learning about the market and Internet environment in Japan has been a challenge, as well as staying motivated to do the daily work for promotional purposes.

What has been (or is) the most difficult aspect of running your own business?

Needing to learn more Japanese, faster.

Is there anything that makes running your own business easier here?

Japanese are used to the inconvenience of payment for services through bank deposit—if I were in the US, NO ONE would be bothered to make a trip to the ATM to pay for online services—and many still worry about the security of credit card payments online. Thank goodness the Japanese are used to and accept this inconvenience, or I'd have a much bigger struggle to get established and collect payments—I'd need a merchant's account as well as a security system on my site for accepting credit card payment. This has made being in Japan a huge advantage in getting started. Also, Japan is not yet saturated with Internet businesses the way the US is, so there are ways to get your site noticed on the Web.

What are your plans for the future?

At this point, I'm content to maintain my base and grow through good word of mouth; the next step is to get investment and expand throughout Asia.

Any issues specifically relating to being a foreign woman?

Not as a woman, just that I've got more credibility in my field, being an American who has been through the same process my clients are going through and being experienced in my field.

Advice

Just do it! I meet many people who talk about starting a business, but seem to think they have to wait for someone's approval or interest in the idea or some official sanction—you never know how good your idea is until you give it a try.

Recommended resources

SOHO and entrepreneurial resources are big in Japan now and do sometimes have good ideas that are worth checking out.

A portable business

Name	Sheila Donnell
Company name	The International Executive (now based in the US)
Nature of business	Intercultural adjustment and personal business skills, coaching, training
Working hours	7:00 a.m. to 10:00 p.m., 7 days a week

When, why, and how did you start your own business?

Moved to Japan in 1990 after retiring from a great career in financial sales in the US. In Japan I identified a need for Western executive training, specifically in American interpersonal business skills such as presentations, etiquette, and general cross-cultural understanding. I noticed that this was being done by English teachers who had little or no business experience, let alone at the executive level.

Did you need investors or did you use your own money to start?

I only had a couple of thousand dollars when I first came to Japan, so I started doing executive training to pay my rent while I was looking for a niche to create a business.

How helpful were the Japanese banks to you?

You must be kidding. When I first came to Japan there was no English anywhere in the banks, and no real help. Constant aggravation. It was the most difficult part of my life in Japan. It was one of the reasons I never grew my business. Dealing with the banks was such a nightmare.

Are you reaping the financial and emotional benefits of your business yet?

The primary benefit I got from my business in Japan was the feeling when mentees or participants told me how grateful they were for my help. Monetarily it was finally okay after the first few years, but not enough for it to be worth living in Japan.

What did you do before starting your own business?

Sold bonds and other financial products in the US.

What do you think are the differences in running a business in Japan when compared with your home country?

Even the smallest things were a royal hassle in Japan—things such as banking, finding places, trying to get something done with the Japanese. The Japanese really did not want to do business with a foreigner unless they could get a big cut or, in the case of foreign companies, if their Western management insisted.

What kind of visa did you have?

I had a work visa, but had to prove to immigration every year that I had contracts equal to ¥250,000 a month. It was one of the main things about living there that I didn't like.

420

What was the most difficult aspect of running your own business?

The various hassles and outrageous expenses with the government: immigration, taxes, and Japanese health insurance. Drove me crazy!

Was there anything that made running your own business easier in Japan?

Clearly there is more demand in Japan for Western executive coaching and training for cross-cultural personal business skills than any place else in the world right now.

What are your plans for the future?

Currently I am in New York City and thrilled to be here! Continuing my coaching and training in Japan now and then, and also conducting workshops in presentation skills and corporate etiquette here.

Any issues specifically relating to being a foreign woman?

Nope. Just being a foreigner in Japan in general was often demeaning.

Advice

Any other country—except in the Middle East—would surely be easier to live and run a business in. It also would be much easier if you are either married to a Japanese or are an ex-pat wife. Offer a product or service that is not provided by the Japanese and they make competing with them, on their turf, next to impossible, especially for an individual with no corporate support.

Recommended resources

Fortitude, determination, and patience. Support from other foreigners I found a great deal more useful and timely than that from Japanese.

Staying power: A 20-year-old company

Name	Charlotte Kennedy-Takahashi
Company name	Oak Associates KK
Nature of business	Human Resources Consultancy
Working hours	Depends on the time of year and what's going on in the company—maybe 12 hours a day. But if you count all the groups and things that I'm involved in, maybe it's more than that.

When, why, and how did you start your own business?

Everyone in my family owns their own company except my mother. Owning a business was second nature. I wanted to do it, but I wanted to do it overseas and sometimes I can't believe that I have done it. I started it in 1980 and incorporated in 1981. There are probably two reasons why I started my own business. First, the human resources field in Japan was highly underdeveloped back then. I wanted to provide a service with a Western approach, yet that would be adaptable to Japan. Second, it was clear to me in 1980 that foreign companies were not hiring foreign women, they said a foreign woman couldn't work in Japan and be successful. Also, Japanese companies were hiring only English speakers or support people. The two different kinds of companies had different problems.

What were the initial start-up costs?

Who remembers?! I guess maybe we had a contract to begin with which was our money for the year. We incorporated with ¥3 million and with that money set up a small office. We broke even in the first year, but my partner and I sacrificed our salaries—I went from ¥10 million a year to ¥50,000 a month. We donated our labour as the capital investment, although it doesn't show in the books.

Did you need investors or did you use your own money to start?

All my own money. And my partner's money too, but she sold out to me about seven or eight years later.

How easy do you think it is to find investors in Japan?

I never tried. I had a feeling that if I had asked, then I would have got it from friends. I have had people offer, but I have never taken them up on it. Each year we have invested the profit. I have never had the need and one of the philosophies I had was for very steady growth.

How helpful have the Japanese banks been to you?

I was the first foreigner to ever get a Japanese bank loan. It was big press. But of course they only gave me the money when they saw that I was making a profit. They never give you anything if you really need it. I owe them a great deal of gratitude, so I shouldn't complain. Not a lot of banks were willing to support foreigners in the eighties.

423

Are you reaping the financial and emotional benefits of your business yet?

Since year four to five I've had a very good salary. I raised my salary gradually as the profits increased. I didn't really set out to make a huge amount of money but, at the same time, one advantage of being a business owner is tremendous financial benefit. Financially I have no concerns. I've been able to make a choice about whether I get the money or the company gets the money. Frankly, most of the time I choose the company. I'm very satisfied. There were times when things were tight and I was quite worried. Emotionally—this is much more difficult to answer! I really get a high from starting things. During the early entrepreneurial years (until year seven) I was really high on everything. But after the seventh year something changed and we had to concentrate on policy—the company went into managerial crisis. I wasn't very happy during that transition period. When we had got over that, again, I was extremely satisfied. Then I got bored and needed a new challenge, and I made the decision to expand overseas—I am going into this process now. I plan to make the company grow five times in the next five years. I need that sort of thing. I don't like the frustration when you've achieved what you want and don't know which direction to go in next. I like forcing the company to burst its borders each time. I have had incredible staff and I've been blessed with some very proactive people, but on the down side I've always been surprised with how people accept boundaries, how people limit themselves. One of the most exciting things is that I have seen a lot of my people develop. That has been very satisfying for me. Emotionally there are so many different levels on which I have been rewarded.

Do you have another job?

I quit my job when I started. I decided that this had to be it. I am on boards of directors for other companies. I advise people. I also have Oak International in the US.

What did you do before starting your own business?

I was originally a high school and college teacher. I taught in Kansas, Latin America, Korea, and the Philippines. I taught history and I have one master's degree in Chinese history and another one in international management. My entire goal was to go into international business. When I came to Japan I taught at a business school here. I did some really exciting things there as it was the most prestigious one at that time. Through that I could see what was needed in my field. It was a combination of education and business, and it really opened the doors for me to get started.

What do you think are the differences in running a business in Japan when compared with your home country?

There are differences because of being a foreigner rather than because of being a woman. I think being a foreigner you have tremendous privileges. In the eighties I used to play that. I think now that has disappeared a bit. As a foreigner you see things other people don't see. You can see where there is a need. Another difference is that when I incorporated in the States it took a couple of days and was very simple—in Japan the cost of doing everything and keeping up with all the requirements is very high. Another thing that's different is in the area of marketing. When marketing to Japanese, they're resistant to change and slow to accept a new idea, but, when they do, they all jump on the boat at the same time. It can be frustrating trying to get people to accept it, but when they do, you can find yourself right in the middle of something big.

What kind of visa do you have?

Spouse.

What kind of challenges have you overcome regarding running your own business?

I think the whole area of legal requirements for reporting and the complicated bureaucracy are incredibly overwhelming. I still believe that the amount of regulation here is an incredible barrier. Another huge barrier is attracting quality Japanese staff who really know how to work in an international environment. I think my business would be bigger if I had found them. I think in the eighties people were reluctant to work for a small company and this industry had a bad image. Now it's difficult to find a Japanese who really knows how to work in a truly international context. I have had some wonderful staff, but I could use a few more!

Any issues specifically relating to being a foreign woman?

I guess the humorous thing is that everyone assumes that my husband owns the company. I know one time I went to a conference with a male fifteen years my junior and they spent the whole time talking to him. He'd been working for me for a week. I was thinking: didn't they read my name card? I ended up laughing—as long as the guy got the job done, I didn't care really. I think that being a woman has been a great advantage. I guess foreign women are a bit easier to deal with than foreign men. Building trust with the Japanese has been easier being a woman. I don't consider the fact that I am a woman has a serious negative aspect. I think when you're a professional and have good knowledge, then the Japanese respect that above anything else.

Advice

I think my major advice is that if you really want the adventure of starting a business and you're willing to take a calculated risk, then take one step at a time and soon you'll be there. The best way to develop a good business is to take it step by step. As long as you go forward two steps and go back only one, then you're still winning.

Recommended resources

Good business credentials and experience. Be the best you can be in your own country, study as much as you can, be the top of everything, then you'll have a whole bunch of knowledge to pull from. Other: the American Chamber of Commerce; FEW (Foreign Executive Women); and a really good mentor—someone you really trust—my husband was this for me.

Useful Japanese

business .... *bijinesu/shigoto/*
                     shoobai
home-based .... *zaitaku no*
start-up capital .... *shihonkin*

bank loan .... *(ginkoo no) yuushi*
guarantor .... *hoshoonin*
investor .... *tooshika/tooshisha*

I'd like some legal advice (in English) about
starting my own business. .... *Bijinesu o hajimeru ni atatte, (eigo de) houritsu-kankei no adobaisu ga itadakitai no desu.*

I'd like to hire an (English-speaking)
accountant for my tax returns. .... *Zeikin-taisaku no tame, (eigo no wakaru) zeirishi o yatoitai to omotte imasu.*

I'd like an application form for a bank
loan. .... *Ginkoo yuushi no moushikomisho o itadakitai no desu ga.*

I need to print some business cards. .... *(Gyoumu-you no) meishi o tsukuru hitsuyou ga arimasu.*

Resources

Legal
Japan Golden Club 03-3358-8521
Nakai Immigration Service 03-5282-7654
Tokyo Administrative Office ... 03-3379-2251
JOS Enterprise 03-5330-3300
Onedera Office 03-3590-7511

Support
Association for New Entrepreneurial Women (ANEW) 0721-98-3265
Japan External Trade Organisation (JETRO) 03-3582-1775
       Promotes importing, industrial cooperation, and international
       exchange. Two libraries in Tokyo.
       http://www.jetro.go.jp/iv/e/japan/pandc/cont2.html
Manufactured Imports Promotion Organisation (MIPRO) 03-3984-5960
       http://www.mipro.or.jp
Otsubo International Inc 03-3753-4779
       Corporate communications provider: translation, design,
       DTP, printing.
       http://www.iac.co.jp/~cataldo
Civic Entrepreneur's International Network
       http://www.cein.org/en/entop.htm

Chambers of Commerce
American Chamber of Commerce in Japan (ACCJ) 03-3433-5381
       http://www.accj.or.jp

Australian and New Zealand Chamber of Commerce 03-5214-0710
    http://www.anzccj.org
British Chamber of Commerce in Japan (BCCJ) 03-3267-1901
    http://www.uknow.or.jp/bccj
Canadian Chamber of Commerce in Japan (CCCJ) 03-3556-9566
    http://www.cccj.or.jp
French Chamber of Commerce and Industry in Japan 03-3288-6921
    http://www.ccifj.or.jp
German Chamber of Commerce and Industry 03-5276-9811
    http://www.ahk.de/de/jp

Business Services

Dear Cards 03-3473-6245
    Printing
    http://www.dearcards.co.jp
Harachi Printing (see display ad, page 428) 090-3420-7345
    Printing. Yokohama area only.
Kinkos 0120-001-966
    Photocopying, binding, business cards, lamination, DPE film
    service, computer access, printing. 24 locations throughout Japan.
    http://www.kinkos.co.jp
Mail Station Ebisu 03-5469-1408
    Mailbox, secretarial services, translation.

Resources and Further Information

These books generally address the needs of people travelling to Japan on business, but entrepreneurs based in Japan also find them useful.

Business Japan: A Practical Guide to Understanding Japanese Business Culture
    By Peggy Kenna and Sondra Lacy, NTC Publishing Group: 1994.
Doing Business With Japan: Successful Strategies for Intercultural Communication
    By Kazuo Nishiyama, University of Hawaii Press: 2000.
Doing Business With Japanese Men: A Woman's Handbook
    By Christalyn Brannen (Contributor) and Tracey Wilen, Stone Bridge
    Press: 1993.
Doing Business With the Japanese: A Guide to Successful Communication,
    Management, and Diplomacy
    By Alan Goldman, State University of New York Press: 1994.
Doing Business with the New Japan
    By James Day Hodgson, Yoshihiro Sano, John L. Graham and James Hodgson,
    Rowman and Littlefield: 2000.
International Business: A Basic Guide for Women
    By Tracey Wilen, Xlibris Corp: 2001.
Japanese Business Etiquette: A Practical Guide to Success With the Japanese
    By Diana Rowland, Warner Books: 1993.
Japanese Etiquette and Ethics in Business
    By Boye Lafayette De Mente, NTC Publishing Group: 1994.
Setting Up an Office in Japan
    American Chamber of Commerce in Japan publication.

Volunteer Work

Most Western women don't have the time to do voluntary work whilst living in Japan, but those who do find it very rewarding. Voluntary work in Japan opens up new opportunities for meeting people (Japanese and foreign) and brings a sense of caring and community to an otherwise work- and money-dominated lifestyle. Western women say that they also welcome the opportunity to give something back to Japan, either to the foreign community or the Japanese. Aside from the conventional idea of voluntary work, many of the networking organisations listed in this book are non-profit and run entirely by volunteers. These have the added benefit of not only helping a community, but also helping you in your life here now and possibly later when you leave Japan. Being a board member in one of these organisations is a valuable experience and one you may feel you are missing if your present job limits your decision-making skills, especially if you are working for a Japanese company. Also, watch out for one-off events where the organisers are looking for people who want to get involved.

Useful Japanese

volunteer .... *borantia*   volunteer work .... *borantia katsudou*

I'd like to volunteer. .... *Borantia (katsudou) ga shitai desu.*
I'd like to register as a volunteer. .... *Borantia to shite touroku shitai desu.*

Resources

Much of the following resource information is based on that found in *Foreign Executive Women's Volunteering Directory.* For a copy of the directory contact FEW at few@gol.com or view it on their website at http://www.few.gol.com

Check the resources listed in the sections below for other volunteer opportunities:
Safety in **Chapter One: Survival** (women's shelters)
Labour Laws and Disputes in this chapter (trade unions and support groups)
All of **Chapter Nine: Women's Organisations**

Volunteer Organisations
Key   A: Activities
        S: Skills required
        J: Japanese language ability

AMDA International Medical Information Centre 03-5285-8086
        A: Helps foreigners use the Japanese medical system by
        providing a telephone information service including interpreta-
        tion, publishes multi-lingual medical guide books, holds
        seminars and symposia. S: Office and telephone. Training
        about the Japanese medical system provided. J: Necessary.
        http://www.osk.3web.ne.jp/~amdack/
Amnesty International, Japanese Section 0467-23-7018
        A: Promoting the international protection of human rights;
        lobbying; campaigning; public relations; consultations for
        asylum seekers; fundraising via bazaars, concerts and other
        events. 140 local AI groups have adopted an individual
        prisoner of conscience. S: Letter writing, envelope stuffing,
        fundraising, public relations skills, and general management.
        J: Not necessary.
        http://www.amnesty.or.jp
Artists Without Borders 03-3550-7053
        A: Bring entertainment and art to victims of war throughout the
        world. S: Creativity in any area, teaching art, experience in
        working with children. J: Preferred but not necessary.
        http://www5a.biglobe.ne.jp/~artWB/
Caring For Young Refugees 03-3724-7525
        A: In Thailand and Cambodia: providing day nurseries, training
        teachers, and rebuilding schools. In Japan: promoting

international understanding and exchange between refugees from Indochina and Japanese people. Newsletter. S: Translation and clerical work. J: Some required.

Citizen's Network For Japanese-Filipino Children (JFC Network) 03-3264-4272
A: Providing legal aid to Japanese-Filipino children whose fathers are not paying support and helping to obtain recognition, child support, Japanese nationality, etc. for them; counselling for mothers so that they can be independent; and searching for and negotiating with fathers. S: English and Japanese. Tagalog if possible. Computer. Translation. J: Required.
http://www.jca.ax.apc.org

Dobutsutachi No Kai 0425-84-4354
A: Improving the living conditions of animals; spaying and neutering of cats and dogs; finding homes for pets; writing petitions; visiting local administrations; holding rallies, demonstrations, information events, and bazaars. S: Clerical, financial, transportation, marketing, writing, translation, design, animal care, and horseback riding. Japanese, English and/or German. J: Useful.

Earth Day Japan Tokyo Office 03-3263-9022
A: International exchange of information with Earth Day participants; newsletter and publications regarding environmental issues. S: Computing, networking, interpreting. J: Preferred.
http://www.earthday-j.org

Foreign Nurses Association In Japan 03-5469-0966
A: Teaching CPR and first aid, medical information   03-3370-3415
brochures, newsletter, lectures, health booths. S: Health care background, nursing, teaching, office, and CPR and first aid courses. J: Helpful.

Foundation for Global Peace and Environment 03-5442-3161
A: Global peace and environmental education; International Contest and Exhibition of Children's Environment Paintings, publication of books and newsletters, environmental education materials, international conferences for young people, symposia and seminars, Save the Sea campaign projects, Tennis Forum and Rice Forum for Global Environment, exchange programs for youth in developing countries, planning and support of projects of international organizations and eco-tourism. S: Translation, interpreting, writing, computer, and project planning. J: Required.

Franciscan Chapel Centre 03-3401-2141
A: Serving the needs of the international community in Tokyo; assisting foreign prisoners, refugees, foreign workers, and sexually abused children; Rice Patrol feeding program for Japanese homeless; Support in Grief Program; 'moms and tots' support group; FCC Women's Group charities; and teaching catechism and bible studies to grade school children. S: Counselling, teaching, telephone reception, fund raising. English, Japanese, French, Spanish, or Filipino language ability also useful. J: Useful.

431

Friends of the Earth Japan 03-3951-1081
    A: Promoting environmental, ecological, cultural, and ethnic
    diversity issues; Aid Impact; wetlands preservation; Russian
    forests conservation; Amur Leopard Fund; hiking program,
    Ecotour; and newsletters. S: Office work, writing, proofreading,
    rewriting, translation, and transportation. J: Useful.
    http://www.foejapan.org

Global Village 03-3705-0233
    A: Campaigning on environmental and north-south issues;
    supplying greener alternatives for everyday lives; fair trade
    operation; newspapers; Fashion and Living Earth catalogues;
    study meetings; study tours to India, Bangladesh and Kenya;
    education/outreach booths at events; information on organic/
    health food shops, restaurants and hotels; library resources.
    S: Friendly, flexible. J: Useful.

Greenpeace Japan 03-5351-5400
    A: International activities to stop environmental destruction,
    lobbying at conferences, and non-violent direct action against
    environmental destruction. S: English teaching, translation,
    interpretation, driving car or boat, and clerical work. J: Useful.
    http://www.nets.or.jp/GREENPEACE

Hand-in-Hand Chiba 043-224-2154
    A: Helping foreign workers; projects serving women—
    assistance with marriage/divorce, childbirth, citizenship, and
    health insurance issues; projects serving men—assistance
    with unpaid salary, labour accidents, etc. S: Counselling,
    interpretation, translation, and transportation. Japanese,
    English, and other Asian languages. J: Helpful.

International Education Resource and Innovation Center (ERIC) 03-3800-9416
    A: Increasing awareness of the environment, human rights,
    peace, and other global issues in Japan and worldwide
    through educational media; educational publications,
    seminars, and information services; human resources
    development in Japan; and sending volunteers to Cambodia.
    S: Training of educators and local facilitators in participatory
    learning; editing; translation; and volunteer training. Japanese
    and English or Cambodian languages. J: Useful.
    http://www.try-net.or.jp/eric-net/

International Living Craft Association (World Family Fund) 03-3262-5033
    A: Enabling poor women in developing countries to earn
    income through production of handicrafts; fair-trade policies.
    S: No special skills required. English and Japanese
    languages. J: Helpful.
    http://www.asahi-net.or.jp/~pg3s-aso/ilca/

International Movement Against All Forms of Discrimination
and Racism 03-3586-7447
    A: Eliminating discrimination against ethnic minorities,
    indigenous peoples, persons with disabilities, migrant workers,
    and other groups subject to discrimination; Project Against
    Trafficking in Women; Lobbying of the United Nations;
    seminars; information network; and projects for the

empowerment of indigenous peoples in Guatemala and
Argentina. S: Translation, writing, and computer skills
(Macintosh). English, Spanish, French, German, and
Japanese languages. J: Useful.
http://www.imadr.org

International Social Service Japan 03-3760-3471
A: Facilitating adoption of children; counselling foreigners on
marriage, nationality, and adoption issues; networking
worldwide on adoption issues: telephone services; publication
of *Intercountry*. S: Translation, office skills, and sales. English,
German, Spanish, Tagalog, and other Asian languages.
J: Useful.

Japan AIDS Prevention Awareness Network (JAPANetwork)
A: Designing and disseminating EFL teaching materials to
teachers around the country, maintaining a video lending
library, producing free HIV/AIDS lesson plans at three
language levels, producing a quarterly newsletter, sending
speakers to lecture or do workshops at events, holding an
annual World AIDS Day (December 1) Memorial Candlelight
Walk in downtown Nagoya (and other cities if volunteers are
willing). S: A willing heart, some extra time (depending on the
project you'd like to do). Need people who'd like to work on our
newsletter: film reviews, student-produced AIDS-related
stories, poems, artwork or research; and also help us develop
teaching ideas. J: None.
http://www.japanetwork.gol.com

Japan Braille Library 03-3209-0241
A: Providing braille books, talking books, and face-to-face
reading, as well as a reference service; selling aids for the
blind; publishing braille books; teaching braille to the newly
blind and others; volunteer education of braille transcribers
and narrators; newsletters; annual movie shows and concerts
to raise funds; and training workshop for computerized braille
production in ASEAN countries. S: Braille transcription and
narration of talking books. J: Required. Occasionally other
languages are needed.

Japan Environmental Exchange 0424-88-8943
A: Sharing information from international and local environ-
mental groups through bilingual reports, booklets, and regular
public meetings; environmental projects, meetings, and
discussions; and Green Talk English Classes. S: Research,
teaching, public relations, desktop publishing, and event
planning that includes outdoor activities. J: Spoken and written
Japanese useful, but not necessary.
http://www.web.kyoto-inet.or.jp/org/s-world/jee

Japan International Volunteer Centre 03-3834-2388
A: Promoting self-reliance in the Third World through
development cooperation projects; environmental protection;
encouraging understanding between Japanese and foreign
communities in Japan; international projects in Asia, Africa,
Latin America, and the Middle East: rural development,

reforestation, sustainable agriculture, improvement of living conditions, vocational training, social welfare services, and health care. In Japan: information services, lectures and study meetings, and study tours; selling JVC calendars and postcards. S: Computer, translation, marketing, public relations, fundraising, and research and report writing. Japanese, English, Thai, Cambodian, Vietnamese, Laotian, Arabic, and Spanish language skills. J: Useful. http://www.jca.apc.org/jvc

Japan Israel Women's Welfare Organization (JIWWO) 03-3400-2559
A: Supporting the care and education of mentally and physically handicapped children in Japan and Israel; promoting cultural exchange between the two countries through fundraising and social programs. S: Event planning, fundraising, and sales. Occasional need for legal, financial, writing, and translation skills. Japanese or English language skills. J: Useful.

Japan Tropical Forest Action Network (JATAN) 03-3770-6308
A: Centre for the exchange of vital information; various projects that research, publicise, and campaign with regard to the tropical deforestation crisis. S: Translation, research, rewriting, interpreting, and general office. J: Japanese preferred, but English is also needed.

Jhelp.com 03-5780-1113
A: Providing 24-hour emergency telephone hotline and follow-up services, and the Jcard. Affiliated organisations include: AIDS Hotline, Volunteer Hotline, and Japan Emergency Team for disaster relief. S: Website development, counselling, design, and public relations. As many languages as possible. J: Useful.
http://www.jhelp.com/en/home.html

Knowing Is Doing Something (KIDS) 03-3787-6255
A: Supporting children with special needs, those who are mentally or physically challenged, or at social/economic disadvantage; promoting volunteering in the business sector; annual Tokyo Disneyland project; ongoing visit (monthly) and ad hoc visit program at homes/organisations in Tokyo and its suburbs; and publishing a newsletter. S: Interest in working with children, event planning, newsletter editing, and fundraising. Also opportunities to use other business skills for special projects. J: Not essential.
http://www.bekkoame.or.jp/~suzuki-k/

Kobokan Community Centre 03-3611-1880
A: Children's Home (Karuizawa, Nagano) for children and youth in need of assistance due to divorce, mental illness, or other family problems; day care nursery including after-school care; child and youth camps; program for the elderly; and an international exchange program and training for Asian social workers. S: Teaching, people skills, and counselling; organising functions, meetings, and fundraising events.

Make-A-Wish of Japan 03-3221-8388
>A: Granting wishes for children between the ages of 3 and 18
>years who have life threatening or terminal illnesses.
>S: Clerical, fundraising, event planning, and public relations.
>J: Useful, but not required.
>http://www.erde.co.jp/~wish_japan

Meguro Unesco Association 03-3717-3931
>A: Promoting peace through educational, scientific, and
>cultural activities; international cooperation and cultural
>exchange; Japanese, English, French, and Chinese language
>classes; youth summer retreat; study tour; lectures; charity
>concert; bazaar; newsletter in Japanese and English;
>collecting and preparing miswritten postcards for reuse; and
>other activities. S: Translation, proofreading, and teaching of
>English. J: Useful.
>http://www.web.infoweb.ne.jp/meguro-unesco

Missionaries of Charity 03-3876-2864
>A: Helping others through Christian activity, feeding program,
>and clothing distribution. S: No special skills required, just a
>willingness to give of one's time. J: Not necessary.

Pacific Asia Resource Centre 03-3291-5901
>A: Promoting harmony and ending discrimination in Asia,
>publications (English and Japanese), audio-visual materials,
>Freedom School, and advocacy work. S: Translation, editing,
>and rewriting. Japanese and English language skills. J: Useful.
>http://www.jca.ax.apc.org/parc

Peace Boat 03-3363-8047
>A: Organising educational voyages; building a global network
>of NGOs and individuals committed to the creation of a more
>peaceful and humanitarian society; providing a forum to
>discuss and learn about peace, human rights, and
>environmental issues while enjoying the diversity of cultural
>exchange with people in all parts of the world. S: A high level
>of language skills for interpreting, translating, and teaching.
>J: Language teachers should have conversational Japanese
>ability. Interpreters should be fluent in Japanese and English
>or Japanese and Spanish.
>http://www.peaceboat.org

Refugees International Japan 03-5500-3093
>A: Helping refugees by funding emergency, basic assistance,
>and self-help programs; raising awareness of refugee issues;
>fundraising through holding concerts and other special events,
>and through sales of Christmas Cards as well as crafts made
>by refugees; publishing a newsletter; and organizing speakers'
>programs about refugee issues. S: Public relations, event
>planning, and office work. J: Depends on type of
>volunteer activity.
>http://www.d-plug.com/rijapan

Sanya Kyodai No Ie 03-3875-9167
>A: In the spirit of Christian ministry, providing assistance to
>day-labourers who work on a day-to-day contract basis, and to

the poor, elderly and homeless in the Sanya area. S: Interest
in Sanya area. J: Helpful, but not necessary.

Sanyu Kai 03-3874-1269
A: Operating a medical clinic; distributing blankets and food;
and managing a centre providing daily activities, meals, and
shelter to the homeless. S: No special skills are required
(except for clinic work). J: Necessary.

Seishonen Fukushi Centre 03-3856-2728
A: Providing care and services for 15- to 18-year-old youths
who lack parents or guardians to raise them; organising
fundraising bazaars and other programs. S: Teaching, word
processing, meal preparation, and collecting items for bazaars.
J: Mostly needed.
http://www2s.biglobe.ne.jp/~center/

Services for the Health in Asian and African Regions (SHARE) 03-5800-4778
A: Supporting every person's right to better health through
provision of medical care, training, and advice; health
education and training (Cambodia); AIDS prevention and
education (Thailand); counselling for foreign workers; 'AIDS
Talk' monthly meetings and other events (Japan); newsletters.
S: Health care professionals are needed for the counselling
project; no special skills required for other projects.
J: Preferred.
http://www.asahi-net.or.jp/~HV5E-USD/

Setagaya Volunteer Association 03-3426-8001
A: Promoting volunteerism at Setagaya social services
facilities; operating a volunteer center that includes education,
collection and dissemination of information, as well as
consultation on volunteer activity; operating a shop featuring
crafts made by disabled, elderly, and other volunteers;
operating a day care service for the handicapped and staffed
play parks. S: Varies. J: Some helpful, but not essential.
http://www.setagaya.net/setagaya/vol

Together with Africa and Asia Association 048-832-8271
A: Educating needy young people, especially those in
disadvantaged communities who were victims of the former
apartheid regime, and by doing so supporting the new
democratic South Africa; collecting and sending educational
English-language books; sending mobile libraries; and
assisting, primarily through donations, the Chinese and
Korean school in Kobe that was damaged during the January
1995 earthquake. S: Knowledge of English-language books
and libraries; knowledge of South Africa useful, but not
required. J: Useful.

Tokyo Caritas House 03-3947-9365
A: Based in the spirit of Christianity, aim to improve social   03-3943-1726
welfare in the Tokyo area; consultation and assistance with
family problems; referrals to legal and other professional help;
occupational therapy programs; and fundraising.
S: Counselling, teaching, transportation, translation, and
fundraising. J: Useful.

Tokyo English Life Line (TELL) 03-3498-0261
> A: Supporting and counselling the foreign community,
> fundraising, community newsletter, professional face-to-face
> counselling, presentations and training, information services,
> and telephone counselling. S: Bilingual Japanese/English and
> Tagalog (other Filipino languages also useful); general office,
> computer, writing, editing, marketing, fundraising, and
> organisational skills; counselling skills (training provided by
> TELL); teaching skills; community workshop experience.
> http://www.tell.gol.com

Tokyo International Learning Community (TILC) 0422-31-9611
> A: Providing educational and special services for the English-
> speaking community in the Tokyo area, especially for children
> with developmental delays and disabilities and their families;
> school programs and related services for children with
> developmental disabilities who are not able to attend a regular
> international school full time; a Toy Library for neighbourhood
> preschool children; and a Saturday learning disabilities
> program to support students in their regular schools.
> S: Experience or interest in working directly with children;
> fundraising; public relations; and general office.
> J: Not necessary.

Tokyo Union Church Women's Society 03-3400-0942
> A: Volunteer referrals to nonprofit organizations, homeless
> food program, visits to detainees through prison ministry
> program, and fundraising for outreach programs.
> S: No specific skills necessary.

Tokyo YWCA International Language Volunteers 03-3293-5421
> A: Promoting international communication through interpreting
> and translation, supporting human rights and dignity, working
> towards maintaining peace and justice in the world on a basis
> of Christian faith, translating reports and papers, and
> interpreting (for example, when medical and social workers
> visit welfare institutes in Tokyo). S: Editing, translation, and
> interpreting (Japanese/English, English/Japanese). J: Useful.

U.S. Greens Abroad
> A: Providing American citizens overseas with information
> about the USA Green Party and Green activities; providing
> information on Green candidates and how to vote absentee;
> engaging in political work in Japan, including campaigns and
> networking with Japanese and foreign groups, such as
> environmental groups, women's groups, labour unions, and
> others. S: None. J: None.
> http://ultra3.misasa.okayama-u.ac.jp/~pru/usga/USGreens.htm

World Wide Fund For Nature (WWF) Japan 03-3769-1711
> A: International conservation projects (over 11,000 projects in
> 130 countries) through WWF International, domestic
> conservation projects in Japan, grant programmes supporting
> over 400 research programmes. S: Interest in nature/wildlife
> conservation, environmental education, and rewriting.
> J: Useful.

437

Yamate YMCA 03-3202-0321
      A: Camping program for children, English instruction for
      children, and counselling for foreigners. S: Counselling, playing
      with children, teaching, and office skills. Any language.
      J: Not necessary.

Groups Promoting Volunteer Activities or Providing Information

Asia Foundation 03-3441-8291
      http://www.asiafoundation.org
Global Environment Information Centre (GEIC) 03-3407-8107
      http://www.geic.or.jp
International Association of Volunteer Effort (IAVE) 03-3351-5130
Japan NGO Center for International Cooperation (JANIC) 03-3294-5370
      http://www.jca.ax.apc.org/janic/
Japan Youth Volunteers Association 03-3460-0211
      http://www2.coi.te-tokyo.co.jp/~jyval
Tokyo Voluntary Action Centre 03-3235-1171
      http://www.tvac.or.jp/

Resources and Further Information

The Institute of Cultural Affairs: Japan
      Listing of links to Japanese non-governmental and volunteer organizations.
      http://www.icajapan.gol.com/icajapane/link.html
Japan Information Network Website by Ministry of Foreign Affairs
      Listing of non-profit organisations.
      http://jcic.or.jp/jd/
NGO Café
      Information on NGOs worldwide, including Japanese organizations
      and activities.
      http://soc-info.soc.titech.ac.jp/ngo/ncafe-bj.html
The Volunteer Network News
      Volunteer opportunities in Kansai.
      http://www.tr-108.co.jp/KAIGO/VN/Html/VN-E_2.html

Directory of Japanese NGOs Active in International Cooperation
      By Japan NGO Center for International Cooperation (JANIC).
      Call 03-3294-5370 or visit http://www.jca.ax.apc.org/janic/
Tokyo English Life Line (TELL) Calendar
      Lists non-profit organizations and contact information.
      Call 03-3498-0261 or visit http://www.tell.gol.com
Volunteering Directory
      By Foreign Executive Women (FEW).
      Can be viewed online at http://www.few.gol.com

SHANE
ENGLISH SCHOOL

SHANE ENGLISH SCHOOL - The largest British English School in Japan. Requires qualified professionals for TEFL positions in the Kanto, Nagoya and Kyushu regions.

We recruit native English speaking individuals with a minimum of a University Degree and a CELTA or recognised equivalent qualification. Applicants who do not meet all these requirements may be considered. Successful candidates will be recruited from a native British or Commonwealth English speaking background and will preferably have at least some EFL teaching experience.

A competitive fixed monthly salary is offered and varies dependent on further qualifications and experience. Bonus schemes, visa sponsorship, furnished accommodation and generous holidays are also a part of the complete employment package.

Employees will benefit from comprehensive training and development schemes with the opportunity for future promotion and career development within Japan and in other countries in which we have operations.

Teacher welfare is a major consideration and as such there are regular company subsidized events for teachers. In the past these have included skiing trips to Hokkaido and to see the Sapporo Snow Festival, cultural trips to Kabuki and Tokyo Bay Cruises.

Shane English School operates an equal opportunities teacher recruitment and promotion program and there are currently a number of women in more senior positions in the company. We are especially mindful of safety and security issues with respect to women, ensuring that female teachers never leave schools alone at the end of a working day and that they are placed in apartments within reasonable walking distance of train stations.

Shane Language Services (SLS) also has openings for native English speakers, including American English speakers, for Business English lessons, kindergarten lessons and for in-company and ALT work. Both part time and full time positions are available throughout the year.

Contact: Director of Recruitment and Personnel
FAX: (03) 3869 2636
E-Mail: course@shane.co.jp
WEB: http://www.shane.co.jp

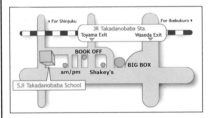
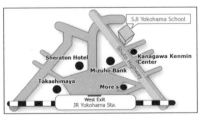

Learning 7

Japanese
Graduate Programmes
Other Classes

Japanese

You won't be able to avoid picking up some Japanese while you are here, but you will need to make an effort in order to become a competent speaker, and a huge effort to be able to read *kanji*. Kanji is a form of writing that consists of Chinese characters and you need to know about eight hundred just to read a newspaper. *Hiragana* and *katakana* are the other forms of writing; there are about forty-five symbols in each syllabary, which are quite easy to learn. These phonetic alphabets (or syllabaries) are used for particles and words 'borrowed' from other languages. For example, katakana is used for 'beer' and 'door'. Your name will be written in katakana. *Romaji* is Japanese words written with the English alphabet, as in the translations in this book. Hiragana is used a lot at the end of verbs to complete them.

You can study Japanese wherever you live in Japan, but in the big cities, especially Tokyo, actually practising what you have learnt requires real effort. Friends of mine lived in the countryside and after two years they returned to their home countries fluent in Japanese. On the other side of the coin, some Tokyo friends who have been in Japan for over ten years still speak only basic Japanese, but find that it doesn't limit their lives at all. Basic English is so widely spoken in Tokyo that it can be difficult to justify the effort of learning Japanese while managing a hectic lifestyle.

The benefits that learning Japanese can bring to your life are clear; I've already discussed the increase in job prospects. In addition, some Japanese ability can help you navigate your way through the meetings and paperwork involved in so many 'simple' procedures. Relationships with colleagues, neighbours, and in-laws will generally improve when they see you making an effort in what the Japanese perceive to be an incredibly difficult language to learn. Knowledge of the most basic phrases will often result in admiration from those around you.

Knowing which words to use with respect to status and gender can be problematic; however, pronuniation and basic grammar are not that difficult to grasp. Most Western women find their greatest obstacles are the teachers and the lack of opportunity to practise, especially if they work with other foreigners:

> *I have been trying to learn Japanese for a number of years but I seldom have an opportunity to practice what I know except for office Japanese and telephone messages.*

Teachers

Many Western women wanting to learn Japanese feel that Japanese teachers are unable to teach in a way that encourages foreigners who are interested in communication rather than rote memorisation:

> *I do not think the Japanese are equipped to teach their language because they have such difficulty communicating in it themselves.*

I found that some teachers were so rigid in their lesson planning that they couldn't cope when I wanted to try a 'normal conversation' or had grasped something quickly. It just didn't feature in their plans. Time to actually practise what one has learnt has been missing in English education in Japan; hence the boom in English conversation schools. Unfortunately, it can be just as difficult for foreigners learning Japanese to find a place where they can practise 'real' Japanese conversation, or to find a method of studying that will allow them to do this.

Schools

There are many schools established to teach foreigners Japanese. Class size varies, as do tuition fees, but they are usually reasonable. Hours are usually flexible, and some schools have many different programs to suit your level and schedule, including intensive courses. Many of the universities offer Japanese courses that are regarded with more respect than the language school courses:

> *Rather than language schools, apply for one of the university programmes—it looks better on your CV, works out cheaper (in many cases) than language schools, gives you a great social life and/or network of contacts for jobs, and because of more contact hours, etc., you learn faster. In addition, after graduating from their language programmes, you are qualified to attend the university as a regular under- or post-grad student.*

Although one woman pointed out that:

> *... attending university presumes (a) an independent income or (b) a part-time evening job lucrative enough to keep you financed.*

See the list below for recommended university programmes and the next section for general information about graduate programmes. Each ward also holds very cheap Japanese classes for foreign residents. Generally, with all schools, you are taking a risk regarding finding a teacher or style with which you will be happy. You may even get a different teacher for each lesson. As with so many things, it's best to go to a recommended school—ask friends and check out the Resources and recommendations at the end of this section.

Private lessons

Private Japanese teachers are not much more expensive than enrolling in a school and, if you choose carefully, you may find one who is flexible and experienced enough to meet your needs. Some Western women found that their Japanese teachers became good friends and general 'guides' to living in Japan:

> *She patiently withstood all my blunt questions about Japanese culture and put up with my bad moods! She chose appropriate readings and got me into modern Japanese writers like Banana Yoshimoto (who's considerably more challenging a read in Japanese than in the English translation). She's familiar with the test material, but also is good with language needed for practical situations.*

Again, it's best to ask around for recommendations, but be sure to check the list at the end of this section, too.

Language exchange

Another option may be the 'language exchange' system. You often see classified advertisements for people who want to practise their English and let you practise your Japanese. Exchanges may be useful for making friends, but the system rarely works to improve your Japanese. You will likely find that most of the language exchange time is spent speaking English—you will not have much Japanese taught to you, never mind a chance to practise speaking it. In some cases, 'language exchange' is just a euphemism for 'looking for a foreign date', so if you're single and want to date Japanese men, this can be a good way to meet them without the date itself being the focus of your time together.

Self-study

Many Western women recommend self-study as the best method for learning Japanese:

Instead of spending money on schools or teachers, use it for opportunities to practise what you know. Travel alone. Read a lot and just plain do the hard work of studying.

I think I learned Japanese in spite of school rather than because of it. Basically, I learned what I know from individual study of kanji cards, listening to the people around me carefully, and refusing to speak English with Japanese people unless (a) their English is better than my Japanese or (b) I'm being paid to teach them.

My friend Sue learnt all her Japanese by finding a traditional Japanese restaurant/bar near her home and hanging out there every night, absorbing everything around her. It does seem like rather a lot of time and effort (and alcohol), but that is what it takes if you are going to study alone. If you are really determined, then surround yourself with Japanese friends who speak a minimum of English:

My advice to anyone wanting to learn Japanese is to find Japanese friends, and just start speaking and listening. For my first six years in Japan I didn't have a single Western friend. I figured that I came to Japan to learn the language and culture, so I just threw myself into it whole hog.

It's obvious that having a Japanese partner will provide you with an in-house teacher, providing you are insistent, because your partner probably wants to speak English at home as much as you want to speak Japanese.

Useful Japanese

Japanese	nihongo	to speak	hanasu
to study	benkyou suru	to listen	kiku
beginner	shoshinsha	language	
intermediate	chuukyuu	exchange	otagai ni kotoba o oshie au
advanced	joukyuu		
to read	yomu	private teacher	kojin kyouju no sensei
to write	kaku		

446

private lesson	*kojin/puraibeeto* *ressun*	to be absent	*kesseki suru*
text book	*kyoukasho/kyouzai*	lesson fee	*jugyouryou/* *koushuuryou*
drill book	*renshuu chou*	refund	*haraimodoshi*
homework	*shukudai*	cancellation	*kyanseru*
to attend	*shusseki suru*		

I'd like to study Japanese.	*Nihongo o benkyou shitai desu.*
How many students are in one class?	*Hitokurasu ni seito wa nanmei desu ka.*
Please send me some information in English.	*Eigo de kakareta shiryou o okutte kudasai.*
How much does it cost?	*Ryoukin wa ikura desu ka.*

Resources

The Tourist Information Centre can arrange visits to Japanese homes throughout Japan to introduce foreigners to Japanese culture and to give you the opportunity to practise Japanese. Call them on 03-3485-6827.

Schools
Check your ward office handbook for your local international association or international friendship association. These groups organise Japanese lessons for the ward's foreign residents at very reasonable prices, sometimes for free.

Academy of Language Arts 03-3235-0071
    Iidabashi, Tokyo. Group intensive classes. All levels.
    http://www.kbic.ardour.co.jp/~newgenji/ala/

Active Learning School 03-5282-8705
    Kanda, Tokyo. Private, group, and intensive classes. All levels.
    http://www.als.co.jp

Alpha Japanese School 03-3769-4945
    3 locations in Tokyo: Mita, Toranomon, Shibuya. Private
    classes for beginners.
    http://www.alpha.ac.jp

Akasaka Japanese Language School 03-5413-7450
    Akasaka, Tokyo. Can do home visits. Private, group, and
    intensive classes. All levels.

Asahi Culture Centre 03-3344-1965
    Shinjuku, Tokyo. Private, group, and intensive classes. All levels.

Association of Japanese Teachers (AJT) 03-3918-0876
    Home classes in Tokyo and surrounding areas. Private and
    intensive classes. All levels.

Educational Information Institute (EII) 03-5366-7201
    Shinjuku, Tokyo. Private, group, and intensive classes. All levels.
    http://www.skyboom.com/eii

Evergreen School 03-3713-4958
    Yutenji, Tokyo. Private, group, and intensive classes. All levels.

Hiroo Japanese Centre 03-3444-3481
    Hiroo, Tokyo. Private, group, and intensive classes. All levels.

International Christian University 0422-333-058
    Mitaka, Tokyo. Group intensive classes. All levels.
    http://www.icu.ac.jp
Japan Airlines Language (JAL) Academy 03-5412-2671
    Harajuku, Tokyo. Private and group classes. All levels.
    http://www.jaca.co.jp
Japanese Language Institute 03-3359-9600
    Yotsuya, Tokyo. Private, group, and intensive classes. All levels.
    http://www.iec-nichibei.or.jp
Kai Japanese Language School 03-3205-1356
    Shin-Okubo, Tokyo. Private and group classes. All levels.
    http://www.kiaj.co.jp
Kansai Gaigo Senmongakko 06-6621-8115
    Tennoji, Osaka. Group intensive classes. All levels.
    http://ss5.inet-osaka.or.jp/~tgjapan
Keio University 03-5427-1614
    Tamachi, Tokyo and Hiyoshi, Yokohama. Beginner and
    intermediate group intensive classes.
    http://www.keio.ac.jp
Kichijoji Language School 0422-47-7390
    Kichijoji, Tokyo. Private, group, and intensive classes. All levels.
    http://www2.gol.com/users/kls/
LIC 03-3770-5344
    Shibuya, Tokyo. Private, group, and intensive classes. All levels.
Sendagaya Japanese Institute 03-3232-6181
    2 locations in Tokyo: Takadanobaba and Shimo Ochiai. Private,
    group, and intensive classes. All levels.
    http://www.jp-sji.org
Tokyo Galaxy Language Academy 03-3473-3251
    Ebisu, Tokyo. Private, group, and intensive classes. All levels.
    http://www.jade.dti.ne.jp/~galaxy
Tokyo Language School 03-3350-0317
    3 locations in Tokyo: Shinjuku Gyoenmae, Okubo, and
    Ikebukuro. Group classes. All levels.
Urban Academy 03-5469-8641
    2 locations in Tokyo: Omotesando and Ikebukuro. Also 1
    school in Shiki, Saitama. Private and group classes. All levels.

Study Materials Recommended by Western Women
A Guide to Learning Hiragana and Katakana
    By Kenneth G Henshall and Tetsuo Takagaki, Charles E Tuttle Co: 1990
Decoding Kanji: A Practical Approach to Learning Look-Alike Characters (Power Japanese Series)
    By Yaeko S Habein and Gerald B Mathias (Contributor), Kodansha International: 2000
English Grammar for Students of Japanese: The Study Guide for Those Learning Japanese (English Grammar Series)
    By Mutsuko Endo Hudson, Olivia & Hill Press: 1994

*Essential Kanji: 2,000 Basic Japanese Characters Systematically Arranged for
Learning and Reference*
By Patrick Geoffrey O'Neill, Weatherhill: 1981
*Guide to Writing Kanji and Kana, Books 1 and 2: A Self-Study Workbook for Learning
Japanese Characters (Tuttle Language Library)*
By Wolfgang Hadamitzky and Mark Spahn, Charles E Tuttle Co: 1991
Japanese for Busy People I, II and III
By the Association for Japanese-Language Teaching (AJALT). Available online at
http://www.ajalt.org/index-e.html
Kana Workbook: The First Step to Learning Japanese
By Yoshiko Saito, McGraw Hill College Division: 1994
Speak Japanese Today: A Self-Study Program for Learning Everyday Japanese
By Taeko Kamiya, Charles E Tuttle Co: 1989

Easy Web Japanese
http://www.enteract.com/~sonobe/japan/
Japanese Online
http://www.japanese-online.com/
Japanese Tutor
http://www.japanesetutor.cc/
Learn Japanese
http://www.thehaucks.com/learn.html
Learn Japanese on the Internet
http://www.georgetown.edu/users/caplanj/
Learn Japanese Online
http://falcon.laker.net/apoc/japanese/
Learning Japanese: games, dictionaries, and other resources
http://www.nanana.com/japanese.html
Teach Yourself Japanese
http://www.sf.airnet.ne.jp/~ts/japanese/index.html

Tips from Other Western Women

- *My best teacher was Japanese television. Although it can be difficult to understand
at first, the constant barrage of Japanese means that eventually some of it sticks in
your brain.*
- *Listen to the radio.*
- *Kanji cards.*
- *Make a point of refusing to speak English unless it is absolutely necessary.*
- *Use your* [Japanese] *partner as a 'walking dictionary'.*
- *Original Japanese books, novels, children's kanji books.*
- *... about kanji—use the first to sixth year primary school books that Japanese kids
use—as this way you learn it a la native.*
- *Manga—Japanese comics—are good for Japanese study because the words used
are conversational and there is often yomigana (hiragana characters to indicate
how to read the kanji).*

Resources and Further Information
Association for the Promotion of Japanese Language Education 03-5386-0080
Information on Japanese language schools throughout Japan.
http://www.rim.or.jp/nisshinkyo
Association of International Education, Japan Testing Division 03-5454-5215
Japanese language proficiency test inquiries. Branches
throughout Japan.
Bonjinsha Resource Centre 03-3239-8673

Guide to Japanese Career and Vocational Schools
By the Tourist Information Centre. Call 03-3485-6827 for a copy.
Guide to Japanese Schools
By the Bonjinsha Resource Centre. Call 03-3239-8673 for a copy.
Japanese and Japanese Studies
By the Tourist Information Centre. Call 03-3485-6827 for a copy.
Onna Rashiku (Like a Woman): The Diary of a Language Learner in Japan
By Karen Ogulnick, State University of New York Press: 1998

Japanese Language Resource Centre
http://www.kanjistep.com
Japanese Language Resources
http://www.nihongo.org/english/language/education/
Japanese Language School Guide
http://kbic.ardour.co.jp/~newgenji/jls/index.html
Study Abroad Guide: Japan
http://www.istudy.com/japan/elist.htm
YMCA Japanese Language Schools
http://ymcajapan.org/japanese/

Graduate Programmes

Instead of studying a correspondence graduate programme offered by your home country, you may want to investigate one of the several graduate programmes for foreigners available throughout Japan that are conducted in English. Apart from the sense of personal satisfaction, completing a graduate programme can greatly increase your job prospects both in Japan and at home. Western women value the insight it has given them into Japan and the opportunity to study with people from a variety of countries, especially if their lives have otherwise been work-dominated:

Being a graduate student gave me the opportunity to meet Japanese people (especially women) who were interested in improving themselves. It was reassuring to see that not everyone is ready to lie down and die for their company.

Not only can you discover a Japan outside of the hustle and bustle of Tokyo's business world—NOT the real Japan—but you can meet people from SO many cultures while advancing your own studies.

A variety of courses are available, although those most popular with Western women are business, Japanese language, or education related. You can study full time or part time, for several weeks or for years. Non-degree courses are available, as well as master's or doctorate degrees. Some courses are online, which one woman felt had benefits that other correspondence courses don't have:

I feel like I have people to talk with if I have problems or just want to discuss something. I couldn't do that if it were just a regular correspondence course. Being in Japan you have two obstacles to doing a grad school programme, though: lack of libraries and lack of contact with other students (if you're in a rural area and can't go on campus for your classes). The latter is solved with this online programme!

Short courses (e.g., eight weeks) resulting in certification tend to be reasonably priced (around ¥40,000), although degrees tend to be expensive. For an MBA you can expect to pay several million yen. Some companies sponsor employees, although they tend to choose their Japanese staff as they are likely to spend their whole life at the same company and that makes it seem like a good investment. Check with your company to see if you are eligible. Sponsorships are also available; check with the individual universities and organisations in your home country.

A word of warning though: despite the fact that a foreign university may have a great reputation at home, its branch in Japan may not be recognised by the Japanese Ministry of Education. These courses may not be the best choice if your reason for studying is to improve your job prospects in Japan.

Useful Japanese

I have not included Useful Japanese in this section, as the main point of it is to show you that you can study graduate programmes in English.

Resources

Universities

International University of Japan (see display ad, page 454) 0257-79-1111
       Niigata. Programmes: International Management;
       International Relations.
       http://www.iuj.ac.jp

McGill University
       Tokyo. Programmes: MBA International Business
       Management.
       maltby@management.mcgill.ca

Newport Asia Pacific University 03-5302-5010
       Online. Programmes: International Business; International
       Communications; Education (TESOL, TJFL).
       http://www.asiapacificu.edu/apuindex.html

Sophia University 03-3238-4004
       Tokyo. Programmes: MA Comparative Culture.
       http://www.sophia.ac.jp

Temple University Japan 0120-86-1026
       Tokyo. Programmes: Executive MBA; Law; TESOL. Also
       has continuing education, corporate education and
       certificate programs.
       http://www.tuj.ac.jp/

University of Maryland 042-358-2733
       Online. Programmes: Business Administration, Distance
       Education, Education, International Management, Computer
       Systems Management, Electronic Commerce,
       Telecommunications Management, Environmental
       Management, Technology Management, Engineering,
       Management. Also have undergraduate programmes and
       certificates, and graduate certificates.
       http://www.umuc.edu

Resources and Further Information

Foreign Student Advisory Centre 03-3946-7565
　　　http://www.abk.or.jp/eng/index.htm
Foreign Students Information Centre and Helpline 03-5454-5216

ACCESS—The Database of Japanese Universities
　　　http://www.yamasa.org/access/indexe.html
Association of International Education Japan (AIEJ)
　　　http://www.aiej.or.jp/index1e.html
Universities in Japan
　　　http://www.st.rim.or.jp/~liliko/univ.j.html

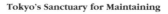

Other Classes

As in your home country, you will find a wide range of classes for just about anything you want to learn. More specific to Japan are classes such as Japanese cooking, flower arranging, and the martial arts, which seem most popular with Western women. Some classes are held in English, but these tend to be expensive when compared with classes held in Japanese that Japanese people attend. Most Western women prefer the Japanese classes, finding that the classes in themselves are a good way to learn Japanese in a natural environment and to meet non-English-speaking Japanese people that they would usually never encounter. Ward offices hold a variety of classes at really cheap prices, sometimes for free.

Useful Japanese

classes .... *naraigoto/kurasu*	Chinese ink brush
Japanese cooking .... *nihon ryouri/*	painting .... *sumi e/suiboku-ga*
washyoku	calligraphy .... *shodou*
flower arrangement .. *kadou/ikebana*	chi gong .... *kikou*
Japanese dance ...... *nihon buyou*	oil painting .... *abura-e*
tea ceremony .... *sadou*	water color painting .. *suisai-ga*
martial arts .... *budou*	

What classes do you offer? .... *Douiu kurasu ga arimasu ka.*
I'd like some information on the classes
you hold. .... *Jyugyounaiyou o shiritai no desu ga.*
How much does it cost? .... *Hiyou wa ikura kakari masu ka.*
Where are the classes held? .... *Kurasu wa doko desu ka.*

Resources

The best resources for classes are your ward office and your local English-language newspapers or magazines. Many of the ward office classes are free, and if not, they are very reasonably priced. Large hotels hold tea ceremony classes. The following classes are all held in English.

Arts
Acting (The Light Company) 03-5458-8065
       Location varies, but always in Tokyo. Theatre, movement, voice
       classes.
Calligraphy 03-5478-8234
       Yoyogi-Uehara, Tokyo.   03-5351-0062
Drawing on the Right Side of the Brain (see display ad, page 459) 03-5484-3719
       Azabu Juban, Tokyo. Workshops and various art classes.
       http://member.nifty.ne.jp/RBR or http://www.rightbrain-art.com/
Japanese Calligraphy 03-3941-3809
       Otsuka, Tokyo.
Japanese Traditional Arts and Crafts 03-3403-2460
       Gaienmae, Tokyo.
Painting 03-3477-6277
       Shibuya, Tokyo. Watercolours, oil, pastels, chalk, acrylic.
Photography 090-3439-8798
       Harajuku, Tokyo. One-to-one classes. Group exhibitions.
Tokyo Photography Club
       Members throughout Japan. For beginners and intermediate.
       Tokyophotoclub@egroups.com

456

Tokyo Union Church 03-3400-0942
        Omotesando, Tokyo or at people's homes in the Tokyo area. 03-3400-0047
        Crafts, drawing, painting, flower arranging.
        http://www2.gol.com/users/tucwf.html

Cooking

A Taste of Culture
        Tokyo. Tasting programmes, market tours, Japanese cooking,
        Japanese culture.
        http://www.tasteofculture.com
Harajuku International Cooking Club 090-9825-4154
        Harajuku, Tokyo.
Konishi Japanese Home Cooking Class 03-3714-8859
        Meguro, Tokyo. Japanese and Chinese cooking.
Yuka Cooking Studio 078-802-4199
        Hankyu Roko, Kobe. Japanese cooking.

Flower Arrangement

Ikenobo Ochanomizu School 03-3292-3071
        Kanda Surugadai, Tokyo.
Japanese Flower Arrangement Club 090-2460-4646
        Sangenjaya, Tokyo.
        http://members.aol.com/ajpflower/
Ohara School 03-3499-1200
        Aoyama, Tokyo.
        http://www.ohararyu.or.jp
Sogetsu School 03-3408-1151
        Akasaka, Tokyo.

Martial Arts

Aikido World Headquarters 03-3203-9236
        Schools throughout Japan.
        http://www.aikikai.or.jp
All-Japan Judo Federation 03-3818-4199
        Schools throughout Japan.
All-Japan Kendo Federation 03-3234-6271
        Schools throughout Japan.
Seidokan Aikido of Tokyo 03-5994-1185
        Schools throughout Tokyo.
        http://www.ne.jp/asahi/chris/home/dojo.html

Other

Archery Federation of Japan 03-3481-2387
        Schools throughout Japan.
Aromatherapy 03-3225-6376
        Yotsuya Sanchome, Tokyo.
International Yoga Centre 03-5397-2741
        Ogikubo, Tokyo.

Japanese Culture 03-3484-7898
    Setagaya-ku, Tokyo.
Maiko Henshin Studio Shiki 03-5459-1230
    Shibuya, Tokyo. Dressing in kimono.
Massage Therapy 03-3478-5898
    Harajuku, Tokyo.
Meditation 03-5458-8065
    Daikanyama, Tokyo, and Yokohama.
Scottish Country Dancing.. 070-5080-8105
    Nakano, Tokyo.
Tai chi 075-213-3204
    Kyoto City, Kyoto.
Tokyo International Amateur Radio Association 03-3718-2461
    Jiyugaoka, Tokyo. Provide information for self-study; can assist
    you in getting a licence.
    http://www.tr.com
Tokyu Seminar 03-3477-6277
    Shibuya, Tokyo. Language, calligraphy, arts, dance, sports.
Tuesday Morning Chorus 03-5380-6070
    Nogata, Tokyo. Singing.

Leaving Japan

8

Before You Go

Each year, seventy percent of all foreigners leave Japan and make their homes in other countries. The turnover is very high. Having had a wealth of information to help them navigate their way into and around Japan, there is very little to help them either prepare to leave Japan or arrive in another country, especially if that country is their original home. Don't make the mistake of thinking that returning home is an easy experience; think about how much needs to be done when you just go home on holiday, and the strange feelings you have when you get there. Leaving Japan for good carries those same feelings, plus the inevitable sadness that comes with leaving something behind, however good or bad your life in Japan has been. Western women who have left Japan recommend preparing as far in advance as possible.

Perhaps you have been considering leaving for some time or perhaps you always knew that your time here was limited due to your job contract or for family reasons. If you are in control of your leaving date, make sure that you really are ready to leave:

Leaving Japan was easy for me, and a killer for my dearest friend who left at the same time. A person needs to be not only ready to leave Japan, but ready to be somewhere else.

Bad times come and go in Japan, just like anywhere else. It is tempting to think that being in Japan is the reason you are unhappy, but it's probably best not to see leaving as a solution to negative feelings. Leave Japan when you feel good about it, yourself, and your experiences. If you are having a bad time, think carefully: is it Japan you want to leave or is it a situation, a feeling, or yourself?

Don't leave Japan when you are hating it. My fifth year was horrible. I hated everything about my life in Tokyo: the noise, the pollution, the costs, the crowds, EVERYTHING. I really wanted to return to my cabin in the US. I decided to celebrate my last year in Japan knowing I was leaving and make each day special in some way. I soaked up every moment of the summer and reveled in those splendid moments in the sticky heat when crowds of hungover businessmen breathed on me for almost an hour. I left Japan yearning to stay.

This celebration of your life in Japan in giving yourself time to do everything you wish you had done and spending time with those who have made your life here good, bearable, and/or interesting is something that all ex-Japan Western women highly recommend:

I left Japan after eighteen months because my stint as a Foreign Service Employee for HP Japan was up. I looked forward to leaving because I lived alone in Japan and felt lonely and alienated a lot of the time. But as my departure day approached, I began to regret that this unique experience was ending and that I hadn't made more of it. (Hence the title of my book, *Too Late for the Festival.) Leaving was an intensely bittersweet experience and I can still recapture the feeling of it.

* *Too Late for the Festival: An American Salary-Woman in Japan* by Rhiannon Paine, Academy Chicago: 1999.

463

Give yourself ample time to do and see all the things you missed but wanted to do. Forget about the expense—just go do it. It's not likely you will be back for a visit as soon as you think. Go to Kyoto, see the Hiroshima Memorial, ski the Alps, scuba in Okinawa, see the ice festival in Hokkaido, and party in Roppongi. Don't miss these places and activities. AND give yourself ample time to offer proper goodbyes to friends and people you have come to love in Japan.

As my friend Cath said at her farewell party, "Grieve before you leave". And take that trip to the souvenir shop that you always do for your friends and family when you go back on holiday—this time stock up for yourself.

Before you leave, research your destination as well as you researched Japan before coming, whether you are returning home or going to a different place. Let people know you are coming well in advance, including prospective employers, as well as friends and family. Your now well-developed networking skills will help you in your transition and you can't start too far in advance.

My online searches through local newspapers did help me get an idea of what I was dealing with. If you're going to be on your own, get a job lined up first, unless you have family to rely on while you get settled. Generally speaking, it takes a few months to find a satisfying position, even in the current US economy where everything is supposedly 'booming'. Be patient, don't panic, and enjoy your new surroundings. See it as an adventure, or an extension of your long list of adventures that might have begun in Tokyo or even earlier. Keep in mind that your fresh perspective will provide interesting contrast material in the future, so write down your impressions and review them after a month or two.

In terms of practicalities, you may need to hand in your notice for your job and apartment—it is polite and in some cases mandatory that you do this about three months in advance. Unnecessarily leaving in a rush and on bad terms won't help your feelings when you look back on your life in Japan (and it won't help you get any references you may require). Utility companies need to be contacted, bills settled, bank accounts closed, and debts paid (including ward tax). Your telephone line and household furniture you will not be taking with you can be sold via classified advertisements. Plan this well in advance and just give it away if you can't sell it. There are several companies that provide shipping services if you have too much stuff to carry; allow three months for it to arrive at your destination. One woman recommends that you complete all household practicalities several days before your leaving date and then find a place to relax:

> *We allowed three days after moving out of our apartment to stay in a hotel in downtown Tokyo. After the stress of moving out, this was a necessary break before our return overseas. Also, because it was the Keio Plaza hotel in Shinjuku, they had all the facilities I needed (like a fax machine and a messaging service) to tie up loose ends. We had some people up to our room on the last night, had drinks and relaxed! It was easy for our friends to meet us since it was so central, and we didn't have to worry about getting rid of our stuff at the last minute. Then, on the last day, we took a bus directly to Narita.*

You are supposed to submit your alien registration card at the airport, one final act showing that you really are leaving Japan, so if you think you may return as a resident:

> *... consider the investment of a re-entry permit. I left on the day my visa expired (no problem). It surprised me that I had to return my alien registration card at the airport. I came, I saw, I conquered!*

When you submit your alien registration card, your ward tax record will be checked and you will be required to pay any money owing. A re-entry permit will also prevent this check and you get to keep your alien registration card as a souvenir (illegally of course).

Useful Japanese

I'm leaving Japan.	*Watashi wa nihon o demasu.*
Do I owe any ward tax?	*Juuminzei no mibaraibun wa arimasu ka.*
I need to ship my belongings to	*Watashi no nimotsu o ... ni okuritai no desu ga.*
My leaving date is	*Shuppatsubi wa ... desu.*
Thank you very much for everything.	*Iroiro o-sewa ni narimashita.*

Resources

See the resources section in **Getting Around** in **Chapter One** for airport information, transportation of luggage to airports, and travel agencies. Also see the resources section in **Utilities** in **Chapter Two** for customer service centres that can provide information about leaving your apartment and their services you have used. Please note: Unless you arrange and pay for door-to-door shipping services, be prepared to receive a large bill from the freight company in the country you move to. This will be in addition to the bill you pay to the shipping company in Japan before you leave.

International Shipping Companies
Econoship 0120-222-111
Japan Luggage Express 0120-48-0081
        http://www.jluggage.com
Nihon Systems Service (NSS) 0120-29-1200
Nippon Express 03-3572-4301
Pakmail 052-232-8988
        http://www.pakmail.co.jp/
Premier Worldwide Movers 03-3663-2685
Valuemove 0120-682-444
        http://www.occidental.co.jp/valuemove

Back Home

Most Westerners experience reverse culture shock upon returning home that can last up to a year. Being prepared for this can help:

I couldn't cope with supermarkets (too big and too many choices). It took me days to stop saying "domo" and "dozo" and "ohayo gozaimasu," all the automatic little things that you learn to say. It took me weeks to stop bowing.

It was FAR harder to readjust to life in the States than it was to adjust to life in Japan. I had no expectation that I would suffer culture shock.

Life seems either too easy since you are fully literate all of a sudden, or too hard because some services are not as smooth as in Japan.

The pace of life is different—hard to describe. But if you are NOT ready for it, then it is very unsettling.

The main thing to remember, especially with respect to old friends and family, is that you have changed. You will probably have experienced some uncomfortable feelings or a sense of not belonging if you have been home on holiday during your time in Japan, but these feelings are easy to dismiss when you are just visiting. Going home for good is another matter entirely:

You are not the same person, but your friends and family will expect you to be. It's a gradual process of reacclimation. And always the gnawing at your heart for what you've left behind.

You are NO LONGER different and special. No one CARES that you were in Japan and most cannot relate to your experience. You will probably NOT know the new slang, the TV shows to watch or what is happening in them—I never realized before what a HUGE topic of conversation this is.

You will be bursting with stories of your adventures and your wonderful foreign friends but, unfortunately, most will not listen for very long and will never truly understand. It can be disappointing, but expect it. You were undoubtedly a star while you were abroad—the only blonde or the tallest or the only foreigner in certain groups. Sorry to burst your bubble, but you are just Plain Jane again.

If you are in a relationship with someone you met in Japan, this means your relationship is 'Japan-defined' and you may have specific issues to deal with. If you are single and have felt somewhat 'ignored' during your life in Japan, you may find the possible burst of attention a welcome relief. You may have to relearn your sense of personal safety; your hometown is probably not as safe as where you lived in Japan. If you have children, then remember that they are experiencing the same reverse culture shock that you are, but may be quicker to adapt to their new surroundings. Ex-Japan Western women recommend seeking out new friends, especially others who have spent time in Japan:

> *Seeking out new friendships while maintaining dear friends is one of the best things you can do. I am back in my hometown after seven years away, including university. It was a strange feeling at first, but I am making the most of it. Seeking out other returnees is a good way to meet people who have done similar things and who understand you. I found the Toronto chapter of the Canada-Japan Society and they have social events once a month. There are groups of former JETs and other similar clubs in major cities. I started by asking a friend and by contacting the closest Japanese embassy. Even if it is just someone to eat sushi with once in awhile, that is great!*

Focus on the positive aspects of your new life:

> *I loved seeing huge trees again, sidewalks that weren't covered with people, and land with nothing built on it. And being able to drive (I didn't in Tokyo). Walking into a bookstore and being able to read the books was magic.*

It is common to develop confused feelings towards your home after being in Japan, and it is difficult to justify them. It seems natural for you to have strange feelings when you come to Japan because it is so different from home; nobody expects to feel like an alien in their hometown with the people they have known all their lives. But remember that Japan has become your home, especially for long-timers, and that you are not the same person:

> *It is OKAY to see your home culture differently, critically, and to reject things that once were commonplace to you. It is okay to question your own culture just like you questioned and judged Japanese culture when you first arrived.*

You made a life in Japan; you can make a life at home again too.

9

Women's Organisations

Association for New Entrepreneurial Wo+men (ANEW)
By Hershey Wier, Founder

ANEW's main purpose is to provide a forum through which new and potential entrepreneurs can share information. We define a new entrepreneur as one with zero- to five-years of entrepreneurial experience. However, the group is open to all (except for those involved in multi-level marketing businesses), regardless of gender or length of entrepreneurial experience. If you want to start a business, but have so many questions that you don't know where to start, this is the place!

ANEW issues a quarterly email newsletter and welcomes articles and input from all of our participants. Topics sometimes focus on unique challenges that female entrepreneurs face. Quite a few of our participants enjoy reading about challenges specific to women: gender discrimination, juggling home and professional responsibilities, and, last but not least, the journey of finding and fulfilling one's dream.

- New entrepreneurs: If you've got a business up and running, we'd love to hear about it, and maybe highlight it in our newsletter.
- Seasoned entrepreneurs: Share your experience with us, while creating goodwill for your enterprise. Members like to focus on the small business owner having to deal with every aspect of running a business.
- Business consultants: We welcome articles that educate our participants. If you are published in our newsletter, we'll include your contact information so that potential clients may inquire further.

Meetings are held in the Kansai area on an irregular basis. A seasoned entrepreneur or consultant 'mentors' participants in a particular area of expertise.

More information
Hershey Wier　　Tel/Fax: 0721-98-3265
　　　　　　　　　Email: joy@gol.com

Association for Women in Finance (AWF)
Compiled by Cheryl Rodriguez

AWF was founded in 1996 by six women in Tokyo's financial marketplace. It represents the first international association for women in finance in Tokyo, and today serves a membership of over one hundred women.

AWF's mission is to support and meet the needs of women in finance in Tokyo, providing members with increased awareness of their achievements and their potential for advancement. Career growth, access to an extensive network, and membership in an association with creative, accomplished, ambitious, and dynamic women are just a few of the benefits offered by AWF. The Association is devoted to the professional development of Japanese and non-Japanese women in finance, and is committed to serving members' needs.

Our members are women who work, have worked, or are interested in working in all sectors of the financial industry. Areas of expertise include commercial and investment banking, portfolio and personal finance management, risk advisory, insurance, research, accounting, consulting, and financial journalism.

The Association for Women in Finance sponsors a variety of programs involving finance and business, career development, and lifestyle issues. AWF also aims to encourage university students to pursue careers in finance by providing educational counselling.

More information
Website: http://www.noriko.com/awftokyo.html

Association of Foreign Wives of Japanese (AFWJ)
By Natasha Uemura, AFWJ PR Coordinator

Women living in Japan who are, have been, or will be married to a Japanese man are special. They qualify for membership in a unique organization. The Association of Foreign Wives of Japanese is the only group of its kind to represent the interests of the women from many national, ethnic, racial, religious, and economic backgrounds who are married to Japanese men.

Founded in 1969, AFWJ provides a network of information for newcomers and long-term residents in Japan. We offer our members friendship, support, and mutual help in adapting to Japanese culture and society. We also offer opportunities for social, emotional, educational, and professional growth.

AFWJ gives members a chance to meet in their localities for a variety of social activities. We also have special interest groups and hold luncheons with guest speakers, an annual two-night national convention, and smaller mini-conventions in local districts.

AFWJ publishes a bimonthly magazine, the AFWJ Journal, that is sent to all members, and is largely produced by and composed of members' own creative and professional contributions. We also publish a yearly directory for members. Local 'branches' provide newsletters with calendars of upcoming events. We produce handbooks on a variety of themes such as legal issues, bilingualism, finance, education, and cookery. There is also a very active email list, which provides opportunities to make friends, seek support, and 'talk' to other members in Japan and overseas.

More information

Natasha Uemura   Email: public-relations@afwj.org
Chris Ishikawa   Tel/Fax: 045-753-7485
                        Email: membership-sec@afwj.org

Website: http://home.att.ne.jp/surf/cei/AFWJ.html

College Women's Association of Japan (CWAJ)
By Helen Capper

CWAJ recently celebrated its 50th anniversary. It is a well-respected club with a long waiting list for Japanese members, but is relatively easy for foreigners to join. Partly due to the scheduling of the activities, most members tend to be in their older years, and there are many wives who came to Japan because of their husband's work. Although younger members are the minority, they are not made to feel unwelcome. CWAJ holds monthly information meetings for women interested in joining (a reservation is required). The membership fee is ¥10,000 per year.

CWAJ organizes numerous voluntary activities in which members can participate, or help organize, and there is a monthly luncheon that gives members a chance to get together. Most activities tend to be conducted during the day, although there is a Night Owl group that meets once a month and includes presentations from members and guests, and evening and weekend outings to museums or gardens. CWAJ has many special interest groups: ceramics, cooking, cross-cultural discussion, Japanese conversation, French conversation, music, hiking, reading, and tours. Regular volunteer activities include the Children's English Circle, Volunteers for Blind Students, and Language and Education Services. CWAJ also holds an annual series of lectures and a print show that has been called Japan's 'foremost exhibition and sale of contemporary Japanese print art'.

Membership requirements include: fluency in written and spoken English; completion of a minimum of two years at an academic institution; residency in Tokyo or accessible commuting area; and participation in at least one volunteer committee yearly.

More information

The CWAJ Center   Tel: 03-3444-2167   Fax: 03-3444-2204
Susan Kreuer   Tel: 03-5443-5870   Fax: 03-5484-7117
Keiko Hayashi   Fax: 03-3309-35151

Cross Cultural Women's Club (CCWC)
By Michiko Moritomo, CCWC President

The CCWC was established in 1981 to encourage cultural exchange and friendship between foreign and Japanese women. We do this by holding activities based on different aspects of Japanese culture, while simultaneously sharing and developing an appreciation for different cultures around the world. CCWC also provides scholarships for women pursuing intercultural educational goals in Japan.

Meetings are usually held on Fridays, two or three times a month, and consist of a lecture or hands-on demonstration of an aspect of Japanese culture. This may include traditional theatre, sumi-e, ukiyo-e, ceramics, bonsai, Japanese art history, as well as other areas of cultural interest. We also organize tours to temples, shrines, gardens, museums, antique markets, and other sites of interest—English explanations are available. We hold cooking and craft classes, based on a variety of cultures, and celebrate together during traditional holidays. Past activities have included: lectures on sumo by NHK commentator Ms Simmons, and ukiyo-e by Ms Fukuhara from Waseda University; classes in Japanese decorative ball making and washi card making; a Bunraku backstage tour; a performance by the Ogawa Kyogen Players; museum tours; New Year, welcome, and farewell parties; and tours to various parts of Japan.

To support our scholarship program we organize fundraising activities such as a yearly bake sale and performances of traditional Japanese theatre in English. We also publish a monthly newsletter in English.

Membership fees are ¥6000 per year (September through August) and new members are welcome throughout the year.

More information
Michiko Moritomo   Tel: 03-3718-7726
                          Email: tane@highway.ne.jp

Digital Eve Japan
By Kristen Elsby and Kristen McQuillin, co-leaders

Digital Eve Japan dedicates itself to helping women and girls reach their personal and professional goals through the use of new technologies.

The Japan chapter of Digital Eve launched in February 2001 from the Japan Webgrrls group, which disbanded at that time. Digital Eve, a global non-profit organisation, strives to support its members by building a strong community of like-minded peers who share their knowledge and skills in a wide range of technology-related subjects. More than 7000 women from fifteen international communities belong to Digital Eve worldwide.

Our members come from all backgrounds and professions, including designers, educators, students, housewives, researchers, managers, programmers, writers, and artists. Digital Eve Japan members communicate in English and Japanese—some using both languages and some only one. Currently, most members reside in Tokyo, although many active participants live in other parts of Japan and outside Japan as well.

We invite you to join Digital Eve Japan. Benefits of our free membership include participation in an email discussion list with almost two hundred other members who share career advice, offer tips for hardware and software troubleshooting, and discuss a wide range of computing and net-related issues.

Our monthly meetings, held on the 10th of every month at various central Tokyo locations, offer an opportunity for face-to-face networking, another important activity for the group.

Digital Eve Japan also runs monthly workshops aimed at skill levels from novice to expert. Topics for 2001 include: web design basics, digital video production, maximising office applications, introductory Photoshop and desktop publishing, computer maintenance, intermediate level web publishing with Dreamweaver, and database design.

More information

Email: digitaleve@gol.com
Website: http://www.digitalevejapan.org

477

Foreign Executive Women (FEW)
By Sacha Solomon

FEW is a networking organisation whose aim is to help foreign women in Japan achieve their full professional and/or personal potential. Reaching beyond the confines of 'executive women', FEW welcomes women from all professional backgrounds and at all stages of their careers, and focuses on networking, information exchange, and educational and social activities. FEW is a non-profit organisation solely funded by membership dues, meeting fees, and sponsorship.

FEW was founded in 1981 and has evolved tremendously since its inception, with a current membership of over 250 women. There are now two chapters, one in Tokyo and another in Osaka. A cross section of professions is represented, ranging from attorneys and bankers to journalists, public relations and marketing specialists, freelance photographers, and entrepreneurs in many industries.

Monthly meetings are FEW's main forum. Guest speakers who are experts in their fields are invited to address a diverse range of topics, including Japanese business, entrepreneurship, media, politics, art, health, the environment, and cross-cultural issues. Meetings are usually held on the second Thursday of every month from 6:30 p.m. at the Foreign Correspondents' Club, Yurakucho. No advance reservation or payment is required—just turn up!

FEW also organises an annual one-day Career Strategies seminar for foreign women in Japan. We hold special projects events that include financial seminars, summer hikes and barbecues, trips to art galleries, kabuki visits, and members' brunches. In addition, members have become actively involved in fundraising for various charitable causes, including womens' shelters, hospitals, and children's welfare.

We produce several publications, including a monthly newsletter and an annual membership directory for our members, the *Career Resources Guide*, and the FEW *Volunteering in Tokyo* directory.

More information
Tel: 090-7216-5171

Email: few@gol.com   Website: http://www.few.gol.com

Foreign Executive Women (FEW) Kansai
By Sonja Condon

FEW Kansai offers foreign professionally-focused women in Japan an opportunity to meet and share experiences with other women in similar situations. The objective of FEW Kansai is to provide a solid foundation for networking, knowledge and information exchange, skill enhancement, and friendship. We welcome all foreign women—whether currently employed, previously employed, or seeking employment—to join and enjoy the same kind of support that is an important part of life in our home countries. FEW Kansai was established in 1991 as the Kansai branch of Tokyo's FEW to serve the growing number of professional women living in the Kansai region.

FEW Kansai holds a regular monthly dinner meeting featuring a guest speaker or presentation. In addition to monthly meetings, the group sponsors social activities that provide opportunities for relaxation and networking. Activities vary slightly from year to year, but often include a spring brunch, a summer get-together, a weekend retreat, and a year-end party. Periodically, FEW Kansai sponsors special events such as seminars on career planning or personal finances. FEW also provides its members with opportunities to interact with other organizations in the Kansai area. FEW Kansai is committed to working with local charities and volunteer organizations, with members selecting projects and fundraisers on a yearly basis.

Members receive a monthly newsletter, a membership directory, discounted fees for meetings, use of our book and audiotape library, and are eligible for positions on the Board of Directors. Membership in FEW Kansai averages about one hundred, with members from countries around the world. Our members include accountants, administrators, artists, consultants, educators, entrepreneurs, executives, lawyers, social workers, and students. They are working in environments ranging from Japanese and multinational companies to government organizations, universities, and home offices.

More information
Tel: 06-6441-2581   Email: fewkns@gol.com

Foreign Nurses Association of Japan (FNAJ)
By Karen Smith, Membership Director

FNAJ is an association of nurses from various nations who are living in Japan. The association started in 1988, and has grown from a handful of foreign nurses who gathered to share thoughts and experiences to a respected and active resource in the community. We also have Japanese nurses who are members.

FNAJ has monthly meetings, usually with a guest speaker, on the last Friday of the month (except July, August, and December) from 10:00 a.m. until 12:30 p.m. at Tokyo Women's Plaza, Omotesando. We also organise day trips to hospitals and other places that deal with health-related issues.

As a member you will receive a monthly newsletter to keep you informed about association activities as well as events and opportunities in Japan.

More information
Karen Smith, Membership Director   Tel: 03-5469-0966

Foreign Women Lawyers Association (FWLA)
By Kelli Longworth

From its inception, FWLA has been a very special organization, fulfilling a wide range of needs for foreign women lawyers in Japan. Most important, FWLA provides the perfect opportunity for meeting and networking with other professional women with legal training. Many FWLA members are the only woman lawyer, the only foreigner, or the only foreign woman lawyer in their workplaces. Newcomers to Japan find a wealth of information from fellow FWLA members and, for many of its members, FWLA has been a lifesaver.

Since 1992, FWLA has been meeting monthly, with a regular schedule of speakers and special seminars, as well as annual holiday and summer parties. FWLA also has a number of committees that work on particular areas or issues.

Each monthly member meeting features a presentation, usually on a legal topic, by an interesting speaker. The FWLA also serves a light dinner and drinks and there is plenty of time for getting to know each other. The regular meetings are open to all interested persons, including men.

One of the principal purposes of FWLA is to assist its members in finding employment, and a substantial percentage of FWLA members have found their jobs through FWLA. Through FWLA member and alumni contacts, FWLA is often first to hear about legal positions available in Tokyo. One of the special benefits of being an FWLA member is the personal attention that the Career Pursuits Chairwoman gives to each member who is searching for work.

FWLA publishes a monthly newsletter providing summaries of talks given by speakers at the monthly meetings; news about members and alumnae; job listings; information about continuing legal education classes; announcements of seminars and other events of interest; book reviews; travelogues; and the regular Member Profile, which focuses on one of FWLA's members.

More information
Website: http://www2.gol.com/users/fwla

Gender Awareness in Language Education (GALE)
By Diane Hawley Nagatomo
Based on information compiled by Dr. Jacqueline D. Beebe

GALE, established in 1998, is a Special Interest Group of JALT with approximately eighty women and men who are interested in gender issues in language education. Since its formation there has been a significant upswing in the number of gender-related topics presented at the national JALT conference, which has contributed to the growing recognition in the academic community in Japan that gender is an important and valuable topic for teaching and research. In addition to newsletters published three times a year, there is also a yearly GALE conference. In 1999 GALE jointly sponsored with WELL a one-day mini-conference with forty-two people attending. GALE also had its own room at a one-day conference of the College and University Educators within JALT in May 2000. GALE had its first two-day Symposium and Retreat in Hiroshima in June 2000. GALE's positive evolution was seen in the much-increased participation of men as conference organizers, presenters, and even as the topic of presentations. GALE also appears to be an increasingly international group, with presentations in Hiroshima by scholars visiting from Canada. A conference with the theme of Gender and Minorities in Japan is to be held in September 2001 and will feature well-known scholars on East Asian Studies who are based outside of Japan.

Yearly dues are ¥1500 for JALT members, and ¥2000 for non-JALT members.

More information
Email: dsnagatomo@bekkoame.ne.jp

International Dyke Community of Japan
By Laura Seidman and Chu

We are an informal and loosely connected group of women who have come together to create a diverse, international community in Japan of women who love women. The group was born about fifteen years ago when a small group of lesbians got together to talk at a feminist workshop near Tokyo. They realized the need to bring Japanese and foreign women together, to deal with concerns specific to the lesbian community. Soon the founders were organizing weekend retreats (which continue to this day), as well as frequent, more informal gatherings. The group, open to all women who love women, has several hundred unofficial members—both Japanese and foreign—all over Japan. Small satellite communities of women who reunite in other world cities, such as San Francisco and Melbourne, after leaving Japan also exist. We hold a wide variety of activities throughout the year and throughout Japan, although it is important to note that some activities are specifically geared toward more limited groups, some activities include men, and the majority of activities are held in Tokyo.

We currently offer the following:

- An email list, Nihon Dykenet, to share information and organize gatherings. The list is open to all women who love women.
- Bilingual weekend retreats take place three or four times a year, usually just outside Tokyo, and include a variety of workshops, sports, celebrations, etc. Weekends alternate between being open to lesbians only, or open to all women who love women.
- Informal and formal gatherings of all sorts, including the annual pride parade, music festivals, reading groups, writing groups, jam sessions, weekly pool playing nights, Brazilian barbecue feasting, square dancing, ski trips, camping trips, film festivals, and much more.
- A list of resources for queer women in Japan.

More information

Nihon Dykenet   Email: loseidman@hotmail.com
General information   Tel: 090-3045-9778 Email: chu@t3.rim.or.jp

International Women in Communications (IWIC)
By Tanya Clark, President

International Women in Communications is a Tokyo-based bilingual non-profit group, founded in 1993 to promote professionalism, the free flow of information, and the advancement of women in communications. IWIC's main purpose is to bring women together to mentor and learn from each other. We were inspired by the US organization Women in Communications, founded in 1909, now called the Association for Women in Communications (AWC).

Our members include professionals in every field that fits under the 'communications' umbrella. Some work for major news organizations, public relations firms, advertising firms, multimedia businesses, or Internet service providers. Others are freelance interpreters or translators, Website designers, writers, or photographers. Still others are communications students, or people considering a career change.

IWIC members value a network of professional women committed to similar goals. We meet to discuss professional issues, learn new skills, become better informed about each other's areas of expertise, and have fun! We believe a sense of community is crucial to advancing the status of professional women, and to enjoying our work.

The IWIC mailing list is our main form of communication. It is free of charge and open to anyone who supports our goals. Announcements include events, job leads and articles of interest, and they reach over two hundred professionals of various nationalities working in Japan.

Most of our events are held in the Tokyo area. Membership fees are ¥10,000 per year for professionals and ¥5,000 per year for students.

More information
Email: iwic@gol.com
Website: http://www.iwic.gol.com

International Women's Club (IWC)

A former director of UNESCO in Minato-ku established the International Women's Club in 1982. Through her work with UNESCO, she organised lectures on international relations, but these lectures were for Japanese people only. She wanted to extend her work to include foreigners living in Japan, so she founded the International Women's Club. The International Awareness Circle (IAC) was later added as a group which is open to women and men.

IWC and IAC work towards international understanding by assisting foreigners in their lives in Japan through the organisation of events, lectures, and tours that provide information and social opportunities. Japanese members often volunteer to assist foreigners through teaching Japanese to foreign children attending Japanese schools and by interpreting for foreigners in hospital.

There are about one hundred and fifty members throughout Japan (one-third being non-Japanese), although activities usually take place in Tokyo or the surrounding prefectures. There is an initial registration fee of ¥1000, and an annual membership fee of ¥3000.

More information

Mrs. Ito   Tel: 03-3773-4836
Email: iwciac@onyx.dti.ne.jp

Japan Exchange Teaching (JET) Women's Group
By Eileen Storey

The Women's Group is a Special Interest Group (SIG) within the Japan Exchange Teaching (JET) community and was started to inform, support, and communicate with women on the JET program. The Women's Group aims to provide both a forum for discussions of the problems and obstacles encountered by female JETs and opportunities to exchange ideas about the positive aspects of being a woman in Japan. The Women's Group hopes to create an atmosphere for discussion of women's issues in their broadest sense, ranging from sexuality, sexual harassment, and women's position in society both here and abroad, to women's health and travel issues.

The Women's Group publishes a monthly newsletter, sponsors prefecture-based support groups, provides information at JET conferences, and organizes other activities beneficial to women on the JET program. In recent years, the Women's Group has organized a trip to the Philippines for Habitat for Humanity and a Women's Group Retreat. The newsletter, Amaterasu, is theme-based and is full of timely, pertinent articles on women's lives in Japan, Asia, and abroad.

Membership is open to any woman, or man, inside or outside the JET program; the cost per year is ¥2000 for non-JETs in Japan and ¥3000 for international members.

More information
Eileen Storey
Address: 127 Tamakura-cho, Nakagyo-ku, Kyoto-shi 604-8211
Tel/Fax: 075-252-0575
Email: estorey@sisf.minoh.osaka.jp

Kobe Women's Club (KWC)
By Lynn Thompson Bryant

The Kobe Women's Club began in the spring of 1914 as the Saturday Morning Club, formed by a group of women who felt the need for an organization that would give English-speaking women of all nationalities a chance to become acquainted. In 1922 the name was changed to the Kobe Women's Club (KWC).

Our purpose is to give members an opportunity to share the cultural experience of living in Japan and to study subjects of interest to progressive women from all over the world.

The KWC general meetings are the second and third Tuesdays of each month and are held at The Kobe Club in Kitano-cho. Since we are an international group, we have the pleasure of enjoying very diverse programs: Indian fashion shows and dancers, Belgian chocolate tastings, and Hawaiian dancers. Of course, the majority of our programs enlighten us on the culture in which we live. We have lectures on topics like sumo wrestling, Japanese gardens, Iai do (sword play), and Noh drama. Or we learn how to make origami cranes, 'Hashioki' jewelry, and sumi-e. A favorite was 'Rakugo' or Japanese comedy. All programs are in English, or skillfully translated by our fluent English-speaking Japanese members.

The fourth Tuesday provides an opportunity for very interesting field trips, and we usually take the full day to experience something of interest in the Kansai area. Excellent guides have taken us on adventures to Bunraku and Kabuki theaters, a washi paper factory where we made our own washi paper, and on terrific seasonal outings to Arashiyama and Nara for 'momiji' or 'sakura' viewing at famous temples and shrines.

The annual membership fee is ¥12,000. All women are welcome to attend any program, and there is a fee of ¥2000 to non-members. Membership is also immediately available at a person's first attendance.

More information
Akiko Umezawa, Vice-President   Tel: 078-742-1296

Stonewall
By Eileen Storey

The Stonewall group, officially a Special Interest Group (SIG) within the Japan Exchange Teaching (JET) community, is for men and women of gay/lesbian/bisexual orientation and their friends. Membership is open to all people, JET or non-JET, in Japan or abroad, and membership rates vary. Members receive a Contact List, and because privacy is of utmost importance, members can choose to be on the Out List, so that everyone in the Stonewall group gets their contact information, or be on the Confidential List, so that only the coordinators have the contact information.

Stonewall began in 1994 as a small, unsponsored group among queer members of the JET community and received SIG status in 1997. The group supports gay, lesbian, and bisexual JETs and other foreigners in Japan, and provides a forum for discussion, debate, and ideas among the queer community. Gay, lesbian, and bisexual people often find living in Japan to be very frustrating and isolating. Stonewall offers emotional and social support, as well as relevant information on queer activities, night-life in various cities, and other GLB groups in Japan.

Stonewall's monthly newsletter, Brix (formerly Stonewall News, and before that Ataglo), offers poetry, art, comics, essays, and stories by members, as well as international news articles of interest to the GLB community. Stonewall also offers the Queer Tatami Timeshare, a listing of members across Japan who are willing to offer space in their homes for overnight accommodation to other Stonewall members. The coordinators of the Stonewall group try to organize seasonal retreats for members; recent ones include beach weekends on Niijima (an island off the coast of Tokyo), Kyushu mountain weekends, a Sapporo Snow Festival trip, a Nagano ski weekend, and trips to the annual Pride Parades around Japan.

More information
Eileen Storey
Tel/Fax: 075-252-0575   Email: estorey@sisf.minoh.osaka.jp
Address: 127 Tamakura-cho, Nakagyo-ku, Kyoto-shi 604-8211

Women Educators and Language Learners (WELL)
By Diane Hawley Nagatomo

WELL is open to all women of all nationalities who are teaching at any level or at any kind of language institution, and/or learning any language. It was established in 1995 at the national JALT (Japan Association of Language Teachers) conference by a group of fourteen women who saw a need for a women's group that is a combination of both a professional organization and a support group. Women are encouraged to write and present academically, some for the first time, through WELL-sponsored activities.

Currently there are approximately 132 members, both Japanese and non-Japanese. Women who are battling sexual harassment and/or discrimination at their school or workplace can turn to WELL for emotional support. Women who are interested in incorporating gender-related or feminist issues into their classroom teaching can find a wealth of ideas from fellow members. Unlike other academic organizations within Japan, WELL strives to be bilingual (Japanese and English) in its newsletter (published twice a year) and its three-day retreat (customarily held at the end of January). A party is usually held every year at the JALT conference, and occasional meetings and get-togethers are arranged several times a year. WELL activities reflect a feminist approach ranging beyond intellectual discussions of language learning to include activities that integrate body, mind, emotions, spirit, and the larger social systems we live in. At the retreat there may be sessions of meditation, hatha yoga, aikido, stand-up comedy, or dance, and workshops with spiritual topics or political content (once we had a report about a Japanese court case on racial discrimination). Child care is provided.

Dues for WELL are ¥1000 for a discount membership, ¥2000 for a regular membership, and ¥5000 for a supporter membership.

More information
Website: http://www.onelist.com/community/welljapan

Women's Network Kyoto

Women's Network Kyoto is an informal group of foreign women who meet once a month to provide support, share information, discuss problems, and socialise. Members enjoy the opportunity to express their feelings and needs in a purely English-speaking environment.

Women's Network Kyoto started in 1990 when two foreign women took a counselling course and wanted to use their skills in a support group setting. It began as a large group of friends, many of whom had been in Kyoto for a long time, but membership has since decreased and is now made up of a mixture of newcomers and old-timers.

Meetings take place at the founder's home, with anywhere from five to twenty women attending. Meetings consist of a potluck dinner, personal introductions, and plenty of time to talk in small groups. There is no formal membership system and English-speaking women of all ages and from all countries outside of Japan are welcome to attend.

Women's Network Kyoto also holds a small Christmas dinner for those away from close friends and family, or those with a Japanese family who would like to celebrate a Western-style Christmas.

Meetings take place near the YWCA in Muromachi, Kyoto, and are open to women throughout the Kansai area.

More information
Lois Karhu   Tel: 075-415-0606

Women's Sports Foundation (WSF) Japan
By Akiko Takahashi

WSF Japan was founded in 1981 to discuss and find solutions for problems affecting women in sport, following the lead of WSF in the United States, which was founded in 1974. Women's involvement in sports increased worldwide during the seventies, but there was a lack of opportunity to discuss the problems and challenges that these women faced. WSF also encourages and expands women's sports through investigation and research from a female perspective. In 1980, Yoko Mitsuya organized the first World Women's Sports Congress in Tokyo. WSF Japan grew from this event. WSF publishes newsletters, holds seminars and luncheons, and facilitates the exchange of information about women and sports. Events usually take place in Tokyo.

Women and men who are interested in women and sports are eligible to join WSF Japan. Members include students, teachers, athletes, and sports fans. Most are Japanese, but non-Japanese are welcome. Annual membership fees are ¥5000 for students, ¥8000 for individuals, and ¥15,000 for groups.

More information

Akiko Takahashi   Tel: 03-3467-4360
                       Fax: 03-3467-5455
                       Email: takahashi@sports-21.com

Women's Studies Society of Japan
By Emiko Takei

The Women's Studies Society of Japan was established in 1978 by a group of people who wished to study the difficulties faced by women in the present and the past. Today we still ask why such difficulties exist and want to change the present situation for women.

Our aim is to encourage people who are conscious of women's difficulties to exchange ideas and cooperate. We try to develop workable ideas, theories, and methods for solving problems. Through this, we try to link scholarship and everyday life, theory and practice, in ways that will support the movement for women's liberation. Our group has no representative or leader, because we reject the top-down authoritative structure that generally prevails in present society. The activities of our group are based on discussions among equal individuals. Through thinking, talking and acting together, we can change ourselves and society at large.

We hold regular meetings (monthly in principle) in various places, mainly in the Kansai area, where members can report their research and activities, exchange ideas, and socialize. These meetings are announced in our newsletter and on our homepage. We also hold meetings for members working on specific projects.

We have two publications: *Voice of Women*, a monthly newsletter in which members plan regular meetings and report on their activities; and *The Annual Report of the Women's Studies Society of Japan*.

Annual membership is usually ¥5000, but we also have a sliding scale system based on income.

More information
Address: Office Alternative, MF Tenmabashi Building 6F, 1-7-4, Tanimachi, Chuo-ku, Osaka 540-0012
Tel: 06-945-5146 (9:30 a.m. to 5:30 p.m., Monday to Friday)
Fax: 06-920-8167
Email: wssj@jca.apc.org
Website: http://www.jca.apc.org/wssj/

Yokohama International Women's Club (YIWC)
By Chris Ishikawa

YIWC was founded in 1929 for the promotion of international good-will through cultural and social activities. At present it is a non-profit volunteer group of English-speaking Japanese and foreign women, with 180 members from 17 different countries. The strength of the organization is its friendship. From that firm base, members reach out with charitable support for various welfare projects in Yokohama City and Kanagawa Prefecture. YIWC finances its welfare activities through fundraising events throughout the year. YIWC took on its current role amid the disruption following World War II. By the mid-1950s, YIWC was aiding Japanese students through loan grants for study abroad, and supporting local orphanages, as well as supplying food and clothing to the less fortunate.

YIWC's Welfare Committee works throughout the year among the local communities of Yokohama and Kanagawa, as well as worldwide, to identify the needs of less-privileged individuals and organizations. YIWC provides substantial help to two children's homes and a home for the elderly on a continuing basis. Donations and support are also given to organizations that support the homeless, disabled, refugees, and disaster relief.

We hold meetings and luncheons, with programs focusing primarily on Japan, its traditions, arts, antiques, foods, etc. Speakers include authors, designers, historians, specialists, shop owners, adventurers, and artists. Interest groups are organized yearly and currently include: Let's Talk, Tennis Troupers, and Music Lovers. YIWC is governed by a 24-member board, with Japanese and foreign members sharing chairs on the board. In addition, YIWC periodically compiles a cookbook of Japanese and international recipes. The latest available edition, published in 2000, is titled *Food for Furoshiki*.

More information
Chris Ishikawa   Tel: 045-753-7485
                    Email: cei@yhc.att.ne.jp
Website: http://home.att.ne.jp/surf/cei/

Women's Centers in Japan
By Tracey Delaney

Every so often I work at Forum Yokohama, a women's center in Yokohama, that is part of the Yokohama Women's Association for Communication and Networking (YWACN). The activities of YWACN, like those of other women's centers in Japan, cut across many areas in life. The ten main activities are information exchange, self-development programs, employment support, health services, life skills development, community based activities, counselling services, research, public education, and international cooperation and exchange. YWACN is not simply a center for women only: it strives hard through its programs and lectures to promote gender equality, getting men involved in its activities as well. YWACN believes that equality will never occur if the only people involved are women.

A History of Women's Centers in Japan

The first center was built in 1900 by the Japan Women's Temperance Union to be used as a base for their anti-prostitution activities. In the following decades similar centers were built by private women's organizations. However, it was not until after the Second World War that these centers began to flourish across the nation. With the support and encouragement of the policy of the General Headquarters of the Allied Powers (GHQ), these centers, called 'Fujin Kaikan', provided numerous educational programs to women. Although built by public organizations, the centers were run, however, by private organizations and focused on the specific and special needs of women in each center's area. The Fujin Kaikan was a multi-faceted facility serving at times not just as an education and resource center, but also as a hotel and inexpensive wedding facility. By the 1960s there were approximately one hundred Fujin Kaikan across the country.

1976 saw the UN's Decade for Women, and the Japanese Prime Minister's Office organized the 'Planning and Promotion Committee for Women's Problems'. 'National Programs for Action' started

494

the following year and each local government subsequently responded with its own 'Programs for Action for Local Women'. It was not until the UN Convention on the Elimination of All Forms of Discrimination against Women was ratified that the country saw a rush in the construction of women's centers.

What Is Happening Now?

At last count, the National Women's Education Center (NWEC) said there were almost eight hundred women-related centers and facilities in Japan. What follows is a directory of 38 centers for women in prefectures and designated cities (*seireishireitoshi*)* as compiled by Yokohama Women's Forum. While these centers do not always offer services in English, guidance and referrals can be sought through a Japanese speaker. I found that quite a number of my Japanese friends knew nothing of these centers and first found out about them through me. The centers are also great sources of (mostly Japanese) information for those concerned with the ever-evolving status of women in Japan.

Resources

Prefectural Women's Centres

Aichi 052-962-2511	Niigata 025-285-6610
http://www.pref.aichi.jp/joseicenter	Okinawa 098-866-9090
Chiba 0471-40-8602	Osaka 06-6910-8615
Ehime 089-926-1633	Saga 0952-26-0011
Fukui 0776-41-4200	Saitama 048-728-7111
Fukuoka 092-584-1261	Shiga 0748-37-3751
Hiroshima 082-242-5262	Shizuoka 054-250-8107
Hokkaido 011-251-6329	Tochigi 028-665-7770
011-251-6349	Tokyo 03-5467-1711
Ishikawa 076-234-1112	Toyama 0764-32-4500
Kanagawa 0466-27-2111	Yamanashi (Kofu) 0522-35-4171
Kyoto 075-692-3433	Yamanashi
Mie 059-233-1130	(Minami Kyoma-gun) 0556-64-4777
Nagano 0266-22-5781	Yamanashi (Tsuru) 0554-45-1666

*A designated city (*seireishireitoshi*) is defined as a city with a population of over one million people. These cities have specific characteristics designated by government ordinances.

Designated City Women's Centres

Chuo-ku, Kobe 078-361-6977
Higashiyodogawa-ku, Osaka 06-6320-6300
Hirano-ku, Osaka 06-6705-1100
Joto-ku, Osaka 06-6965-1200
Kokurakita-ku, Kitakyushu 093-583-3939
Konohana-ku, Osaka 06-6460-7800
Minami Ward, Fukuoka 092-526-3755
     http://www.culture-dome.or.jp/AMIKAS/
Nakagyo-ku, Kyoto 075-212-7460
     http://web.kyoto-inet.or.jp/org/wings262
Sapporo City, Hokkaido 011-621-5177
Sendai City, Miyagi 022-268-8300
Yokohama City, Kanagawa (Nishi-ku) 045-224-1133
     http://women.city.yokohama.jp/
Yokohama City, Kanagawa (Totsuka) 045-862-5050
     http://women.city.yokohama.jp/

National Women's Centre

National Women's Education Center (Saitama) 0493-62-6711

Reading List

With comments by Jeanmarie Todd

Women-specific

Books

36 Views of Japan: On Finding Myself in Japan
> By Catherine Davidson, Plume, 1994.
> In a series of essays based on her ten years off and on in Japan, the author tries to understand the country through different facets of life there. The title is taken from a famous set of woodblock prints of views of Mount Fuji.

An Inn Near Kyoto: Writing by American Women Abroad
> Edited by Kathleen Coskran and CW Truesdale, New Rivers Press: 1998.
> Third in a series of travel anthologies by women, this collection of 45 essays and stories illuminates the meaning of being "at home in the world" and an American in a place both ordinary and exotic.

In The Empire of Dreams
> By Dianne Highbridge, Soho Press: 1999.
> Captures the frustrations, pain, and pleasures of expatriate life in ten accounts of foreign women in Japan.

The Accidental Office Lady
> By Laura J Kriska, Yenbooks: 1998.
> The author's account of her two years as a trainee for Honda Motor Co in Japan, struggling to resist fitting into a rigid life, in a rite of passage that's both funny and insightful.

The Only Woman in the Room: A Memoir
> By Beate Sirota Gordon, Kodansha International: 1999.
> The daughter of a Russian Jewish pianist, raised in Vienna and educated in Japan and America, the author was tasked by General Douglas MacArthur when she was just twenty-two to help draft the new Japanese constitution.

The Clay That Breathes
> By Catherine Browder, Milkweed Editions: 1991.
> Beautifully written collection of stories moving between Japan and America giving account of the lives of Americans, Japanese, and Cambodian and Lao-Hmong refugees.

Too Late for the Festival: An American Salary-Woman in Japan
> By Rhiannon Paine, Academy Chicago: 1999.
> A year and a half of culture shock experienced by a spontaneous young woman hired by Hewlett-Packard Japan as a technical writer, working in an office full of smoke, bad lighting, and people she didn't understand. You think you're lonely and frustrated?

Unbeaten Tracks in Japan
> By Isabella Bird, Virago Books: 1894.
> An account of an 1878 trip to Japan by Isabella Bird, exploring a Japan that few foreigners, let alone a woman on her own, had yet to see.

General

Books

Culture Shock! Japan (Culture Shock Series)
> By Rex Shelley, Graphic Arts Center Pub Co: 1992.
> Part of a series written by experienced expatriates in various countries, this how-to guide highlights the importance of picking up on often subtle signals and learning to communicate across cultural boundaries.

Japanese Etiquette Today
> By James and Michiko Vardaman, Charles E Tuttle: 1994.
> You know that Japanese etiquette differs from that of other countries, but do you know how? Become familiar with subtle rules to guide you through both formal and informal situations.

Learning to Bow: Inside the Heart of Japan
> By Bruce S Feiler, Ticknor & Fields, reprinted 1992.
> With keen insights gleaned from a year teaching at a rural school where he was hired to impart "internationalization," the author amuses and enlightens the reader with his encounters.

Living for Less in Tokyo and Liking It!
> ASK Kodansha Co Ltd: 1991.
> A handy book in question-and-answer format, indexed. Sample questions: "I left my bicycle parked near a train station, with a wheel chained. When I came back, it was gone. How can I get it back?" and "Where can I get some documents translated?" Some of the information is useful.

Max Danger: The Adventures of an Expat in Tokyo
> By Robert J Collins, Charles E Tuttle Co: 1987.

More Max Danger: The Continuing Adventures of an Expat in Tokyo
> By Robert J Collins, Charles E Tuttle Co: 1988.
> Fun for Tokyo-ites familiar with the places and the 'types' of characters, or who want to experience the life of an expatriate company manager. Regardless of your job or circumstances, you'll laugh in recognition.

The Broken Bridge: Fiction from Expatriates in Literary Japan
> Edited by Suzanne Kamata, Stone Bridge Press: 1997.
> Literary works from the Occupation to the '90s by 36 non-Japanese writers in Japan, exploring the balance of fitting into a conformist society and maintaining individual identity, plus universal themes of love, despair, humor, happiness, and pain.

Tokyo For Free
> By Susan Pompian, Kodansha International Ltd: 1998.
> One of the best-organized guidebooks about any city, this one packs an incredible amount of information in 450 pages on enjoying the Big Mikan without going broke.

Tokyo Night City: Where to Drink and Party After Work and After Hours
> By Jude Brand, Charles E Tuttle Co: 1993.
> Tokyo's party expert gives you a tour of her favorite night spots. Some clubs have changed names, moved, or gone out of business, but you may find some places here you'd never find on your own.

Tokyo Q 2000-2001
> By Tokyo Q, Stone Bridge Press: 1999.
> An annual guide to Tokyo compiled by a city-loving gang of foreigners with collectively more than 250 years' experience in Japan, covering everything from intimate hotels, hip galleries, and happening theatres to stunning new architecture, cool cafes, unexpected back streets, and yummy restaurants.

Journals
Kyoto Journal—Perspectives on Asia
> Heian Bunka Centre http://www.kampo.co.jp/kyoto-journal

Printed Matter—Tokyo's English language literary journal
> Call 03-3394-9348 for a copy.

Magazines
Eye-Ai 03-3433-8602
> Japanese entertainment and culture.
> http://202.218.99.221:80/user/river/zeyefr.htm

JapanZine 03-3791-3534
> Humour and information.
> http://www.japan-zine.com

Japan Traveler Magazine 03-5255-3090
> Travel, music, art, and culture.
> http://www.japantraveler.net/

Kansai Time-Out 078-232-4516
> Kansai information.
> http://www.kto.co.jp

J-Select 03-3442-0211
> General information for the international community.
> http://www.jselect.net

Time Magazine 03-5470-6952
> Asian news.
> http://www.timeasia.com

Tokyo Classified 03-3423-6932
> Information and classifieds.
> http://www.tokyoclassified.com

Tokyo Journal 03-3980-0029
> Travel, arts, events.
> http://www.tokyo.to

Tokyo Notice Board 03-3475-0640
> Living information.
> http://www.tokyonoticeboard.co.jp

Tokyo YY 03-3980-0029
> General information.
> http://www.tokyoyy.com

Newspapers

International Herald Tribune Asahi Newspaper
  Japanese news, world news, business, culture.
  http://www.asahi.com
Asian Wall Street Journal 03-3292-1458
  Asian business and financial news.
  http://www.wsj.com
Daily Yomiuri 03-3217-9984
  Japanese and world news, features, sports.
  http://www.yomiuri.co.jp/daily
Eibun Nikkei 03-5255-2310
  Japanese economy, business, finance, politics;
  Asian-Pacific news.
  http://www.nni.nikkei.co.jp
Financial Times 0120-341-468
  World financial news.
  http://www.ft.com
Japan Times (see display ad, page 504) 03-3453-4350
  Japanese and world news.
  http://www.japantimes.co.jp
Mainichi Daily News 03-3212-0321
  Japanese and world news.
  http://www.mainichi.co.jp/english/index.html
Shipping and Trade News 03-3542-8521
  World shipping and trade news.
Tokyo Weekender 03-5689-2471
  Expatriate community news.
  http://www.weekender.co.jp
USA Today 03-3270-8650
  American news, some Asian news.
  http://www.usatoday.com

Websites

Dayline and This Day
  NHK Asia news.
  http://www.nhk.or.jp/daily/
Gate 39
  General information and news.
  http://www.gate39.com/
Insite Tokyo
  Information, interviews, and classifieds.
  http://www.insite-tokyo.com/
Japan Echo
  Translations of essays, interviews, and discussions.
  http://www.japanecho.com/
Japan Information Network
  Useful links on almost everything.
  http://www.jinjapan.org/

Japan Today
> Japanese news.
> http://www.japantoday.com

MixPizza
> Searchable databases of businesses and services.
> http://www.mixpizza.co.jp/mp/svc/html.index_c

Neo-tokyo.com
> Japanese popular culture.
> http://www.neo-tokyo.com/index.html

NewsOnJapan.com
> Daily news and resources.
> http://www.newsonjapan.com

Nikkei BP AsiaBizTech
> Technology business information in Asia.
> http://www.nikkeibp.asiabiztech.com/

Schauwecker's Guide to Japan
> General information about modern and traditional Japan.
> http://www.japan-guide.com/

Tokyo Q
> Weekly entertainment and culture updates.
> http://www.nokia.co.jp/tokyoq/

TokyoCrier
> A digest of news from Tokyo and the rest of Japan, weather, book and movie reviews, etc.
> http://www.tokyocrier.com

Afterword

I wrote *Being A Broad in Japan* because I wanted to help other Western women living in Japan. I wanted to prepare you for living here, to minimise the bad times, to show you some great opportunities, and to let you know that you are not alone. I've trusted you with some of my story—like all girlfriends do—and I've been trusted with the stories of hundreds of women. I'd love to hear YOUR story: how you feel about living in Japan, how this book has helped you, and if there is anything else that you wish had been included. Send me your ideas, as well as any additions to the Resource sections and the Reading List, and I'll be happy to incorporate them in the next edition.

Index

Alexandra Press

Publisher of Number One Bestseller, Being A Broad in Japan: Everything a Western Woman needs to survive and thrive, Alexandra Press is an innovative, independent publisher of English and Japanese books, offering a wide range of services and advice to those interested in self-publishing and creative projects. The unique philosophy and positive attitude of the Alexandra Press team has established us as the publisher of choice for both authors and organizations. Alexandra Press provides more than just books - we create communities and help people fulfill their potential, as readers and writers.

Alexandra Press
*Independent Publishing from
the International Community in Japan*
Chuo Iikura Bldg 7A, 3-4-11 Azabudai
Minato-ku, Tokyo 106-0041
Tel: (03) 5549-2038
Fax: (03) 5549-2039
Email: info@alexandrapress.com
URL: http://www.alexandrapress.com